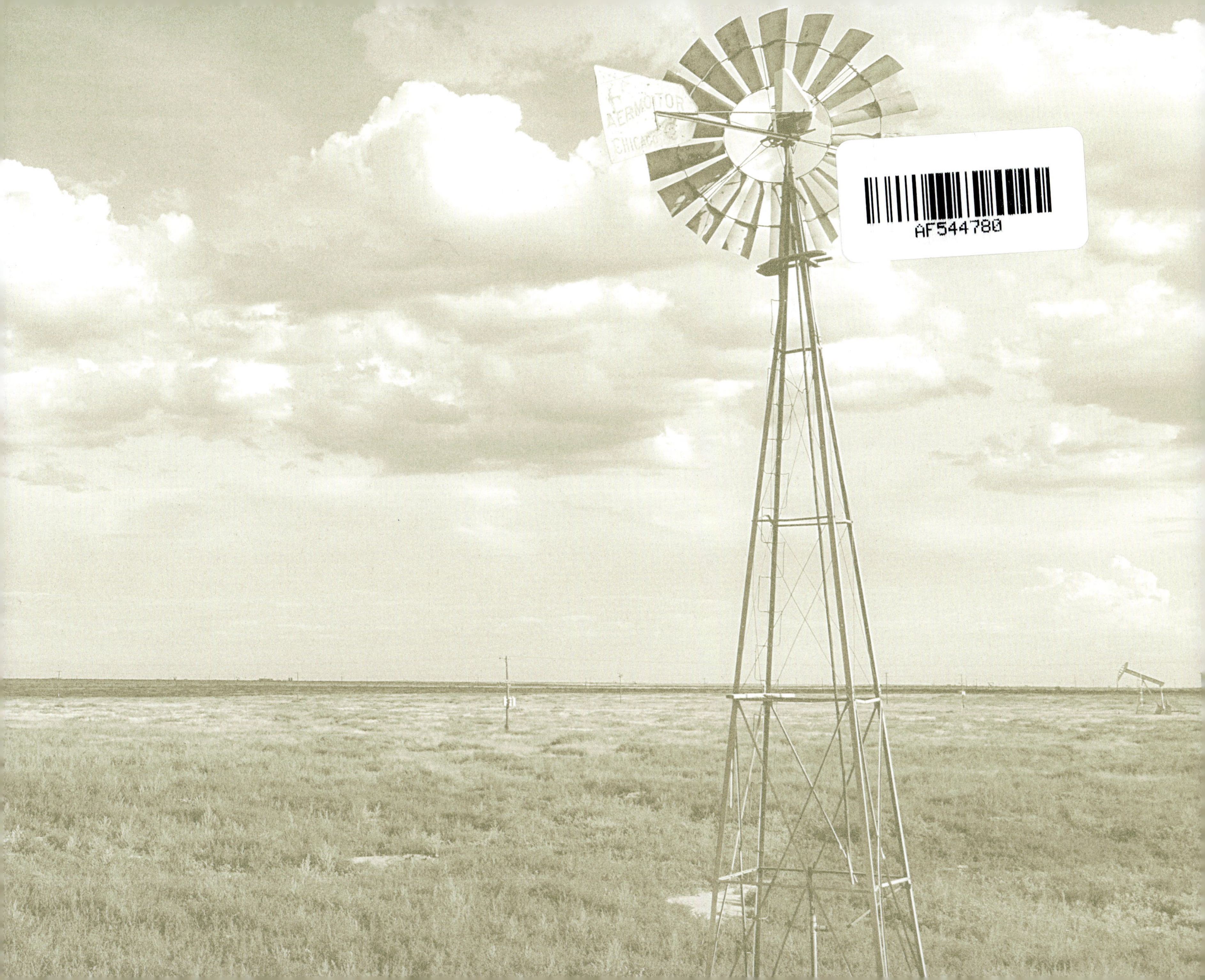
AERMOTOR
CHICAGO

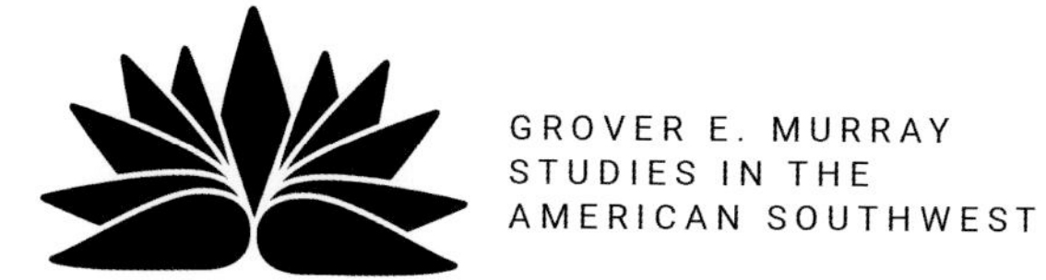

Also in the series:

Agaves, Yuccas, and Their Kin: Seven Genera of the Southwest, by Jon L. Hawker

Between Two Rivers: Photographs and Poems Between the Brazos and the Rio Grande, by Jerod Foster and John Poch

Brujerías: Stories of Witchcraft and the Supernatural in the American Southwest and Beyond, by Nasario García

Cacti of Texas: A Field Guide, by A. Michael Powell, James F. Weedin, and Shirley A. Powell

Cacti of the Trans-Pecos and Adjacent Areas, by A. Michael Powell and James F. Weedin

Cowboy Park: Steer-Roping Contests on the Border, by John O. Baxter

Dance All Night: Those Other Southwestern Swing Bands, Past and Present, by Jean A. Boyd

Dancin' in Anson: A History of the Texas Cowboys' Christmas Ball, by Paul H. Carlson

Deep Time and the Texas High Plains: History and Geology, by Paul H. Carlson

"Don't Count the Tortillas": The Art of Texas Mexican Cooking, by Adán Medrano

Equal Opportunity Hero: T.J. Patterson's Service to West Texas, by Phil Price

Finding the Great Western Trail, by Sylvia Gann Mahoney

From Texas to San Diego in 1851: The Overland Journal of Dr. S. W. Woodhouse, Surgeon-Naturalist of the Sitgreaves Expedition, edited by Andrew Wallace and Richard H. Hevly

The Frontier Centennial: Fort Worth and the New West, by Jacob W. Olmstead

Grasses of South Texas: A Guide to Identification and Value, by James H. Everitt, D. Lynn Drawe, Christopher R. Little, and Robert I. Lonard

A Haven in the Sun: Five Stories of Bird Life and Its Future on the Texas Coast, by B. C. Robison

A Kineño's Journey: On Learning, Family, and Public Service, by Lauro F. Cavazos, with Gene B. Preuss

Kit Carson and the First Battle of Adobe Walls: A Tale of Two Journeys, by Alvin R. Lynn

In the Shadow of the Carmens: Afield with a Naturalist in the Northern Mexican Mountains, by Bonnie Reynolds McKinney

Javelinas: Collared Peccaries of the Southwest, by Jane Manaster

Land of Enchantment Wildflowers: A Guide to the Plants of New Mexico, by LaShara J. Nieland and Willa F. Finley

Little Big Bend: Common, Uncommon, and Rare Plants of Big Bend National Park, by Roy Morey

Lone Star Wildflowers: A Guide to Texas Flowering Plants, by LaShara J. Nieland and Willa F. Finley

My Wild Life: A Memoir of Adventures within America's National Parks, by Roland H. Wauer

Myth, Memory, and Massacre: The Pease River Capture of Cynthia Ann Parker, by Paul H. Carlson and Tom Crum

Opus in Brick and Stone: The Architectural and Planning Heritage of Texas Tech University, by Brian H. Griggs

Pecans: The Story in a Nutshell, by Jane Manaster

Picturing a Different West: Vision, Illustration, and the Tradition of Austin and Cather, by Janis P. Stout

Plants of Central Texas Wetlands, by Scott B. Fleenor and Stephen Welton Taber

Seat of Empire: The Embattled Birth of Austin, Texas, by Jeffrey Stuart Kerr

Texas Natural History in the 21st Century, by David J. Schmidly, Robert D. Bradley, and Lisa C. Bradley

Texas, New Mexico, and the Compromise of 1850: Boundary Dispute and Sectional Crisis, by Mark J. Stegmaier

Texas Quilts and Quilters: A Lone Star Legacy, by Marcia Kaylakie with Janice Whittington

Truly Texas Mexican: A Native Culinary Heritage in Recipes, by Adán Medrano

The Wineslinger Chronicles: Texas on the Vine, by Russell D. Kane

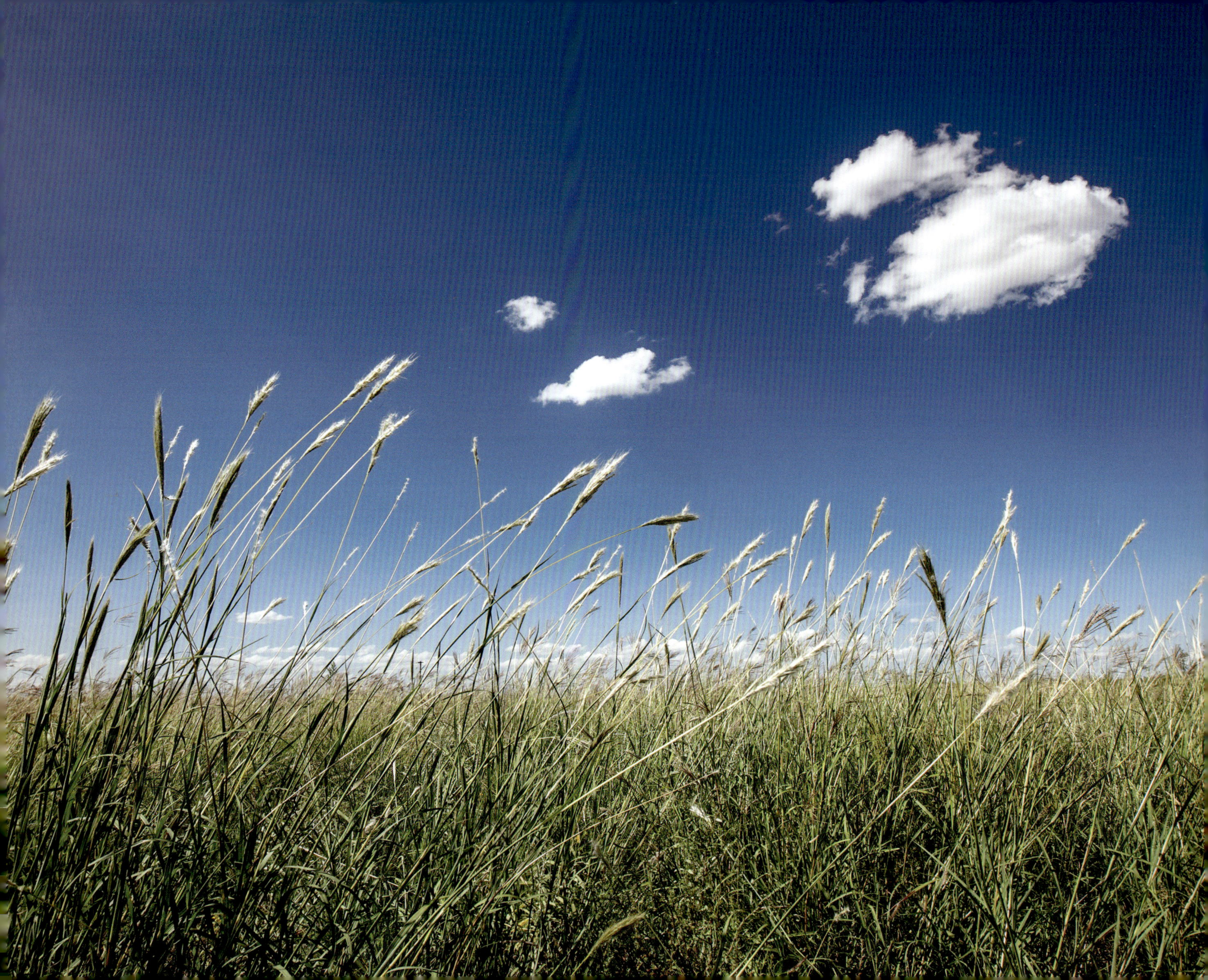

MORE THAN RUNNING CATTLE

THE MALLET RANCH OF THE SOUTH PLAINS

M. SCOTT SOSEBEE

FOREWORD BY JIM BRET CAMPBELL

TEXAS TECH UNIVERSITY PRESS

Publication of this book was made possible by the generous support of the Helen Jones Foundation, Inc.

This book is typeset in EB Garamond. The paper used in this book meets the minimum requirements of ANSI/NISO Z39.48-1992 (R1997). ♾

Designed by Hannah Gaskamp
Cover design by Hannah Gaskamp
Cover photo by Wyman Meinzer
Jacket back cover photos © Wyman Meinzer (left top and bottom), © Casey Dunn (right)

Library of Congress Cataloging-in-Publication Data

Names: Sosebee, M. Scott, 1961– author. Title: More Than Running Cattle: The Mallet Ranch of the South Plains / M. Scott Sosebee. Description: Lubbock, Texas, USA: Texas Tech University Press, [2023] | Series: Grover E. Murray Studies in the American Southwest | Includes bibliographical references and index. | Summary: "The history of the Mallet Ranch and the DeVitt family, scions of a West Texas legacy"—Provided by publisher.
Identifiers: LCCN 2022050648 | ISBN 978-1-68283-147-2 (cloth)
Subjects: LCSH: Mallet Ranch (Tex.)—History. | Devitt family. | DeVitt, David M., 1836–1934. DeVitt, Christine, 1895–1983. | Ranchers—Texas—Biography. | Ranch life—Texas—Mallet Ranch. | Frontier and pioneer life—Texas—Mallet Ranch. | Women philanthropists—Texas—Biography.
Classification: LCC F394.M294 S674 2023 | DDC 976.4/846—dc23/eng/20221110
LC record available at https://lccn.loc.gov/2022050648

Printed in China
23 24 25 26 27 28 29 30 31 / 9 8 7 6 5 4 3 2 1

Texas Tech University Press
Box 41037
Lubbock, Texas 79409-1037 USA
800.832.4042
ttup@ttu.edu
www.ttupress.org

CONTENTS

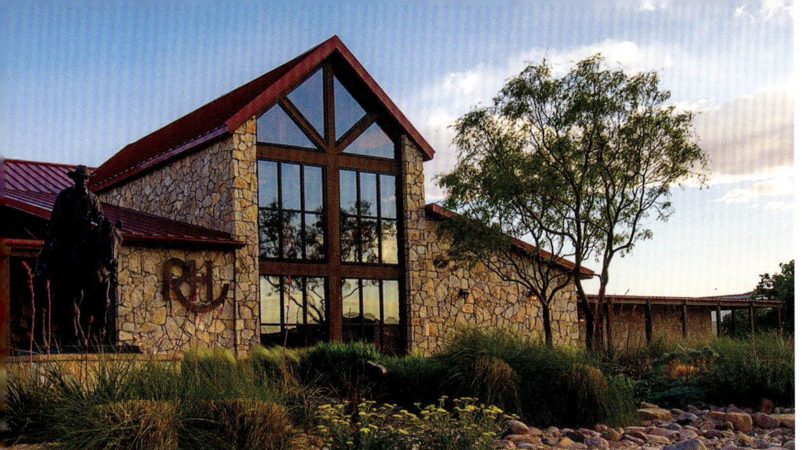

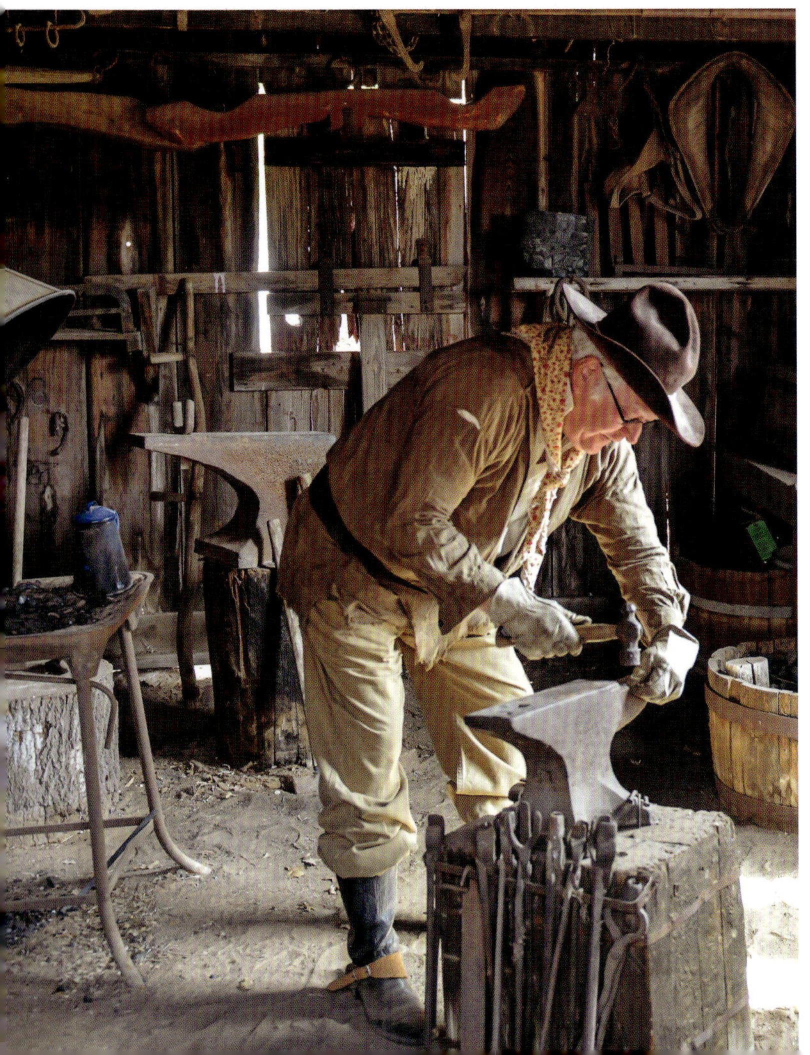

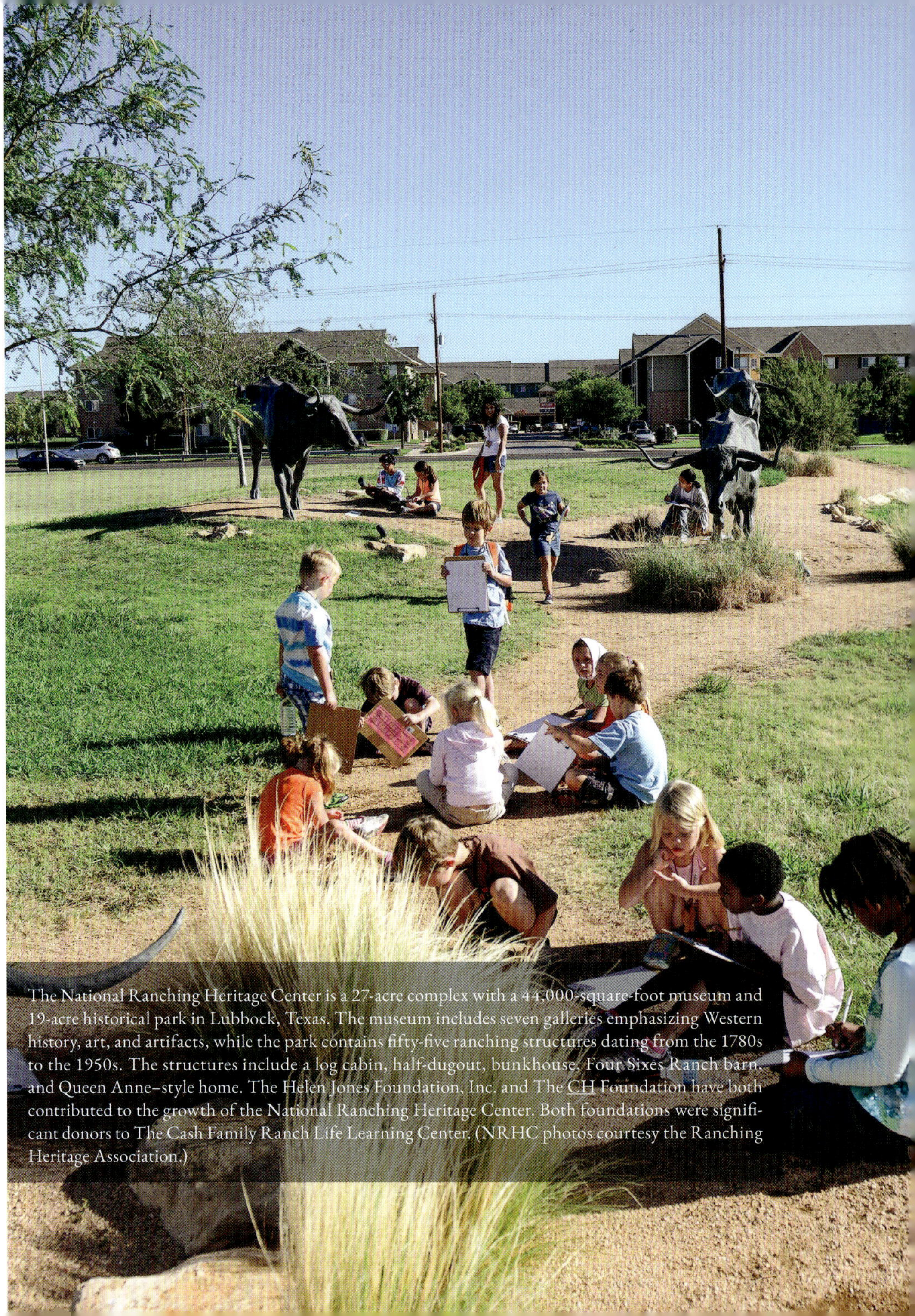

The National Ranching Heritage Center is a 27-acre complex with a 44,000-square-foot museum and 19-acre historical park in Lubbock, Texas. The museum includes seven galleries emphasizing Western history, art, and artifacts, while the park contains fifty-five ranching structures dating from the 1780s to the 1950s. The structures include a log cabin, half-dugout, bunkhouse, Four Sixes Ranch barn, and Queen Anne–style home. The Helen Jones Foundation, Inc. and The CH Foundation have both contributed to the growth of the National Ranching Heritage Center. Both foundations were significant donors to The Cash Family Ranch Life Learning Center. (NRHC photos courtesy the Ranching Heritage Association.)

FOREWORD

What follows is a book that's doing several things. Historian Scott Sosebee documents the history of the Mallet Ranch from its inception through its struggles to its successes, and then he traces the impact of the ranch's wealth throughout the region and beyond. That is the story in the text. But you can also see the Mallet Ranch story through the book's images, which include historical photographs of people and places, beautiful contemporary landscapes by the incomparable Wyman Meinzer, and snapshots of organizations and initiatives that Helen DeVitt Jones and Christine DeVitt have supported over the years. Braided together, these stories form an illuminating picture of struggle and success on the Texas South Plains.

One such initiative, the National Ranching Heritage Center (NRHC), exists to preserve and promote the tradition and history of ranching and address contemporary ranching issues. From its beginning, the two sisters left indelible tracks on the development of the Ranching Heritage Center through their personal commitments and those of their foundations. The NRHC might still exist, but it would not be the world-class facility it is today without Helen DeVitt Jones and Christine DeVitt. A walk through the center reveals how much is owed to the sisters. From the Mallet Ranch Museum Building to the Christine DeVitt Wing to the Helen DeVitt Jones Endowed Director of Collections, Exhibits, and Research and the Helen DeVitt Jones Endowed Director of Education, their names resonate through the halls. In addition, the foundations have funded exhibits, programming, and educational opportunities that have enriched the lives of people across the world.

Cultural institutions across the South Plains have the same story to tell. The sisters' generosity and vision to establish The CH Foundation and the Helen Jones Foundation, Inc. have made generational impacts on arts and cultural organizations across this region, from the NRHC to Texas Tech University to the state-of-the-art Buddy Holly Hall. Their total commitment to Texas Tech University alone exceeds $100 million. But Helen DeVitt Jones's and Christine DeVitt's influence cannot be quantified in dollars and cents. Their dedication and that of their foundations to raising the standard of life for the South Plains community are reflected in their investments from their ranching roots.

Their father, former newspaperman David M. DeVitt, ventured into West Texas and bought land on the vast expanses of the South Plains seeking his fortune in the booming cattle business of the late 1800s. After establishing the Mallet Land and Cattle Company in 1903, the family survived volatile cattle markets, harsh weather, and fluctuating political tides over the next forty years. In 1938, four years after the patriarch's death, oil was discovered on the Mallet Ranch, which had been held together through the Great Depression by the sisters and their mother.

More Than Running Cattle: The Mallet Ranch of the South Plains tells the story of the DeVitt family and the ongoing influence that Helen DeVitt Jones and Christine DeVitt have had on the South Plains community through their personal generosity and that of their foundations. Through the continuing work of the Helen Jones Foundation, Inc. and The CH Foundation, new chapters will be written on their impact on the South Plains community.

JIM BRET CAMPBELL
EXECUTIVE DIRECTOR,
NATIONAL RANCHING HERITAGE CENTER

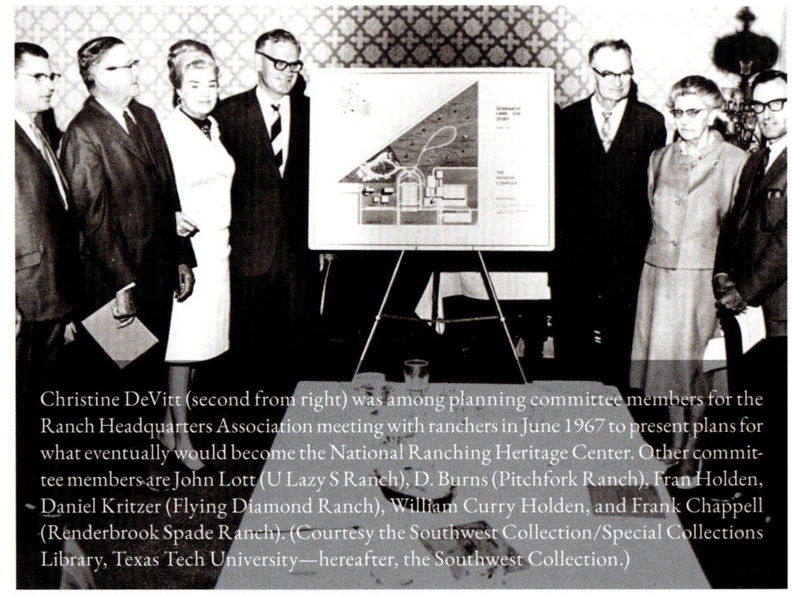

Christine DeVitt (second from right) was among planning committee members for the Ranch Headquarters Association meeting with ranchers in June 1967 to present plans for what eventually would become the National Ranching Heritage Center. Other committee members are John Lott (U Lazy S Ranch), D. Burns (Pitchfork Ranch), Fran Holden, Daniel Kritzer (Flying Diamond Ranch), William Curry Holden, and Frank Chappell (Renderbrook Spade Ranch). (Courtesy the Southwest Collection/Special Collections Library, Texas Tech University—hereafter, the Southwest Collection.)

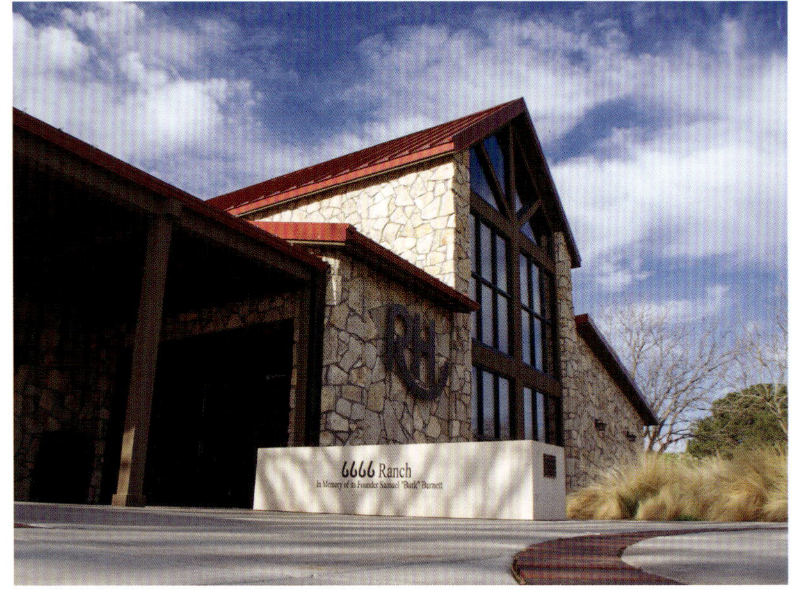

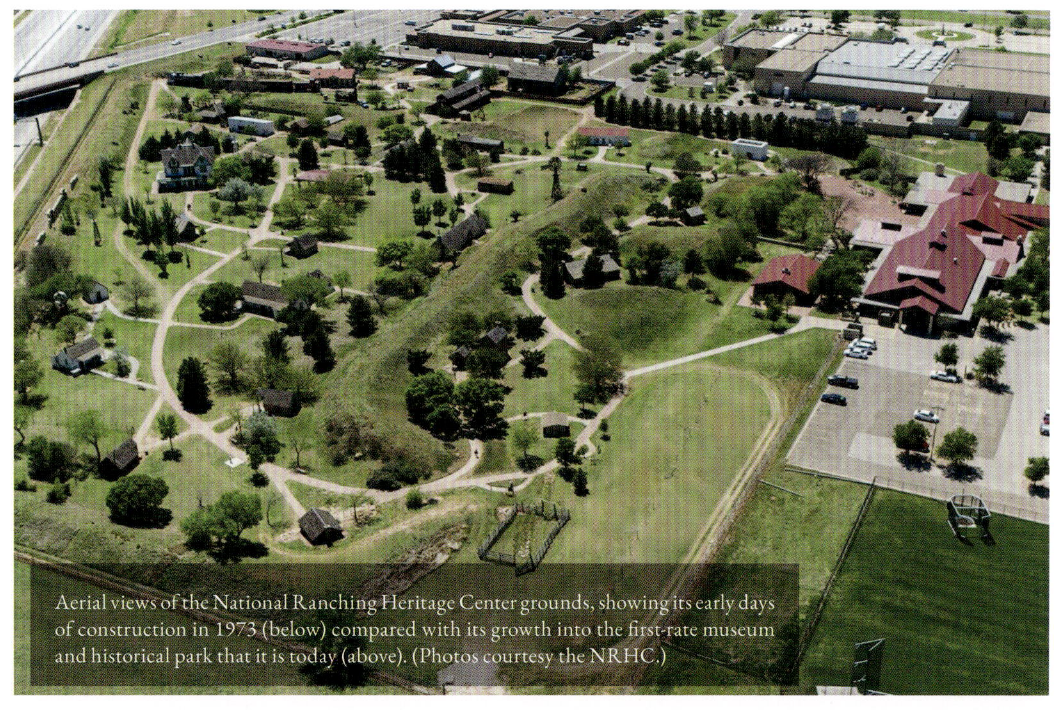

Aerial views of the National Ranching Heritage Center grounds, showing its early days of construction in 1973 (below) compared with its growth into the first-rate museum and historical park that it is today (above). (Photos courtesy the NRHC.)

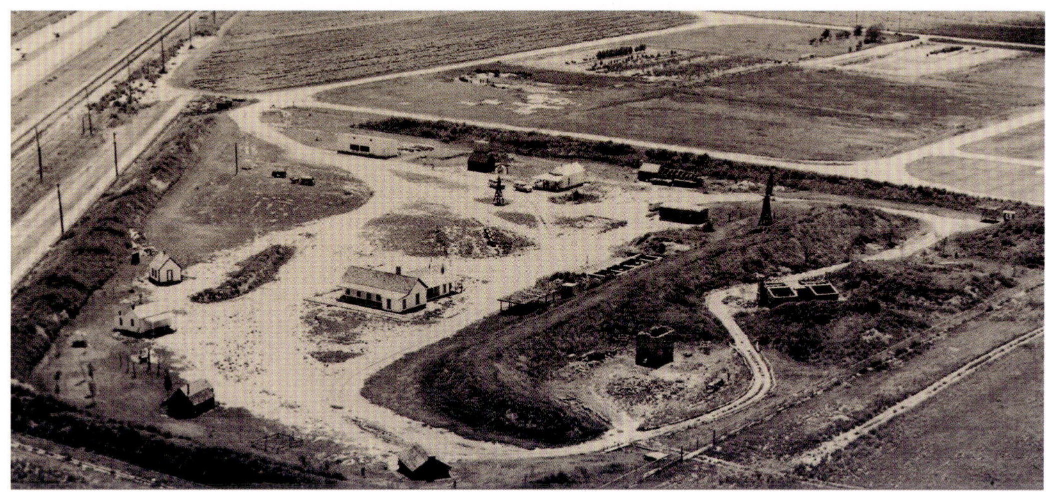

ACKNOWLEDGMENTS

No matter whose name appears on the cover, no author writes a book alone. It takes many people filling many roles to make a written work happen. This work is no different, as multiple people and institutions have helped to make this story of the Mallet Ranch a reality. First and foremost, not one word of text, one single photo, or anything else even begins without the beneficence of the Helen Jones Foundation, Inc. of Lubbock, Texas. Their generous financial support and desire to continue the legacy of the Mallet Ranch and the DeVitt family is what made everything between the covers of this book happen. The National Ranching Heritage Center (NHRC), and specifically its executive director, Jim Bret Campbell, has been the Helen Jones Foundation, Inc.'s partner in this endeavor and equally shares in the efforts to make this book possible. Jim Bret was generous with his time and advice on the direction of the work, and he and his staff provided support during the entire process. Thanks to all involved at the NRHC for their immeasurable assistance. Also, I want to thank Travis Snyder at Texas Tech University Press, first for being very patient with me as I worked through this project, and second for being the epitome of what a good editor is supposed to be: quick with advice and encouragement when he needed to be and steadfast at all other times. He is a big part of the end result.

As I hand out thanks, Dr. David Murrah is high on the list. As author of the wonderful *Oil, Taxes, and Cats: A History of the DeVitt Family and the Mallet Ranch*, Dr. Murrah had already trod every step I took in learning about and chronicling the DeVitt family and the Mallet Ranch. I would not have taken on this project without David's blessing, and whenever I could not quite figure something out or find a direction to take, Dr. Murrah was there to offer guidance. I have tried to come from a different angle than he did, but in many places the works do still mirror each other, so whatever is produced here is just a companion to what he has done before and will never supersede. Thanks, David, for everything you did.

Historical authors are allowed to be the public face of historical works, but every historian worth their salt will tell you that the heroes of the profession are the archivists, and I had some of the best in the business help me. Texas Tech's Southwest Collection/Special Collections Library is one of the finest repositories in the nation, and their staff is second to none, but two—for me—stood out and went above and beyond the call of duty. Archivist Dr. Monte Monroe ran interference for me in making the Mallet records available and also helped to search for whatever I needed to finish this project. He is also a first-rate historian—a requirement for the State Historian of Texas, a role in which he serves—as well as a great friend. In all capacities he bore with my complaints, allowed me to bounce ideas and questions off him, and most of all just listened to and encouraged me as I worked. Weston Marshall, associate archivist at the collection, was there every day to help me in finding the records I needed, arranging for copying, and doing an exemplary job that too often goes unrewarded. Weston, thank you for your cheerfulness and generosity, and for always smiling while this sometimes-clueless historian made another request.

Once again, I have to thank Dr. Paul H. Carlson. He has been and will be a part of anything I produce as a historian because he is the one who, through teaching and observation, taught me to be a historian. He continues to guide me every day, and his advice, as always, helped chart a course for me as I finished. I also must thank my friend and fellow historian Dr. Deborah Liles for being someone I could always "bounce something off," but also for always giving positive encouragement as I worked. Three of my colleagues at Stephen F. Austin State University—Drs. Perky Beisel, Brook Poston, and Paul J. P. Sandul—served in similar roles, and their help and reassurance were invaluable. I offer special thanks to Chris Gill, the secretary of the East Texas Historical Association, who has to share the walls of an office with me. She listened to me wail, yell, cuss, and engage in countless other pleas with nothing but a smile. I know she is secretly grateful whenever I finish a manuscript.

Finally, and certainly not least, all my love and thanks to my wife and life partner Leslie Daniel. She makes me feel like a "star" when I'm decidedly not and props me up twenty-four hours a day with her love and cheerleading. She deserves co-authorship in this and everything I do because I could never ask for a better partner.

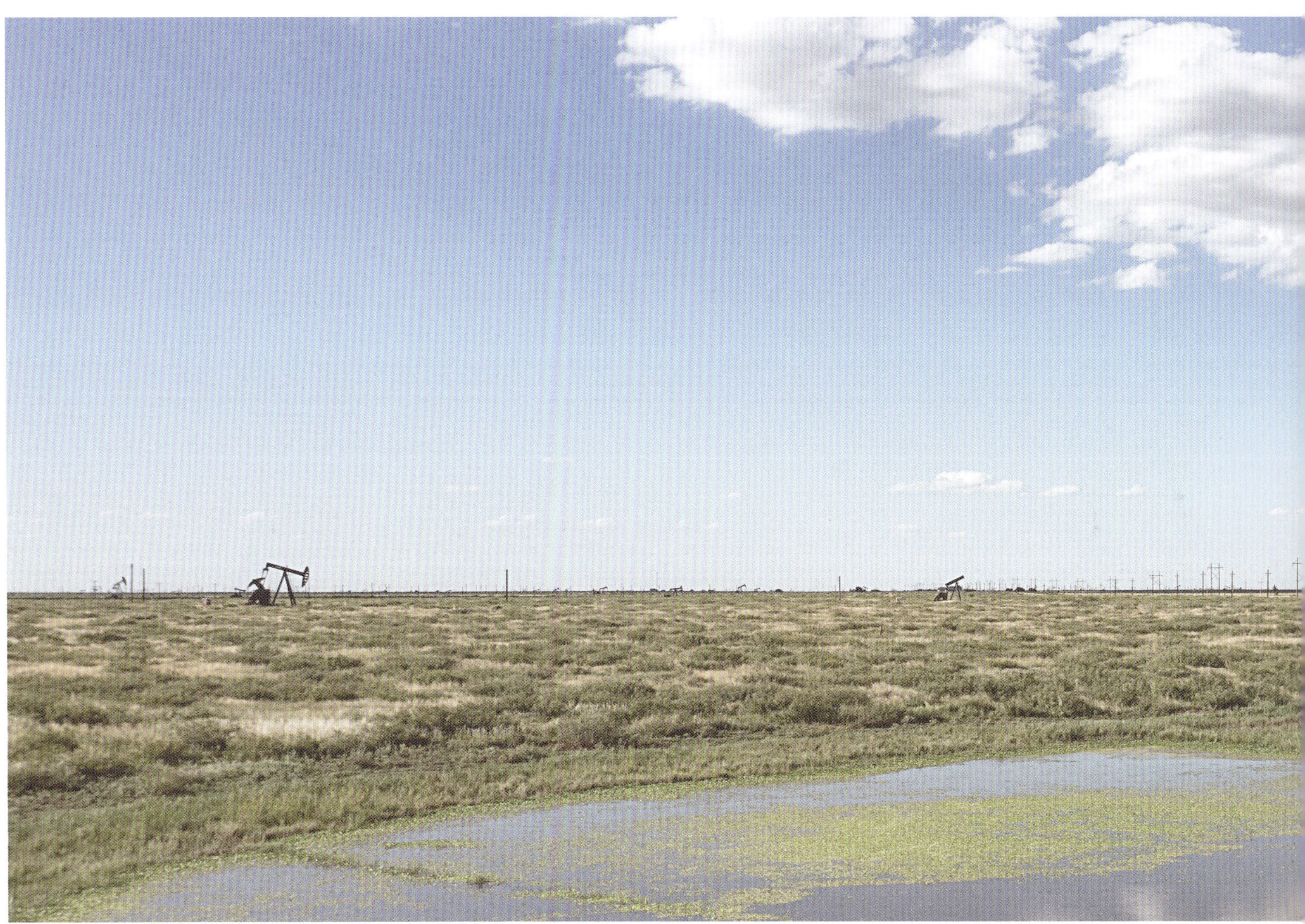

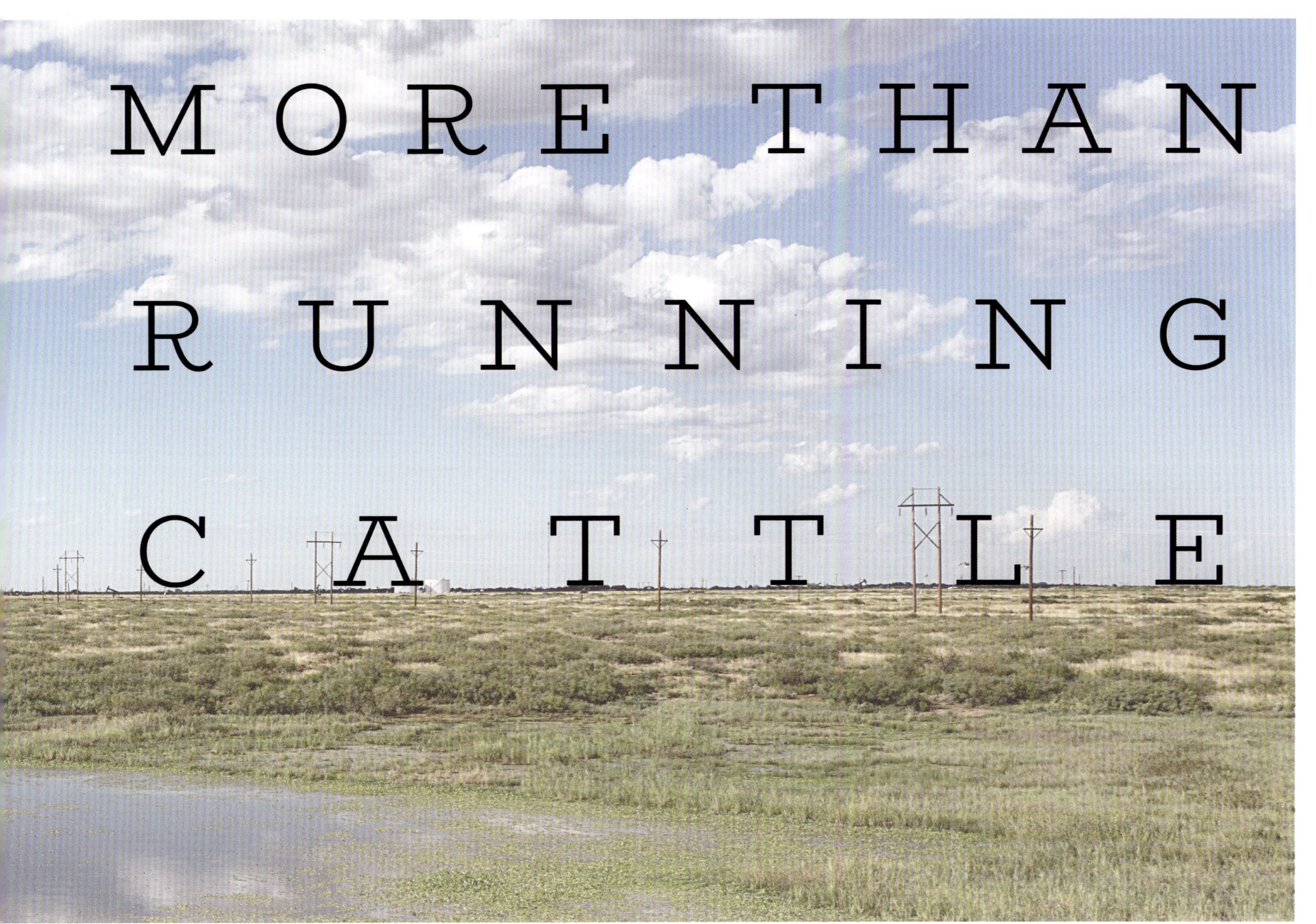
MORE THAN
RUNNING
CATTLE

INTRODUCTION

On one of the rare overcast summer days with threatening thunderstorms in Lubbock, Texas, the Ranching Heritage Center (known since 1999 as the National Ranching Heritage Center) held its official dedication ceremony on July 2, 1976. The center was the brainchild in 1966 of Dr. Grover E. Murray, eighth president of Texas Tech University. Murray had the idea that if European cities could create representations of medieval cities and eastern US municipalities such as Williamsburg could build replicas of colonial towns, Lubbock could take on the preservation and chronicling of the region's most iconic institution—the stock ranch.

The physical remnants of historical ranches in the state and region were crumbling into disrepair and oblivion at that time, and Murray's vision was to create an outdoor complex that would not only record a history of stock raising but also preserve the historic buildings before they disappeared. Texas Tech had recently committed to a center for the study of arid lands, and Murray believed that a complex helping to tell the narrative of ranching in the arid land of the South Plains was thus a perfect fit. He also knew exactly who he wanted to chair the committee organized to explore the idea: William Curry Holden. Dr. Holden had been at Texas Tech University since 1929, first as a history and anthropology professor (he became chair of the department in 1936), then as dean of the graduate school, but perhaps most significantly as the organizer and director of the West Texas Museum (now the Museum of Texas Tech University) since 1936.

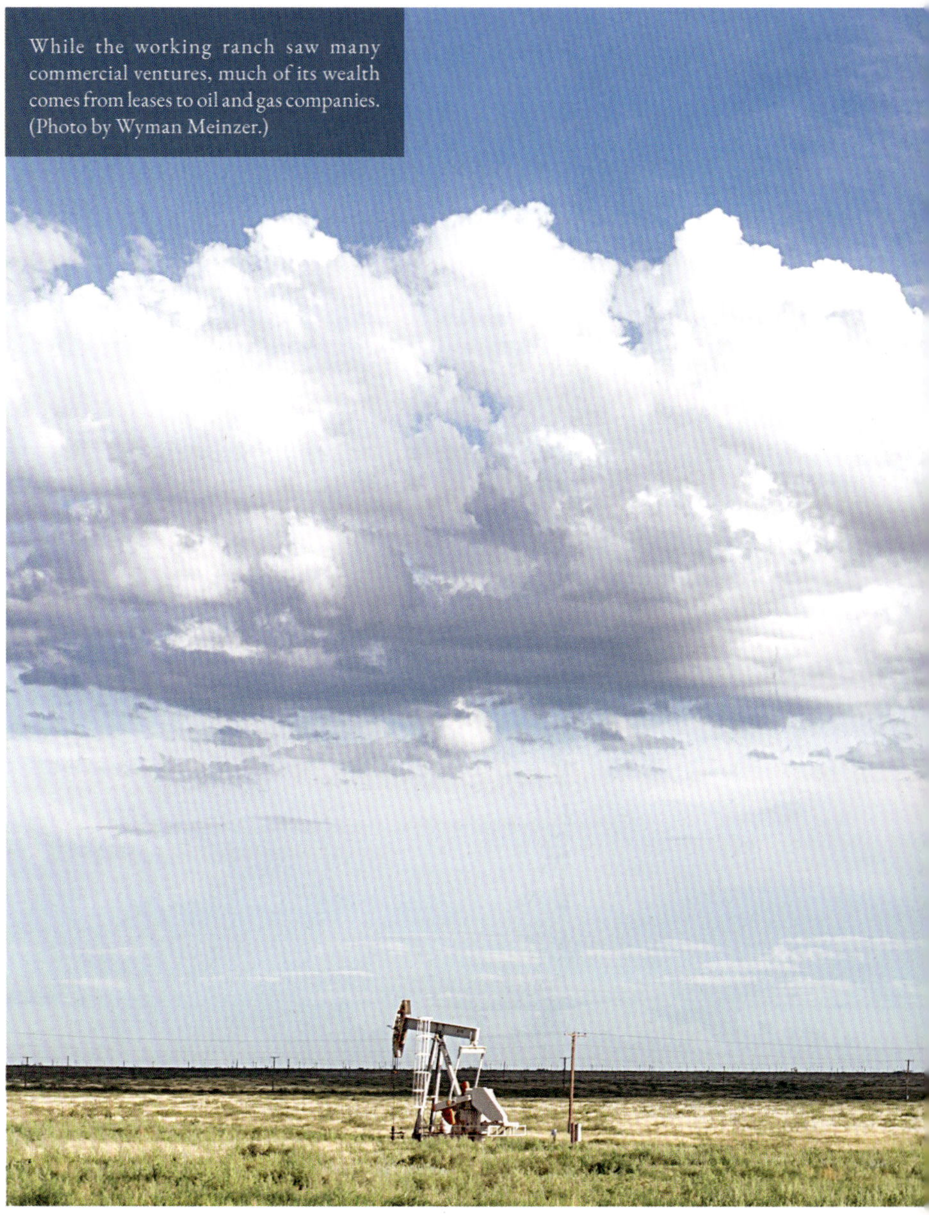
While the working ranch saw many commercial ventures, much of its wealth comes from leases to oil and gas companies. (Photo by Wyman Meinzer.)

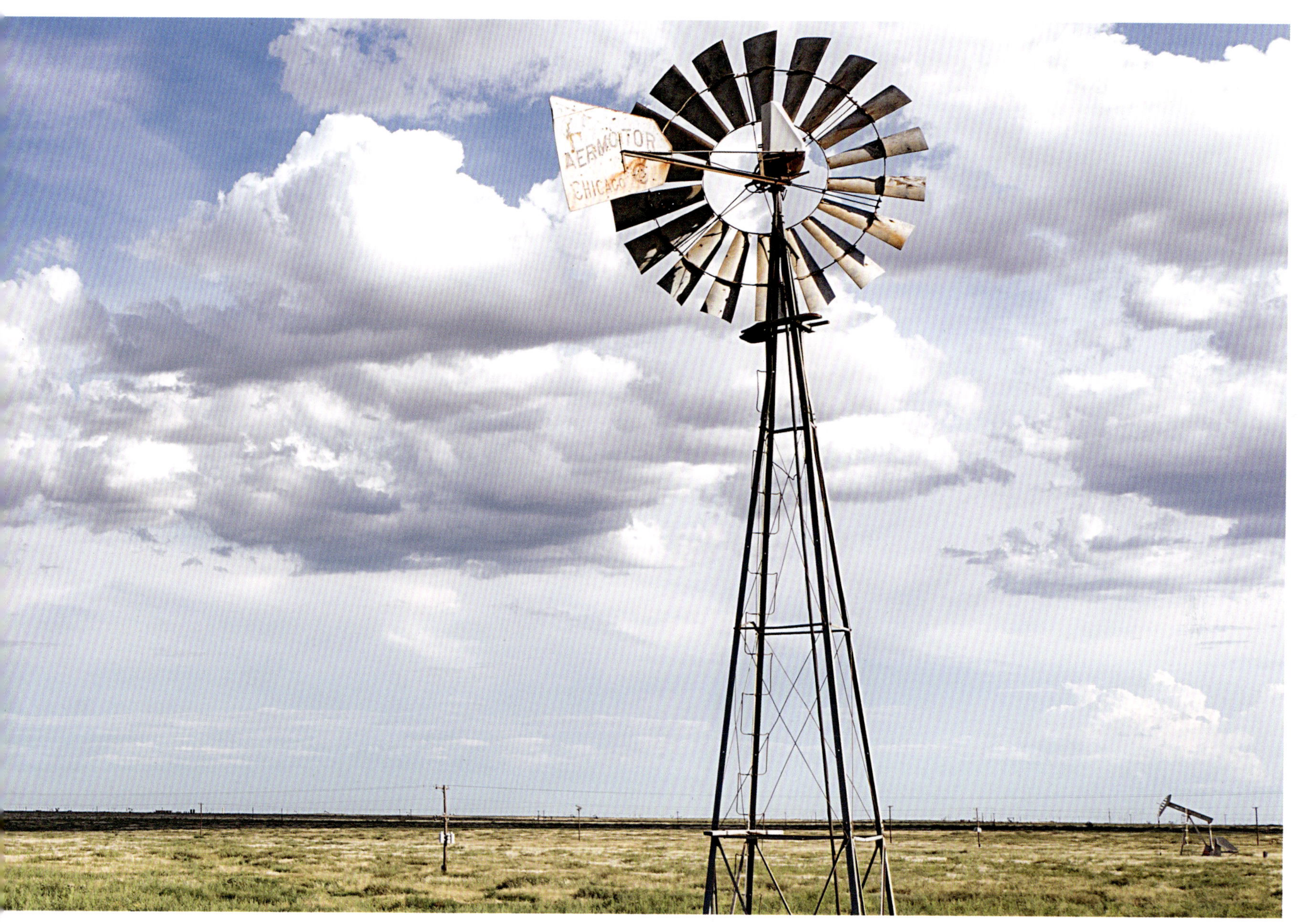
AERMOTOR
CHICAGO

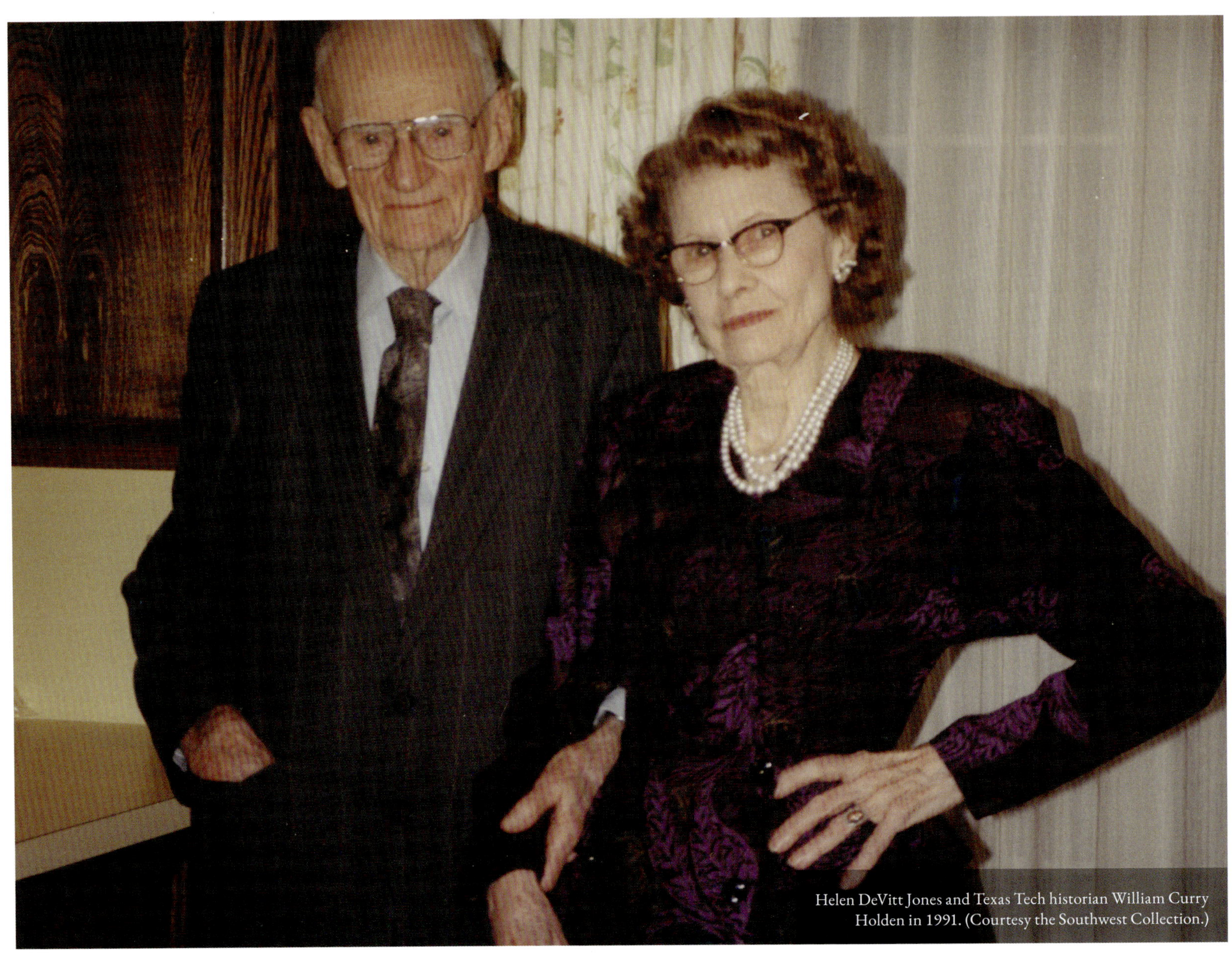

Helen DeVitt Jones and Texas Tech historian William Curry Holden in 1991. (Courtesy the Southwest Collection.)

Holden accepted the charge and in 1966 formed an initial planning committee that would undertake a feasibility study on support for such a ranching center. The membership of that 1966 committee included Holden, with D. Burns, Frank Chappell Jr., Howard Hampton, and John Lott Sr. Texas Tech had designated land it owned near the main campus adjacent to the West Texas Museum to house the project, and for almost a decade the committee located appropriate buildings and arranged for their transport, placement, and preservation. The committee had discovered and placed nineteen buildings and three windmills by 1976. As the work neared completion, they designated an opening ceremony for the park that would be part of the official 1976 United States Bicentennial Celebration in Lubbock. The work of the committee was admirable, but it required funding far above what Texas Tech was able to allocate and the pittance the project received from the State of Texas. If there was actually to be a Ranching Heritage Center, the committee needed to raise money. Holden knew of one person he could surely turn to who would help make that happen, a woman he had known for years, the extant matron of a pioneering family that had established one of the most successful stock operations on the South Plains: Christine DeVitt.

Miss DeVitt—the moniker most people used for Christine—responded generously. Between 1967 and the official opening of the Ranching Heritage Center in 1976, she contributed more than a million dollars to the project, was a member of the first Board of Overseers for the museum, and was the primary funding arm of the historical project. Her largesse also led to naming the main building the David M. DeVitt and Mallet Ranch Museum Building and designing the structure to resemble the Mallet Ranch headquarters in Hockley County. Today more than 62,000 visitors a year view exhibits in this building and walk through the doorways to enter the 27.5-acre historic park.

Christine DeVitt's health would not allow her to attend the July 2 park dedication, but she was a central figure in Grover Murray's speech at the opening. Murray related to the audience that he had called her that morning and she had sent a message that was, to those who knew her, pure Christine DeVitt. Murray said, "She is thankful to her parents for the selection of land on which the Mallet Ranch and Cattle Company was founded. She's very appreciative to the oil companies and to the oil industry which helped develop that land and which provided the funding. And she's very appreciative of Uncle Sam's magnanimous tax structure which has prevented even greater contributions on her part."

The dedication of the museum building on that July day was in many ways the climax of a story that is now over a hundred years in the making. While the DeVitt family's beneficence—of both Christine and her sister Helen—provided a large portion of the funds that went into constructing and conceiving the most impressive preservation of ranch life in the nation and played a huge role in the naming of the museum headquarters, the choice of the Mallet Ranch was also appropriate. From its founding to the present, the Mallet has followed the arc of most Texas ranches. It was an open-range operation that transformed into a ranch running blooded-stock Herefords and then dividing into farmland as well as ranch land and then extracting petroleum to help save the operation and enrich the DeVitt family. The Mallet experienced booms and busts and fretted over droughts, floods, and courtroom battles. It progressed to a modern corporation managed by a board of directors and, despite hardships that may have outnumbered successes, perseveres through today. In other words, it is the story of a Texas ranch.

It is more than just a ranch story, however. The Mallet history is both conventional and unique among Texas stock raisers. David Mantz DeVitt, like many before him, was not "born" to be a Texas cattleman. He was born in 1856 in Frederick, Maryland, and began his career as a reporter for the *Brooklyn Daily Eagle* in Brooklyn, New York. He decided to leave that career behind to try his luck with his brother on the ranges of West Texas, a move that must have seemed curious to his friends in the Empire State. His first efforts in the arid lands of the Texas Permian Basin were more hit than miss; tensions between sheepmen and cattlemen caused the two brothers to move their operations north into a region that had until recently supported bison. By the late nineteenth century, the Llano Estacado was in the beginning stages of stocking cattle. DeVitt had to transition from open range to fenced pastures and once again faced adversities that rivaled attainment. Still, he persisted.

Perhaps David DeVitt was just stubborn. If so, he certainly passed this trait on to his two daughters. Although Christine and Helen were raised in Fort Worth and spent a good part of their young adult lives in California, both must have learned the lesson that the land—and the Mallet Ranch—were part of their soul. When David DeVitt died in 1934, the Mallet Land and Cattle Company Board of Directors planned to sell the ranch and exit the cattle business on the South Plains, but they ran into an immovable object at odds with such a strategy: Christine DeVitt. Her mother, Florence, along with Christine and Helen, had inherited David DeVitt's majority share of the Mallet operation. Florence and David had endured a difficult marriage and as a result Florence had spent the better part of the last two decades before her husband's death in California. As a result, she had taken little interest in the business her husband operated in West Texas. The board of the cattle company believed little opposition would exist to its plans of liquidation, but they had not anticipated daughter Christine's tenacity. She urged her mother and sister to keep their holdings and thus together they could control the board and its actions. Furthermore, Christine took on her father's role in operating the stock and farm operations and vowed to continue to support the family on the Great Depression–ravaged profits of the isolated ranch on the semi-arid plains of Northwest Texas. It would not be an easy venture for Miss DeVitt: she would have to endure almost constant opposition from her business partners (involving years of legal fights) and doubt from her mother and sister about such a direction. In the end, Christine's resolve won out, and the Mallet Ranch stayed intact with Christine DeVitt as the operational force.

Fate more often determines the direction of human endeavors than most people realize. Such was the case with the Mallet. When David M. DeVitt established the Mallet Ranch, he had no way of knowing the riches the land held beneath its bedrock. Christine DeVitt, when she and her sister were fighting for control of their inheritance, likely had no clue of those same potential fortunes. The Mallet Ranch was not the only historic Texas ranch saved by the discovery of oil and gas beneath its surface, but it is one of the most spectacular examples. Despite Christine DeVitt's insistence on continuing to operate the Mallet as her father had done before her, the ravages of the Great Depression, the vagaries of the cattle industry, and the capricious climatological challenges of agricultural pursuits in such an environment might very well have ended the operation or forced Christine and the board of directors to divide it into sections to sell, a fate that had befallen numerous stock operations in Texas during the period. The Mallet found a savior underneath the harsh lands upon which the owners had scattered cattle. Discovery of oil on the ranch and the subsequent drilling of more than a thousand oil wells over the next few decades transformed the Mallet from a struggling enterprise into one of the most profitable ranches in the nation.

Christine DeVitt directed much of her energies toward operating the Mallet Ranch and dealing with the oil companies whose royalties built the family's fortune, but she also began to use part of her ranch proceeds for philanthropy. She formed The CH Foundation in 1969 using the CH brand her father designated for cattle owned by Christine and her brother Harold, who died in 1901. The brand subsequently became that of the cattle she owned with her sister, Helen, who was fourteen years younger. Helen was married to Tom Jones until his death in 1955. In 1984 she incorporated her own foundation—the Helen Jones Foundation, Inc. Both sisters gave millions of dollars in philanthropic gifts before their foundations were ever formed, but the two foundations combined have given more than $367 million to South Plains hospitals, public and private schools, higher education institutions, museums, libraries, human and health services, youth leadership, and a multitude of fine arts programs and projects. The charitable arms of the DeVitt sisters embraced the region they and the Mallet Ranch called home. As a result, the Mallet story has no ending as long as the accumulated wealth of the family members spreads over the South Plains into the lives of those who reside where the bison once roamed.

Few operations like the Mallet Ranch have survived for a lengthy time, and even fewer have maintained not only a record of continuing operation on their original tract but also a profile of philanthropy and benevolence. The Mallet story in this volume will feature some twists and turns that echo those of a fictional novel but will be more enticing and engaging because it is real life. By design it also will be the study of a Texas ranch—how it was formed, the land that made it all possible, the hardships that accompanied each new decade, and the journey to becoming one of the most recognizable enterprises of its kind in Texas history.

CHAPTER 1

GO WEST, YOUNG MAN

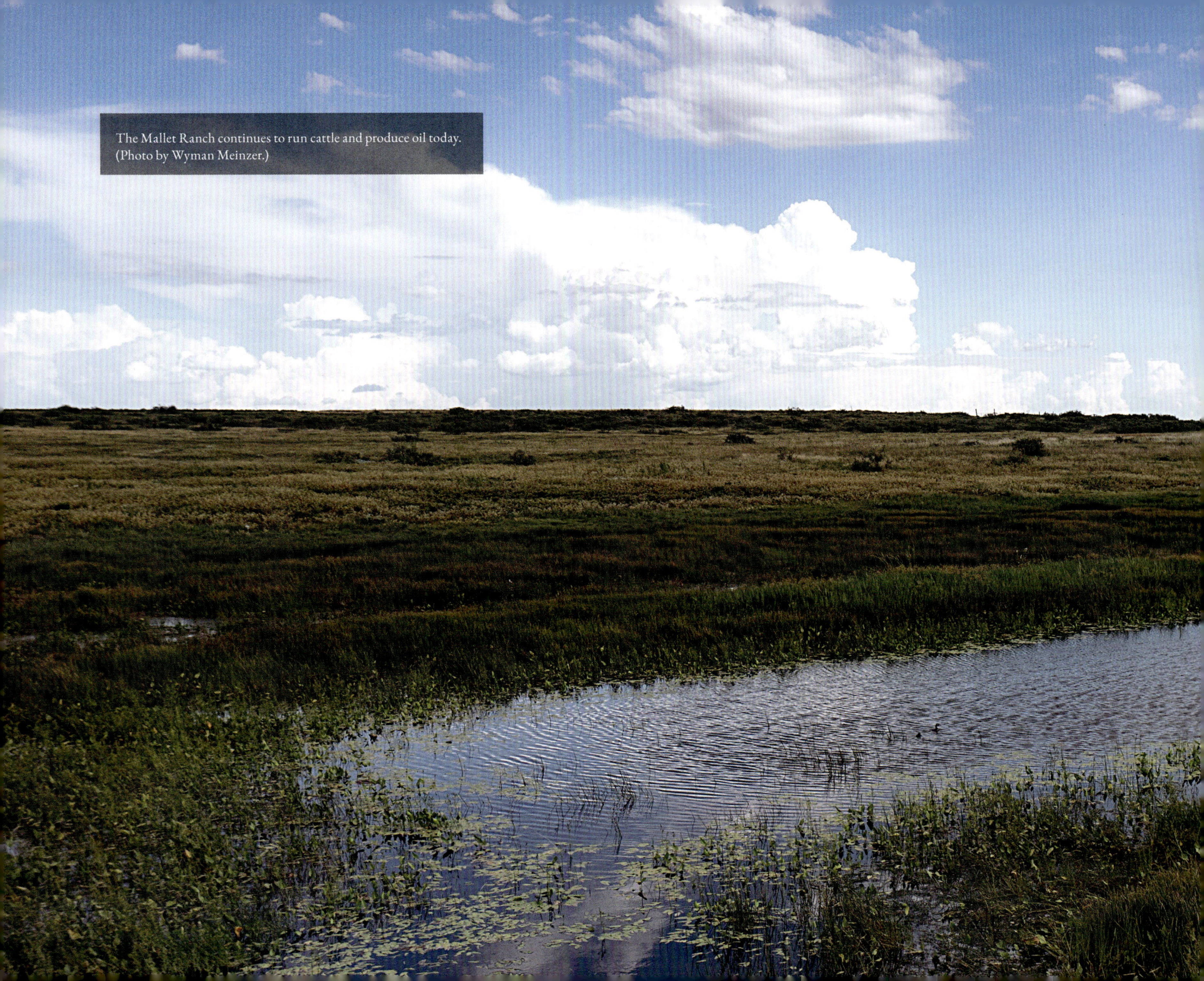
The Mallet Ranch continues to run cattle and produce oil today. (Photo by Wyman Meinzer.)

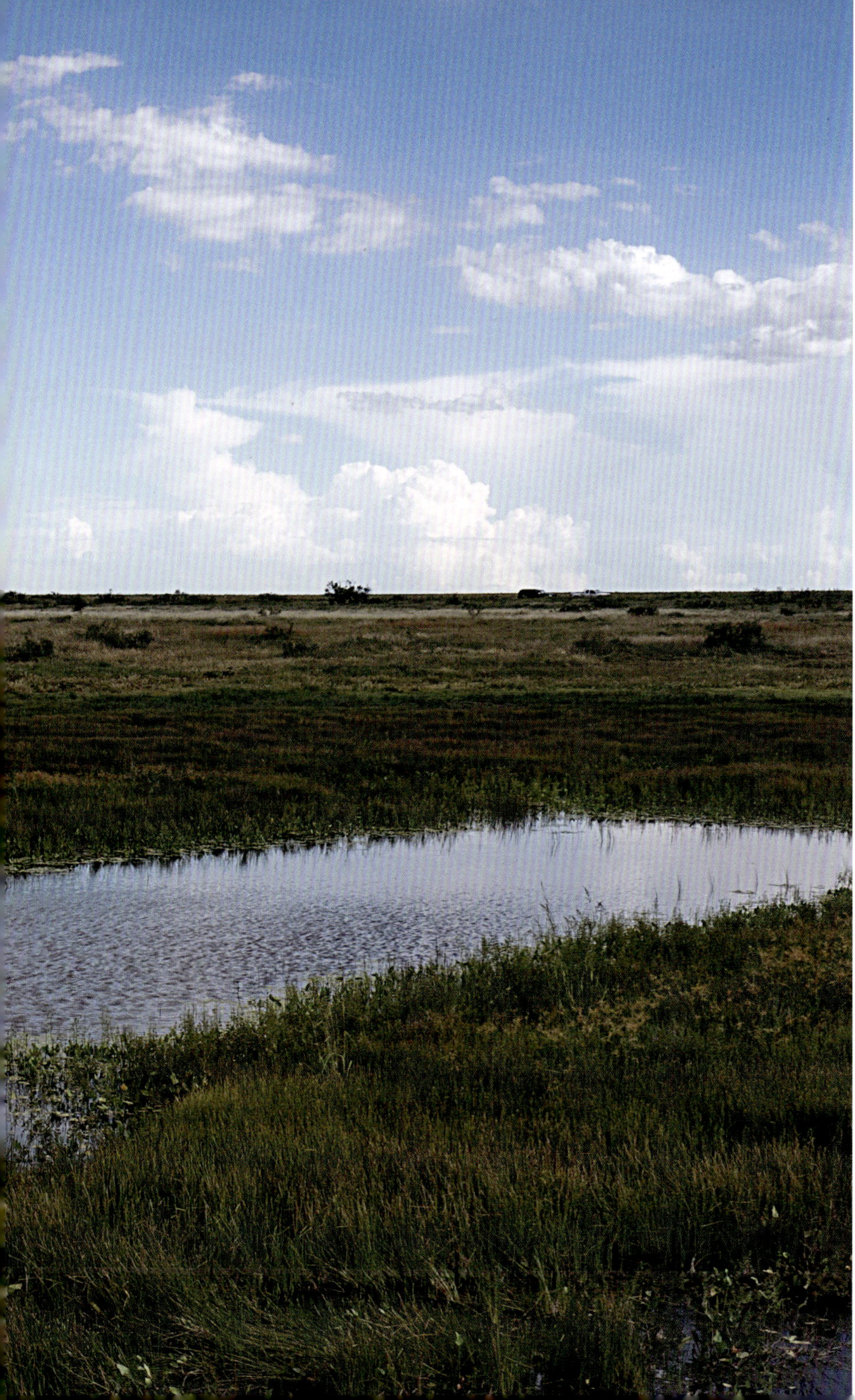

David Mantz DeVitt Jr. took a circuitous route to becoming the majority owner of an iconic and historic Texas ranch. Like a good number of Texas residents in the late 1800s, DeVitt was not, as many like to trumpet these days, a native Texan. But, as one often sees on bumper stickers and social media in the present, he did get here as fast as he could. Tragedy cloaked DeVitt's early life. David Mantz DeVitt Sr., his father, died at age 30 in a carriage accident while his mother, Elizabeth, was pregnant. Named after his father, David Mantz DeVitt was born six months after his father's death in 1856. Elizabeth and her sons—David and his older brother Phillip—moved to Washington, DC, soon after the Civil War. When he was just fifteen, David went to work as a page in the United States House of Representatives, which led him into contact with the press and an early effort to be a journalist. He apprenticed for a number of outlets in Washington, DC, before moving to New York and becoming a reporter for the *Brooklyn Daily Eagle* in the late 1870s.

Brooklyn, New York, must have been a heady experience for a young journalist in the 1880s. Originally a small village across the East River from its more famous cousin on Manhattan Island, Brooklyn had both a population and economic surge after completion of the Erie Canal in 1825. Numerous industrial factories and shipping firms were located in the city. The population went from not quite 10,000 in the 1820s to nearly 80,000 by 1845 and more than 200,000 by the time David DeVitt was born. When David moved to the metropolis,

Brooklyn had more than 800,000 residents, which made it the third largest city in the United States.

While David DeVitt toiled as a reporter in New York, his older brother Phillip became one of the hundreds of thousands who had "gone to Texas" after the Civil War. Phillip and his wife moved to the Lone Star State in 1876 to try their hand at the booming business of raising livestock. Phillip wrote his brother glowing reports of the land in Texas—most of them imploring him to join him. They must have worked, as David traveled to see his brother in late 1878. After returning to Brooklyn, David wrote a number of articles for the *Eagle* in which he described the abundant and fertile land in Texas, the great opportunities in raising stock for anyone willing to try ranching, and the "frontier waiting for those with the spirit to take a chance to make a fortune." DeVitt's romantic-tinged articles mirrored a number of others extolling Texas's virtues in the late nineteenth century, a narrative that fueled much of Texas's post–Civil War population growth. There is no way of determining how many people DeVitt's writing had convinced to move to Texas, but it obviously persuaded one person to do so: David M. DeVitt himself followed his brother to Texas in 1880. Their mother moved to Fort Worth in 1883.

David and Phillip DeVitt's first venture came in the form of a sheep operation on the western edge of the Edwards Plateau near the contemporary small city of Brady. They had to travel overland from Austin, the nearest train depot to their tract, and in the first year had to live in a tent and subsist on what they could hunt and the meager supplies they could bring with them.

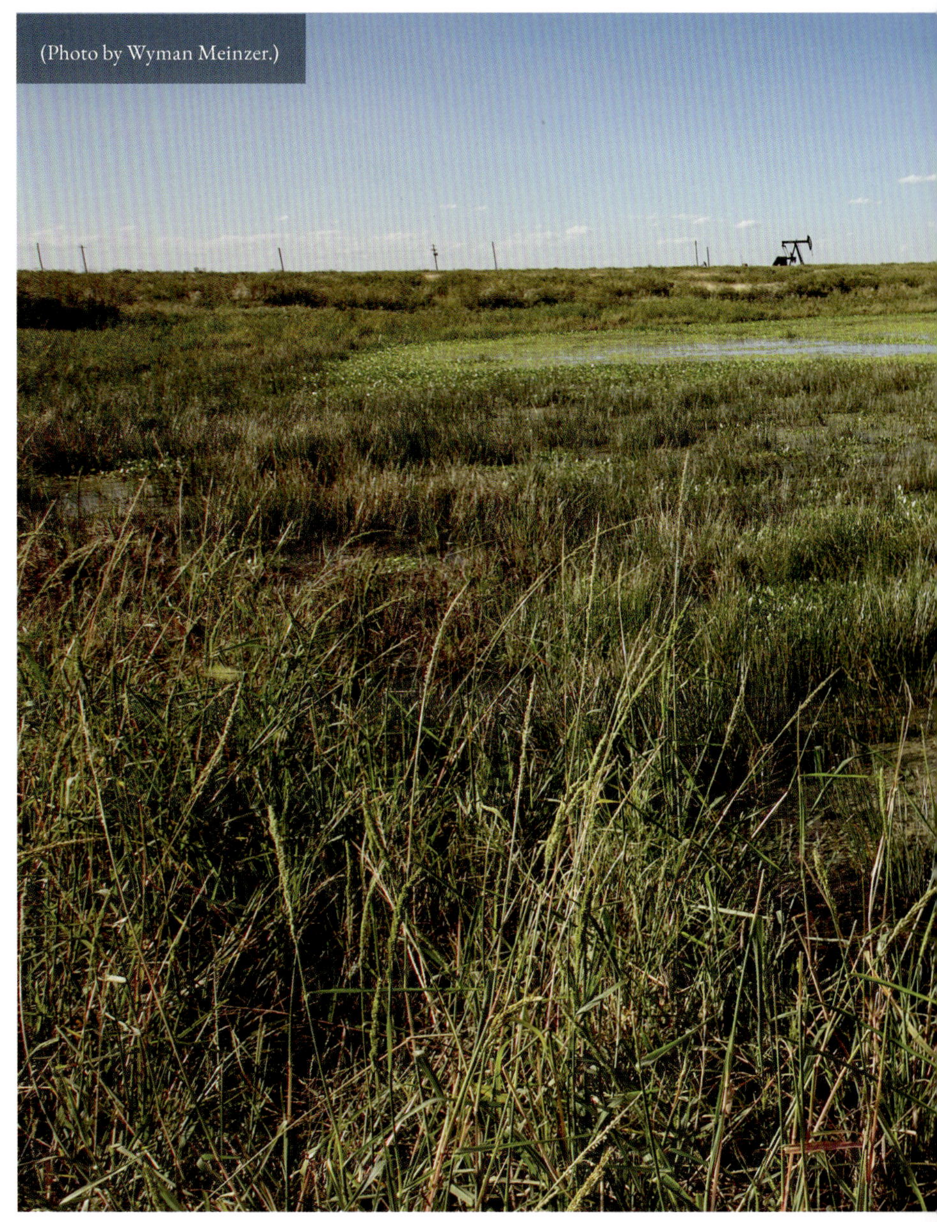
(Photo by Wyman Meinzer.)

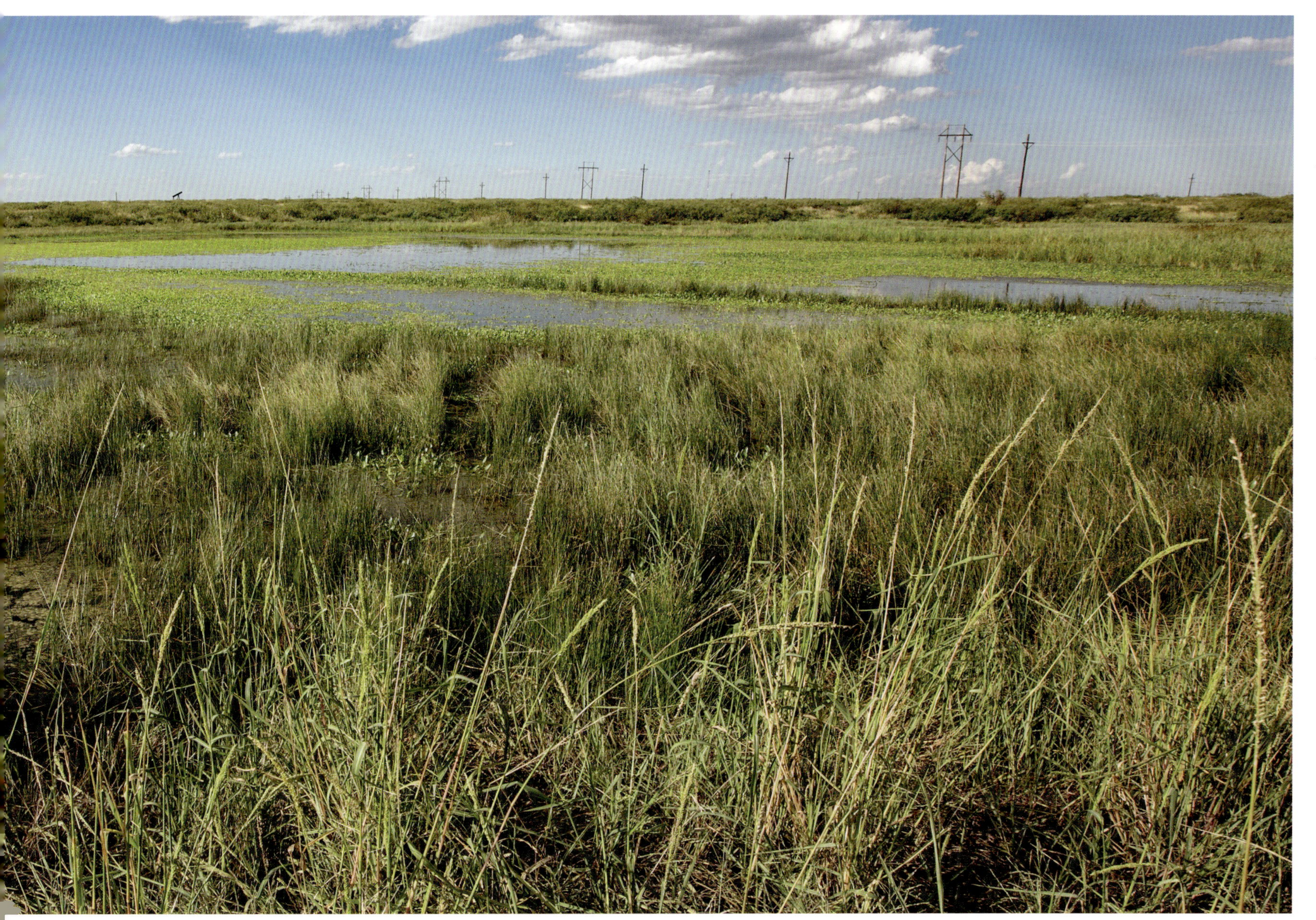

It was a sparsely populated existence, one that had to be a huge change for David, a man who had spent his entire life residing in urban settings in the East. It was a difficult experience for two men not used to living under such spartan—and dangerous—circumstances far away from a populated center. Although the United States Army had built or reoccupied a series of forts along the western frontier line of Texas in 1866–1868 to help alleviate conflict between Anglo migrants and the indigenous Native American dwellers in West Texas, raids did still occasionally occur (although by the 1880s they were rare). More hazardous for the DeVitt brothers were the natural climatic conditions of drought, often followed by floods, harsh winters, and then the broiling heat of summer. Some cattle raisers, who had also begun to move into the region, resented the presence of sheep on the range, which many—erroneously—thought could not occupy the same grazing plots.

The DeVitt brothers had picked a good time to begin to raise sheep in Texas. Although some advantageous factors arose in the years preceding the Civil War, the postbellum years produced a pronounced "sheep boom" in the state. Wool had long been a preferred cloth for many men and women—particularly those in the cooler northern regions of the nation—but cotton was a viable option in the antebellum period. The Civil War changed the equation. War between the regions had cut the supply of cotton available to the dominant New England mills, which caused textile operators to begin to use wool. The reliance on wool also led those manufacturers to develop new techniques in refining the material, processes that not only mechanized

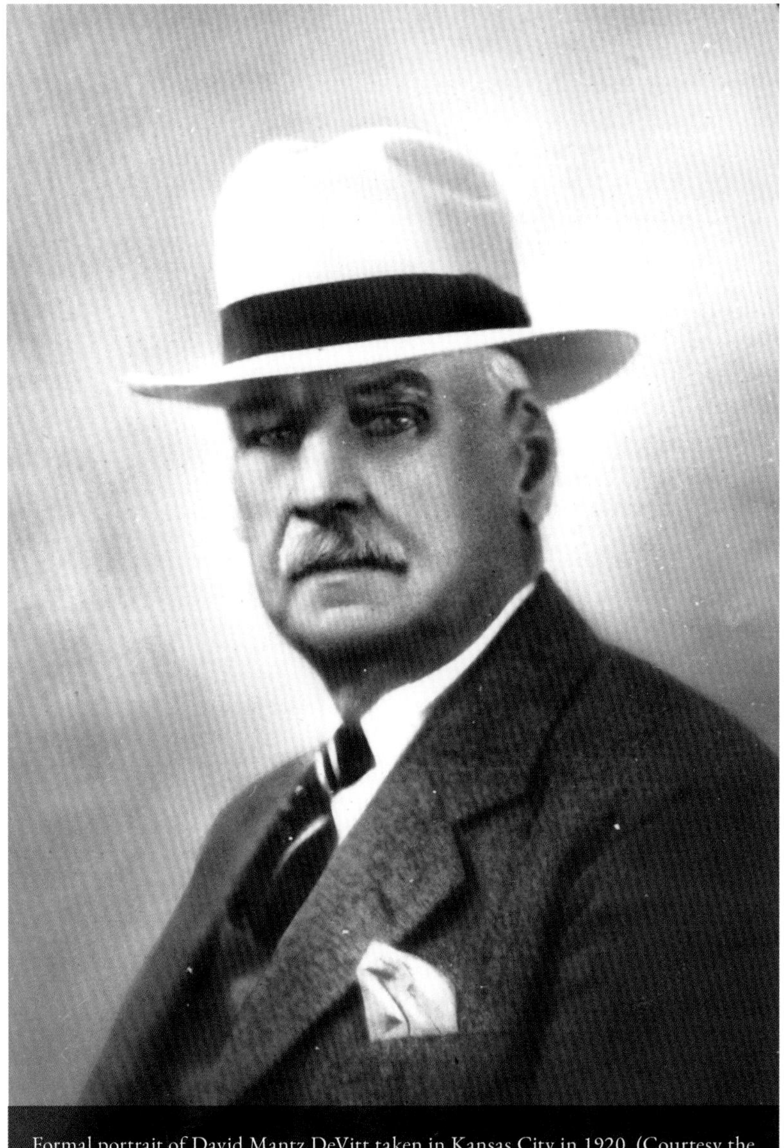
Formal portrait of David Mantz DeVitt taken in Kansas City in 1920. (Courtesy the Southwest Collection.)

many tasks that formerly required manual labor but also made the produced fabric more desirable. At the same time, the end of the war opened up more land in the western reaches of the nation—land that could ably support sheep—with Texas being perhaps the most viable region. Wool processing was ready to take on cotton.

Texas began to lead the range sheep industry. Like the DeVitt brothers, migrants flocked to Texas in huge numbers after the war. The influx of people to Texas—with all of them looking for land and opportunity—caused a natural expansion of the state's populated areas. Such a developing scenario is what caused the United States military to reoccupy and increase their presence in forts and in harassing Native Americans in West Texas. The population followed the Army into the region.

East of the Texas frontier line, sheep shared the land with cotton, cattle, and those who raised all three. Sheep on farms were penned rather than free-range, and because the farmer, his family, and perhaps a few laborers did all the work on an agricultural homestead, sheep flocks were relatively small. Thus, sheep were more of a supplemental stock endeavor, a way to extend a farm income that was often as much bust as it was boom. What that meant was that in Texas heads of sheep were relatively limited, and even when wool prices rose, the number of sheep in the state remained relatively stable at between two and two-and-a-half million through 1876.

Those numbers began to change in the late 1870s. The US Army had by that time either effectively pushed Native Americans onto reservations in Indian Territory or reduced their resistance to white invasion to little more than token. Thus, thousands of people moved west of the old frontier line—including David and Phillip DeVitt—and began to establish both farms and stock operations. Land was plentiful and affordable in West Texas, allowing stock raisers to place animals across open ranges. Wool demand and prices rose even more, which permitted stockmen to profit handsomely from wool clip alone. They could then keep their lambs to expand their flocks and even further serve the increased demand for wool across the nation. The number of sheep on Texas ranges by 1887 had risen to over five million. Texas was certainly in the midst of the sheep boom, one of which the DeVitt brothers hoped to become a part.

Sheepmen began entering what Texans often refer to as the Hill Country in the late 1860s and early 1870s, with settlement of the region generally proceeding from east to west. The DeVitt brothers were late to the migration and thus settled on the western edges of the Edwards Plateau. The Texas Hill Country lies within the Balcones Escarpment, a fault zone of uplift and small hills that separates the coastal plains to the east from the Edwards Plateau to the west. Culturally, geographers often include the eastern edge of the Edwards Plateau in the classification of the Hill Country. The DeVitts' plots were on the Edwards Plateau which, geologically, is the southernmost extension of the Great Plains, that vast, treeless tract that dominates the middle of the North American continent. It is referred to as a plateau because it is an erosional bed of the Great Plains—which exposes the limestone underneath the tablelands

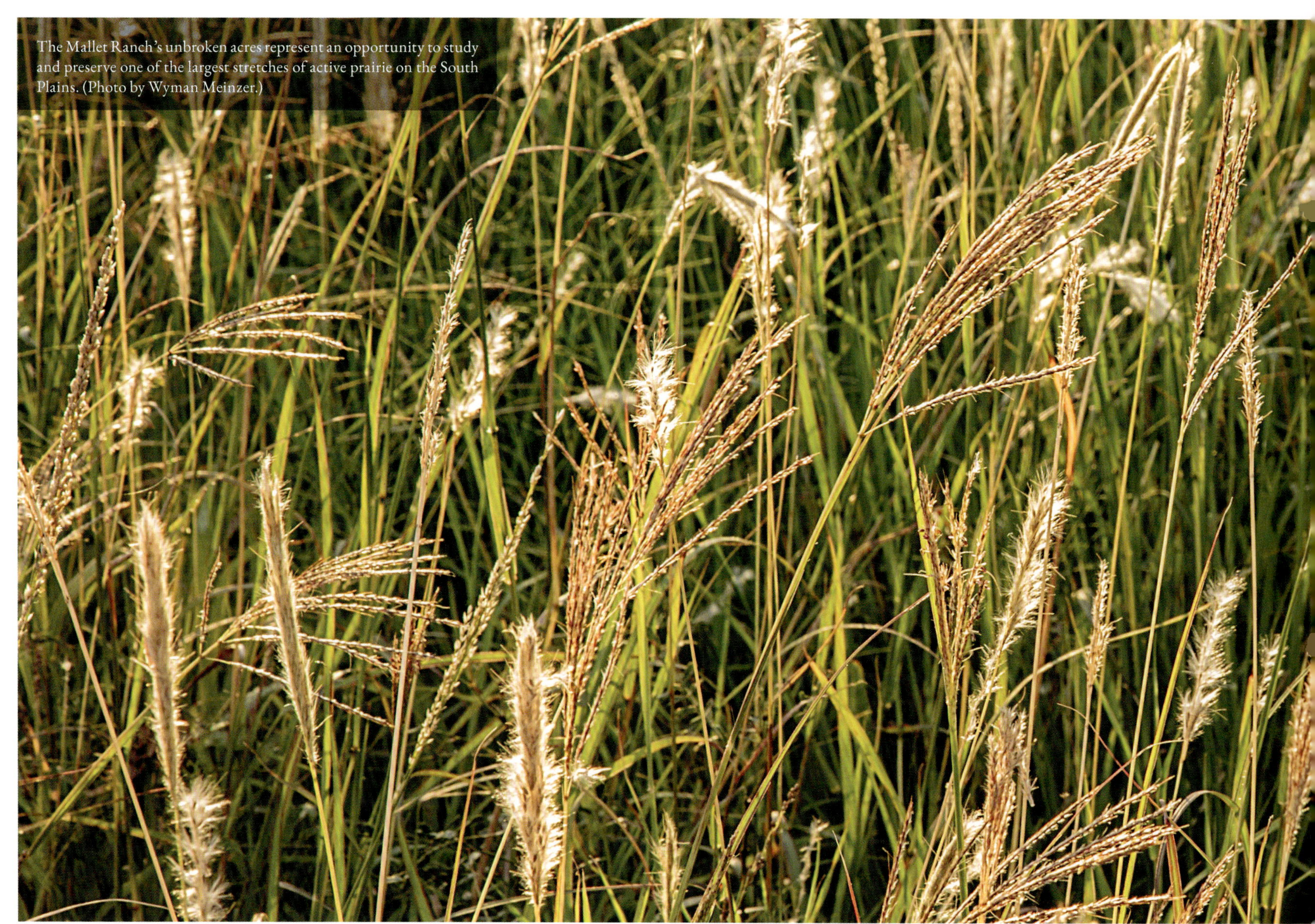

The Mallet Ranch's unbroken acres represent an opportunity to study and preserve one of the largest stretches of active prairie on the South Plains. (Photo by Wyman Meinzer.)

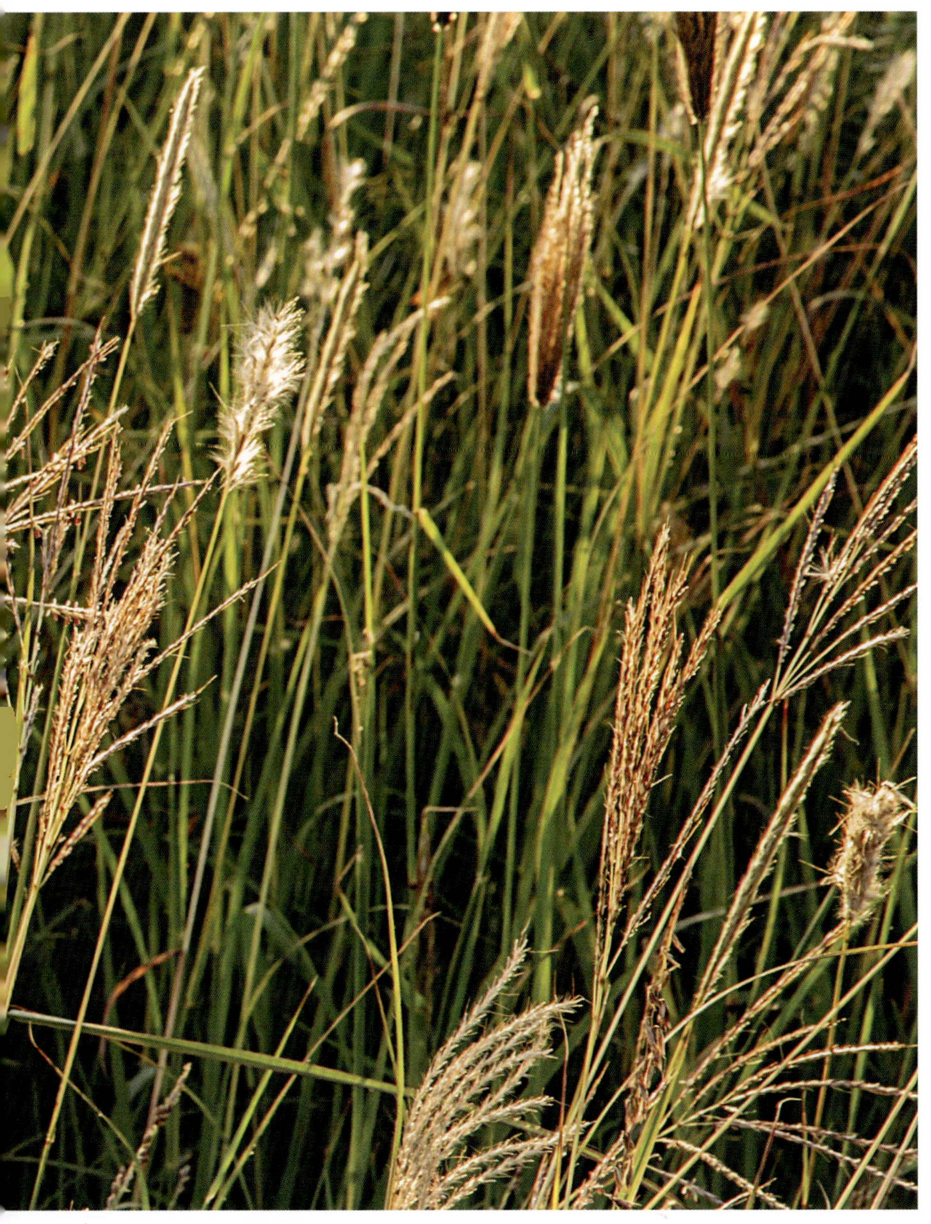

of North America—and is just east of the lower-level Permian and Triassic ancient seabeds. Its distinctive feature is thin soil over the rocky outcrop, making it essentially inconducive to large-scale farming but particularly suited for stock grazing.

When the earliest sheepmen in the Edwards region moved in during the late 1870s the area was far from hospitable to their efforts. For one thing, they were not the first to establish stock operations. Cattlemen had moved into the eastern portions in the late 1850s and continued out onto the Plateau in the 1860s, and even more in the decade immediately after the Civil War. Cattlemen saw the sheep raisers as a nuisance, unwanted competitors on what they considered their range. Also, sheep were even more prone to predators such as wolves, coyotes, and the occasional mountain lion, which attacked and took sheep isolated from shepherds. There remained also a Native American threat. Although by the late 1870s the vast majority had been forced onto reservations and extirpated from Texas, the Edwards Plateau was close enough to Mexico that the occasional raid of hunting parties threatened settlers' flocks. Such obstacles and hardships, as damaging as they were, did not include one of the most persistent challenges for sheepmen: the lack of water.

The DeVitts persevered as best they could under such conditions, but it was a constant grind. The brothers had originally stocked their range in 1881 with approximately fifteen hundred sheep and by 1883 could boast of more than three thousand head in their flock. When shearing season approached, the DeVitts hired experienced *tasinques* (shearers) from Northern Mexico. It was difficult work—an experienced shearer often handled as many as one hundred animals a day—and for that the DeVitts paid their contractors between three dollars and fifty cents and five dollars a day, depending on their experience. Shearing usually took place in the spring and the DeVitts shipped their wool out of San Antonio, which shippers then moved to Galveston for transport to textile mills. The DeVitts had turned a profit on their sheep, but not without difficulties. Cattlemen erected newly invented barbed wire to keep the DeVitts' flocks from drifting, something sheep—who closely clip their range—need to do to survive. David DeVitt once related that he and his brother had to guard their range to keep men hired by local cattlemen from "scattering their flocks" and hired guns from shooting at their herders.

The DeVitts remained in McCulloch County for two years but in 1882 decided they needed to be someplace less violent, less contentious, and—possibly most critical—with greater access to a shipping railhead. The nearest carriage point for them in McCulloch County was in the growing town of San Angelo, a journey of sixty-plus miles. The Texas and Pacific Railroad changed the equation for the brothers. By 1882, the line had reached through Big Spring and on into Midland, and a new locale would make shipping their wool clip a much easier—and likely cheaper—alternative. The DeVitt brothers moved their sheep more than 150 miles to Howard County, which had been created in 1876 but had yet to be organized. The trailers and sheep paused for some time in San Angelo then made their way to the land the two had chosen that, while it was then within the confines of Howard County, was closer to the newly platted West Texas city of Midland.

The land on the Edwards Plateau where David and Phillip DeVitt lived was not the lushest and could be difficult terrain, but many would claim that it was a garden spot compared to the new location the brothers had found. Their new ranch was on the eastern edge of the Permian Basin, once a vast, ancient, shallow sea that stretched over 300 miles in length and almost 250 miles in width. When the ancient Permian Sea finally receded, it left behind a number of minerals that would become valuable in the modern era. The first of those was potash—mostly found in the western reaches of the basin, largely between modern-day Pecos, Texas, and Artesia, New Mexico—which was a sought-after military and industrial commodity in the late nineteenth and early twentieth centuries. But the subsurface mineral that would make the most difference in the Permian Basin—and make it economically viable—would be one that the DeVitt family, in another location, would become familiar with: petroleum. Today, the area is the most productive oil region in the United States.

The Permian Basin that David and Phillip found was an arid landscape with thin soil and native grasses that had evolved to, if not thrive, at least survive in a land that was certainly less than amenable if not altogether inhospitable in places. Indigenous people were the only permanent inhabitants of the region for over a millennium, and by the latter portions of that period occupied the land somewhat reluctantly, pushed there not just by white invasion but through conflict with other Native American peoples. Spanish explorers had traversed the region but felt no compunction to linger and thus the area gained a reputation as nothing more than a place to get through instead

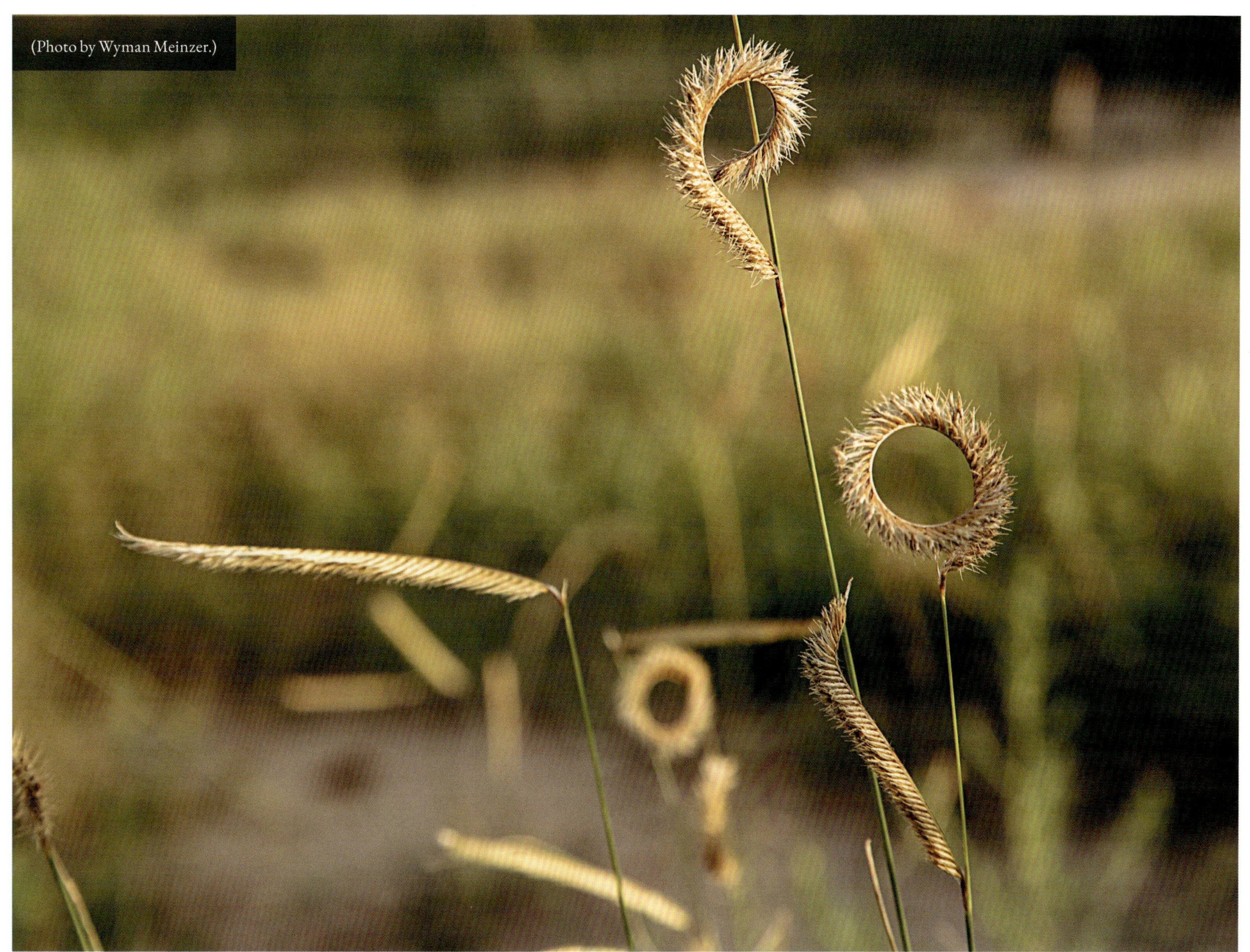
(Photo by Wyman Meinzer.)

of one to stay. The United States Army sent Captain Randolph Marcy east from Santa Fe in 1849 to find a level route in which to one day build a railroad. The route he mapped out, which became known as "Marcy's Trail," would run through the Permian Basin on its way to Fort Smith, Arkansas. The railroad that was supposed to run on his route would have to wait decades to come to fruition, but the Butterfield Overland Mail Company stage line would begin to use it in the 1850s. Still, the Permian Basin remained just a place to traverse until the late 1870s.

The United States Army eventually conquered the Comanche in the mid-1870s, opening the way for white cattle ranchers to venture out to West Texas. These early stock raisers included men such as J. R. Couts and John Simpson, who established the Hashknife Ranch in 1875 near what would become Abilene; Henry C. "Hank" Smith, who pioneered the Cross B Ranch in 1878 just below the Caprock; and Charles Goodnight, whose JA took root in 1876–1877 at Palo Duro Canyon in the Panhandle. The railroad closely followed the cattlemen when the Texas and Pacific, after it came under the ownership of mogul Jay Gould in 1879, began to lay track west out of Fort Worth. The T&P, as Texans came to call it, moved quickly under the stewardship of builder Greenville Dodge, and in 1880–1881 reached Sierra Blanca in far West Texas where it met the tracks of the Southern Pacific. In the process, the railroad established a number of towns including Abilene, Big Spring, and Midland. The latter was so named because it was approximately the midway point between Fort Worth and El Paso.

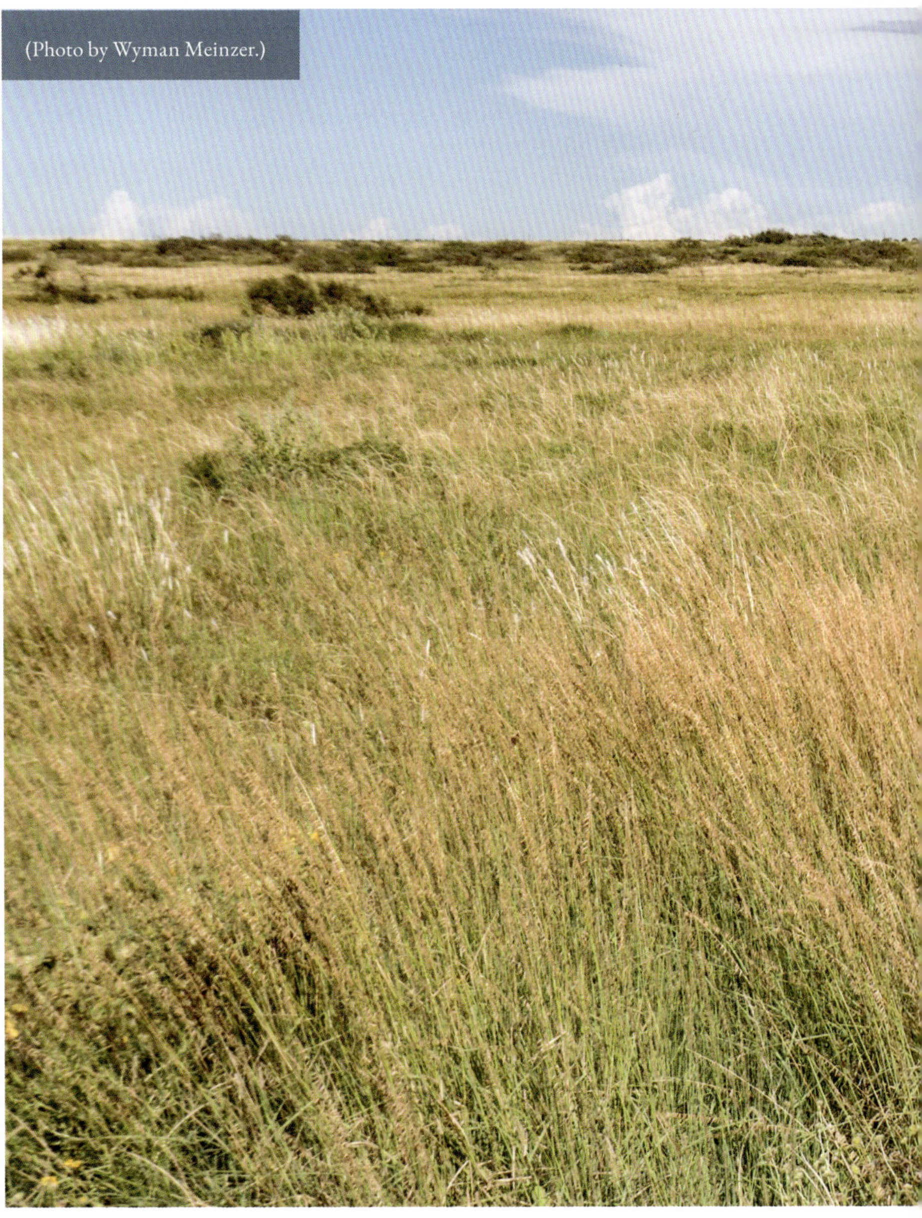
(Photo by Wyman Meinzer.)

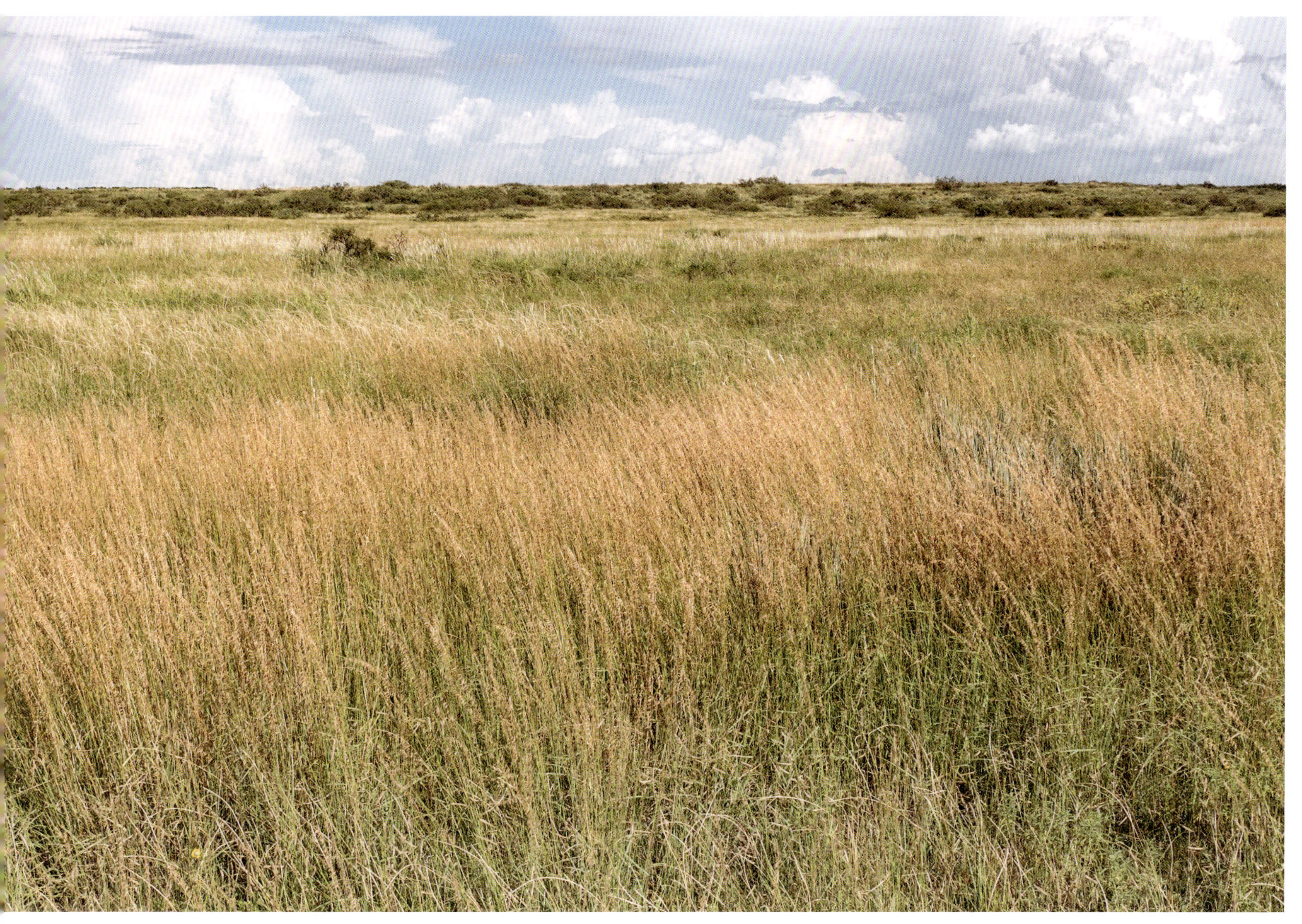

The climate in the Permian Basin is like much of West Texas in that it is unpredictable at best. It classifies as a semi-arid region, meaning that it generally receives 10 to 20 inches of rain annually. The problem is that such rainfall is not consistent. While it may be twenty-five to thirty inches one year, it may be less than ten the next. David and Phillip DeVitt arrived during one of the plentiful periods, and abundant precipitation meant that they found plenty of grassland for their sheep herd. These were mostly public lands, which allowed the DeVitts to move their flock with the seasons and the water. They could take their sheep south to near the upper reaches of the Devils River during the winter, return them to the Permian Basin during the spring, and perhaps move them more northerly during the summer. It did not take long for the DeVitts' sheep to prosper and multiply, and the brothers began to accumulate some degree of wealth. The future seemed bright, but change was certainly in the offing.

David Mantz DeVitt was still a young man when he had made his way to West Texas. Just barely twenty-six, he had already changed careers three times, moved across the nation, and transitioned from a decidedly urban dweller to one who now lived in an area almost devoid of population. Life on an isolated sheep ranch in deep West Texas may have placed too much hardship on young men such as the DeVitt brothers, but they also had another concern. Their mother, Elizabeth, grew up in the East. Although she was not elderly, the late nineteenth century could present a difficult existence for a widow, especially one whose sons lived almost two thousand miles away. The DeVitt boys, now the most financially successful of her offspring, felt an obligation to care for her, but a sheep ranch was no place for her to live. David and Phillip moved Elizabeth to Fort Worth in 1883.

The DeVitt brothers found a home for their mother on Fort Worth's Southside, which at that time was a burgeoning neighborhood for the city's growing entrepreneurial and upper middle class. The zone's primary attraction was that downtown Fort Worth lay between the Southside and the Stockyards, a rowdy region that also carried with it the smell of thousands of head of cattle. When the DeVitt matriarch first moved to the Southside, transportation to and from the growing area was substandard, but the city began to improve the roads that branched into the region in the 1890s, and shortly after the turn of the century the Texas and Pacific Railway constructed a viaduct over its railroad infrastructure that gave the Southside a direct route to downtown. Elizabeth DeVitt, happy to finally find some financial security and a home after the somewhat precarious life she had led after her husband's death, came to enjoy living in Fort Worth. Her sons—especially Phillip—checked in on her often.

Elizabeth DeVitt's life improved in Fort Worth, but that did not mean she did not still worry about her two sons, especially her youngest, David. What she specifically fretted over was the fact that he was still single. Elizabeth's personality had led her to make friends easily in Fort Worth, and she also likely felt some camaraderie with women who faced difficulties as she had in her life. One such person she befriended was Florence Bailey. Bailey, who had come to Fort Worth from Houston with her sister, worked as a domestic servant for a family on the Southside, which is how Elizabeth DeVitt met her. Elizabeth was struck by the events of Florence's life. Florence became an orphan at age five, grew up in an orphanage near Waco, and came to Fort Worth at the age of seventeen to find work. Elizabeth DeVitt had this history in her thoughts as she worried about her son. His ambition meant that he worked—in her mind—far too hard, but equally perplexing to his mother, David DeVitt also "played" just as intensely. She thought that her son needed a wife who could "tame" his tendencies, but also one who would be content keeping a home and raising children. Elizabeth played matchmaker between Florence and her youngest child and made sure they saw each other whenever David came to visit. Her efforts paid off when David proposed. He and Florence married in 1884.

David and Florence lived in a modest home on his Midland range. If Florence DeVitt had any trepidation about leaving Fort Worth and taking up residence on an isolated sheep ranch in the harsh lands of the Permian Basin, she kept it to herself. She and David quickly began to build a family in Midland. Their oldest daughter, Christine, came along in September 1885, followed by a son—Harold—in 1887. The sheep ranch also continued to prosper as the Texas sheep boom entered some of its most profitable years, and the western reaches of the state became one of the prime regions to run sheep. Flocks on the Edwards Plateau—the region the DeVitts left—expanded at the fastest rate, but the Permian Basin and adjacent Trans-Pecos also experienced huge growth. The Permian Basin had virtually no sheep on its ranges in 1880 but could count over 70,000 head in 1890. Texas also,

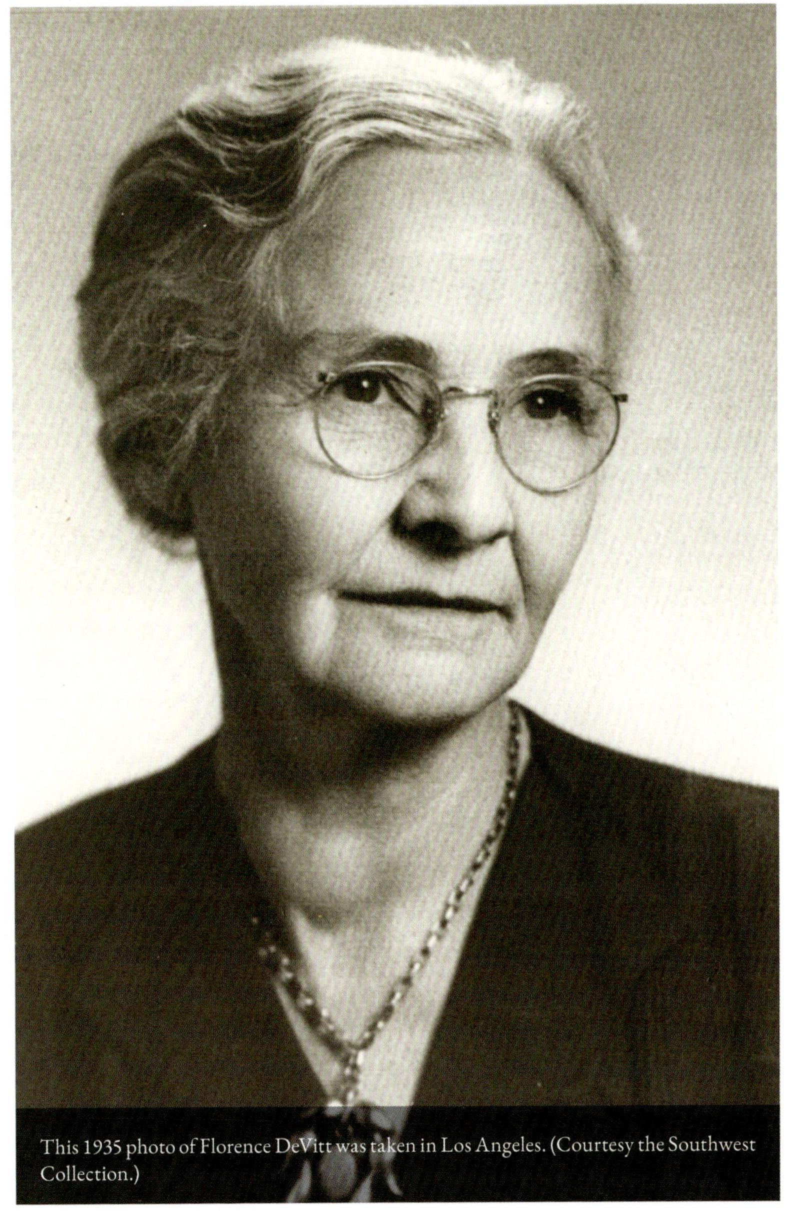

This 1935 photo of Florence DeVitt was taken in Los Angeles. (Courtesy the Southwest Collection.)

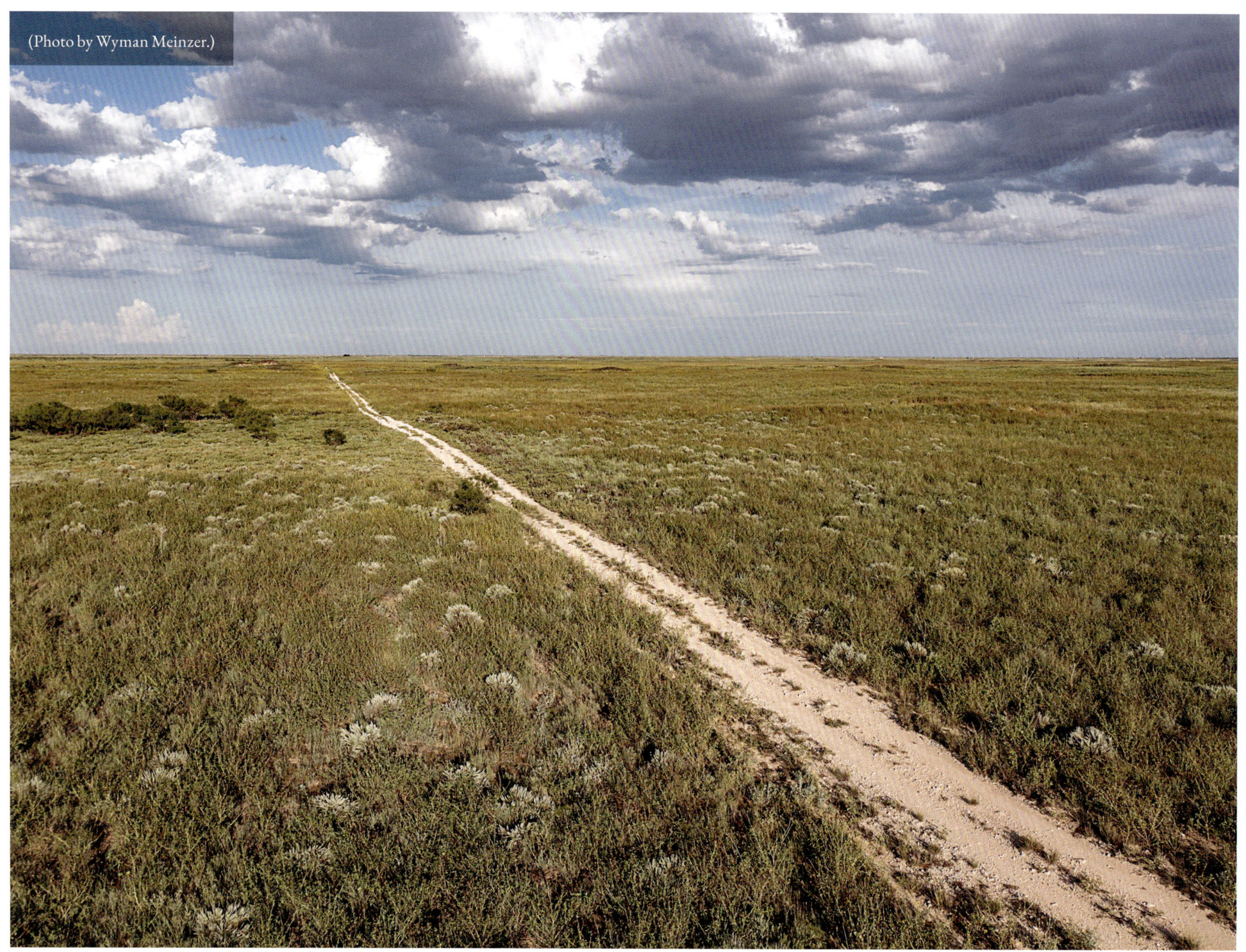
(Photo by Wyman Meinzer.)

naturally, greatly raised its wool production. The DeVitts had bred most of their ewes to Merino rams, a breed that could produce a particularly impressive shear. The DeVitts' sheep, in the latter years of the 1880s, produced an impressive average of over nine pounds of wool per head. They could easily transport their shear to Midland for shipment to markets on the Texas and Pacific. The DeVitts were becoming very successful—and moderately wealthy—sheepmen.

The DeVitts' profits were positive, but life on a Permian Basin sheep ranch was not as much so. Sheep, and the few cows that dotted the range in the region in the 1880s, far outnumbered people, and while the Texas legislature decide to create Midland County from vast Tom Green County in 1885, the little town did not yet even, as the editor of the *San Angelo Standard* noted, have a single saloon. Moreover, the area suffered from a lack of reliable water, even when rain was plentiful, and by the late 1880s the capricious weather had turned toward drought. The sheep boom also meant that more sheepmen had followed the DeVitts to the Permian Basin, with the result of overgrazing the grasses that grew in the fragile soil. At the same time, wool prices began to drastically decline as the abundance of Texas sheep impacted the market. While the DeVitts continued to show a profit each year, as the 1880s moved along those proceeds began to dip.

The DeVitt brothers were prudent with their profits. While they did put some of their returns back into ranch and stock improvements—they made significant enhancement in their stock of rams in 1886—the brothers also began to diversify their holdings. Phillip DeVitt began to speculate in real estate, mostly in Fort Worth, as well as railroad stock. Together the brothers also bought a sizable block of land in the growing West Texas town of San Angelo, which was becoming the primary market for their wool. David DeVitt became one of the largest stockholders of the proposed Abilene, Henrietta, & Red River Railway, a line whose prospectus outlined how it would capitalize on the growing importance of West Texas as a stock raising region. The railway's board of directors next appointed David DeVitt as secretary-treasurer of the new line.

Despite material comfort, the remoteness of the sheep ranch chafed at both brothers, particularly Phillip. Although becoming sheepmen had originally been the elder DeVitt's idea, by 1888–1889 he began to look for a way to disengage from the operation. David's buying out Phillip's share seemed the natural solution, but either the brothers could not agree on a price or David could not raise the funds Phillip asked for, so the elder DeVitt found another buyer in 1890. He sold his share of the Permian Basin operation to another stockman in the region, John Scharbauer. Phillip packed up and relocated to Forth Worth. He moved near his mother and found great success as a real estate developer, becoming one of the pioneers of the Southside development of the city.

David DeVitt had no desire to end his ranching pursuits, but he did want to move his family from the remote ranch. The children were growing and needed the stability of a town, and Florence had likely expressed her desire for more human contact. David DeVitt had become familiar with San Angelo not only on travels there to sell wool and to ship sheep but also

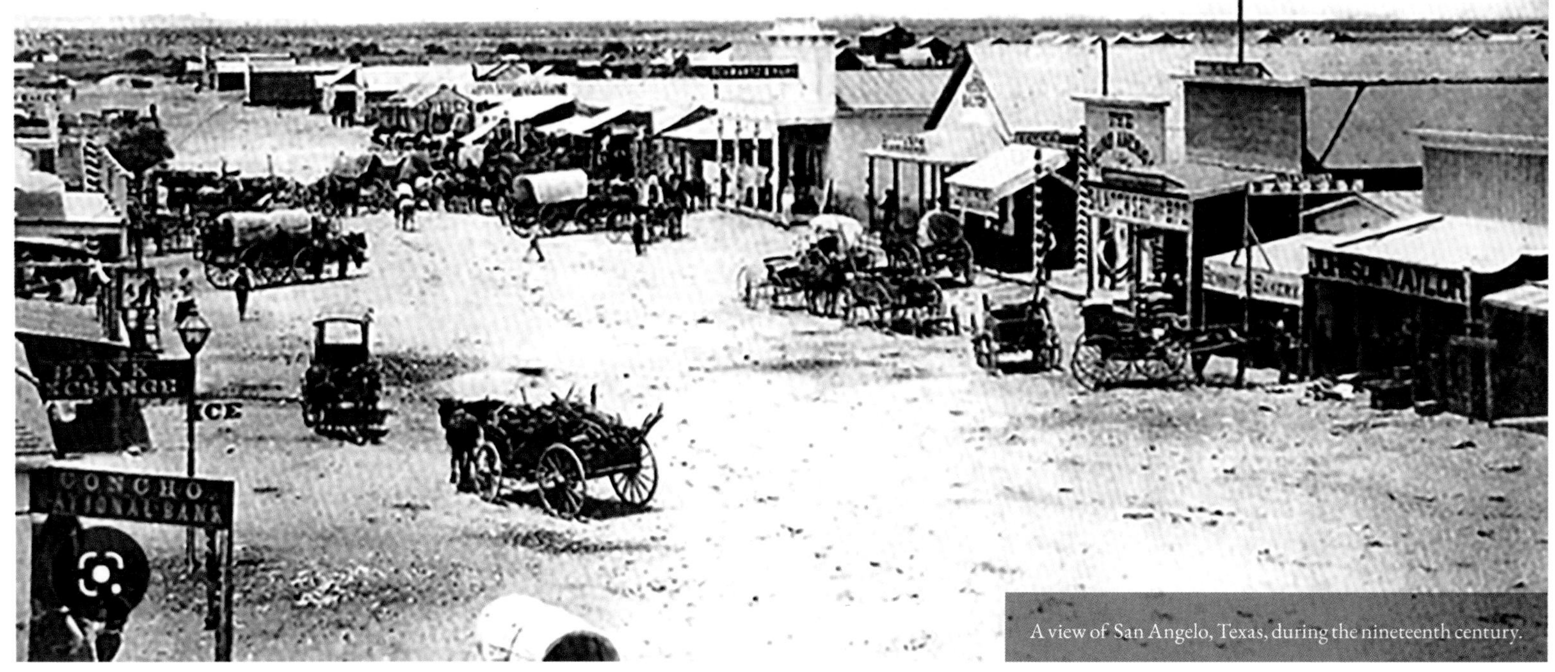

A view of San Angelo, Texas, during the nineteenth century.

in his role with the projected Abilene, Henrietta, and Red River Railway. He liked San Angelo, enjoyed its vitality, and had even invested in town lots. In letters to friends back in New York and in Fort Worth he praised San Angelo as a city on a forward path and one surrounded by fertile lands for both farming and ranching. His attraction to the town that had grown up around Fort Concho made his 1889 decision easy. He loaded his wife and two children onto wagons and moved to San Angelo, where Christine and Harold would begin their education.

San Angelo was about one hundred miles southeast of Midland on the edge of the Edwards Plateau. When the United States Army began to establish a new "frontier line" of forts in 1866–1868, they built one on the banks of the North Concho River that took the name of that stream. Fort Concho played a vital role in the engagements against Comanches and other tribes in the 1870s and was the headquarters at various times for the 4th Cavalry from 1868 to 1873 and the famed 10th Cavalry of "Buffalo Soldiers" beginning in 1875. Soldiers from Fort Concho during various campaigns from the fort scouted and mapped large portions of West Texas—including the DeVitts' ranchlands near Midland—and built telegraph lines, stage roads, and other vital improvements in the region.

A fort's presence means a gathering of young men, who often become bored and restless. Such conditions are perfect for the origins of a "fort town," a development that played out near almost every fort in the west in the years after the Civil War. Those fort towns took a usual form: the primary institutions were those frequented by soldiers and hangers-on near the fort, such as trading posts, saloons, prostitution houses, and gambling halls. Almost as soon as Fort Concho began in 1867, Bartholomew (Bart) J. DeWitt bought over 300 acres on the bank just opposite the fort and launched a trading post. He sold other plots to men who began operations of the other elements of a fort town. He called his new development "Santa Angela" after his wife, Carolina Angela, who had died the year before he moved west to begin his new venture. "Santa" was soon dropped and by 1883, when the little settlement finally got a post office, it had become San Angela and shortly afterward, San Angelo. The town's fortunes grew even more when a devastating flood destroyed the county seat of respectable Ben Ficklin, which meant that San Angelo took over the county seat mantle.

The DeVitts moved to San Angelo in 1889, the same year that the Army abandoned Fort Concho. It was growing, especially after the arrival of the Santa Fe Railroad in 1888, which allowed San Angelo to become a shipping center for stock and wool, also becoming an important market in the region. The waters of the North, Middle, and South Concho Rivers, which meet within the city limits of modern San Angelo to form the Concho River on its last flow to meet the Colorado River near the Runnels and Coleman County line, attracted stockmen as early as 1864 when Richard F. Tankersley introduced longhorn cattle along a spread that fronted the South Concho River. Others followed, and the river became an important watering spot for herds headed west across the arid Trans-Pecos. San Angelo also became a sheep-raising center in 1877 when John Arden and Joseph Tweedy introduced flocks to the region.

Life had moved quickly for David M. DeVitt in the last decade. He had left New York and come to Texas, established two sheep ranches, married and began a family, moved three times, and now had to take on a new partner in John Scharbauer. Partnerships can be contentious, and the potential existed for such a scenario between DeVitt and Scharbauer. Fortunately, this business arrangement would prove beneficial for both men, and David DeVitt would find in John Scharbauer someone whose tutelage would prove vital in advancing his education in becoming a stockman and a businessman.

John Scharbauer's father and mother, Ferdinand and Rosa, left Bavaria in 1846. They boarded a ship in Donauwörth not entirely sure of their destination. The ship docked in New York, after which Ferdinand worked in a leatherworks shop in New York City for two years before moving to and opening his own shop in Albany. He and Rosa raised seven children in New York, and three of them—John, Christian, and Phillip—would eventually make their way to Texas.

Ferdinand and Rosa Scharbauers' middle child John was born in 1852 in Albany, New York, but when he was twenty-eight, he left New York behind and, like David DeVitt, was sure his path to fortune passed through the West, and specifically Texas. He and his wife, the former Katie Thompkins, had scrimped and saved almost $2,500 and in 1880 came to Texas. They boarded

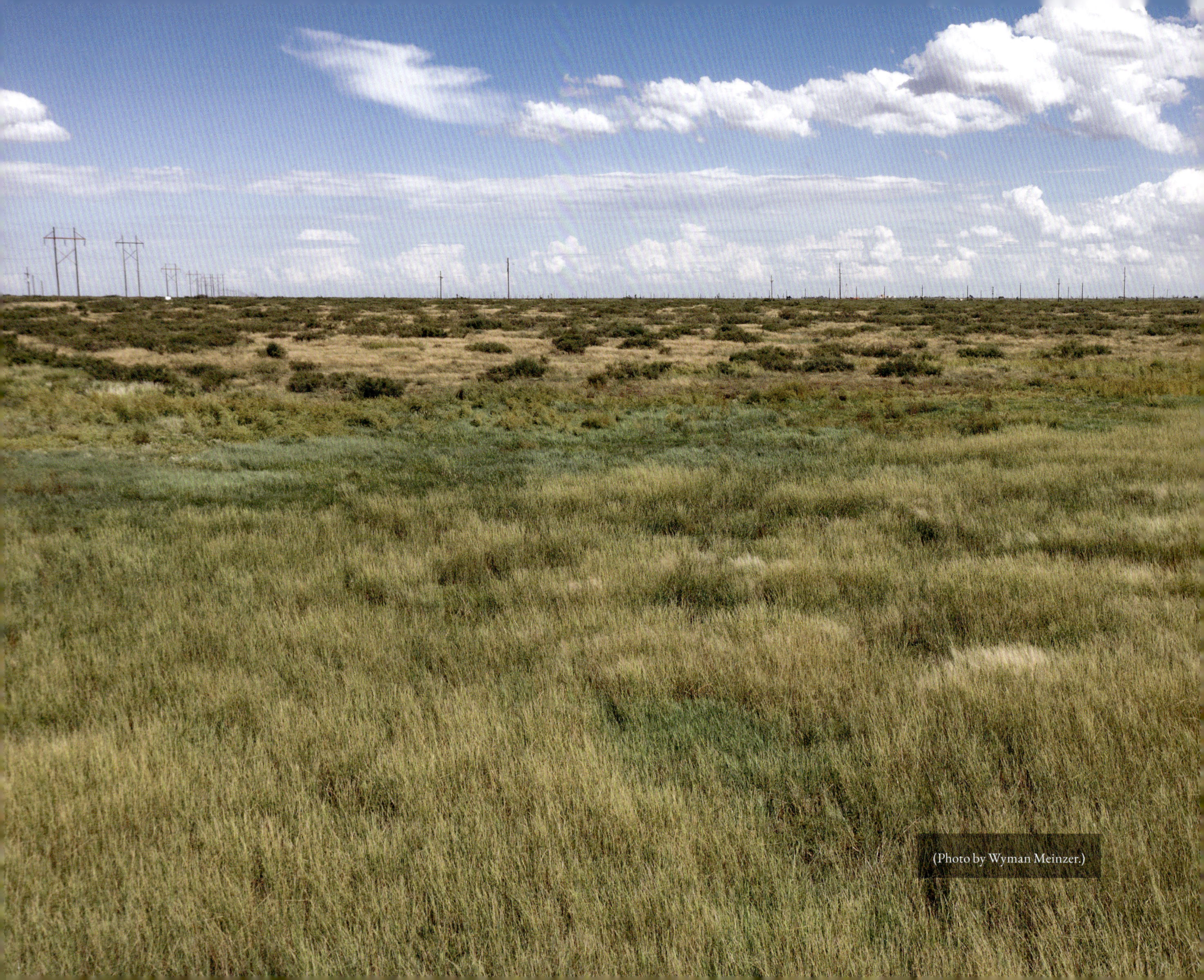

(Photo by Wyman Meinzer.)

the Texas and Pacific (T&P), and when it stopped in the new railroad town of Eastland that is where they decided to settle. They arrived in the same year that the T&P put up lots for sale in order to begin the town, so John and Katie bought five of the lots with their savings and then "flipped" them in the next two years to new residents the railroad drew to Eastland (the town grew to almost 1,000 residents within four years of its founding).

The Scharbauers left Eastland, and moved about fifty miles east to Abilene, another town the T&P had spawned. Ranchers, raising both cattle and sheep, had moved into the area that would become Abilene in the mid-1870s after the United States Army had pushed Native Americans from the region. Enough people had arrived by 1878 to allow for the organization of Taylor County and the establishment of Buffalo Gap as the county seat. When the T&P continued its movement westward in 1881, a group of cattlemen in the northeast corner of the new county hatched a scheme to have the railroad bypass Buffalo Gap and move through land they controlled. Claiborne Merchant, whose 74 Ranch lay near Belle Plain in Callahan County, conspired with John Simpson, who owned the Hashknife Ranch in that corner of Taylor County, to convince the railroad not only to lay track north of Buffalo Gap but also to contribute lots for a new town. Merchant supposedly suggested that the new enclave be named "Abilene" after the notorious railhead in Kansas. Town promoters began to tout Abilene as the "future great city in West Texas."

When the Scharbauers arrived in Abilene, the town had already wrestled the county seat from declining Buffalo Gap and

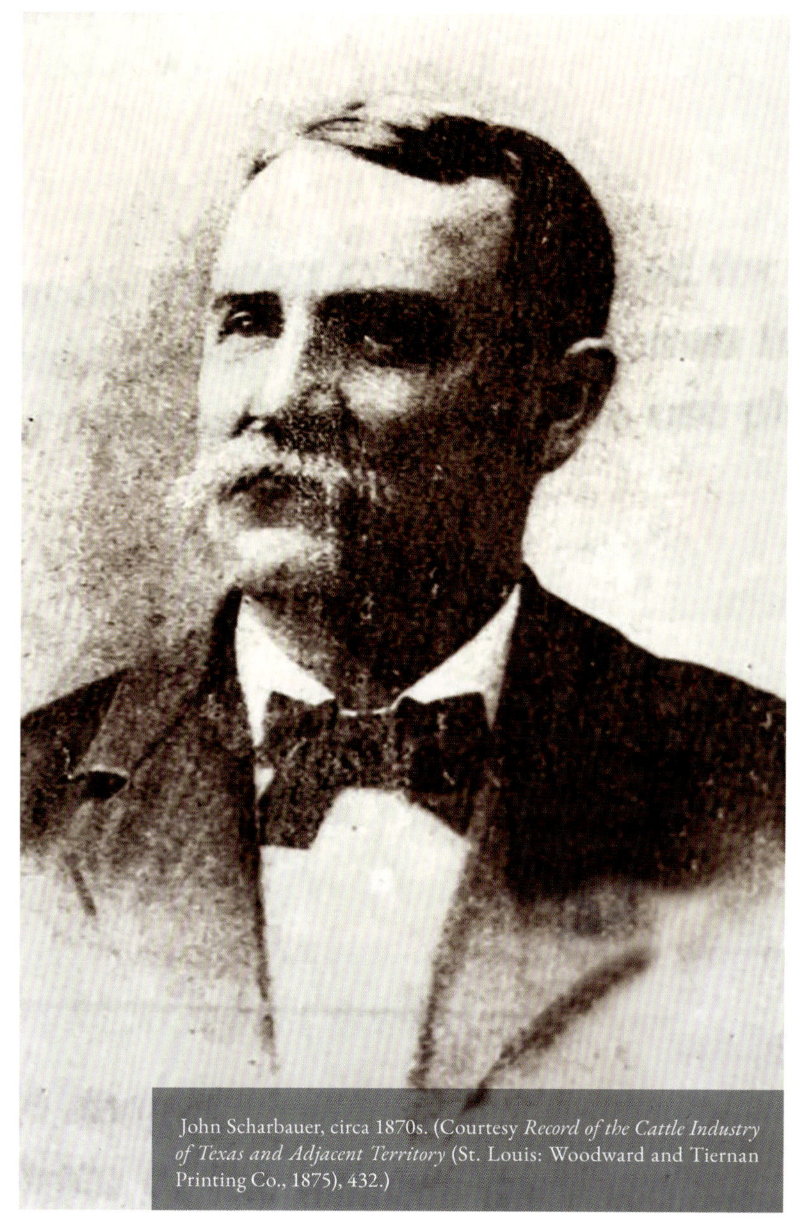

John Scharbauer, circa 1870s. (Courtesy *Record of the Cattle Industry of Texas and Adjacent Territory* (St. Louis: Woodward and Tiernan Printing Co., 1875), 432.)

the population had grown to almost 2,500. Like so many precipitous railroad towns, Abilene was a difficult place for a family to make roots. It had more saloons than churches (quite the change from contemporary Abilene), and the streets were sticky, gooey, muddy messes after rains, which came infrequently but were often downpours. John Scharbauer had concentrated on real estate in Eastland, but he took another direction when he came to Abilene. He noted the abundant grasslands in the area and, given the sheep boom of the era, decided that a sheep operation was his best avenue to make a fortune. Scharbauer secured land and grazing rights to an area almost due west of Abilene on the Taylor and Nolan County line, and he and a partner were soon running almost 1,500 head. The sheep boom was good to John Scharbauer, and with his profits he bought out his partner's interest and looked to expand his holdings and herd. However, the railroad's success in the area had made land cost more than he wanted to spend, so Scharbauer did what he had done earlier in his life: he drove his herd in 1884 to Mitchell County near another new railroad town, Colorado City. Three years later he did the same thing and moved on near Midland, where he formed his partnership with David DeVitt.

Fortune, karma, or just plain luck smiled on David DeVitt when he met and formed a business relationship with John Scharbauer. Phillip DeVitt may have tired of the sheep business in West Texas, but David still believed that his fortune lay in the area. However, the stock business was changing with the times. The sheep boom may have been nearing an end, and in that regard only those who were able and willing to change their operations found success. David DeVitt had learned the sheep and stock market at a quick pace, but his short relationship with John Scharbauer would be somewhat of a completion of his education. Scharbauer was only four years older than David DeVitt, but while the age difference was more akin to that between brothers, David DeVitt—who had grown up fatherless—began to learn from Scharbauer almost as a boy would learn lessons from a father. John Scharbauer taught DeVitt that the key to the stock business was the ability to evaluate the value of the animals and that the successful buying and selling of stock all depended on timing. The effective stockman knew to anticipate when to sell and when to buy: the age-old idea of "buy low and sell high."

David M. DeVitt learned that lesson well. He came to relish his time spent at the great livestock markets, first at Union Stockyards in Chicago and later in Omaha and Kansas City. In fact, his hometown newspaper, the *San Angelo Standard*, went so far as to call him the "great mutton manipulator of the West." Such a skill came in handy within two years of the DeVitt-Scharbauer partnership. The "Texas sheep boom" had begun to decline in the late 1880s for the eternal reason that ends all booms eventually: supply began to outstrip demand. Sheepmen in Texas tried to respond—the number of sheep in Texas declined from a high of 6,620,000 in 1885 to just a bit over 5 million in 1887—but they could not dispose of sheep fast enough to keep proceeds for wool and lambs from falling. DeVitt and Scharbauer began to liquidate their herds in 1892,

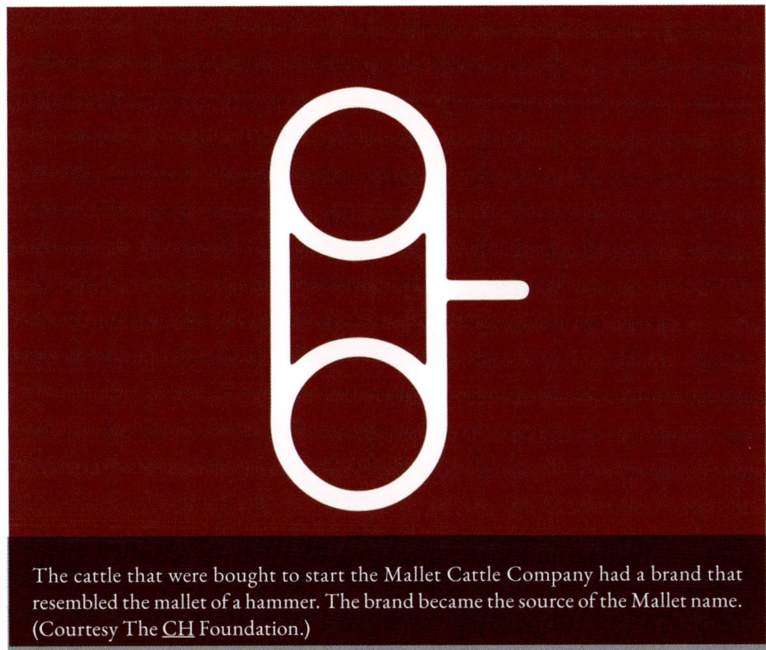

The cattle that were bought to start the Mallet Cattle Company had a brand that resembled the mallet of a hammer. The brand became the source of the Mallet name. (Courtesy The CH Foundation.)

a process that would take almost five years to fully complete. The two men would together sell over 100,000 sheep at market. When the sheep had been disposed of, the partnership ended, although the two remained friends for decades.

Life for all the DeVitts also began to change during the same period. David and Florence had made a life in San Angelo—even after the bulk of the DeVitt herd grazed closer to Midland—but Florence DeVitt had not relished her life in the small West Texas town. She seemed drawn more to life in a larger city, with cultural outlets and opportunities that frontier Texas towns did not offer. She and the children accompanied David on his trips to Chicago and Kansas City, as well as when they traveled to Fort Worth to see Phillip and the DeVitt family matriarch. The DeVitts embarked on a long visit to the East in 1893; after concluding business in Chicago, the family traveled to New York City, not only to see David DeVitt's hometown but also to attend the monumental 1893 World's Fair.

The family returned to San Angelo by the spring of 1894 and immediately made plans to move to New York City permanently, a change that pleased Florence. The family leased their house and went back to New York in May 1894 but came back to San Angelo in mid-September. David DeVitt had changed his mind. He had left New York for a reason, and while he had made money in the sheep business, he was not ready to give up raising stock in Texas. He did, however, concede to move his family from small, isolated San Angelo to Fort Worth, a city that would allow his children to achieve a more well-rounded education and would also make his wife happier. David DeVitt's commercial endeavors would remain in West Texas, but he was done with sheep. At the same time that the Texas sheep boom began to end, it looked as if the other iconic Texas stock animal's fortunes were also on the decline. As David DeVitt had learned from John Scharbauer, quite often the best time to enter a new market was during a decline when you could buy low. So, David Mantz DeVitt in 1895 looked to enter the cattle business. He would find the perfect instrument by buying the assets of a failed operation in the hands of a consortium whose owners were in New Haven, Connecticut. David DeVitt was about to acquire the Mallet Cattle Company.

CHAPTER 2

BUILDING A STOCK EMPIRE

David M. DeVitt had picked a curious time to enter the range cattle industry. Cattle raising in Texas and the western reaches of the United States had flourished in the heady years of the 1870s and 1880s, but the 1890s brought the same ravages that DeVitt had begun to witness with the sheep business: an overabundance of supply had led to a collapse in prices. Land available for stock production in the eastern reaches of Texas had become scarce, which meant that grazing lands available within the region of abundant rain in the state had become expensive. Such conditions—and the extermination and movement of Native Americans in the state—had led ranchers to begin to move onto the vast treeless plains of West Texas. By the time DeVitt decided to move from a sheep operation to a cattle operation, even West Texas was on the verge of being filled with cattlemen and bovines.

The development of the range cattle industry is one that began upon the plains of the Iberian peninsula. The development of an Iberian herding system within Andalusia eventually transferred to the New World, both in practice and in stock. This "Spanish system" of open-range grazing spread up the Mexican peninsula and found its greatest expanse in what would become Northern Mexico, which, by the eighteenth century, included the coastal ranges and brushy plains of South Texas just over the Rio Grande. As the Spanish established missions around the new city of San Antonio, the friars also brought stock—cattle, horses, oxen, and sheep—with them and utilized the same practices that dominated in New Spain:

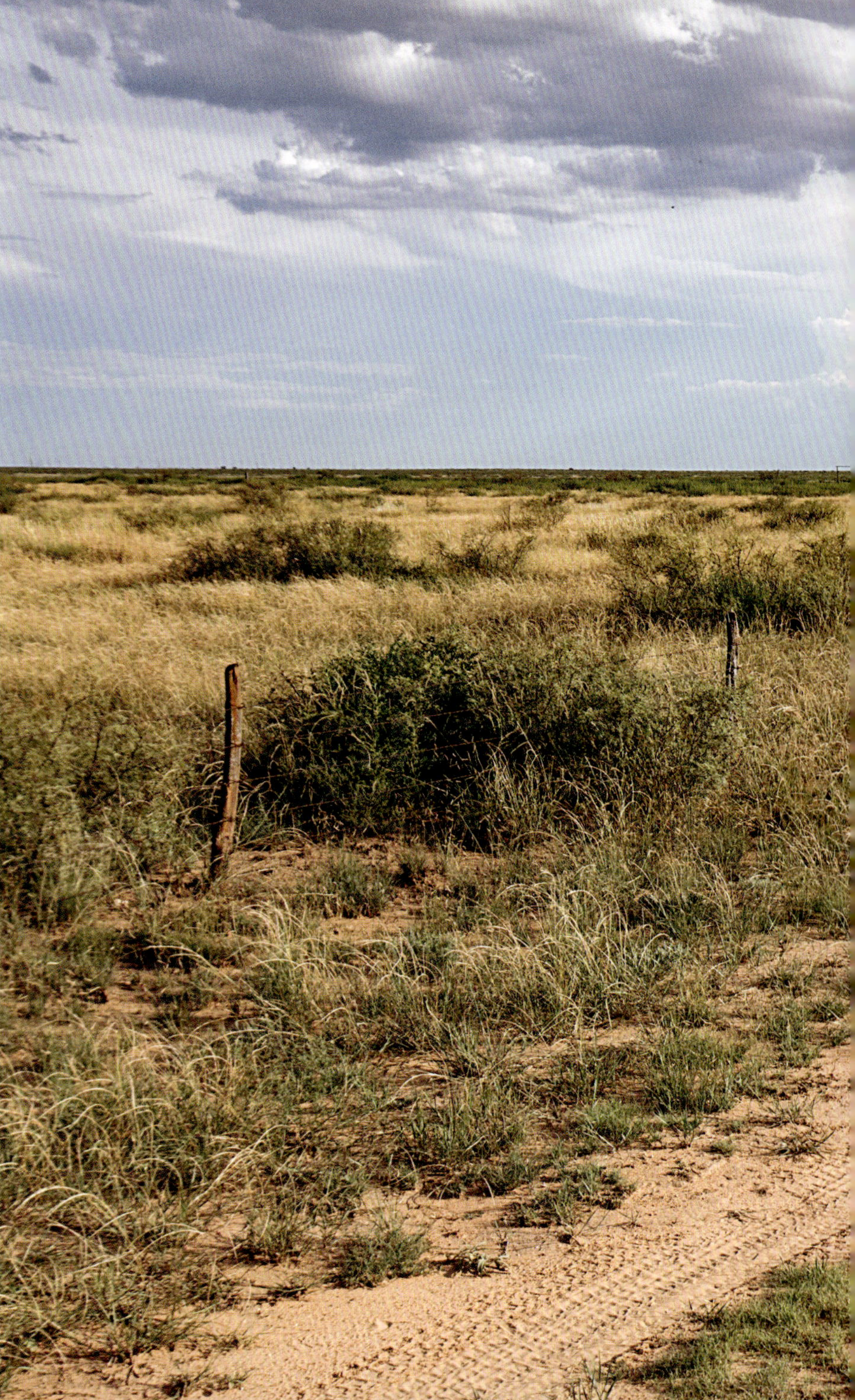

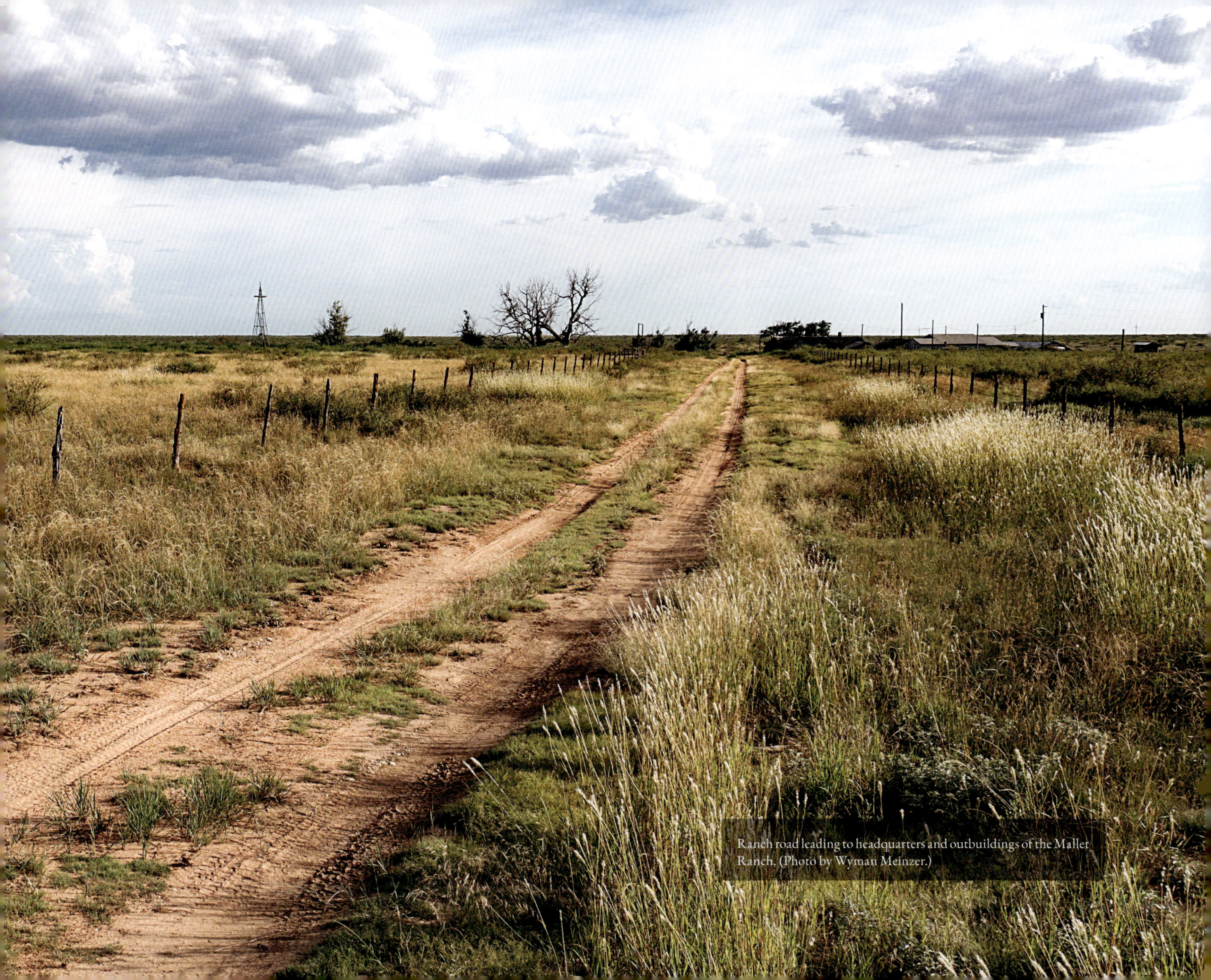

Ranch road leading to headquarters and outbuildings of the Mallet Ranch. (Photo by Wyman Meinzer.)

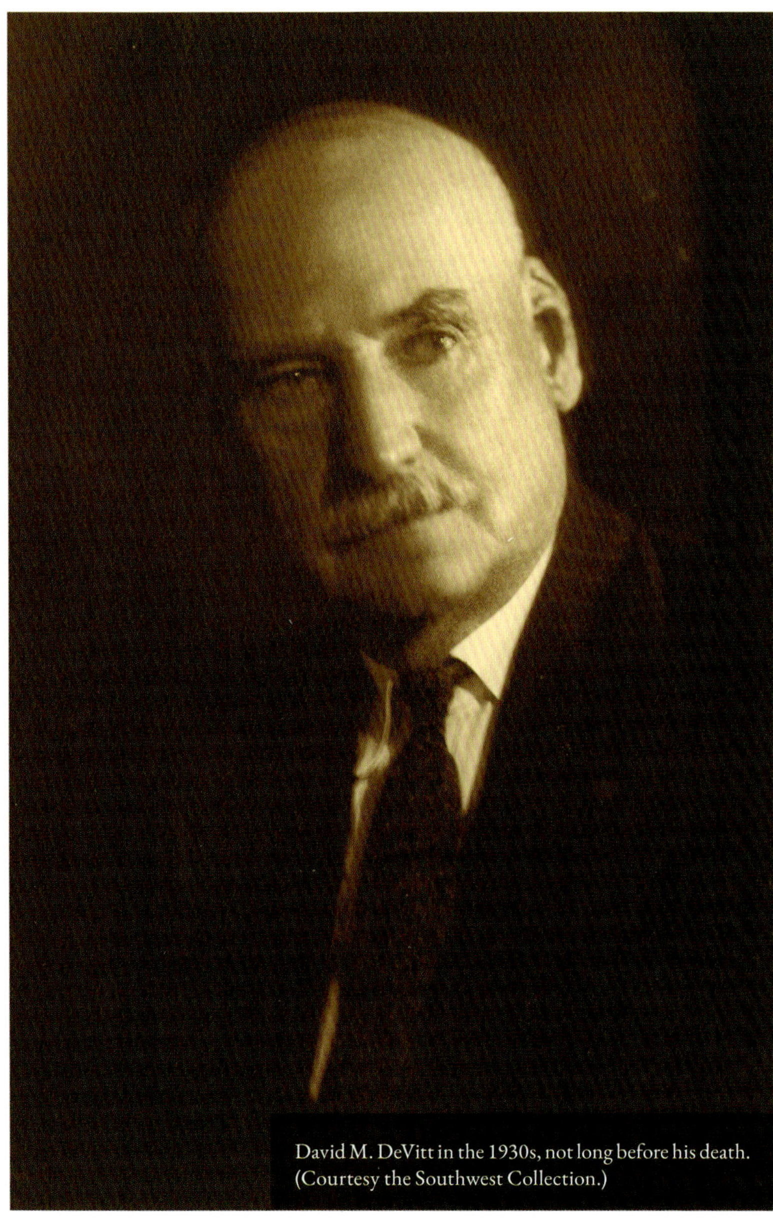
David M. DeVitt in the 1930s, not long before his death. (Courtesy the Southwest Collection.)

those of open-range grazing and tending cattle from horseback. Thus this "Spanish system" became the predominant pattern in Texas.

When Spain, and then an independent Mexico, began to neglect its northern frontier in the late eighteenth century and early nineteenth, Anglo ranchers began to move into the region and exploit the void. They acquired title to Spanish grants—some legitimately, others not so much—and established ranches familiar to the modern Texan, with names such as the King Ranch and the Kennedy operation. Still, despite such outfits, millions of head of now feral cattle began to roam the brushy lands of South Texas south of San Antonio. When the Civil War ended in 1865 there were an estimated five to six million head of these wild animals, descendants of the original Spanish stock with some traces of Northern European breeds mixed in, roaming the range. These bovines, which evolution and natural selection had endowed with distinctive traits to survive in the wild—specifically long, sharp horns and a nasty disposition—acquired the name of "longhorns."

When the Civil War ended in 1865, these longhorns roamed the region, which meant they were not only plentiful but there for the taking by anyone resourceful and tenacious enough to catch them. Enterprising drovers had trailed cattle from Texas in the past. Spanish cattle drives had moved animals to New Orleans, and in the decades since isolated drives had taken Texas cattle to Missouri, Ohio, and even all the way to California during the Gold Rush. But this burgeoning era of cattle drives would be different and would spark a "boom." After the Civil

War, the expanding populations in the eastern cities had created a thriving market that needed to be fed. The abundance of cattle in Texas and other areas provided the sustenance.

The eastern cities had generated the demand, and the supply was in Texas, but there remained an obstacle: getting those beeves to the people who wanted them. Chicago and other northern slaughterhouses were paying high prices, even for tough, stringy, Texas longhorns, but cattlemen had to get those animals to the market. Texas in the late 1860s and 1870s did not have the railroad connections to ship live animals, so they had to be driven to railheads in Missouri and Kansas for shipment to those eastern markets—thus the dawn of the cattle drive era. Sedalia, Missouri, became the first drive terminal, and through the spring and summer of 1866 more than 250,000 head of Texas cattle reached the railhead and were loaded for transport east. Because the trail to Sedalia cut through and destroyed settled land, Missouri farmers complained loudly enough—and formed armed gangs to keep drovers and their herds off their lands—that it became necessary to shift the drives to the west.

The first solution came when Joseph G. McCoy, a cattle buyer for eastern concerns, bought land in the isolated hamlet of Abilene, Kansas. He then convinced the Hannibal and St. Joseph Railroad to build a trunk line to Abilene, built pens and a yard to hold cattle, constructed a new hotel, and then marked a trail beyond the settlement line through Oklahoma and Kansas. The cattlemen now had a preferred destination,

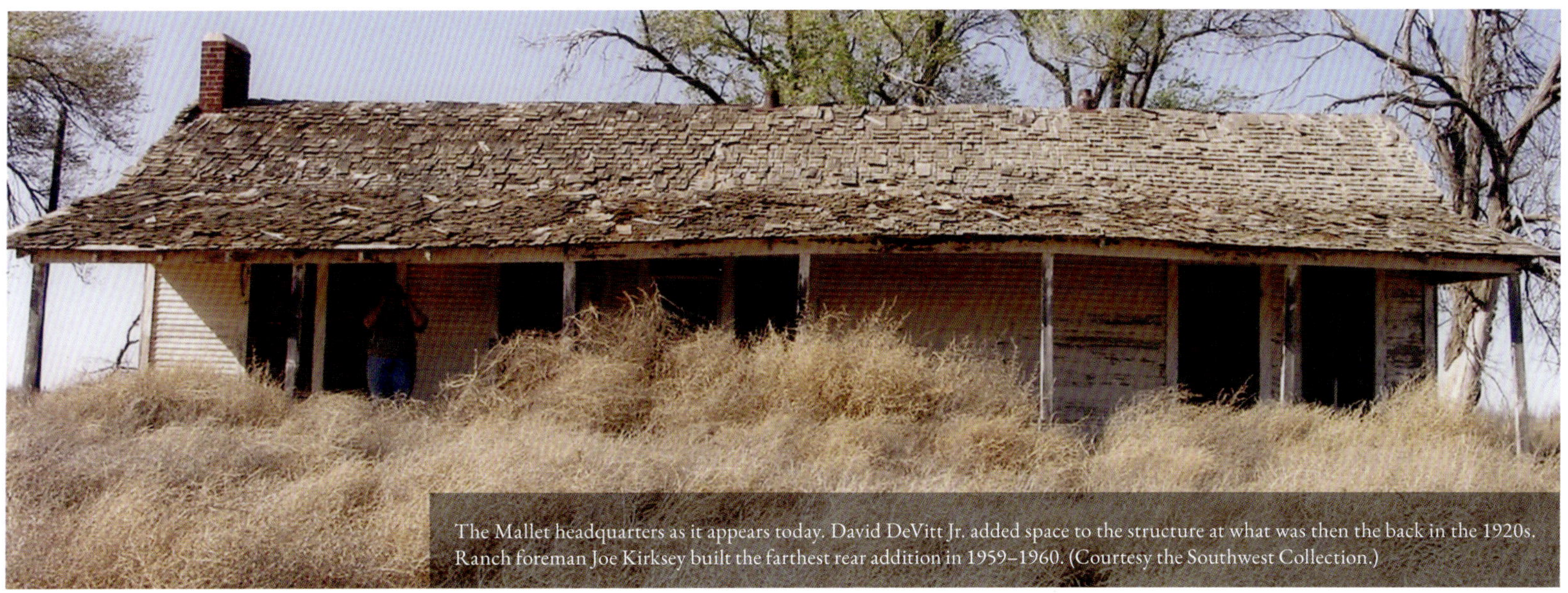

The Mallet headquarters as it appears today. David DeVitt Jr. added space to the structure at what was then the back in the 1920s. Ranch foreman Joe Kirksey built the farthest rear addition in 1959–1960. (Courtesy the Southwest Collection.)

and over the next two decades Texas cattle drovers moved more than six million Texas cattle into Abilene and other Kansas towns such as Dodge City and Wichita.

The cattlemen of the late 1860s and 1870s relied on the cattle drives to get their herds to market, but they also began to see the need to establish ranches; after the US Army pushed the native tribes out of West Texas, an entire domain of public land opened up. The state of Texas, forever experiencing financial problems, was also eager to sell those lands. When the early ranchers began to move into West Texas they claimed, or purchased at greatly accommodating prices, a few hundred acres near a good water source, and then took over the surrounding range. Since this was public land it was open to anyone to use, and thus the earliest operations in West Texas spread their herds across vast expanses and ran cattle under the open-range system.

During the earliest years of open-range stock raising in West Texas, cattlemen continued to send their cattle north on drives, but eventually the rails began to expand across Texas in the 1880s, which, along with the blockade of Texas cattle into Kansas to stem the spread of Texas cattle fever (a tick-borne disease), ended the cattle drive era. Shortly afterward, the era of the open range began to end with the introduction of blooded stock in Texas as well as cheap fencing in the form of barbed wire. Beginning in 1876, the state of Texas began the process of disposing of its public lands in West Texas (most of these had previously been designated as "school lands"). They offered the land at $1.50 an acre for purchase or to lease at just five cents an acre a year. Those who had once utilized the open range to raise stock had no choice but to acquire title to the hundreds of thousands of acres on which they ran stock.

The advent of barbed wire to fence large plots and the end of the open range also allowed ranchers to begin to experiment with and raise purebred livestock, chiefly after 1890. In 1890, the United States Department of Agriculture had estimated that 81 percent of all cattle in the nation were "common" or "native," which was their classification of bovines with multiple genetic backgrounds, most of those descended from some combination of Spanish "blacks," Devonshire reds, Dutch blacks and whites, and Danish yellows. About 19 percent were "mixed blood," and fewer than one percent were "purebreds." Such a finding was only natural since the open-range system meant that it was useless to try to raise stock that would remain purebred. Blooded stock had begun to appear in the East as early as the late 1600s, although they were very limited. Shorthorns arrived in the late 1700s, Herefords in the 1810s, and then Brahmans, or Zebus, in the 1850s. The Angus, a Scottish breed, was a late arrival in the 1870s. Of course, in Texas and the rest of the West, any introduction of these breeds usually led to a mixing with Texas longhorns or other of the "native" bovines.

The seeming golden age of the Texas open-range cattle industry took a huge hit in the late 1880s when all over the North American West a harsh winter devastated the range cattle. Cattle perished by the tens of thousands during successive winters from 1884 to 1887, with the season of 1885–1886 being particularly brutal, as estimates were that as many as 85 percent of all cattle on the southern range died by freezing or starvation. The Panhandle and South Plains of Texas was the

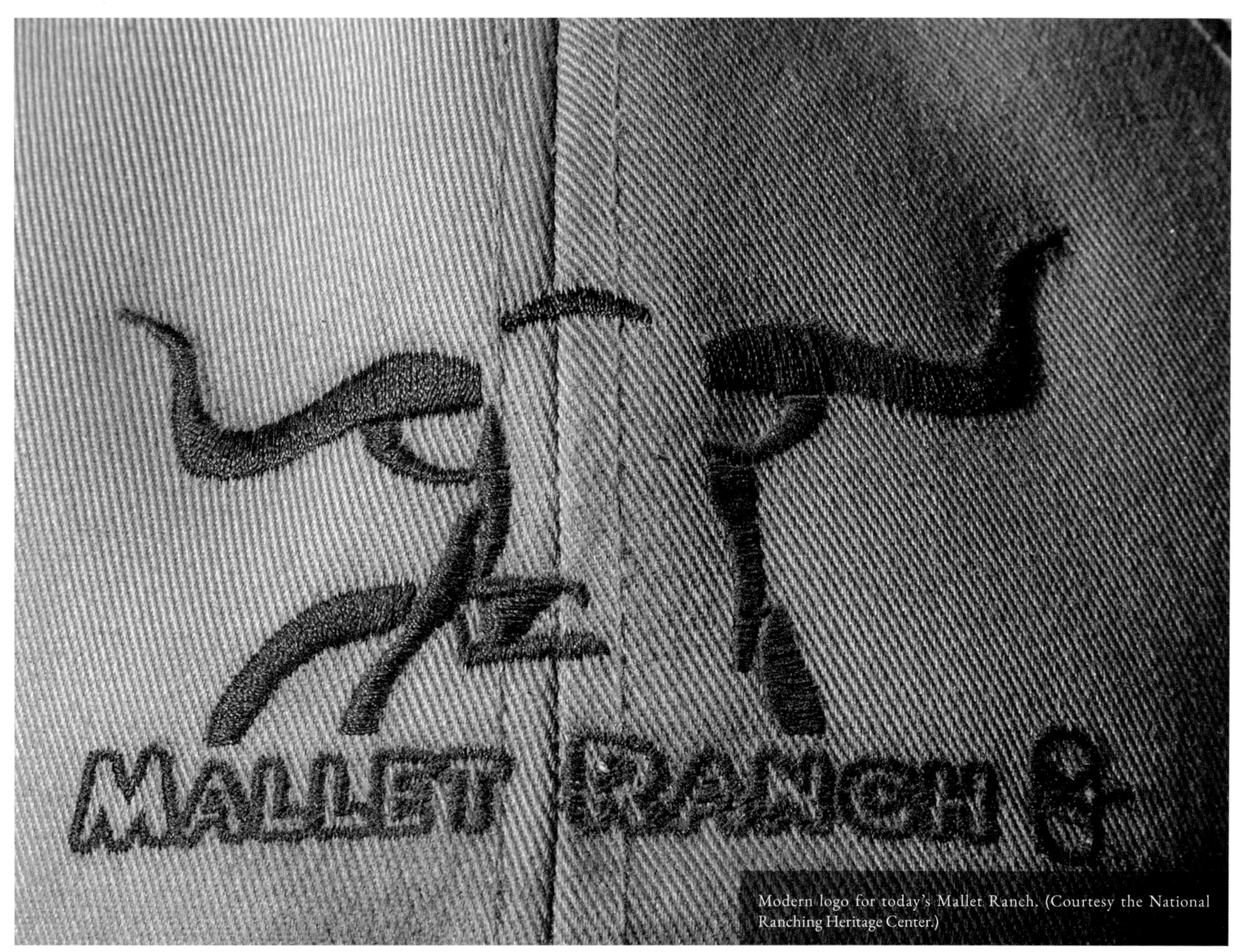

Modern logo for today's Mallet Ranch. (Courtesy the National Ranching Heritage Center.)

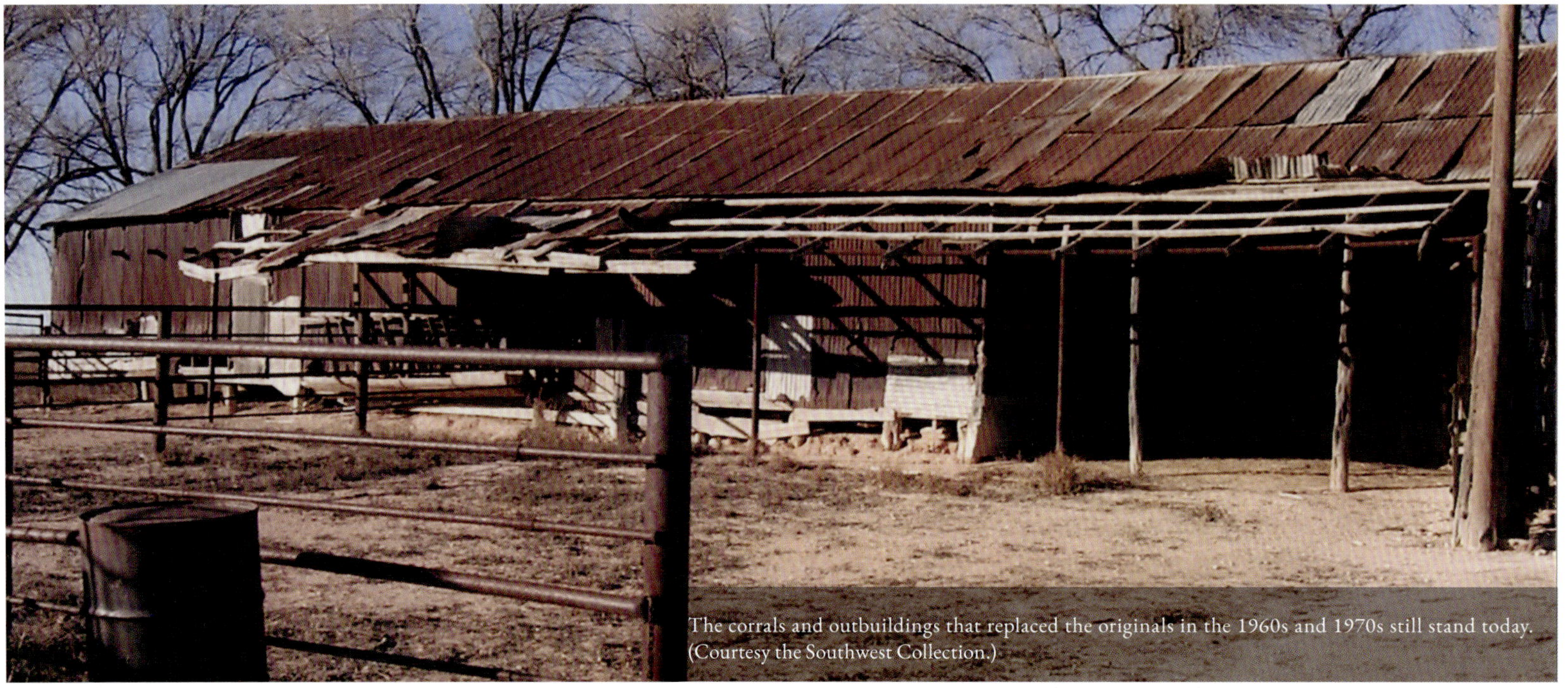
The corrals and outbuildings that replaced the originals in the 1960s and 1970s still stand today. (Courtesy the Southwest Collection.)

hardest hit area. Desperate cattle, fighting bone-chilling temperatures and often blinding blizzards, drifted with the storms, their hindquarters to the wind, looking for any grass or water to survive. In their quest to find sustenance, they would then pile up against the fence lines now constructed across much of the range where they would die. Following herds would then walk over the bodies of the earlier carcasses and then pile up and die at the next barrier.

The succession of deadly winters became known as the "die-up," and it almost ended the cattle industry in Texas. Investors, particularly foreign backers who had invested heavily in large Texas ranches such as the Matador and the XIT, among others, began to pull back from financing Texas cattle ventures precisely when such funding was sorely needed. At the same time, the cattle trails had closed and the range was fenced off. By 1890, the Texas cattle industry approached a precipice, which made it a precarious time for David DeVitt to enter.

DeVitt could have likely continued raising sheep and made a comfortable living; he could have also taken his profits from his Permian Basin sheep operation, left West Texas behind, and partnered again with his brother to make healthier profits speculating on land in Fort Worth. He chose not to pursue any of

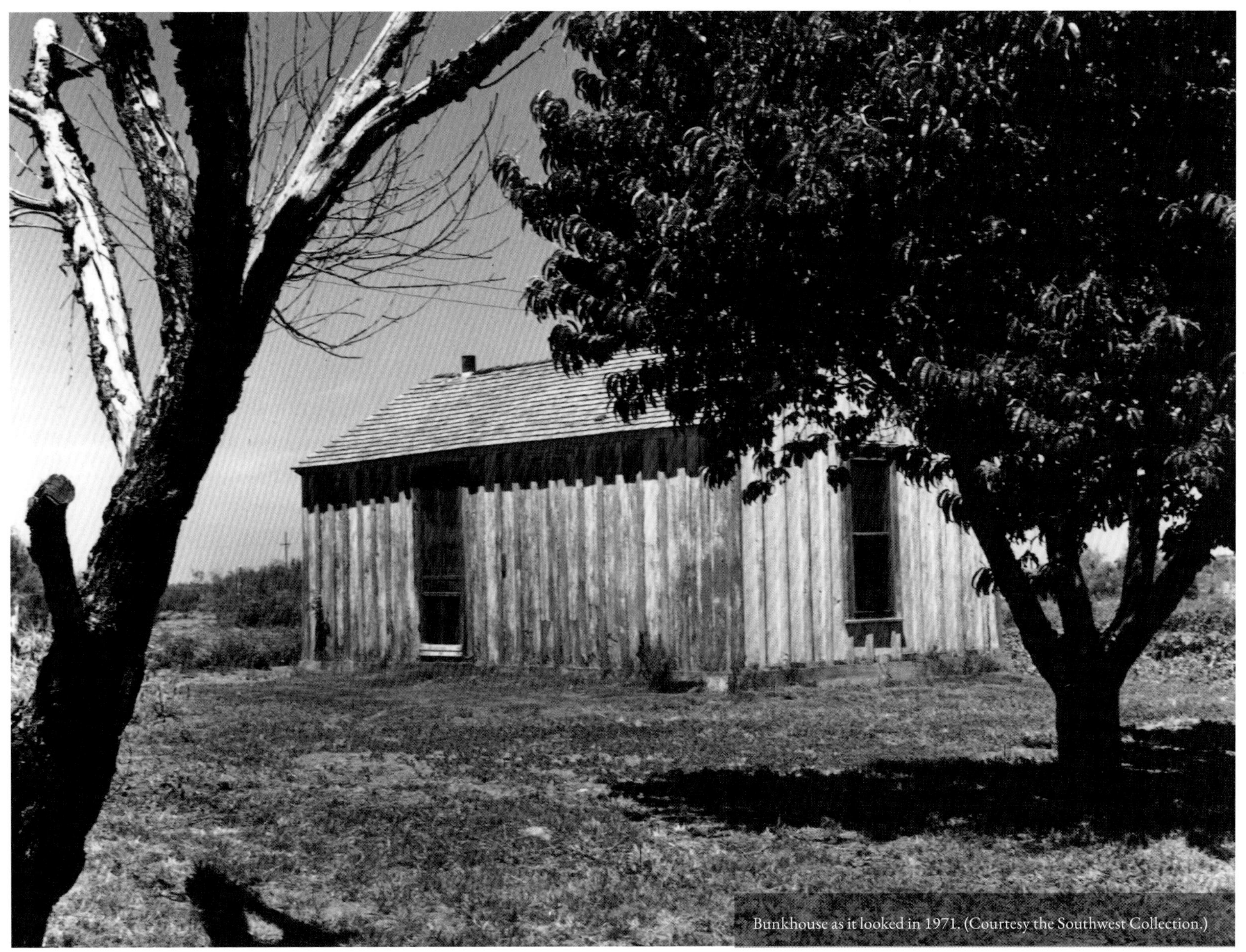
Bunkhouse as it looked in 1971. (Courtesy the Southwest Collection.)

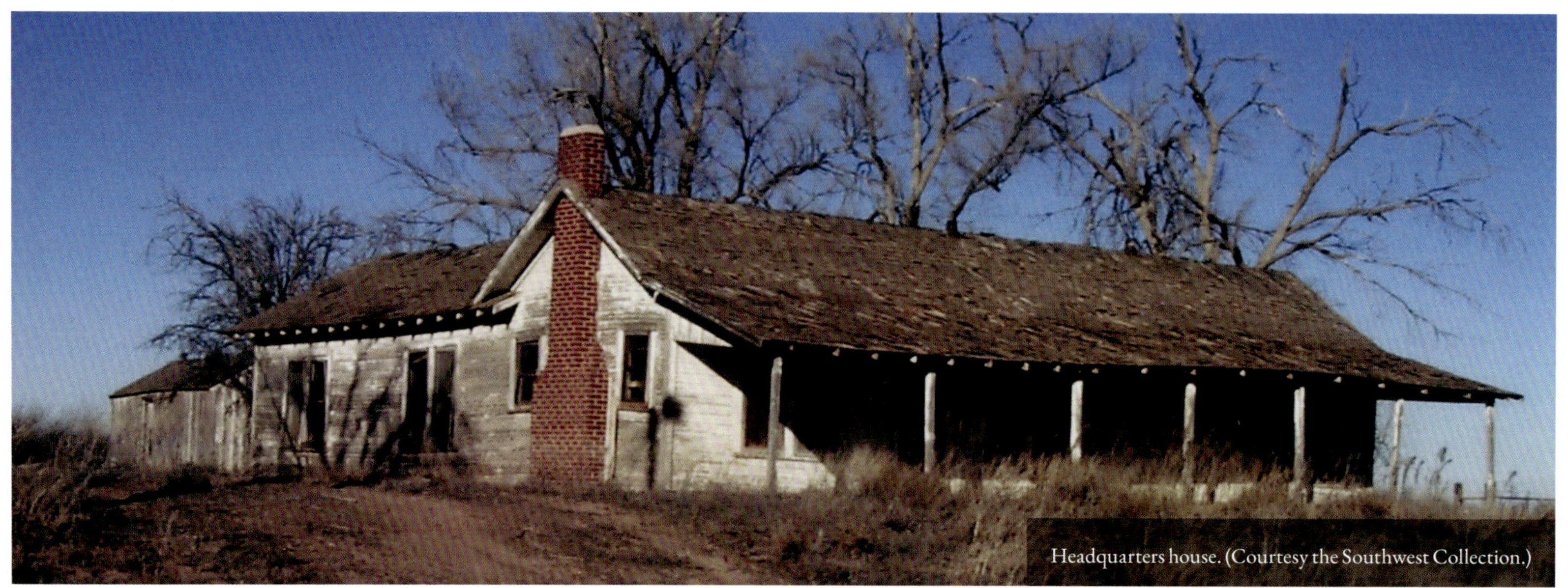
Headquarters house. (Courtesy the Southwest Collection.)

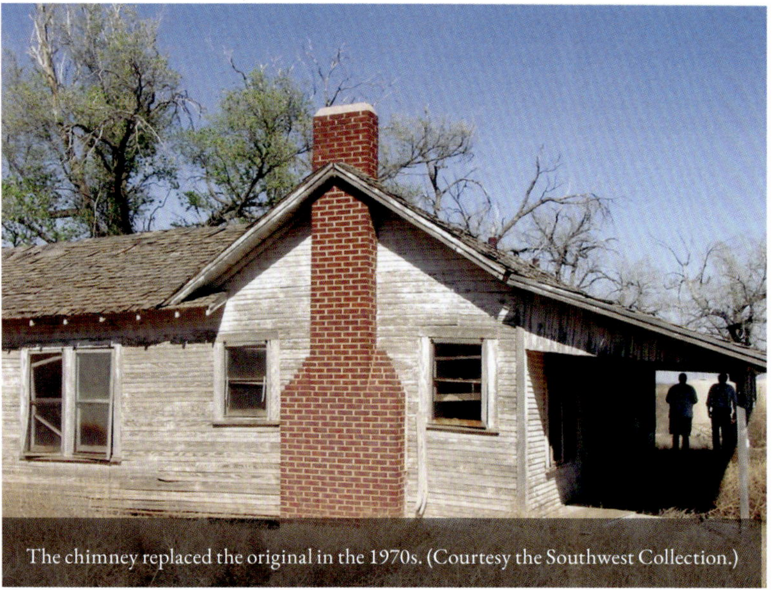
The chimney replaced the original in the 1970s. (Courtesy the Southwest Collection.)

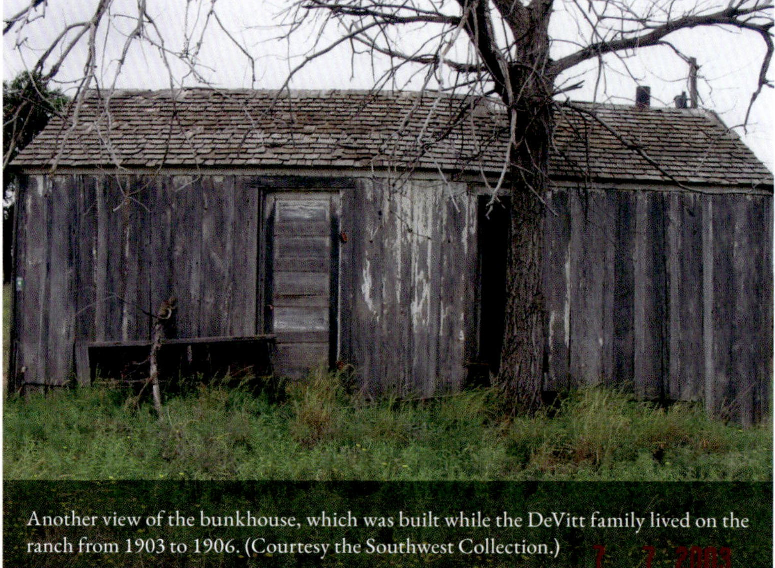

Another view of the bunkhouse, which was built while the DeVitt family lived on the ranch from 1903 to 1906. (Courtesy the Southwest Collection.)

those options because he still believed that a stock operation in West Texas remained his most viable option to what he wanted to acquire: a fortune. He also had come to believe that while sheep could yield him a comfortable, even wealthy, life, cattle ranching was the avenue for him to reach the heights of affluence to which he aspired.

DeVitt left no records that specifically detailed why he made the decision he did, but the men he had met and associated with in the Midland area likely influenced him. John Scharbauer possibly discussed cattle raising with DeVitt as Scharbauer, as well as his brothers and cousins, began to acquire cattle and place them on the range in the Permian Basin. Through his relationship with Scharbauer, DeVitt met influential regional cattleman William Frederick Cowden. Cowden was part of a pioneering ranching family that came to Texas after the Mexican War and eventually followed the traditional migratory pattern of westward movement in the state from initial settlement in deep East Texas to finally reside in Palo Pinto County when the Civil War began. When the Texas and Pacific Railroad completed its line to Fort Worth in 1880 and began to move across the plains, William Frederick (known as Fred), the fifth child of Cowden patriarch George Frederick, made the trek to open a ranch in Midland County in 1883. He established what would be a massive operation that still remains in the hands of the Cowden family.

DeVitt, always a voracious learner, sought advice from these and other men in the region when he began to contemplate shifting from running sheep to cattle. While he absorbed a number of ideas and concepts about the cattle industry that he would make part of his philosophy, perhaps the counsel he took most to heart was that he needed a vast range that had plenty of grass for feed, one much larger than he currently used for his sheep operation. Once again, DeVitt enlisted his mentor John Scharbauer, and the two began to search for either available land—which was difficult to find in the 1890s—or an established operation they could purchase. They would find one in an isolated tract near the New Mexico line.

The spread of the Texas cattle market into the western environs of the state—and the subsequent possible profits from the cattle boom—attracted millions of dollars in outside capital from both foreign and domestic investors. Among the most notable were as follows: the Dundee, Scotland, syndicate that took control of the Matador Ranch just below the Caprock Escarpment in 1882; the Capitol Syndicate company—which built the new Texas Capitol in the mid-1880s after the original burned—that took land as payment for construction efforts that eventually became the XIT Ranch in the Panhandle; and a British concern that purchased the Espuela Land and Cattle operation from Alfred M. Britton in 1885. The success of these operations was mixed, but by 1890 most of these outside investors were looking to exit the Texas market as cattle prices and conditions changed.

One of those investor groups that had hoped to cash in on the Texas cattle boom was the Mallet Cattle Company. Attracted by the potential profits available in Texas cattle ranching in the late 1870s and early 1880s, Dwight P. Atwood and

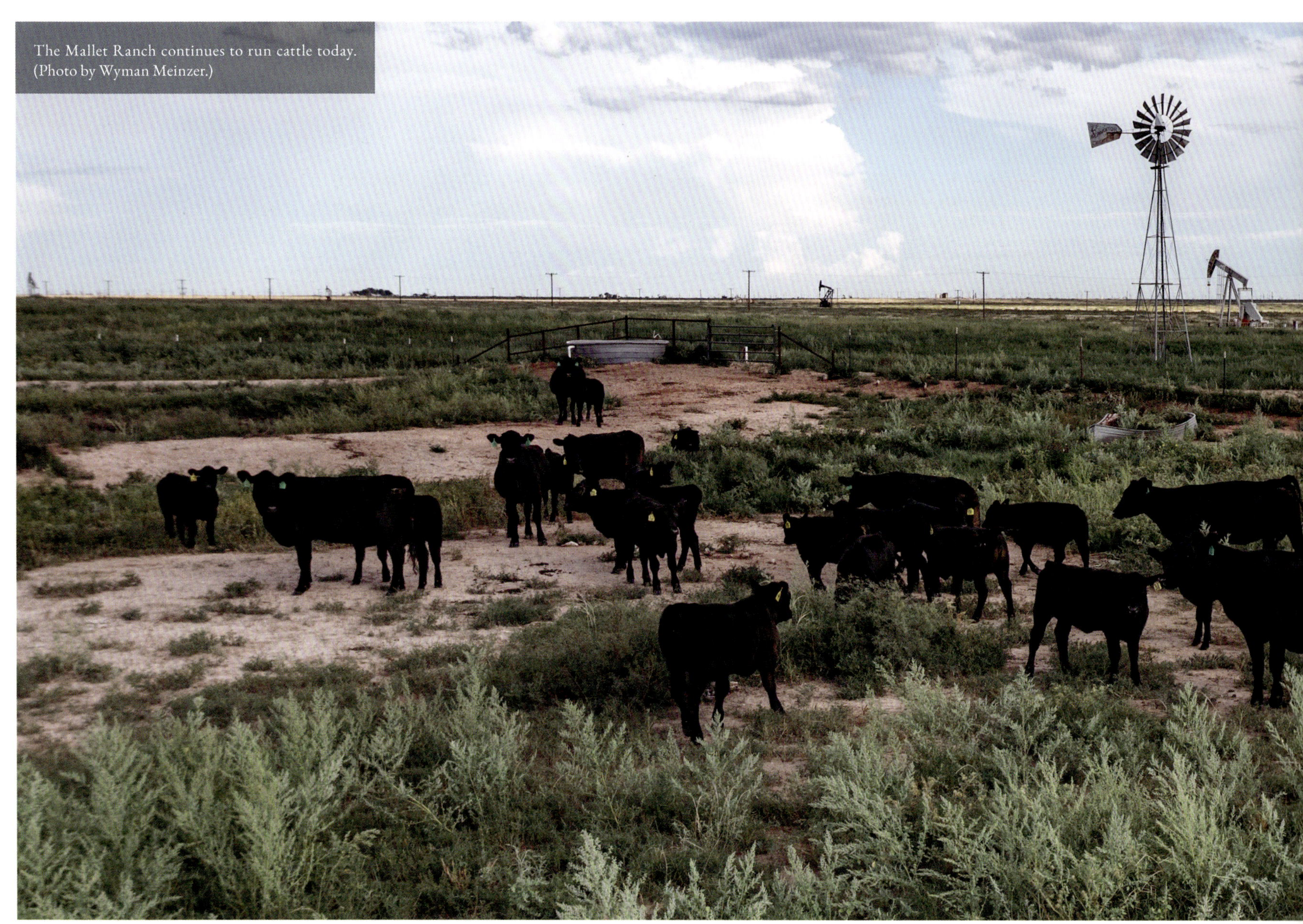

The Mallet Ranch continues to run cattle today. (Photo by Wyman Meinzer.)

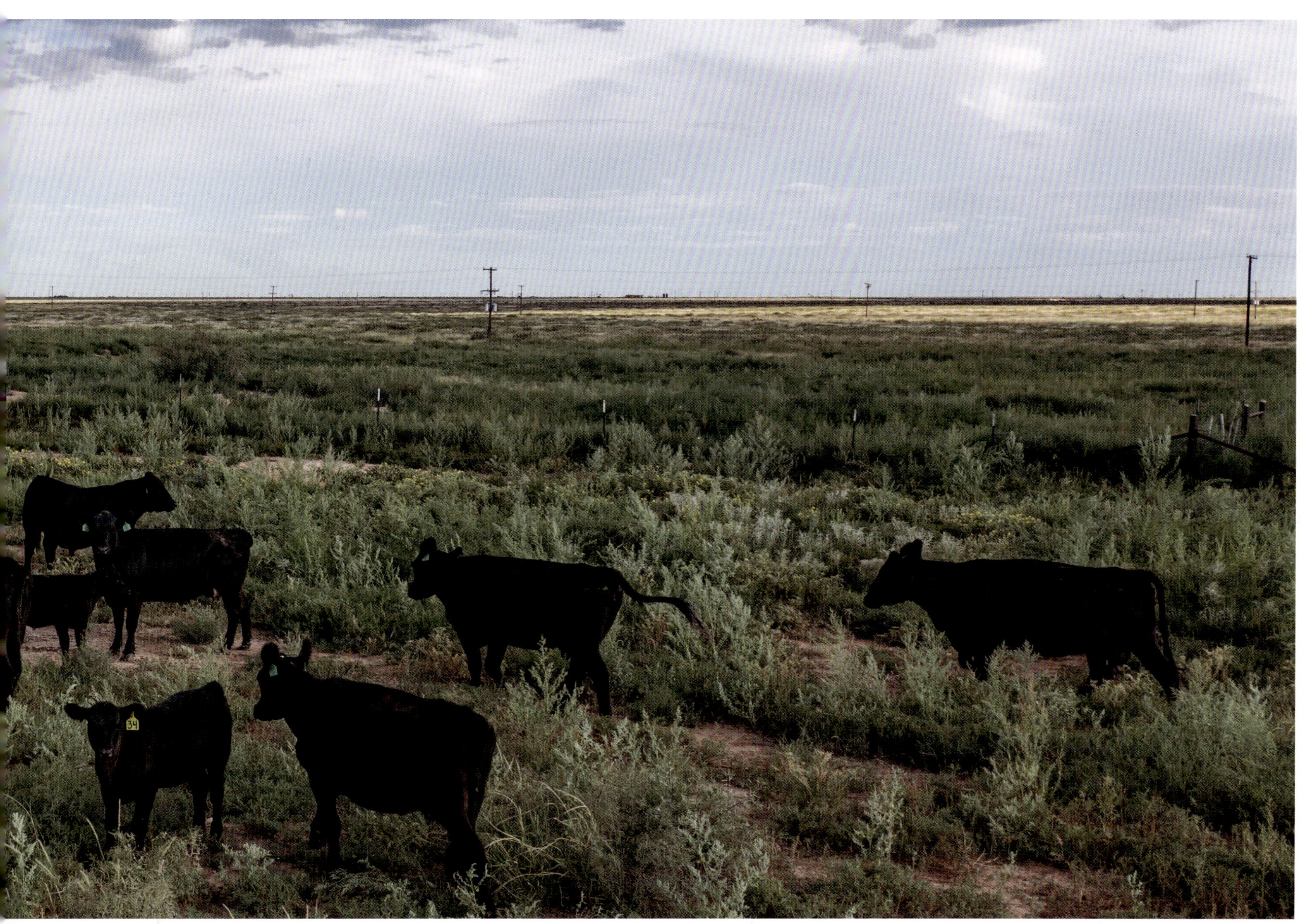
34

A. Neal Harris began to lay the foundation for a company that would invest in cattle operations in the state. The two men acquired part of a large herd from an operation in Mitchell and Howard Counties. The cattle they bought had a brand that resembled a mallet-type hammer, so when they organized their company in New Haven, Connecticut, in 1883, they christened it the Mallet Cattle Company. They advertised their new venture in newspapers and among financial corners of their native New England and had soon recruited seven major investors to add capital to the enterprise. They capitalized their Texas business at $200,000, with which they began to improve their range with fencing and infrastructure.

Atwood took the job of overseeing the ranch, moving to Texas and almost immediately mismanaging the operation. He spent a good portion of the new company's capital to build a ranch headquarters, corrals, and outbuildings and then to fence a ten-thousand-acre expanse to serve as the grazing lands for the herd. The Mallet headquarters, particularly, signaled Atwood's desire to establish a presence in the area and in the stock business. In an era when most operations in the area built small, functional dwellings that were often little more than one room of the most rudimentary design, the Mallet's owners hired George Causey, who had made his reputation as a buffalo hunter, to design and serve as contractor for their headquarters. Causey built a rock house with five large rooms on the highest point of the range. It had a gabled roof—almost unheard on the range—a veranda that commanded a view of the surrounding landscape, and furnishings that rivaled the grandest hotels in Fort Worth. The Mallet looked to establish itself as one of the giants of the region, but despite the grandiose plans the inexperience of the owners would cause the ranch to fail. It took a little more than two years for the Mallet cattle to overgraze the range, which meant Atwood and the company had to find another stretch of grazing land. That necessitated moving west and required, given the aridity of the region, finding a much larger area for their bovines. Atwood bought and/or acquired grazing rights to an almost 100,000-acre tract in Gaines and Yoakum Counties of the Texas South Plains and in Lea County, New Mexico. Atwood also bought more cattle to stock his now larger operation and by 1890 had stocked the Mallet's range with more than 6,000 head of cattle.

Atwood and the Mallet had built what seemed to be an operation on par with some of the larger operations in the region, such as the Matador and Kentucky Land and Cattle operations east of their range, but the ranch manager had failed to anticipate the downturn coming in the cattle business. In many ways the western cattle raisers had been too successful; when combined with a simultaneous increase in cattle production in the Midwestern states—and in such areas the increases were usually in purebred stock that yielded a higher quality of beef than Texas mixed-breed cattle—as well as in some southern states, the price of beef began to decline precipitously. The average price for slaughter-cattle moved from $6.25 a hundredweight in 1882 to less than four dollars in 1890 (prices for slaughter-cattle would not rebound to above five dollars until 1900 and would not return to pre-1865 levels until the market demand years of World War I).

What that meant for the Mallet Cattle Company was that their herd was worth at least a third less than it had been when Atwood acquired it. The range in far West Texas and Eastern New Mexico was also not as robust as Atwood had projected, and that was before drought conditions began to take hold in the late 1880s. The Mallet thus had to buy feed for their cattle, further eroding profits and sinking the operation into serious debt. The Mallet's directors reorganized the company in 1892, bringing in new investors and negotiating some relief with creditors, but it was too little, too late. The Mallet went into bankruptcy in 1893 and came under receivership.

Selling such a large expanse of land and cattle, especially during a bust period, was no easy task, and receivers often had to take offers not near the value of the business; the Mallet proprietors also had to sell their operation in pieces. D. P. Earnest, who had served as the manager, bought the parts in Mitchell and Howard Counties and Meyer Halff, along with his son Henry (who also owned the huge 600-section Quien Sabe Ranch that stretched across Upton, Glasscock, and Midland Counties), bought the Mallet portion in West Texas, which they would use as a grazing pasture for some of their larger ranch's steers. Three other Midland County ranchers—Allen C. Lee, Jesse Heard, and Tom White—acquired the parts of the operation in New Mexico.

The cattlemen that had acquired the majority of the original Mallet Ranch incorporated the holdings into the cattle outfits they already controlled, which meant that they had no desire to buy the stock that grazed on Mallet-controlled acres. Those bovines, along with control of the Mallet Brand, would go to a much smaller operator named Theodore Schuster who lived in Fort Worth. Schuster operated a 150,000-acre ranch that he called the "K," in the southwestern corner of Hockley County. As would be true for many small operators by the 1890s, the surrounding larger operations wholly encircled Schuster's grazing lands. Schuster also did not own the land on which his cattle grazed. While the State of Texas had begun selling off most of its public lands in the late 1870s and the 1880s, some parcels, generally in isolated regions like the western South Plains, remained designated as public range. Texas had turned over management of these lands to the counties, which in this case meant that Schuster practiced what amounted to free-range ranching by the 1890s by leasing grazing rights from Hockley County for his herd.

Schuster would become another casualty of the 1890s cattle bust. There were reasons the large operations were consolidating and obtaining larger parcels: much like for many contemporary businesses, volume is a way to make a smaller profit margin viable. Smaller operators such as Schuster were caught in a squeeze and had to either diversify their stock—such as beginning to raise sheep along with cattle as well as planting and harvesting fruit trees as Henry C. "Hank" Smith did at the Cross B Ranch in Crosby County east of Hockley County—or take on debt and hope to ride out the downturn. Schuster was in no position to do either. He had purchased the Mallet parcel with a loan from Kansas City concerns, and conditions meant that he could take on no more debt nor could he repay the obligation he had. He had only one choice and that was to sell.

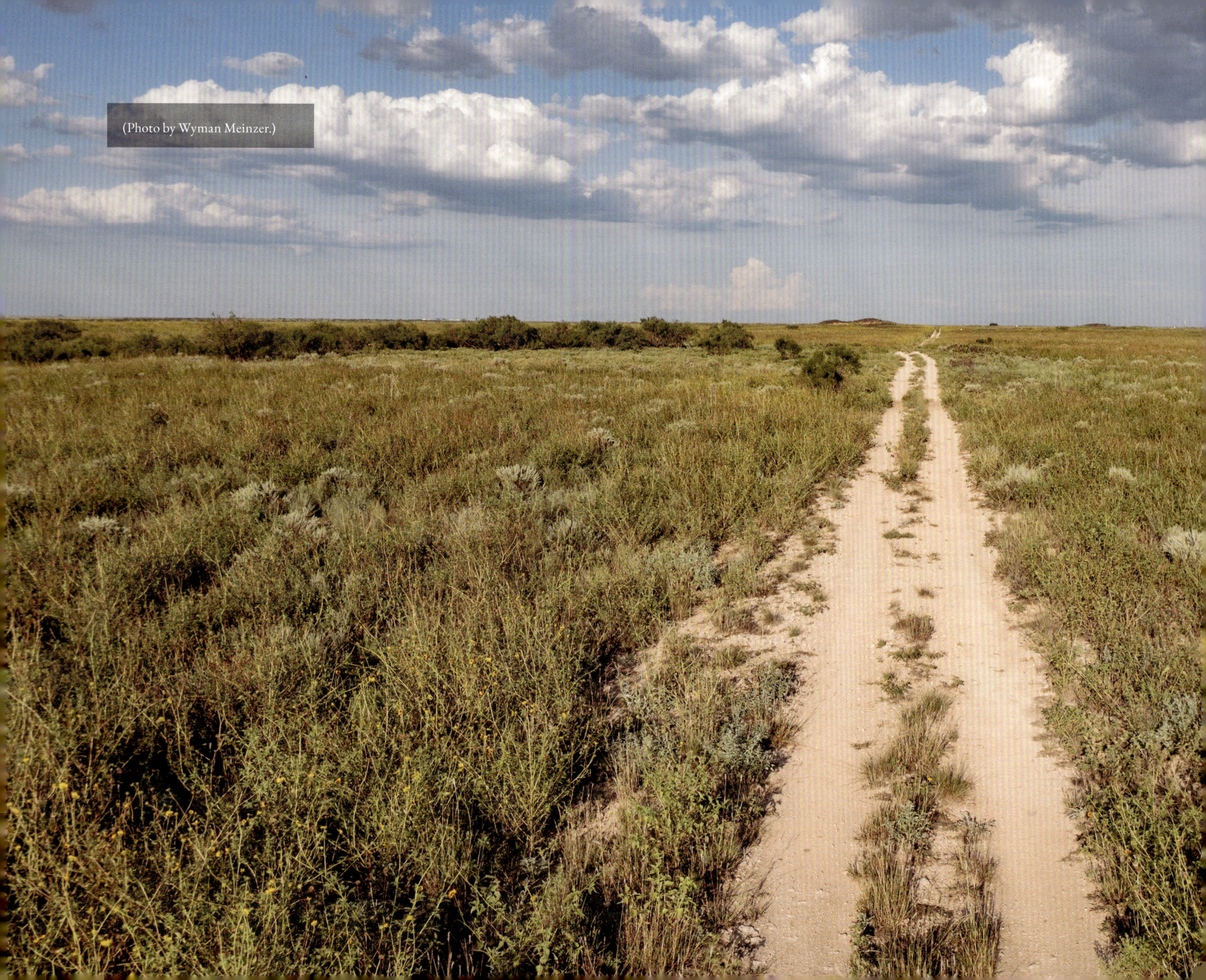
(Photo by Wyman Meinzer.)

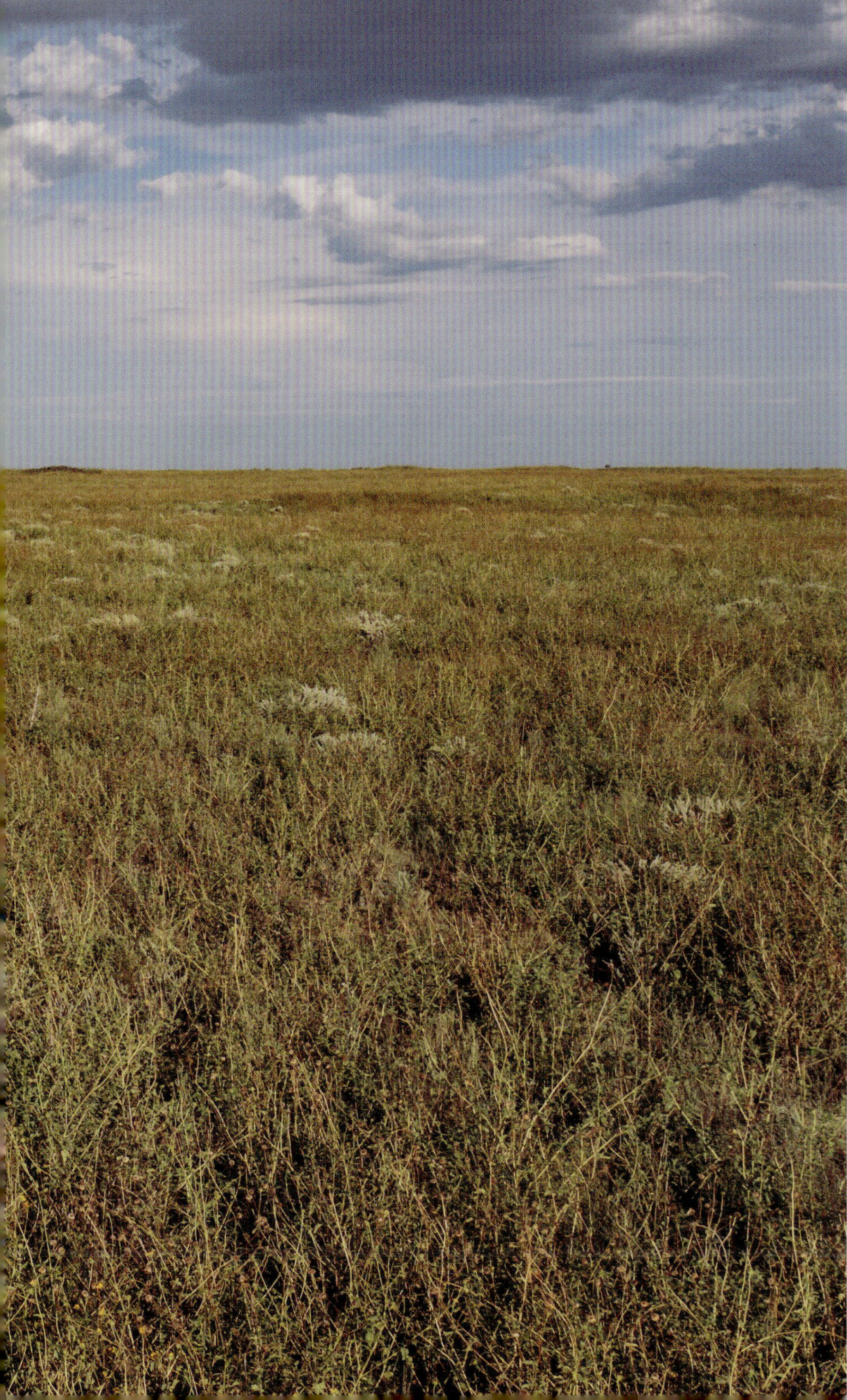

When DeVitt and Scharbauer began to look for land to acquire and begin their new venture, the Mallet lands became an attractive option. The two smaller operators, while successful stockmen, did not have the means to purchase the huge parcels that Halff, Earnest, and the other Midland County ranchers had, so it seemed that they would not be players in the Mallet sell-off. However, because Scharbauer had previously leased pastureland adjacent to Schuster's K Ranch, he kept an eye on his neighbor's new purchase. Scharbauer was also familiar with officials among the Kansas City livestock agents who had lent Schuster the funds to acquire the Mallet herd, so he could have some inside information on the health of Schuster's business. When it became apparent that Schuster had to liquidate his Hockley County herds, Scharbauer and his partner were well positioned to make an offer in the spring of 1895.

There is no record in any collection that details how much DeVitt and Scharbauer paid Schuster for his range, but David Murrah, in *Oil, Taxes, and Cats: A History of the DeVitt Family and the Mallet Ranch*, speculated that it could not have been more than a few thousand dollars. Schuster had no deeds to any of the land on which his cattle grazed—only leases and what little public domain remained—so the value of those acres could not have been much. Besides, the significant part of the transaction was Schuster's cattle, over 4,000 head, many of them prime blooded stock. Since they did not have true legal rights to the land they used to graze their herds, the men began to acquire leases to the land that surrounded their holdings.

David DeVitt and John Scharbauer had together made the decision to move their cattle to the South Plains, but just a few years after they began their venture, Scharbauer decided that he wanted to move on to new opportunities. Scharbauer, who was every bit the entrepreneur as was his partner, had also pursued diversified business interests, and by the mid-1890s came to believe that his best economic option was to pay more attention to those. In 1898, Scharbauer ended his partnership with DeVitt and three years later sold his portion of land on the South Plains to neighboring stockman C. C. Slaughter. Scharbauer then concentrated his business interests in his home of Fort Worth and in banking and real estate development.

David DeVitt sought out a new partner when Scharbauer decided to follow different pursuits. F. W. Flato Jr., while a member of a pioneering South Plains family, lived in Kansas City and ran his own livestock commission firm, Drumm-Flato Commission Company. Flato viewed the Mallet as purely an investment opportunity and an avenue to exploit the movement onto the South Plains to establish stock operations. Flato was also generally content to allow David DeVitt to make the major decisions about the management and direction of the ranch.

DeVitt and Scharbauer, after they had bought Schuster's herd, had to then secure some sort of legal rights to the grazing lands on which they staked the animals. Texas stockmen, as they moved east to west onto Texas public lands, pursued a specific strategy to acquire the use of the range on which they ran their cattle. The first ranchers onto the South Plains did not take the step of purchasing anything more than enough land to establish a headquarters since they could simply let their cattle roam the public lands and practice open-range operations. Most stockmen did designate particular areas in which they would graze their stock, although the vastness of the range and the roaming nature of herds meant that cattle did not necessarily remain in the allocated range. Stockmen, then, had informal agreements with their neighbors about returning cattle to their owners. It was a system that worked as long as the range was not crowded and stockmen took care to honor these agreements. However, as conditions evolved and the cattle industry matured—particularly with the raising of blooded stock and the advent of barbed wire and fencing—such a system began to change. David DeVitt and the Mallet would become caught in the middle, and it would cause controversy and a legal fight.

Christopher Columbus Slaughter today is recognized as one of the most iconic of Texas cattlemen. Slaughter was born into a ranching family in Sabine County in 1837. Almost as soon as he could walk, he began to help his father, George W., in managing and tending their meager herd. When he was just twelve years old, he and his father moved their approximately ninety-head herd to a new plot in Freestone County on the Trinity. After a short education at Larissa College in Cherokee County, C. C. returned to the family ranch and began to fashion ways to raise money that would allow him to stake out a range and herd of his own, from hauling timber harvested in Anderson County to buying and processing wheat grown in Collin County. When he was seventeen, he bought his uncle's share of the family business to become a full partner with his father. He then convinced his father to move their operation to Palo Pinto County where they began to supply beef to the growing United States forts along the western frontier line as well as the Indian Reservation in the Brazos Country the state founded and oversaw.

After the Civil War, the elder Slaughter turned his attention to being a Baptist minister and C. C. turned his to full management of the family's stock operations. C. C. expanded the operation and, after the conquest of native tribes in the mid-1870s, moved even farther west to Mitchell County in 1876, where he established the Long S Ranch on the headwaters of the Colorado River. When he made the move of his herd this time, he also set another pattern. Slaughter had no desire to subject his family to the difficulties of living on the frontier, so they moved and lived in a grand home in Dallas. He would live there the rest of his life and never take up residence on any of his famous ranches. He would eventually move some of his operations to the South Plains in order to avoid new conditions that Texas made on the sale of unclaimed land in the state, a move that would bring him in direct confrontation with David DeVitt.

Texas had begun, in the 1870s, to grant railroads alternate sections of land to aid in railroad construction in the state. This action mirrored federal action but was necessary since there was no federal land in Texas to grant, as Texas had retained its public lands upon annexation. At the same time, the state also designated the remaining sections between railroad land as school lands to fund public education. Stock raisers, particularly in West Texas, had used and leased these school lands, which were mostly unsold and thus in the public domain, for grazing purposes. The Four Section Act changed the equation. The law allowed individuals, most of whom would be looking to establish some sort of homestead, to buy at cheap rates and interest, up to three sections of grazing land as well as another section of agricultural plots. All these new settlers would have to do to gain full title to the land was to improve their holdings and prove residency of three years. What that meant for ranchers in the region is that the state was, essentially, getting out of the leasing business and transitioning to the selling of real estate, which indicated that when stock leases expired the land would be sold and the range "broken up."

C. C. Slaughter was one of those caught in the crosshairs of such a new reality. The range upon which he depended for his herd on the Long S would be broken; it also meant that he would not be able to fence the huge expanses he needed in order to preserve the blooded Hereford stock that had become the most dominant part of his herd. Slaughter had no choice but to look for an alternative, and that was further west in established but unorganized counties. He had definite requirements: first, it had to be a large, contiguous block of land that he alone would control, which meant tracts to which the alternate sections scheme did not apply, and second, it had to be land to which he could cheaply obtain title. He found swathes that satisfied such parameters among the designated school lands in West Texas on the South Plains.

The state of Texas had a long history of using its public lands to substitute for actual appropriation to pay for services. It had done so during the initial phases of the Republic, again in the antebellum years, and in the decades after the Civil War turned once again to such a practice. The legislature, in 1883, dodged designating treasury funds for public schools by passing a law that called for setting aside 325 leagues of land (1,439,100 acres) for public schools in organized counties. Sale of the land, in turn, could be used to support public schools. The law also designated four leagues of land (17,712 acres) in each unorganized county—of which the majority lay in West Texas—for the same purpose. Additionally, since many organized counties could not receive the full grant of four leagues due to competing titles and land in the counties that was already sold, organized county land that the state could not grant was also allocated to unorganized counties, which gave those entities huge blocks of adjacent land available for sale, conditions that were particularly attractive to stockmen looking to expand. The unorganized counties of Bailey, Cochran, and Hockley all had some of such allocated land, upon which Slaughter set his eyes. Another cattleman, F. G. Oxsheer, informed Slaughter of the opportunity and introduced him to John Scharbauer, David DeVitt's partner, who had begun to move toward liquidation of his stock operation. In 1897, Slaughter bought Scharbauer's Hereford herd, and he and Oxsheer agreed that he would graze his herd on Oxsheer's Diamond Ranch in the mentioned counties.

Slaughter traveled from his home in Dallas to examine his herd on Oxsheer's range and came away impressed with the region's potential for raising stock. He thus decided that he would find a way to form his new ranch—which he would call the Lazy S—on the South Plains. Slaughter, however, was a well-known cattleman, and he thought that a move to purchase such a large parcel of land would alarm officials and keep them from selling to him, so he made a clandestine arrangement with Oxsheer and three other men, A. J. Harris, R. S. Ferrell, and W. E. Keys, to be "front men" in making the purchases with the goal of allowing Slaughter to gain control of a huge contiguous tract in which to establish the Lazy S. Slaughter instructed Oxsheer to purchase up to 220,000 acres in Hockley and Cochran Counties. Oxsheer then enlisted a Fort Worth man, W. E. Kaye, to serve as his agent. Kaye, in turn, hired others as agents, and all of them began their clandestine campaign to acquire as much range land on the South Plains as they could, not caring who they may have had to force off the land they wanted in the process.

One of Kaye's moves to acquire land for Slaughter was to approach the commissioners' courts in the counties in which DeVitt (and his new partner F. W. Flato) had leased pastureland—specifically the school lands owned by Zavala, Scurry, and Baylor Counties—and then purchase the tracts and ask the commissioners to void DeVitt's leases. The Zavala County commissioners agreed to Kaye's scheme, while the courts in Scurry and Baylor refused the offer and upheld DeVitt's lease. Kaye, as he was hired to do, turned the Zavala school land he bought over to C. C. Slaughter. DeVitt suspected that something nefarious was taking place, and his suspicions were confirmed when in December 1898 a commissioner for Concho County, which owned a block of land that DeVitt had received in his deal with Theodore Schuster, informed him that an R. S. Ferrell was attempting to buy the land.

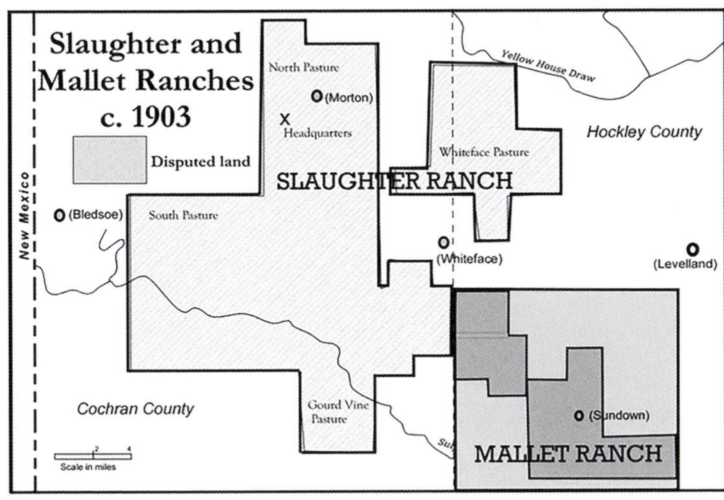

Lubbock Avalanche-Journal

DeVitt reacted angrily, as he viewed such an effort as a violation of the "gentleman's agreement" that had always existed among those on the range that one cattleman would not try to buy and infringe on another's range rights. DeVitt confronted Ferrell, who feigned ignorance and denied that he had made any such bid. DeVitt suspected that Ferrell had lied to him. Ferrell had done so because he had agreed to allow Kaye to use his name to purchase the Concho County lands. DeVitt—who certainly knew how the landmen in Fort Worth operated and who W. E. Kaye was and what he had done in the cases of the other school lands—directly challenged Kaye. The Fort Worth agent repeated his ruse that he was working for Ferrell, to which DeVitt informed him that Ferrell had denied agreeing to such an arrangement and furthermore he knew that R. S. Ferrell could not afford to buy such a large expanse. Kaye claimed then that

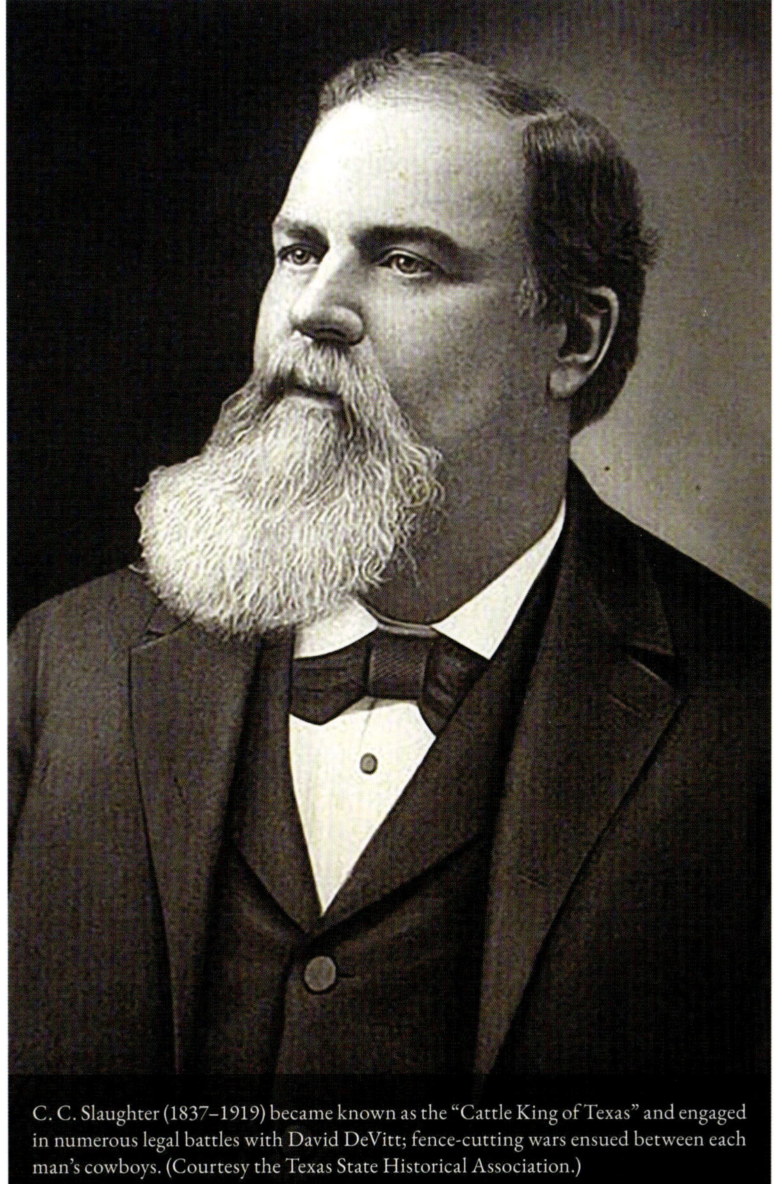

C. C. Slaughter (1837–1919) became known as the "Cattle King of Texas" and engaged in numerous legal battles with David DeVitt; fence-cutting wars ensued between each man's cowboys. (Courtesy the Texas State Historical Association.)

Ferrell's uncle was fronting the money for the purchase. DeVitt, fortunately, had a clause in his lease contract that gave him right of first refusal if Concho County was to sell the land, so he and Flato bought the 4,300-acre strip in January 1899. However, DeVitt was not done with his confrontation with those who were helping C. C. Slaughter buy up most of the land in the region for his Lazy S.

W. E. Kaye sent a letter to David DeVitt in May 1899 informing him that he had purchased over 30,000 acres of Maverick, Kaufman, and Edwards Counties land in which the Mallet had leased. Then, in August, another communiqué brought the news that R. S. Ferrell had purchased the entire 17,712-acre holding of Zavala County, which contained the almost 4,300-acre tract that DeVitt and Flato had leased. This portended a disaster for DeVitt because if he lost those lands the Mallet would be split in two and its size would be reduced to approximately 50,000 acres. The men had saved their range from the earlier grab because they had right of purchase, but they held no such privilege to the Maverick and Kaufman lands they had leased, which meant they would lose those 15,000-plus acres. Their lease was due to expire in 1902, at which time they lost the parcels. That set up a confrontation between the Slaughter interests and DeVitt and Flato over the Edwards County lands.

DeVitt and his former partner John Scharbauer had originally leased the 18,000-acre Edwards school lands in June 1898, and this piece passed to the new partnership of DeVitt and Flato. Their contract had a clause that allowed them to re-lease the land at the same price when their current lease expired on June 1, 1903. They also had a purchase option if the Edwards County commissioners chose to offer the parcel for sale. The manner of how this piece became contested was representative of the often-shadowy way that West Texas lands during the era were bought, sold, controlled, and sometimes outright stolen.

Kaye had made a deal in March 1899 with Edwards County in which he became the selling agent for the county. He agreed that he would seek buyers for the land and sell it for eighty-five cents an acre. The agreement further stated that if Kaye had not sold the land by August he would personally buy the entire plot. It also noted that Kaye was granted the right to keep anything over the agreed-upon price of eighty-five cents an acre as his commission. Edwards County had inserted a clause that the current leaseholders—DeVitt and Flato—had "preference right to purchase" as was stated in their original lease, and the Edwards County judge pointed out to Kaye that DeVitt and Flato would have first right of purchase. Kaye ignored the clause and warning—even telling the commissioners court that DeVitt and Flato were near bankruptcy and would not be able to purchase the tract—an action that would cause a direct legal confrontation between the Mallet and C. C. Slaughter.

Kaye's primary fealty was to his Slaughter acquisition scheme, not to Edwards County and certainly not to allowing DeVitt and Flato to acquire the pasture. Kaye sold the Edwards County land to R. S. Ferrell for one dollar an acre in May 1899. Ferrell then—as per the agreement—signed his title over to Slaughter two weeks later. Ferrell would later testify that he had insisted that Slaughter accept all conditions of the contract as it was transferred to him by Edwards County, which would have included the Mallet option to buy the land. Kaye sent a letter to DeVitt in which he likely alluded to the potential Ferrell-Slaughter purchase when he informed DeVitt that "I am not the only one wanting to buy lands within your pasture." DeVitt, suspicious of Kaye and with the intention of protecting his range, wrote directly to Edwards County Judge James M. Hunter to remind him that he and Flato held the first option to purchase. The judge wrote back pledging that the county would abide by all clauses and options of the lease agreement.

David DeVitt considered the matter closed at this point and that the contract would allow him to buy the land he currently leased. F. W. Flato was not as confident. Flato's financial situation was not as stable as DeVitt's, and he may have feared directly confronting a man as well connected, powerful, and wealthy as C. C. Slaughter. Flato approached Slaughter in November 1900 and offered a land trade or division of some kind. Slaughter not only declined but strongly countered that he intended to take the entire parcel. Flato knew that losing the almost 18,000 acres would destroy the Mallet, so he next proposed that Slaughter buy out all of his and DeVitt's interests, but that also was met with a refusal. While Flato was negotiating with Slaughter, the first legal battle between the men began and involved the Zavala and Kaufman County parcels, a case that DeVitt and Flato lost. Upon the conclusion of the case, Slaughter immediately filed suit to remove any Mallet cattle from the land they now owned. He was confident that he would soon obtain the Edwards County acres that he desired as well.

Undeterred by his courtroom loss, David DeVitt became even more determined not to lose the crucial Edwards County 18,000 acres. He exercised his contractual right to purchase the plot in February 1902, and the Edwards County commissioners made no mention of the Kaye-Ferrell arrangement and expressed to DeVitt that they would accept his offer of ninety cents an acre. The problem was that Edwards County *had* allowed Kaye to agree to sell to Ferrell and thus to Slaughter, which placed them in the middle of a burgeoning fight between the two parties and cattle empires. The Edwards County commissioners then tried a Solomon-like solution and voided the contract with *both* Kaye/Ferrell/Slaughter and DeVitt and Flato. DeVitt then decided to increase his offer to one dollar an acre.

While DeVitt, Flato, and Slaughter fought it out in court, both ranches' hands engaged in another kind of war on the ground between the two spreads. When the DeVitt-Flato lease expired on June 1, 1903, Slaughter immediately had his men move onto the disputed land, begin to drill a water well, and construct a fence that would enclose it within the adjacent Slaughter-owned Lazy S. DeVitt sent his foreman, Hall Jarman, in August to the new town of Lubbock to get the courts there to issue an injunction to prevent Slaughter's seizure of the plot before they could finish the fence. Slaughter then sent in his attorney, G. G. Wright, and had the injunction squashed and once again sent his ranch hands into the contested spread and resumed building his fence as well as driving off all Mallet cattle. A pattern developed: the Slaughter hands

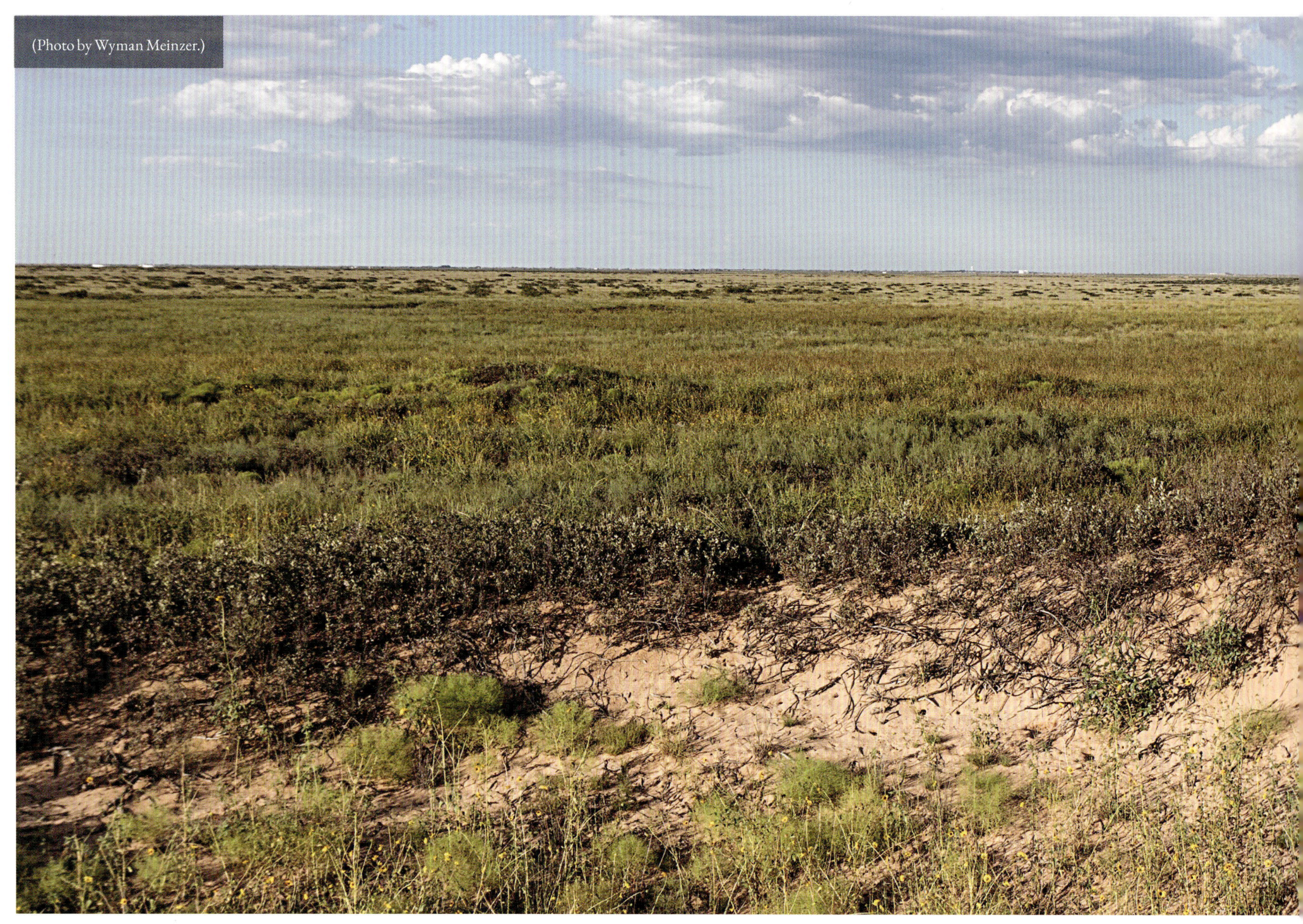
(Photo by Wyman Meinzer.)

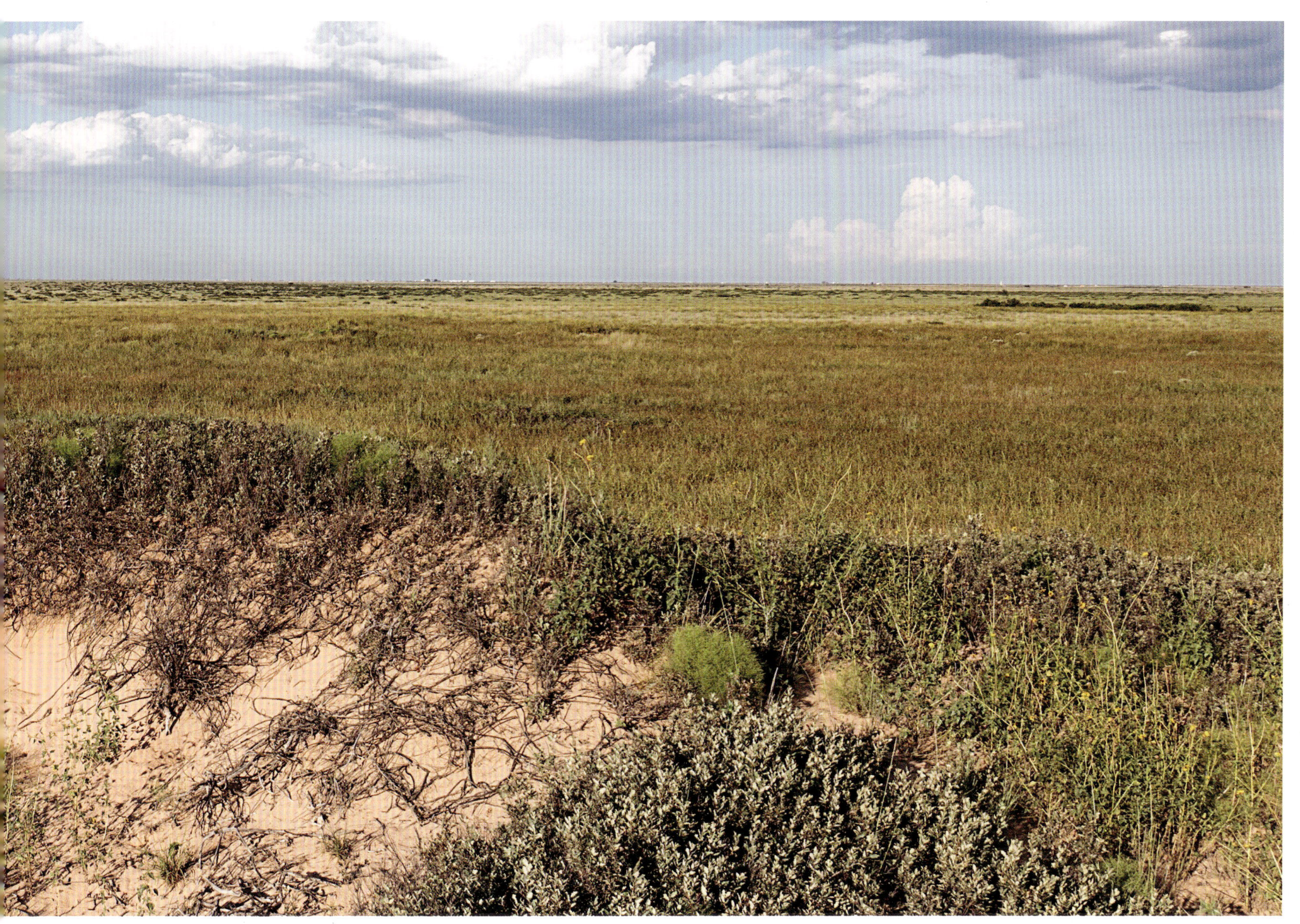

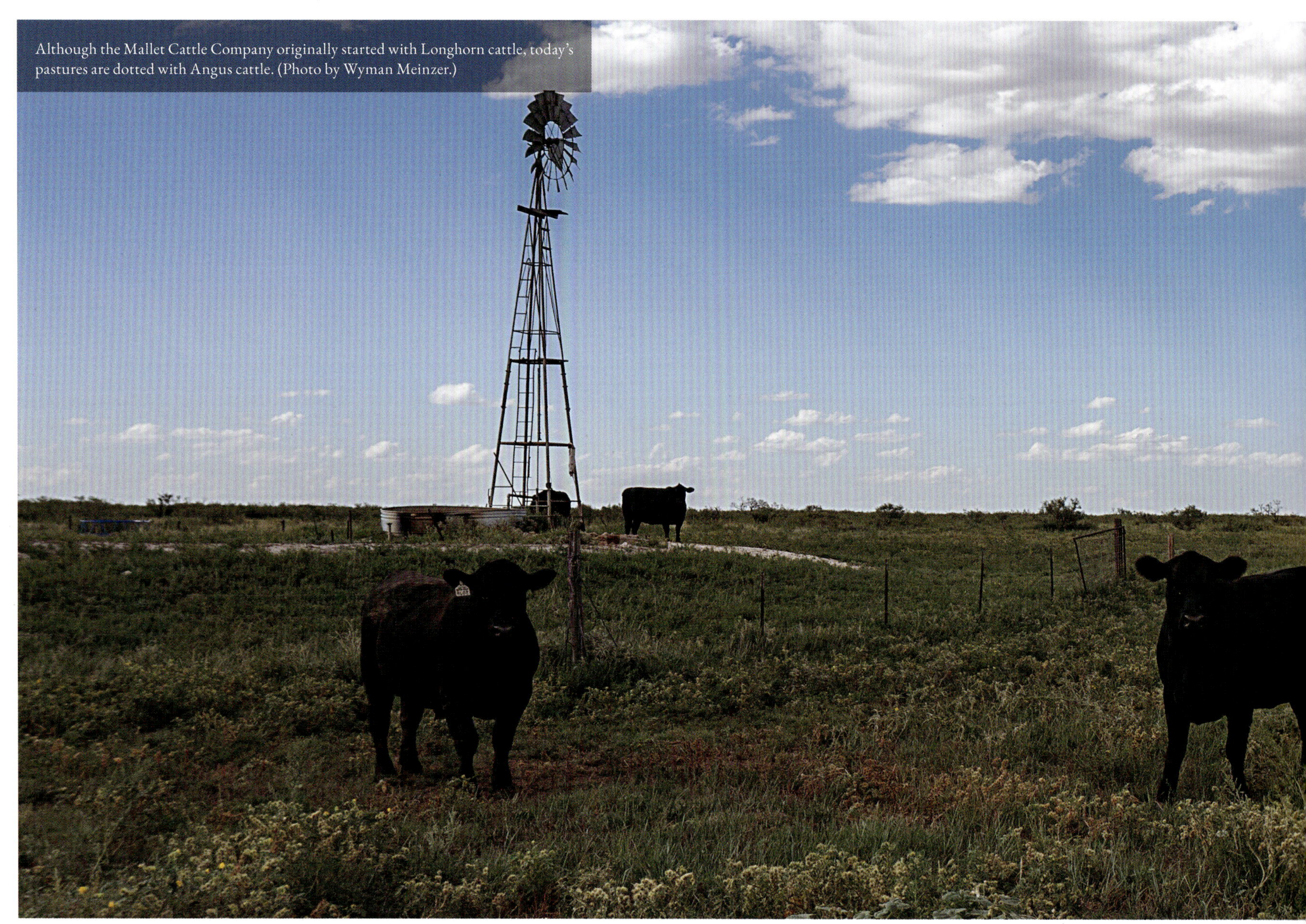
Although the Mallet Cattle Company originally started with Longhorn cattle, today's pastures are dotted with Angus cattle. (Photo by Wyman Meinzer.)

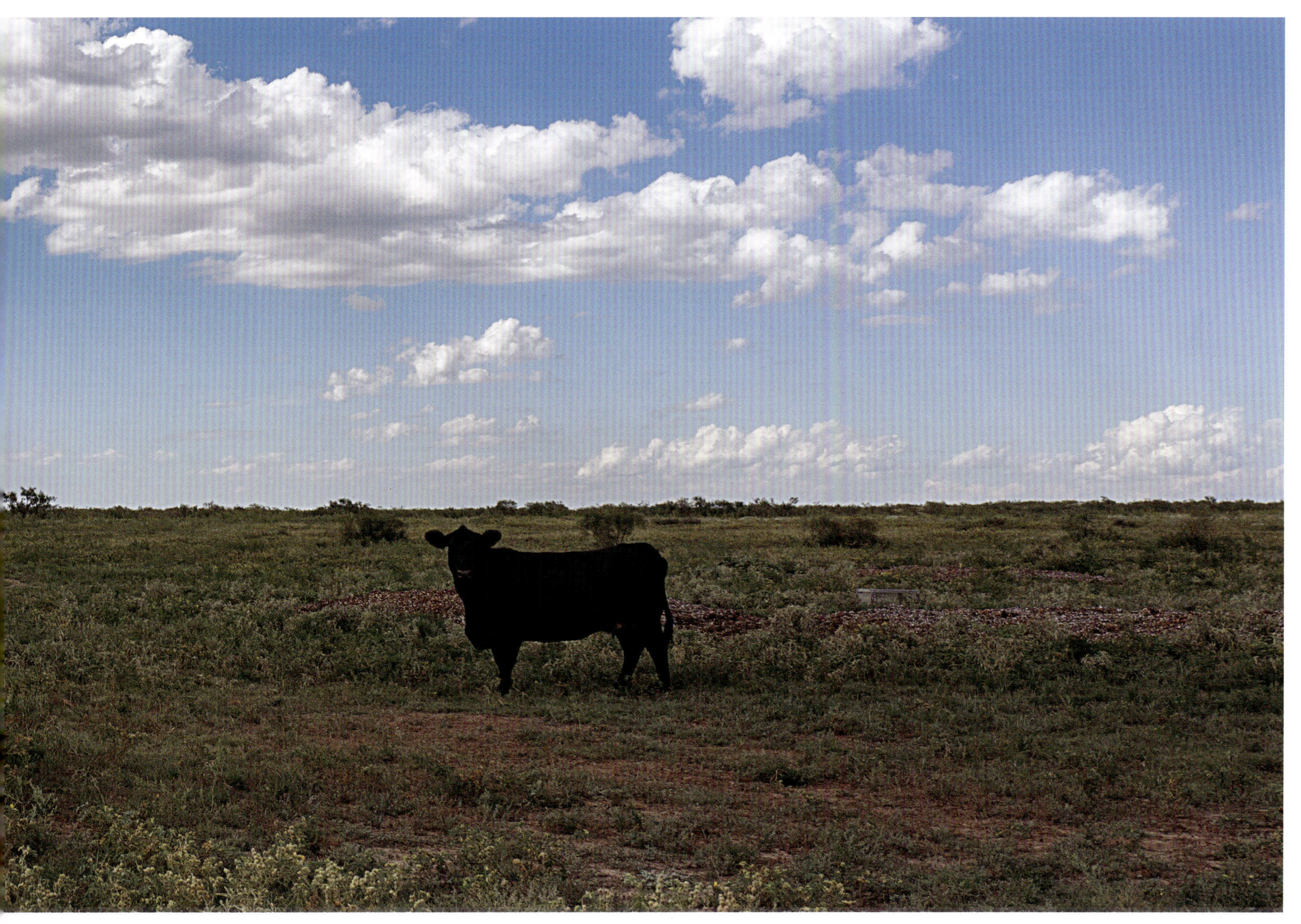

would build a fence, the Mallet cowboys would cut it, and the Slaughter people would build it back, and then the process would begin again.

The Slaughter employees finished their fence and isolated the Mallet herd and lands on October 24. The DeVitt cowboys then cut the fence in at least two places the same day. Meanwhile, David DeVitt and C. C. Slaughter had met on the contested lands in mid-October. Slaughter, in a bit of bombast and confidence, had essentially dared DeVitt to challenge his claim in court, telling him that he "was going to take the land any way." DeVitt took the cattleman up on his taunt and on October 24 once again received an injunction from the Lubbock district court ordering Slaughter to stop all activity on the Edwards County lands. On the ground, the cowboys from each outfit continued their stand-off, with many of them now carrying weapons, portending violence.

DeVitt and Flato, at the same time they received the injunction, had filed suit against Slaughter to "recover damages for trespass." The court ruled in favor of the Mallet men. Also, in November the Edwards County Commissioners Court weighed in and issued DeVitt and Flato a deed to the land. DeVitt traveled to Rocksprings, the county seat, and completed the purchase of the Edwards County school lands at one dollar an acre. Slaughter's response was obliviousness, and he continued drilling the well and fencing the pasture. His actions were seemingly justified when in December the Lubbock District Court overturned their earlier decision, giving Slaughter a full go-ahead to continue his improvements and occupation of the land.

DeVitt and Flato had to counter somehow. On the same day that the Lubbock court issued its December decision, the two men formed a new entity, the Mallet Land and Cattle Company, which they then incorporated in Missouri. The state, in turn, issued a Certificate of Incorporation to the Mallet firm and, on December 25, 1903, the Mallet Land and Cattle Company filed suit in United States District Court against Slaughter "for an injunction to restrain the defendant, C. C. Slaughter, from trespassing upon the plaintiff's land . . . and to remove cloud from title to said land." DeVitt and Flato received their injunction on December 29, and foreman Jarman and three Mallet hands rode to the disputed land, found Slaughter's men, and read to them the injunction. The Lazy S men responded as their boss had continually done before: they renounced the authority of the federal court and were prepared to ignore the order. The Slaughter hands, for the next month, continued building fence, and the Mallet cowboys continued to damage what they had built, often not just by cutting wire but by chopping down posts, which meant that the Lazy S employees had to start digging holes and placing the posts all over again. The Lazy S men also engaged in their share of fence cutting, moving over and cutting Mallet lines along the western edge of the Edwards County pasture. Although the fence was on Mallet land, Slaughter's men claimed that the Lazy S owned the fence and they could do as they pleased. They cut the fence and drove over 1,500 head of cattle onto the formerly enclosed land. The Hockley County fence-cutting war was on the brink of turning violent.

The DeVitt-Flato gambit of incorporating in Missouri and then seeking federal relief in their fight with C. C. Slaughter had shifted the momentum of the battle between the two. Slaughter, a powerful man within Texas political and social circles, held a definite advantage in the courts of the state, but that benefit disappeared in federal court. The more even playing field yielded dividends for the Mallet men in May 1904 when US District Judge Edward Meeks ruled in favor of DeVitt and Flato and voided Slaughter's claim to the disputed land. Slaughter's attorneys then appealed the decision to the United States Fifth Circuit Court of Appeals.

Slaughter's attorneys argued that DeVitt and Flato had used and manipulated the nation's incorporation laws by choosing to form their firm in Missouri instead of Texas solely to move the jurisdiction in the case from Texas courts to federal ones. The Slaughter position was that the dispute should be settled in state court, where they—of course—had already succeeded. DeVitt's lawyers countered that the court case had nothing to do with the incorporation since they had always intended to reorganize and form the new entity but had just delayed doing so for over a year. In their line of reasoning, the new corporation was a result of the two partners having divergent interests that required such action, specifically that Flato had used his interests as collateral for another loan from a Kansas City bank and needed the incorporation tactic to satisfy the bank's need to secure his debt.

The appeals court decided in favor of the DeVitt and Flato position. It ruled that Slaughter had not proved that the incorporation of the Mallet Land and Cattle Company was solely a ruse to move jurisdiction of their dispute to federal court. Furthermore, it rejected the Slaughter claim that Edwards County had no right to include the DeVitt-Flato purchase option in their lease and that the parties certainly retained that right and that it superseded any claim that Slaughter may have. They went on to conclude that Edwards County's contract with W. E. Kaye was null and void because the Texas Supreme Court had ruled, on numerous occasions, that commissioners' courts could make no such contract with an agent who made a commission from the sale of public lands. Therefore, Kaye had sold the land to Ferrell illegally, and thus Ferrell could not transfer title to C. C. Slaughter.

The federal appeals court ruling should have ended the matter, but C. C. Slaughter—true to his obstinate nature and aversion to losing—appealed the ruling to the United States Supreme Court. Slaughter believed that the Edwards County land tract was key to building his operation, but an ulterior motive may have also been to eliminate DeVitt as a competitor. The two men had come to dislike each other, and there may have been a bit of the Fort Worth–Dallas rivalry involved as well. Slaughter thus pushed his suit to the highest level. It did not, however, do him any good as in an April 1906 ruling the United States Supreme Court refused to hear the case. David DeVitt and F. W. Flato had, against large odds, won their case. Ironically, because the Mallet now separated two portions of the Lazy S, which precipitated Slaughter hands having to come across Mallet tracts to switch pastures, relations between the two outfits would actually improve to become cordial in the years after the protracted legal fight.

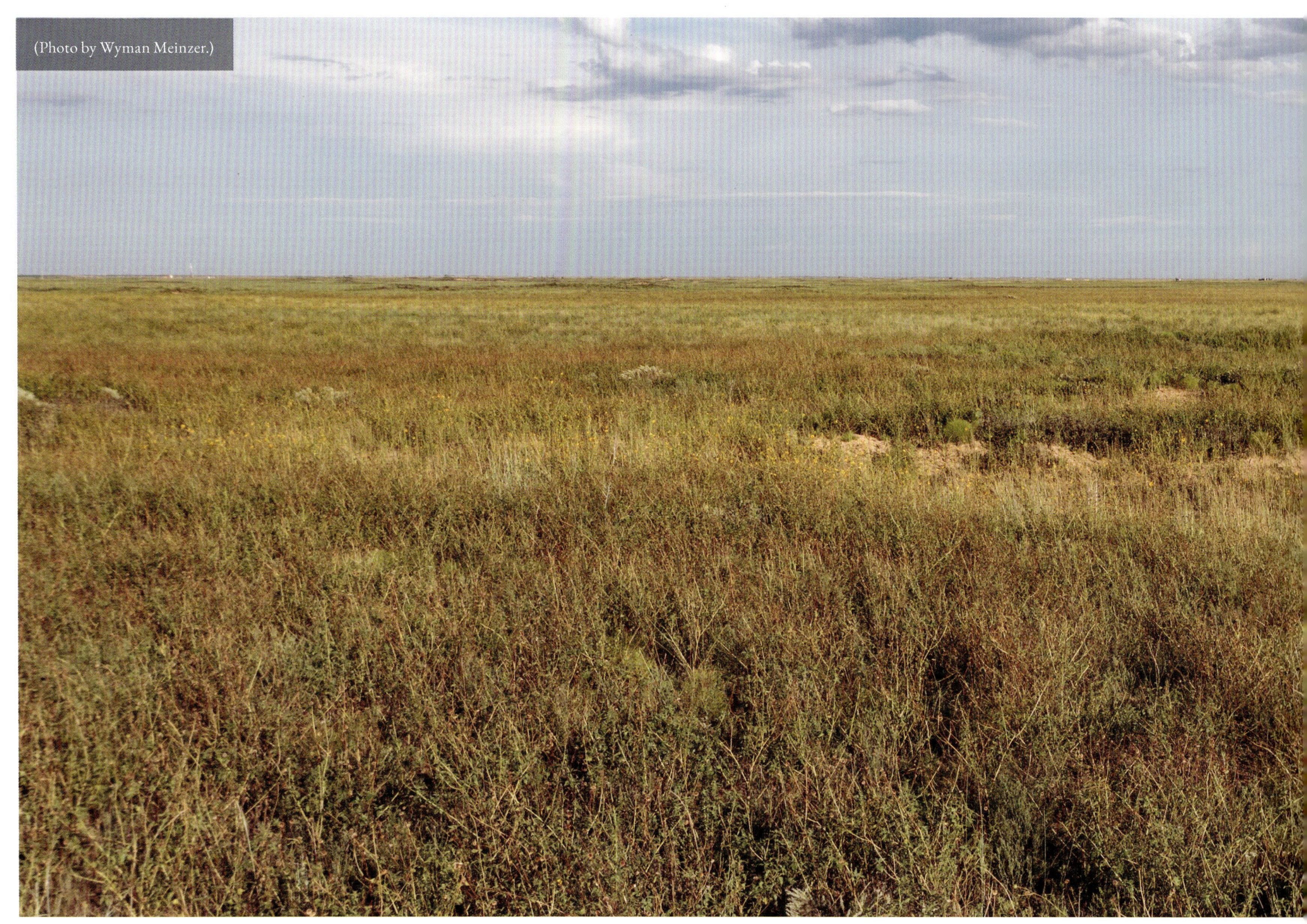

(Photo by Wyman Meinzer.)

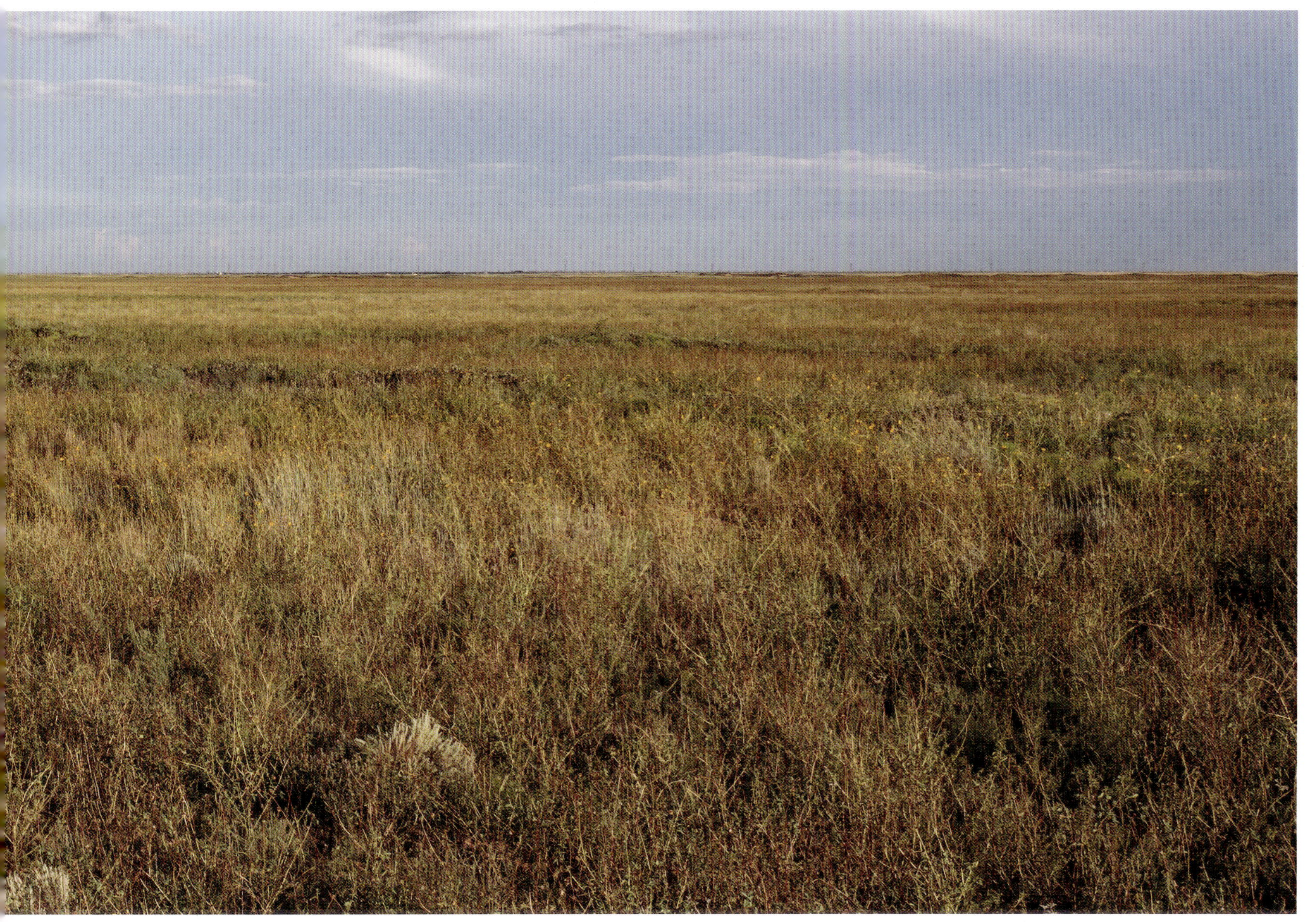

DeVitt needed the acquisition of clear title to the Edwards County land in order to ensure the continuity and success of his operation, but he and his partner faced other challenges in securing their holdings. The Mallet had built its headquarters on a strip of land that the original surveyors of the established South Plains counties had overlooked. The surveys were supposed to meet along the Terry–Hockley and Cochran–Yoakum County lines, but somehow neither one had included land that lay along the southern edge of Hockley and Cochran Counties. The headquarters was within that strip.

The oversight might not have created a problem if an Erath County legislator, Jim Jarrott, had not discovered it. Jarrott, an attorney, recognized an opportunity, so he surveyed the land and organized a group of homesteaders in 1901 to begin to claim land in the parcel. Jarrott's move to secure homesteaded land in the area angered many regional ranchers, and their ire would turn to violence. The lawyer, who had moved his family to the land in question, was murdered by an unknown assailant in August 1902. Jarrott's murder made the homesteaders even more intent on remaining and staking their claims. The farmers also were sure that one of the ranchers in the area had orchestrated the assassination. The murder was never solved, which only added to the mystery, and only reached some closure when, in 1933, Jarrott's widow supposedly learned that a paid killer had confessed to the murder before he was hanged in 1909 in Oklahoma. However, he did not name who commissioned him to do so.

Since the southern portion of the Mallet also lay in the unsurveyed strip, David DeVitt had to act fast to make sure another portion of his ranch was not affected by legal maneuvering, although no homesteaded land came within the Mallet lease and Jarrott had made no plans to claim parcels under the control of DeVitt and Flato. Still, DeVitt quickly began to buy those sections of the newly surveyed land he could in order to make sure that the Mallet remained intact. However, the homestead law required that anyone buying land had to actually reside on the property for at least three years. That meant that David DeVitt had to leave the family home in Fort Worth and move onto the ranch full time; for three years Florence DeVitt and the DeVitt children shuttled back and forth between the Fort Worth home and the Mallet living quarters. DeVitt finally fulfilled the requirement in October 1906, and the State of Texas issued a secure title to the two sections of land contained within the unsurveyed strip.

David DeVitt, also in the early twentieth century, began to move to secure title to more parcels of land and solidify Mallet holdings. He bought four more sections of the formerly unsurveyed strip between 1912 and 1917 and then almost 7,000 more acres of land adjacent to those holdings. South of that line he acquired another 7,000 acres by 1917 in Yoakum and Terry Counties, as well as Oldham, Concho, Atascosa, Garza, Rusk, and Sutton County school lands. Still, despite such efforts, DeVitt could not retain control of all the land with which he had begun. He could not secure title to the Zavala, Maverick, and Kaufman County school lands and had to watch Slaughter gain control of those parcels, which reduced a sizable chunk of the southern portion of the Mallet. He also lost control of other parcels that he had previously leased such as the Baylor and Rains County school lands.

David DeVitt had chosen a prime spot to begin a cattle operation. The land and soil of the South Plains of Texas—located just above the Caprock Escarpment on a high flat plateau known as the Llano Estacado—proved to be an outstanding locale to raise cattle. The flat nature of the region meant that pastureland was plentiful, and in soil that millions of years ago lay on the slopes of the Rocky Mountains before being washed down onto the Llano, rich grazing grasses grew that had fed vast buffalo herds in the centuries before cattlemen learned they could use the same region to fatten their stock. Such prime conditions are what drove stockmen to the region and were also why C. C. Slaughter and DeVitt were willing to go head-to-head to secure grazing lands for their herds.

David DeVitt and his partner F. W. Flato, fresh off their court fight with C. C. Slaughter, had succeeded in securing a formidable and profitable cattle empire on the South Plains, one that was now poised to soar to even greater heights in the next few decades. However, DeVitt had no way of knowing just how bumpy that journey would be, one that would eventually lead to the lowest ebb in the Mallet's history before a change in fortune—literally—would produce one of the most lucrative tracts of land in the state of Texas. It would also produce a new generation of DeVitts who would face a period of fantastic turmoil but also persevere to see the lands that David DeVitt chose for his operation produce one of the most notable fortunes in Texas history.

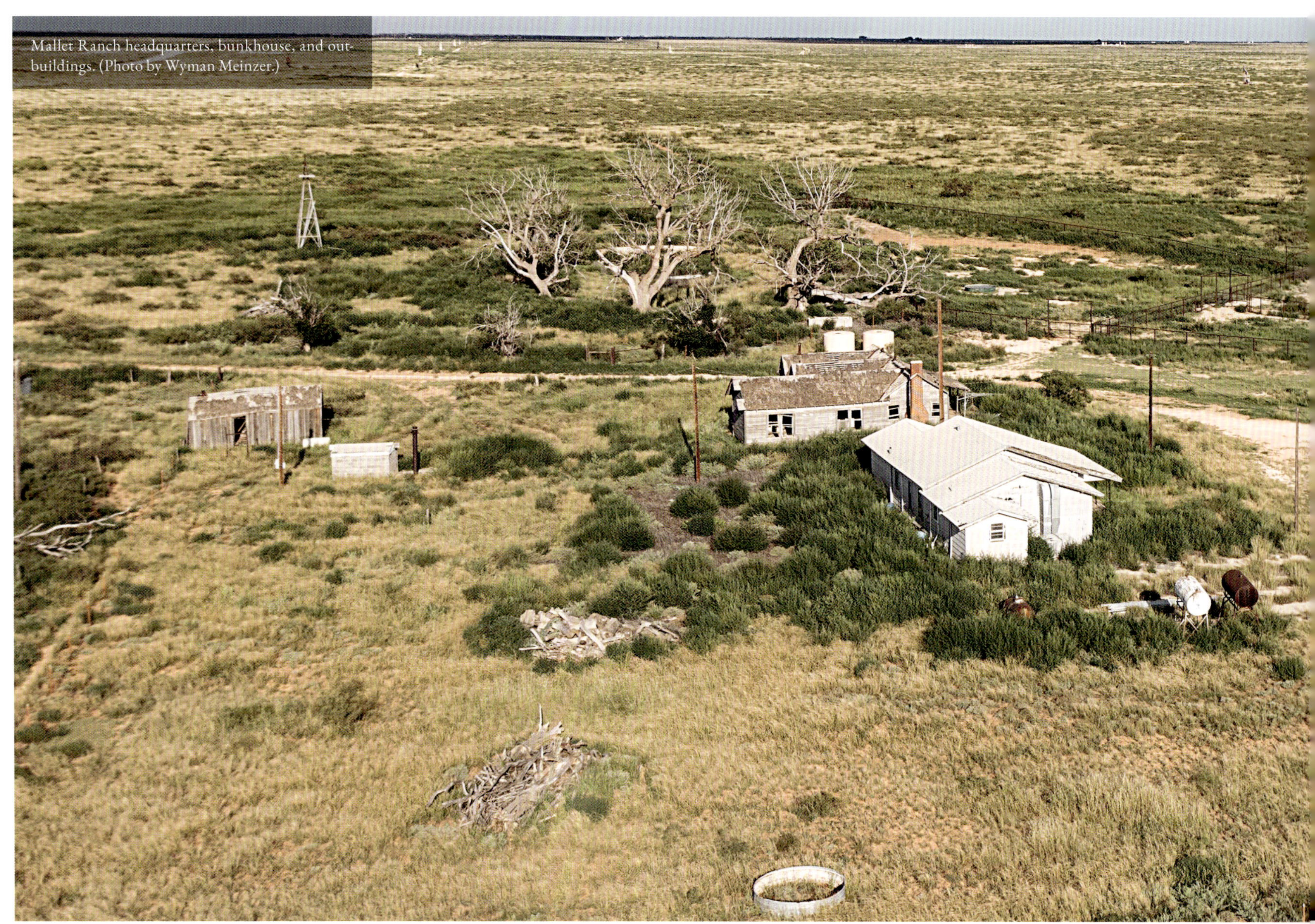
Mallet Ranch headquarters, bunkhouse, and outbuildings. (Photo by Wyman Meinzer.)

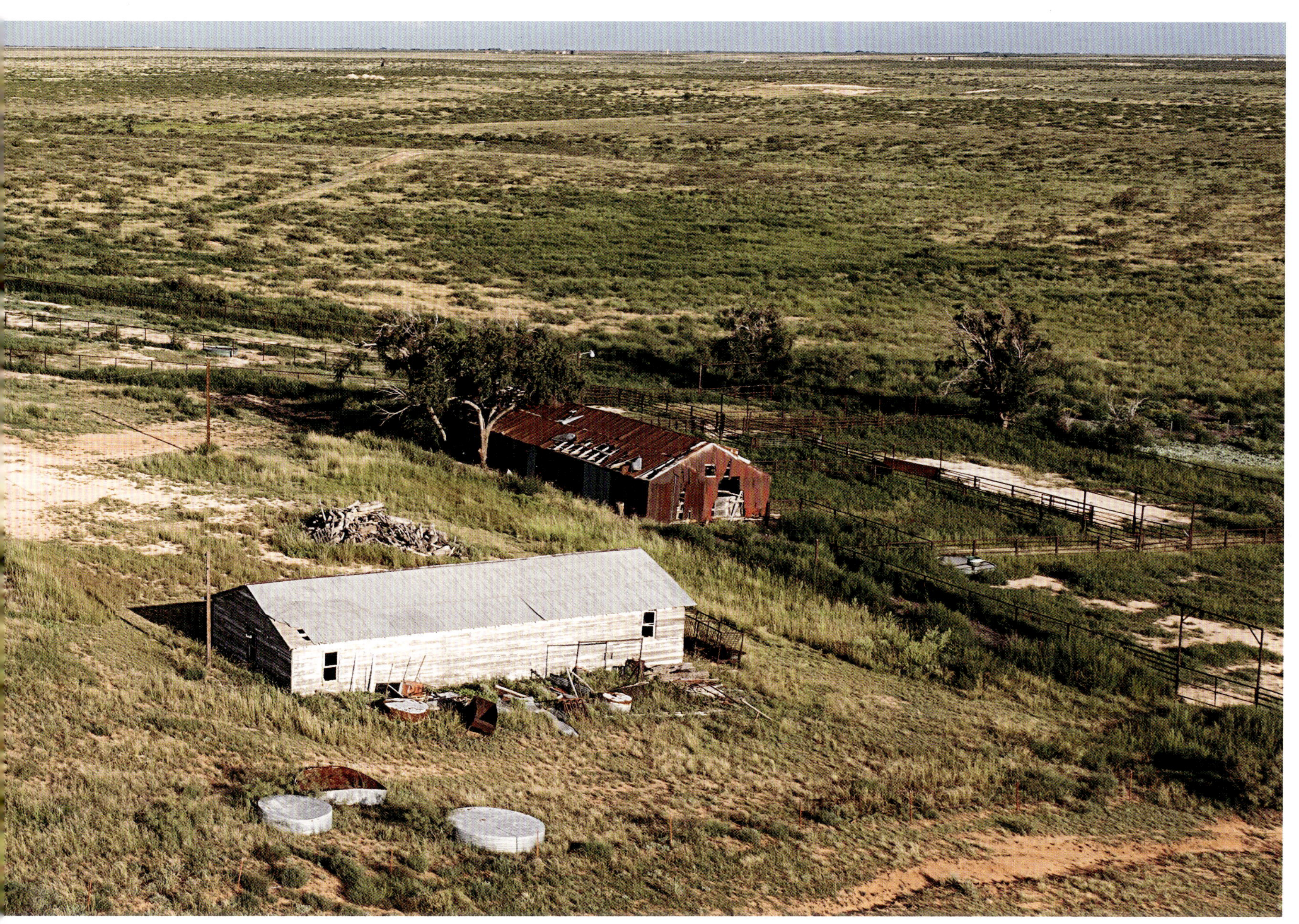

CHAPTER 3

GOOD TIMES, BAD TIMES, AND CHANGING TIMES

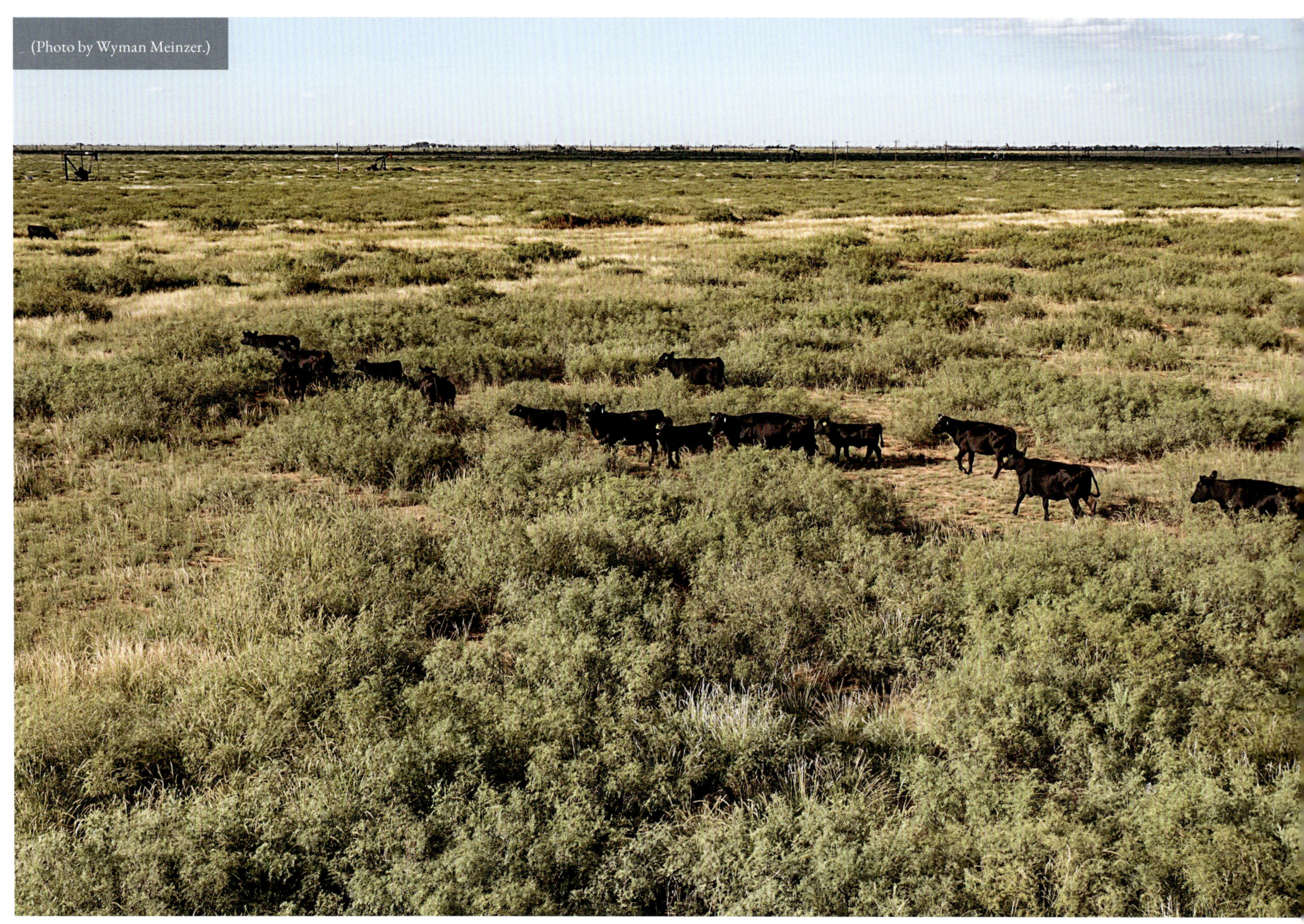
(Photo by Wyman Meinzer.)

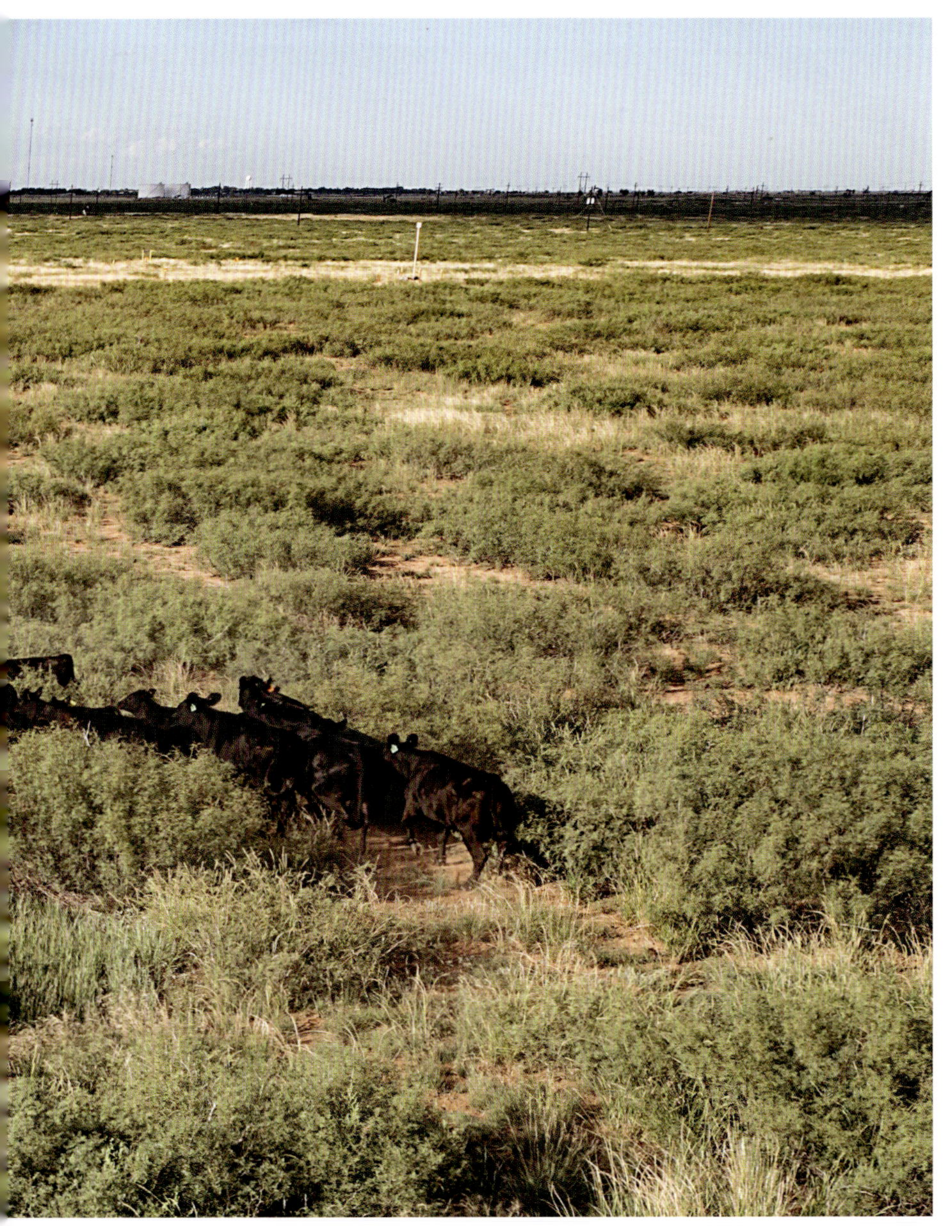

While David DeVitt was building his stock empire, he and his wife Florence were also trying to build a family and a life together—an exercise that proved almost as difficult as the construction of the Mallet Ranch. Florence and David would eventually have four children. Christine, the oldest, was born in 1885 and was followed by a son, Harold, in 1887. There was a large gap between births at that point, which coincided with David's almost constant entrepreneurial moves to build his range, both in the Permian Basin and on the South Plains. Another daughter, Helen, came along in 1899 after they had moved to Fort Worth. Three children may have been enough for Florence and David at that point, as the couple were—in many ways—growing apart. David and Florence DeVitts' marriage was, at best, troubled. David, with time spent building his ranch and consumed with the legal maneuvering required to keep control of it, was frequently gone, especially after the DeVitts had moved to Fort Worth. More strain also developed when their son Harold died in a hunting accident on the ranch in the summer of 1901, just before David moved his family to the ranch for homesteading purposes. Florence was devastated and dearly wanted another child to replace the one she had lost. Thus, the family welcomed another son, David Jr., to the family in May 1902.

The couple then had to face the trauma of living at least six months of the year at the Mallet Ranch in order to prove residency for their homestead claim. Christine was by that time eighteen and had just finished public school in Fort Worth. She looked forward to living on the ranch as she enjoyed riding and interacting with the cowboys and hands on the Mallet, but Florence—who had grown up poor and part of the working class—wanted her daughter to receive a classical education. So, she convinced her husband to send their daughter to Hollins Institute, a boarding school for young women in Roanoke, Virginia. Christine would finish at Hollins in 1905 and then enroll at Forest Park University in St. Louis, where she studied music. She eventually would rejoin her family in Fort Worth.

Florence, who had grown up in cities, was no doubt ill-prepared for life on an isolated Texas ranch on the South Plains, but when her husband had to move his family onto the ranch to establish residency that is exactly what she faced six to seven months of each year. She also had to care for her two young children who were there with her, three-year-old Helen and David Jr., who was not quite one when they moved to the ranch. The stress of raising and providing for two such very young children while her husband attended to ranch business must have added to her loneliness and feelings of isolation.

The family returned to their home in Fort Worth, although David DeVitt, as the manager of the ranch as well as the majority stockholder in the Mallet Land and Cattle Company, had to spend almost half his time away from the family and on the ranch. When David Jr. reached an age at which he could reasonably travel, he would join his father on the ranch to begin to learn how to manage the Mallet in anticipation of one day taking over management of the operation. If Florence DeVitt ever returned to the Mallet acres after she left, the records do not indicate such. Daughter Christine seemed to take after her mother and rarely made the trek to the South Plains and the headquarters house after the family moved back to Fort Worth. Mother and elder daughter seemed to prefer to live in the growing metropolitan Texas city.

The Fort Worth that the DeVitts had moved to in 1898 and returned to in 1905 was a place going through a significant transition. As the 1890s drew to a close, Fort Worth's growth—which had seemed promising in the late 1870s and 1880s—had ground to a halt and the city had entered a period of stagnation. There were some who thought that Fort Worth might go the way of so many other cities in the late nineteenth century that had experienced an initial boom when a railroad line came through only to cease development and try to persevere as a railway crossroads. It was still a county seat and enjoyed some prosperity as a regional trade center, but it had an underdeveloped industrial base and no true direction to build an economy that would bring to fruition any dream of building a "great city" as its late nineteenth century boosters had promised. Any attempts to attract industry had also been devastated when the Panic of 1893 struck the city with a destructive blow.

The city's fortunes began to turn in 1903—while the DeVitts were living on the South Plains—when two major meat packing firms, owned by industry giant Swift and Armour, brought new employment, wealth, and population to the city.

Most significantly, they established a strong industrial base that would help to propel Fort Worth into the new century with hope that it could indeed become the great city that many believed it would become in the heady years of its advancement in the years after the Civil War. While it was a start, Fort Worth still needed diversification to reach its goals.

The packing houses proved to be the key. Their success spurred ancillary businesses such as banks. The railroads also located more facilities in the city, and most of all commercial expansion grew in the downtown area. Most significantly, Fort Worth's population began to grow, almost doubling between 1900 and 1910. Such growth meant that real estate speculation became a booming form of commerce in the city, something of which David DeVitt, like many other investors, took advantage. Phillip DeVitt, David's older brother, had moved to Fort Worth in 1890 when he sold out his stock interests to John Scharbauer. He began to invest in real estate in the Southside area of the city and convinced his brother to make speculations in the same. David DeVitt managed his herd and pastures on the Mallet conservatively, but he pursued potential investments with much greater aggression. He began to buy lots in Fort Worth, mostly on the Southside but also some in the downtown and stockyards area, a gamble that with Fort Worth's new growth and economic prosperity paid handsome dividends.

When the DeVitt family finished their homestead period on the Mallet and returned to Fort Worth, David DeVitt and his partner, F. W. Flato, had built a sizable and profitable operation. Their ranch covered around 50,000 acres, and they had divided it into thirteen pastures. In addition to the headquarters house, the Mallet had two permanent camps for hands and David had built a two-room box and strip house, a bunkhouse for the hands, a blacksmith shop, barns, pens, and a windmill and water tank near the headquarters house. There was also a vat camp (a designated pen for dipping cattle in medicinal chemicals to guard against insect-borne disease) along with another bunkhouse, two more windmills (there were more than twenty on the entire ranch), and shipping pens on the northern portion of the ranch. The Mallet stocked, depending on the year through approximately 1925, between 5,000 and 8,000 head of cattle.

David DeVitt was an effective ranch manager. He rotated cattle between pastures and reduced their numbers when drought or other conditions warranted so that the herds did not overgraze the available grasses. While he had first operated a cow-calf operation in the late 1800s and early 1900s, after 1904 DeVitt switched to a steer enterprise. He sold cattle when they were three years old, usually in Kansas City. He replenished his herd with new calves every year. Running a steer operation was less labor-intensive, so he only employed five, sometimes six, men full time, although he would hire extra hands to help with branding and other duties during spring roundup. While DeVitt was changing his mode of operation, he once again lost a partner and gained another. F. W. Flato had never had DeVitt's resolve during the fight with C. C. Slaughter and the Lazy S. Even before the partnership settled the legal fight, he had begun to look for a way to sell his shares in the Mallet

Land and Cattle Company. Flato, who after some years working for Missouri-based livestock commission firms, formed his own commission company with partners Andrew Drumm and R. G. Head in 1893. Along with operating and acting as the primary agent in his business, Flato had invested in a number of enterprises other than his partnership with DeVitt in the late 1890s and the early 1900s, but not all of those turned out to be profitable. In fact, his finances had so deteriorated by 1902 that his primary partner, Andrew Drumm, had bought Flato's interest in the firm and then—because it was the only way Flato saw to settle his debts—in 1904 he acquired all 400 of his shares in the Mallet. Seventy-six-year-old Kansas City native Andrew Drumm now became David DeVitt's partner.

David DeVitt, the former journalist from New York, had proven to be an apt pupil when it came to learning stock operations because by all accounts he ran a profitable business that even outpaced some of his better-known neighbors on the South Plains. During the earliest years of the Mallet's operations right after the turn of the century, DeVitt was able to squeeze out profits of somewhere between $10,000 and a high of $30,000. However, after 1905 the South Plains entered one of its frequent droughts, which significantly cut into Mallet profits. The lack of rainfall meant that grazing alone could not adequately feed cattle and the ranch had to provide supplemental supplies, usually in the form of cotton-cake. Such expenditures raised the costs of maintaining stock. At the same time, beef prices began to fall, and David DeVitt had no choice but to begin to accumulate debt to keep his operations afloat.

The first drought of the 1900s on the South Plains broke somewhat in 1915 when the region received some of the highest rainfall it had gotten since the early 1890s. DeVitt once again was nimble enough to exploit the new conditions, and he bought more than 3,000 two- and three-year-old steers, which in 1916 and 1917 he was able to sell at relatively high prices. Although he had had to spend almost $100,000 to stock his range in those years, he made a two-year profit in excess of $70,000, and instead of paying a dividend he poured more than 80 percent of those profits back into buying more cattle, primarily because the outbreak of World War I and the United States' subsequent entry into the war looked as though it might cause beef prices to rise even more.

The increased demand for beef during the war—canned beef was a prime provision for soldiers in the field—caused prices to rise, and since DeVitt had positioned his venture as primarily a steer operation he was in a good position to capitalize on the new development. The war did cause beef prices to rise but, once again, the West Texas weather, as well as the market, did not cooperate. Drought conditions returned in 1917 and lingered into 1918. The lack of rainfall caused DeVitt to alter his methods and schedules, but since he had ceased his cow-calf operation earlier and operated only a steer operation he was able to endure the climatological conditions in better shape than many of his neighbors. Practically simultaneously with the reemergence of a drought, the price spike brought on by World War I began to end with the abrupt ending of that war. Even when the drought broke again in late 1918, the war's end pushed

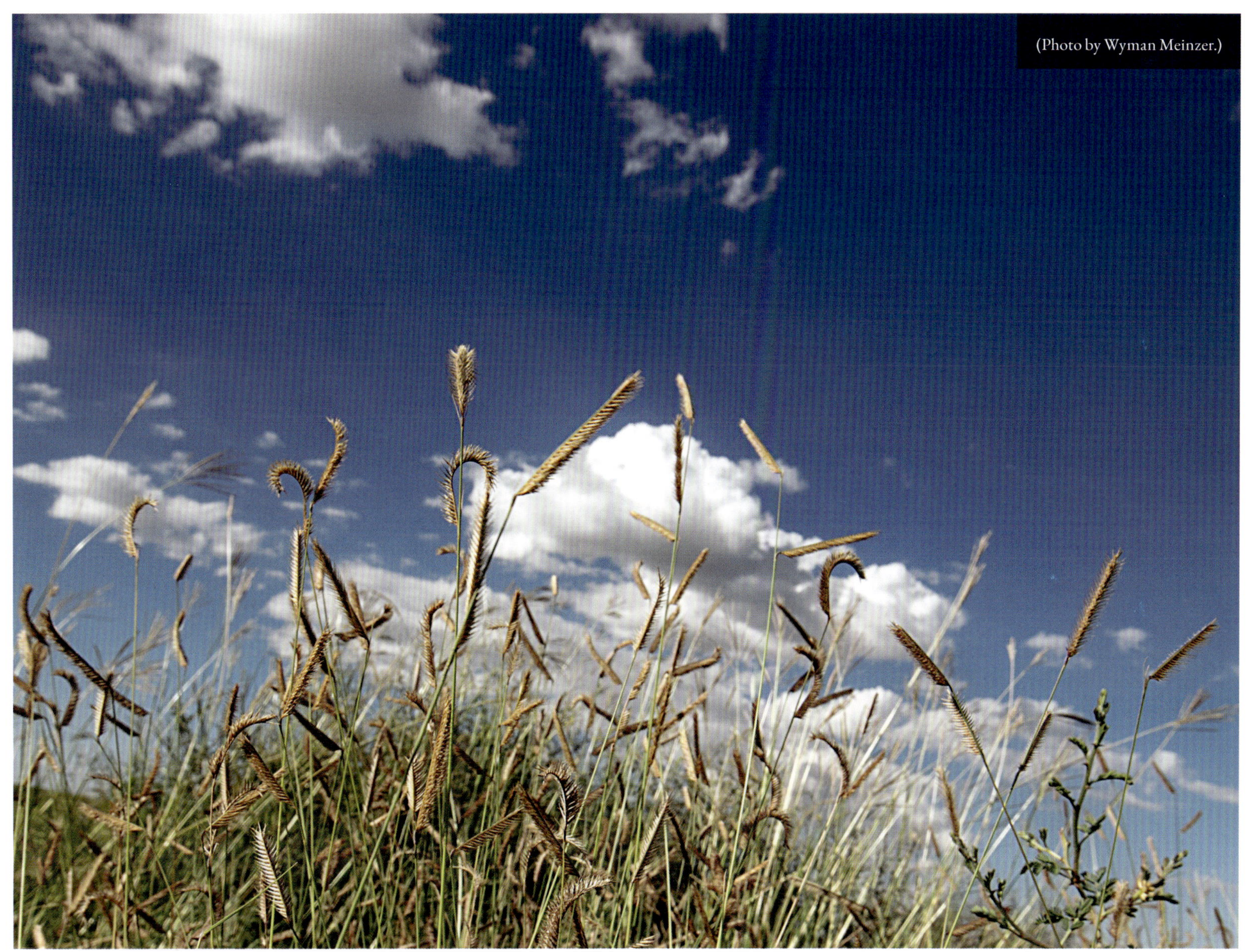
(Photo by Wyman Meinzer.)

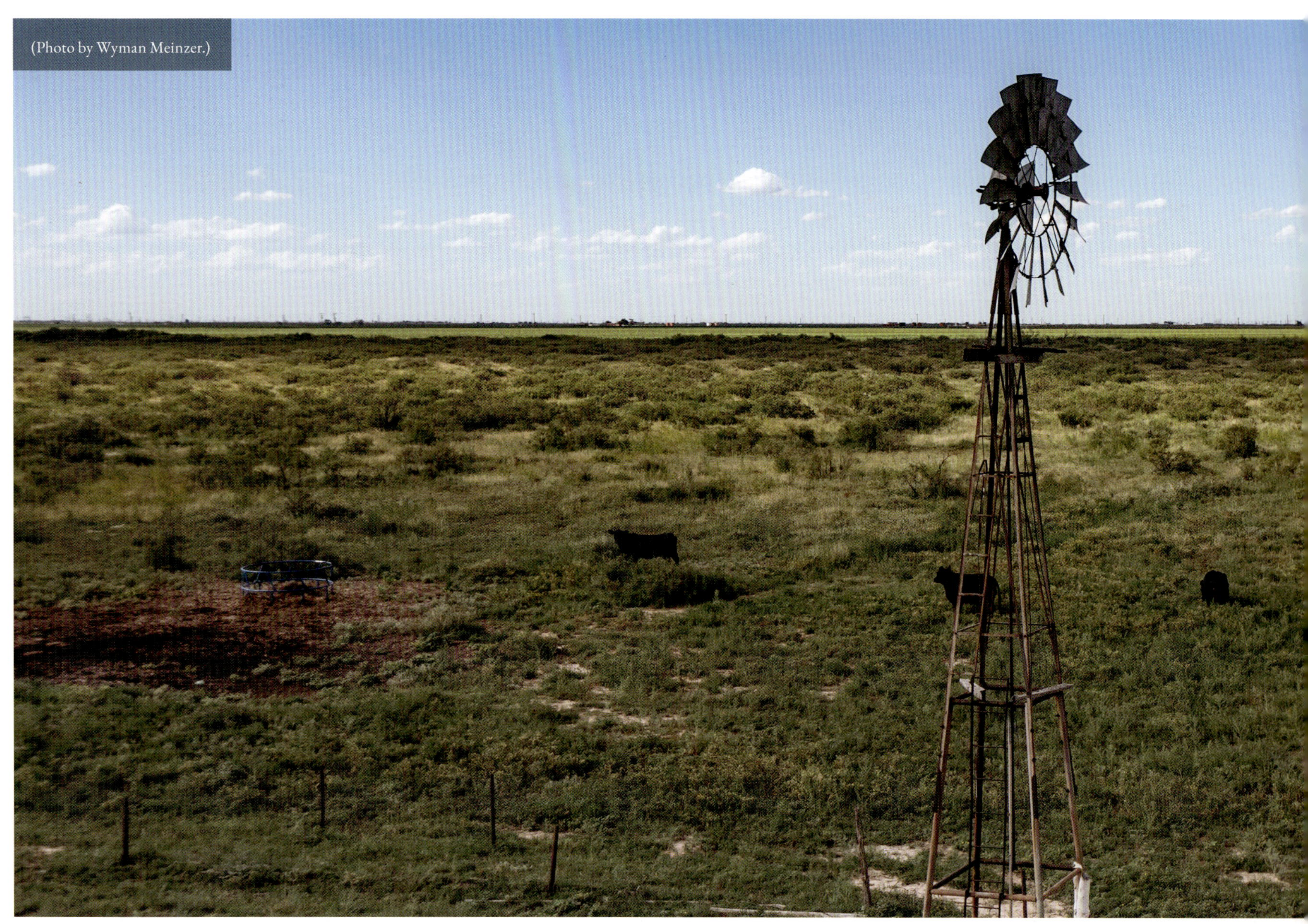

(Photo by Wyman Meinzer.)

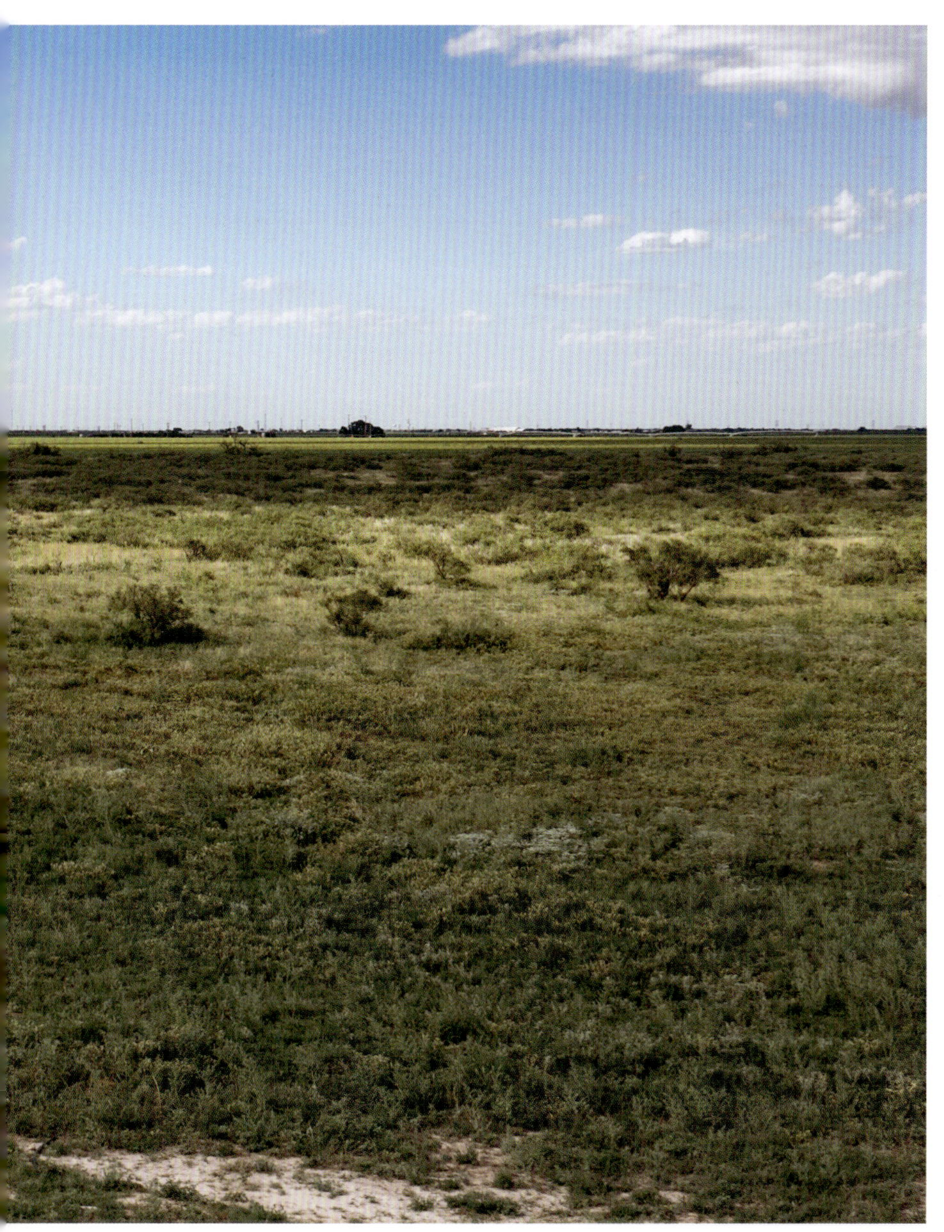

prices down precipitously. DeVitt, like many other ranchers across the United States, dealt with the decline by sending more cattle to market—even a number of steers and breed cows and heifers that he would have likely wished to keep longer—which in many ways further depressed the market and prices. DeVitt, for example, shipped out and sold a record dollar amount for Mallet steers—almost $250,000—but the profits he returned were half of what he had made just five years before. That also meant that he could not stock his pastures with as many animals as he had in the past.

Despite trying conditions, DeVitt continued to improve the Mallet acres. Unlike many of his neighbors, who banked their earnings instead of making upgrades, DeVitt used his profits from the war years to buy more steers as well as property to expand his pasture. He also demonstrated that he had learned to prepare for droughts. He built three new tanks to help water his cattle and—significantly—erected twenty-three new windmills. He fenced and cross-fenced the Mallet, dividing it into sixteen different pastures, which allowed him to move and alternate his herd so as to reduce the stress on valuable grasslands. DeVitt placed his yearlings in pastures on the south and southeast fringes of the ranch near the headquarters house he had built for his family, then moved them to northern pastures to be "finished" for shipment to markets. When the steers were ready to be sold, hands drove them to railheads for shipment, points that changed at various times during the early 1900s. When railroad trunk lines finally reached the new town of Whiteface in the late 1920s—which was only a few miles from the Mallet's most northern pastures—the drive became much shorter, and Whiteface became the primary shipping point for Mallet steers.

DeVitt had overcome a number of serious obstacles—the risk of beginning an operation in a part of Texas that did not guarantee success, the struggle of securing grazing land for his herd, a protracted legal fight with a neighbor, and finally market and environmental conditions that threatened to destroy all he had built—and now seemed on the precipice of finally achieving his dream of controlling one of the most profitable and innovative stock operations in the state. He had the Mallet poised for growth and success as the 1920s began to look toward the 1930s. What David DeVitt likely did not realize was that the most trying and strenuous time of his life was about to begin.

While DeVitt was battling C. C. Slaughter and then improving his herd and pastures, other developments on the South Plains began that would ultimately affect his operation. The drought of the early 1900s had caused some cattlemen to question the long-term future of the South Plains, and they began to look for other ways to make profits from their lands. At the same time, the population of Texas was growing as migrants from other states began to come in looking for land and opportunity. The majority of these new migrants were different than the wave that David DeVitt had been a part of when he came to Texas from New York. Most of these new residents moving to Texas came not to acquire a stock empire but to farm small plats. The new migrants were joined by poorer Texas natives who sought to flee marginal land that many had to sharecrop, also pursuing the dream of land ownership. That opportunity, by the turn of the twentieth century, lay in West Texas.

At the same time that migrants from the east and north were looking to find suitable land to homestead and farm, many of the large ranches in West Texas were experiencing difficulties such as drought, low commodity prices, greater competition—especially from range cattle lands overseas—and a rise in taxes as more counties were organized and the population of the South Plains increased, which all led a number of ranchers to begin to sell off some of their acres to small farmers and smaller operations. With the dawn of the 1920s, the age of the large operations began to close and the era of modern stock operations started to emerge. David DeVitt would now be forced to confront such change.

Drought conditions and drops in commodity prices began to have detrimental effects for Northwest Texas ranches as early as 1900. The huge XIT—the operations set up by the British investors as the Capitol Syndicate since the land was exchanged as payment for rebuilding the Texas Capitol after it had burned in November 1881—had begun to sell off massive chunks of its lands just after the turn of the century. The syndicate sold most of its land to developers and other ranchers such as George Littlefield, who bought about 230,000 XIT acres in the southern Yellow House division in 1901. Other ranchers and land companies would eventually buy nearly 270,000 additional acres in the same area within the next ten years. Many of these developers would ultimately revolutionize the region when they began efforts to bring in small farmers, endeavors that would eventually begin to impact the Mallet Ranch.

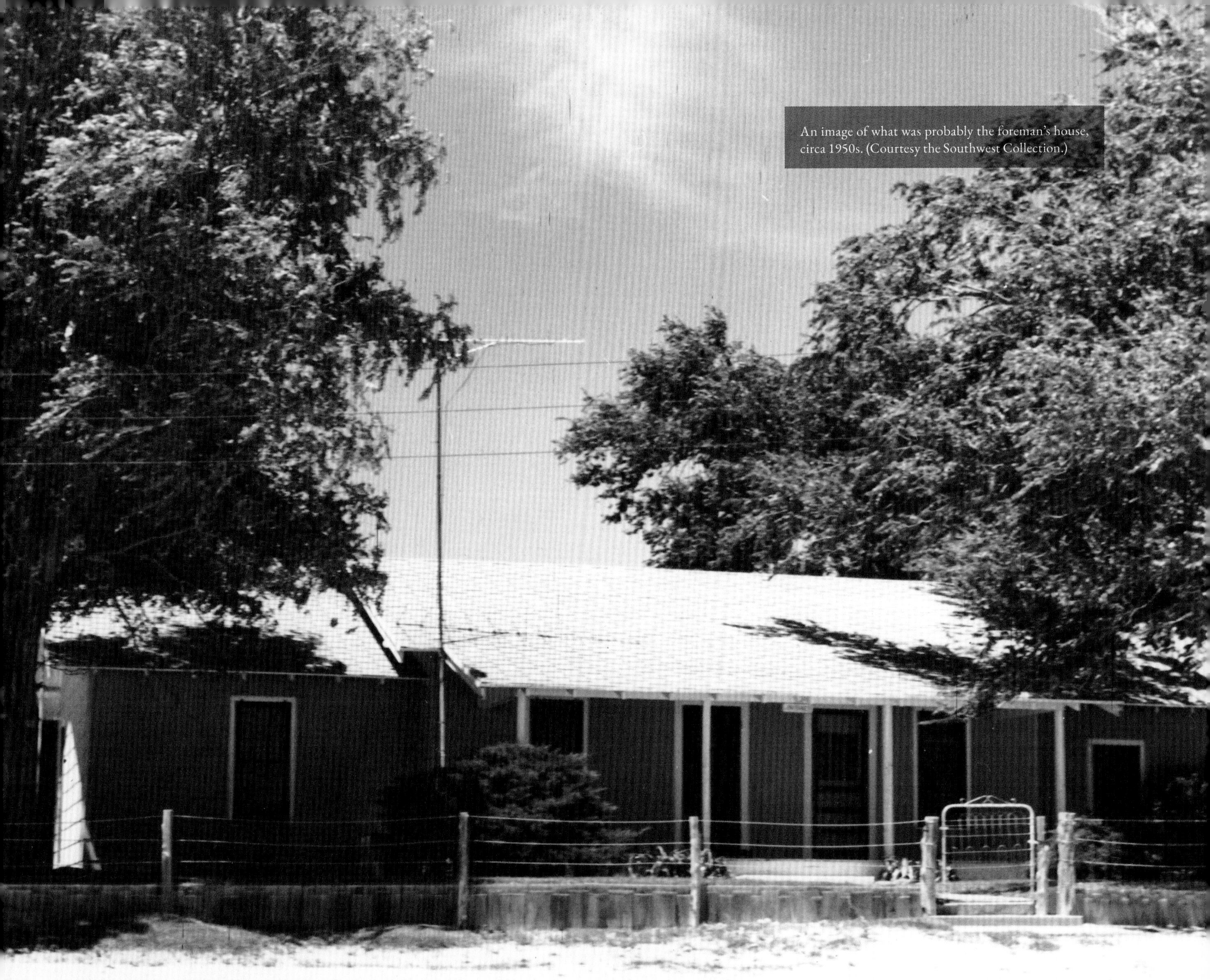

An image of what was probably the foreman's house, circa 1950s. (Courtesy the Southwest Collection.)

Farm operations on the South Plains and the remainder of Northwest Texas had, for decades, been an almost futile endeavor, primarily due to the lack of reliable water. Rainfall was spotty at best, and the creeks, rivers, and streams were swift, narrow conduits ill-suited for traditional irrigation efforts. There were some efforts to make the land productive in the late nineteenth century, such as the Quaker Colony whose endeavor in the 1880s in Crosby County east of the Mallet failed almost wholly due to a lack of sufficient moisture to make their lands arable. There was enough water for farming on the South Plains in the form of the southern reaches of the giant Ogallala Aquifer that lay directly under most of the region: the problem was a lack of technology to bring it to the surface.

The Ogallala is a shallow aquifer confined by sand, silt, clay, and gravel. It is a vast natural reservoir of approximately 175,000 square miles underneath portions of eight Great Plains states: South Dakota, Nebraska, Wyoming, Colorado, Kansas, Oklahoma, New Mexico, and Texas. The problem for those who tried to cultivate the land in the late nineteenth and very early twentieth centuries was that the southern stretches of the Ogallala are not artesian and lie deep under the surface. The technology just did not exist to bring it to the surface in usable quantities. That situation began to change in 1910 when pump equipment that could propel the Ogallala's and other smaller aquifers' water to the surface became available.

The South Plains region was now able to support farm operations, and cultivators quickly began to move onto the plains. A number of ranchers, who still faced difficult times, along with developers, now had another market for their land. George Littlefield became one of the first in the region to begin to colonize his land with small farm operations. Littlefield's Yellowhouse Ranch was mostly north and a bit west of the Mallet in Bailey, Lamb, Cochran, and the western reaches of Hockley County. Littlefield had first decided to begin to dispose of his lands to small farm "colonies" in 1906, primarily so as to convert his property into cash that he could more easily divide among his many heirs. Making a profit from his sales would be all the better, as George Littlefield was first and foremost a committed capitalist. Littlefield's colonization scheme began in 1912, and by the time World War I had begun in Europe he had sold over 30,000 acres, but the coming of the war and the subsequent drought years caused his sales to decrease. He stopped dividing and selling his land in 1918 and did not initiate the process again until 1920. Littlefield died in November 1920, and his heirs finished the liquidation of his holdings in 1924.

The majority of these new farms on the South Plains cultivated cotton, both because it was a needed commodity and because that is what the majority of those who came knew how to grow. After a decline in prices during the late war years, the price of cotton began to rise in 1922 and set new records by the 1925–1926 growing season. Thus, these South Plains farmers increased production and new migrants moved to the region seeking new fields to cultivate. The South Plains had another advantage as well: a general lack of the scourge of cotton farmers—the dreaded boll weevil. Rail access had also increased, so conditions in the 1920s

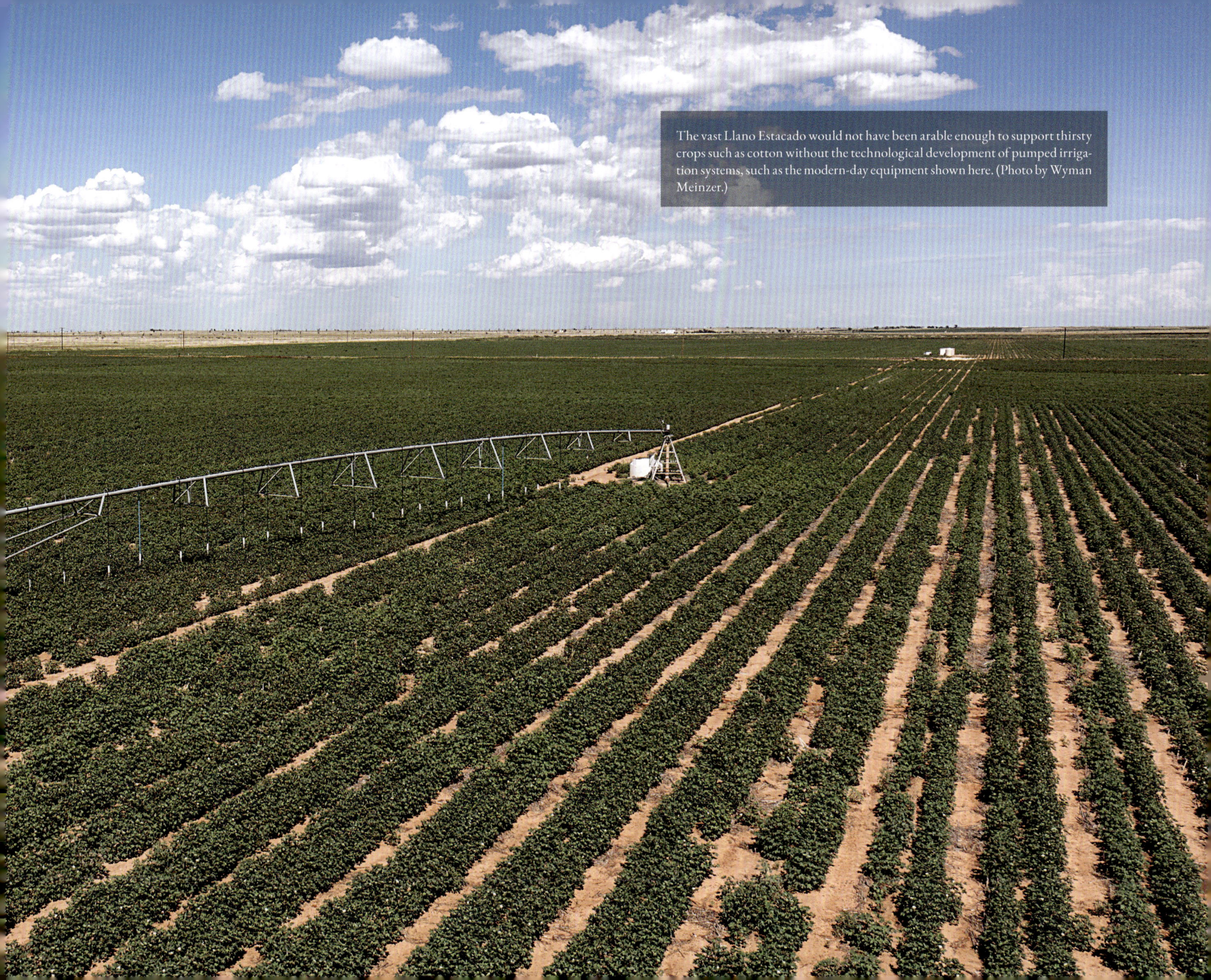

The vast Llano Estacado would not have been arable enough to support thirsty crops such as cotton without the technological development of pumped irrigation systems, such as the modern-day equipment shown here. (Photo by Wyman Meinzer.)

led David DeVitt, one of the last "holdouts" among South Plains ranchers, to also begin to divide some of his pastures for sale to farmers.

DeVitt encountered serious problems in maintaining the profitability of the Mallet in the 1920s. One of the most pressing issues he faced was the increase in the need for (and the price of) cattle feed. David M. DeVitt was a progressive stockman in that he was ahead of the curve in moving cattle from pasture to pasture to save his grasslands as well as in making sure that he did not overstock his range. Still, because of frequent drought and a general shift in climatological and environmental conditions, DeVitt had to turn more and more to buying supplemental feed for his cattle. Mallet records in 1922–1925 show that prices for feed had risen so much, combined with shipping costs and other associated expenses, that DeVitt had to take a loss on many of the cattle that he sold. He wrote to Christine in 1923 that he was worried about the effects on his operation. Faced with mounting losses through 1922, DeVitt had to find a solution, and one soon presented itself right next door.

When C. C. Slaughter died in 1919, family squabbling made the full settlement of his estate difficult, which gave David DeVitt an opportunity to take advantage and buy some of the Lazy S herd. The end of World War I and the crash of beef prices had hit the Mallet hard, with the ranch posting significant losses in 1919, 1920, and 1921. DeVitt, who had significantly cut ranch costs—including his own salary as ranch manager—searched for a solution. The answer he came up with was expansion.

Perhaps he thought that beef prices would rebound from their post–World War I slump. Maybe his competitive streak simply relished the idea of "besting" his old nemesis Slaughter one more time by making part of his stock wear the Mallet brand. DeVitt first partnered with an employee, Pat Ross, to buy 1,100 head of cattle in 1922. He also bought 500 head of former Lazy S cows from Slaughter's son Alex, from whom he also leased 17,000 acres of pasture. Not finished yet, he formed another partnership with another friend, Ed Crocker, to buy over 1,000 head of cow-calf pairs from Carrie Slaughter, C. C. Slaughter's second wife and heir to the now very divided Lazy S. He also leased 25,000 acres of former Lazy S land to pasture his new cattle.

Expansion had forced DeVitt to borrow more than $100,000 from the Fidelity Union Bank and Trust in Kansas City, and when beef prices did not rebound, he had to remedy his personal and the Mallet's debt problems. He effectively dissolved his partnership with Pat Ross and forced his former employee to buy his share of the cattle contained in the partnership, money he actually borrowed from David DeVitt's brother Phillip. He also ended his partnership with Crocker and sold the cattle and his part of the lease at a loss, but at just a bit over $5,000 it was a loss he could manage. Still, the Mallet faced difficulty in making a profit and had to find a way forward.

Faced with such conditions and with no other real choice, the Mallet Board of Directors met in February 1923 to discuss the possibility of selling parts of the ranch. Andrew Drumm, DeVitt's partner after F. W. Flato, had died in 1919, and his final will had left the bulk of his estate to the Drumm Institute, an institution for orphaned boys—most given up by their families after delinquency or other problems—that operated as an almost 400-acre working farm. His will had placed his shares of the Mallet into a trust, which was overseen by Marion L. McClure, who not only represented the Drumm shares at the meeting but also had twenty shares of Mallet stock. The board decided that they could better use the land by selling it than operating it as a stock operation. So, they moved to begin farm colonization efforts, which DeVitt initiated in 1925.

DeVitt enlisted two sales agents, Stanley Watson and R. C. Hopping, to sell up to 44,000 acres of the Mallet by December 31, 1927. Most of the land placed for potential sale was on the edges of the range, including large parts of the Edwards and Scurry County school lands, which were mostly on the northern edge of the Mallet property. The two sales agents, between 1925 and 1926, would sell 5,743 acres of Mallet land at a price of almost $220,000. However, the figure is misleading because most of the small farmers who bought the tracts did so by paying only a small sum down—about $15,000—with the promise to pay the full sums by 1930. When the nearby Spade Ranch offered a huge tract of their range for purchase at much more favorable prices than those Watson and Hopping had listed, land sales on the Mallet range essentially dried up. Eventually, the Great Depression would cause almost 80 percent of those who purchased farmland on the Mallet range to default, which meant that the ranch had to foreclose and take back most of the pastures it had thought it had sold. David DeVitt's increasingly tenuous financial position with the Mallet thus grew even more severe.

While DeVitt certainly operated the Mallet spread with financial caution, in his personal lifestyle he lived more extravagantly. He enjoyed a certain flashy sartorial lifestyle, spending generous sums at Fort Worth, Kansas City, and Los Angeles tailors and clothiers. He traveled to Kansas City often—the Mallet Land and Cattle Company held board meetings in the Missouri city, and the Royal stock shows as well as other smaller such exhibitions were some of DeVitt's preferred places to buy steers—and when he did travel to Kansas City he almost always rented a suite, first at the Cosby Hotel until the late 1920s, and then switching his allegiance to the Presidential Hotel. Both of these hostelries were known as the most luxurious in the city. His personal habits certainly reflected his desire to project an image as a man of considerable means. In fact, his lavishness caused his former partner, Andrew Drumm, to once remark in a telegram to DeVitt that he hoped that he did not "wear the suit too often in Texas" because he would "hate to see the cost to ever replace it."

The DeVitt family also underwent significant changes during the 1920s. DeVitt's mother, Elizabeth, had passed away in 1906, and David and Florence began to at least discuss moving to California, a place in which both desired to live. Florence DeVitt had made frequent trips to the West Coast, where she seemed to think the weather and various health resorts soothed what daughter Christine described as her "various ills." Florence's life as the wife of David M. DeVitt had not turned out quite

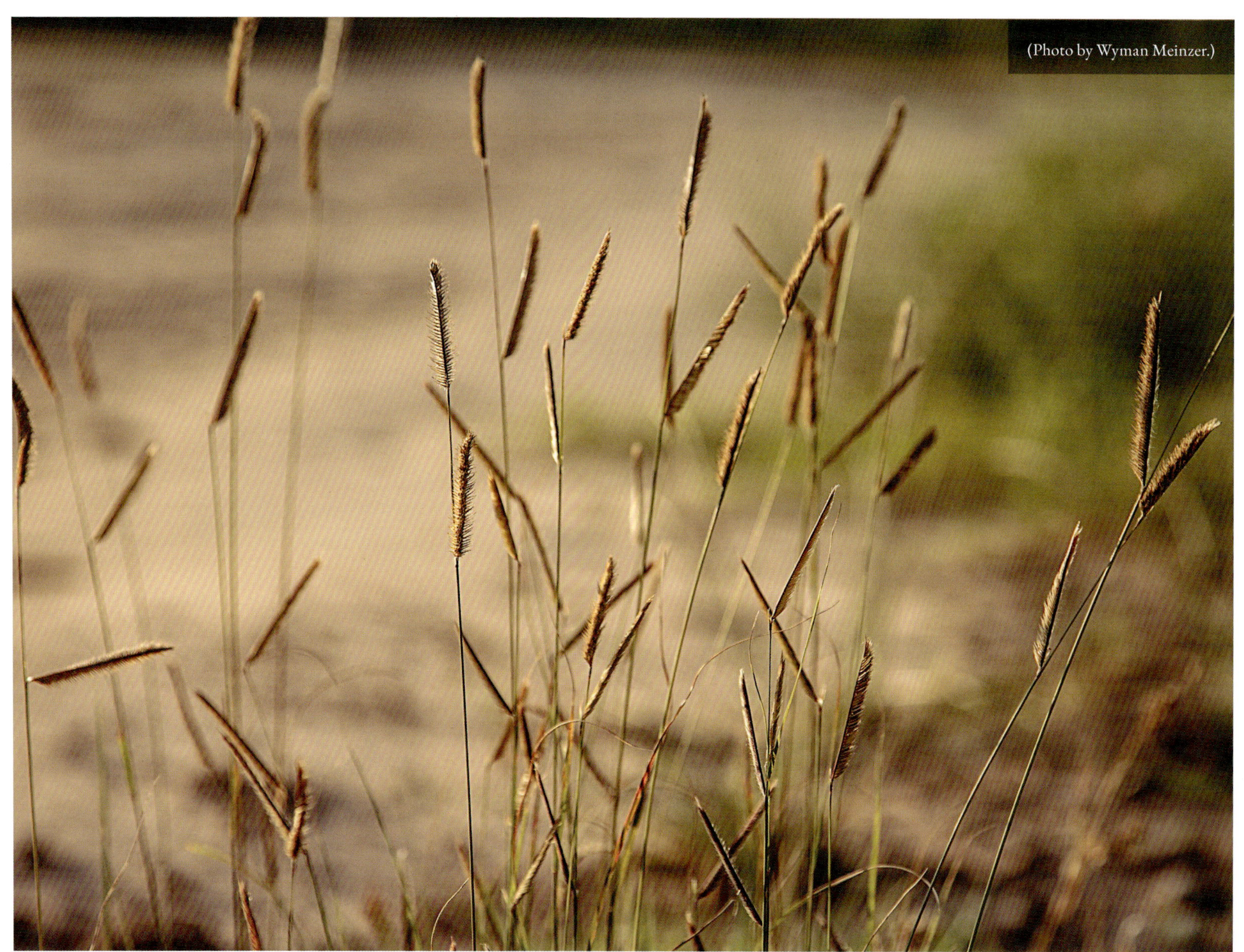
(Photo by Wyman Meinzer.)

like the former domestic worker from Fort Worth had hoped. Her husband was gone from the family for extended periods; in fact, the time they spent together on the Mallet Ranch in the early 1900s was likely the longest they had together in all the years of their marriage. David DeVitt's attention was not always fully on making his wife happy. Running a ranch more than 300 miles from the family home—a trip that in those days took most of a day even on the fastest train—gained most of his focus. Florence's health seemed to deteriorate as David DeVitt's absences grew longer, even though most of the doctors she visited could find very few actual physical troubles with her health.

Florence DeVitt decided to move permanently to California in 1918. David DeVitt, although he had earlier expressed a desire to live in the Golden State, supported the move but made it clear that he would not take up permanent residence in California. Florence had made up her mind and began to lay the groundwork for the family to move. Christine, by this date, had finished her education and was teaching at Riverside High School in Fort Worth. Helen had enrolled at Texas Christian University (TCU) in 1914 and attended that institution somewhat sporadically through 1917. The only surviving DeVitt son, David Jr., had finished his required public education in 1918. The elder David DeVitt was grooming his son to one day take over operations of the Mallet. Since the family had returned to Fort Worth, David the younger had spent almost every summer at the ranch shadowing his father or the Mallet foreman to learn the family business. Florence DeVitt must have thought it was a good time to make her move. Helen, who had expressed a desire to enroll in a California school, accompanied her mother.

Helen decided that she would attend the University of California at Berkeley, so the two DeVitt women first moved to Berkeley and remained there for almost three years. As she did at TCU, Helen enrolled somewhat sporadically in classes but eventually graduated summa cum laude. She and her mother took trips to a number of sanitariums and other such health resorts, with Florence looking for some relief from her maladies.

Helen had suffered since childhood from periods of flare-ups caused by an enlarged colon. This condition resulted in serious complications such as digestive problems, abdominal pain, bloody stool, fatigue, and diarrhea. Throughout her life she experimented with various diets and searched for a doctor and/or health facility that would give her relief from these issues. Trips to doctors and health spas for both Florence and Helen did not come cheap, and while David DeVitt happily sent them a substantial allowance for their monthly expenses, one or the other quite often sent telegrams asking for more money. David usually complied, likely so that there was never any reason for Florence to return to Texas and to also retain some semblance of domestic harmony.

David DeVitt made an occasional trip to California, but he did not usually stay with his wife or daughter. Instead, he lodged at a nearby hotel. Living in hotels had become his blueprint. As mentioned, he stayed at the Cosby or Presidential in Kansas City, which he frequented often. When he was in Texas, he tended to rent a hotel room, usually a suite, in Lubbock. He had also developed as curious a relationship with his children as he had with his wife. He was closest to his son, David Jr., who by the mid-1920s had moved permanently to the Mallet. Young David preferred living in the headquarters house, although he did at times accompany and stay overnight with his father in Lubbock. He took over as assistant ranch manager in 1924 or 1925, and by all accounts his father had taught him well. The Mallet was still having a difficult time making a profit, and the farm sales were ongoing, but the younger DeVitt streamlined some operations, and his father expressed pride in the way his son was learning the business.

The DeVitt daughters had two different types of relationship with their father. Helen adored her father while Christine, on the other hand, had a much dimmer view of him. Perhaps because she was fourteen years older than Helen and had shared the tribulations of the marriage with her mother, or perhaps because she had a somewhat similar strong personality to that of her father, Christine and David DeVitt were distant. They exchanged occasional letters, but these were almost perfunctory in tone and usually dealt only with ranch business or the direction of Christine's economic life. While she and her father discussed the Mallet Ranch, she rarely—if ever—visited her father's spread for almost thirty years after the family left it. Christine worried about her mother and her sister and tended to be protective of both, which also further strained her relationship with her father. She was particularly anxious about how Florence and Helen were making out in California, so in 1921 she decided to take a trip to see them.

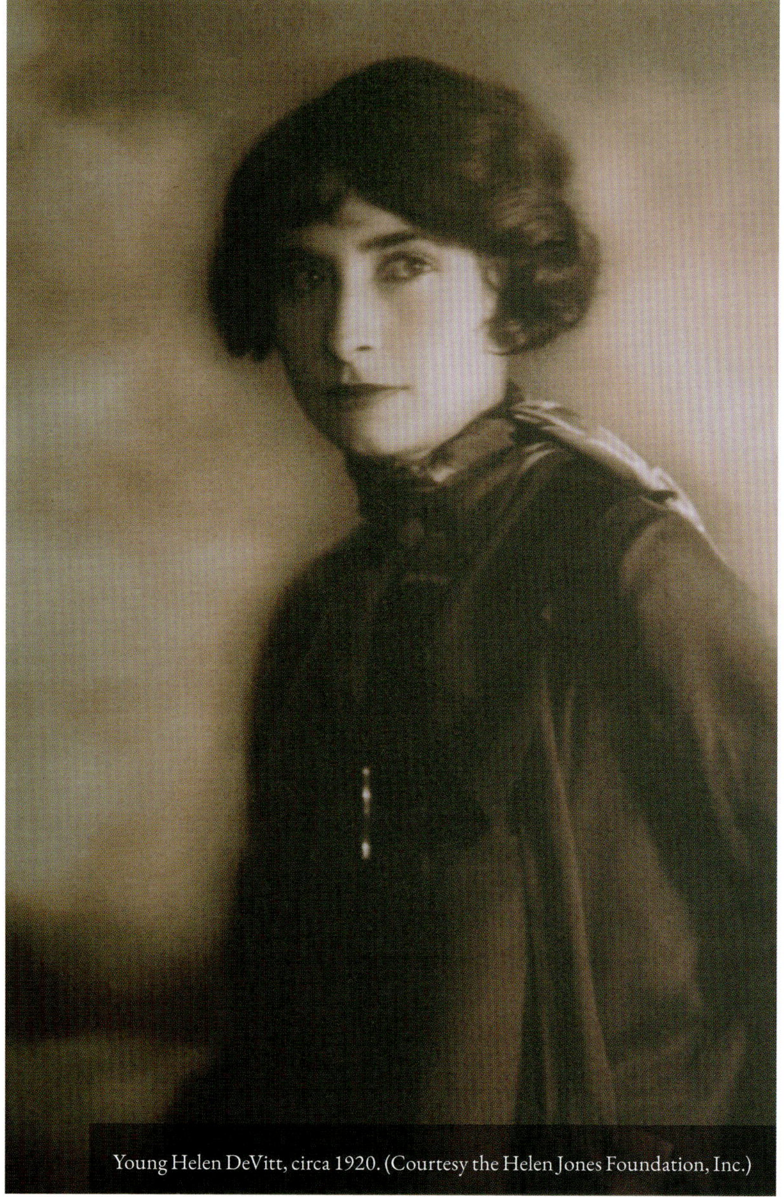
Young Helen DeVitt, circa 1920. (Courtesy the Helen Jones Foundation, Inc.)

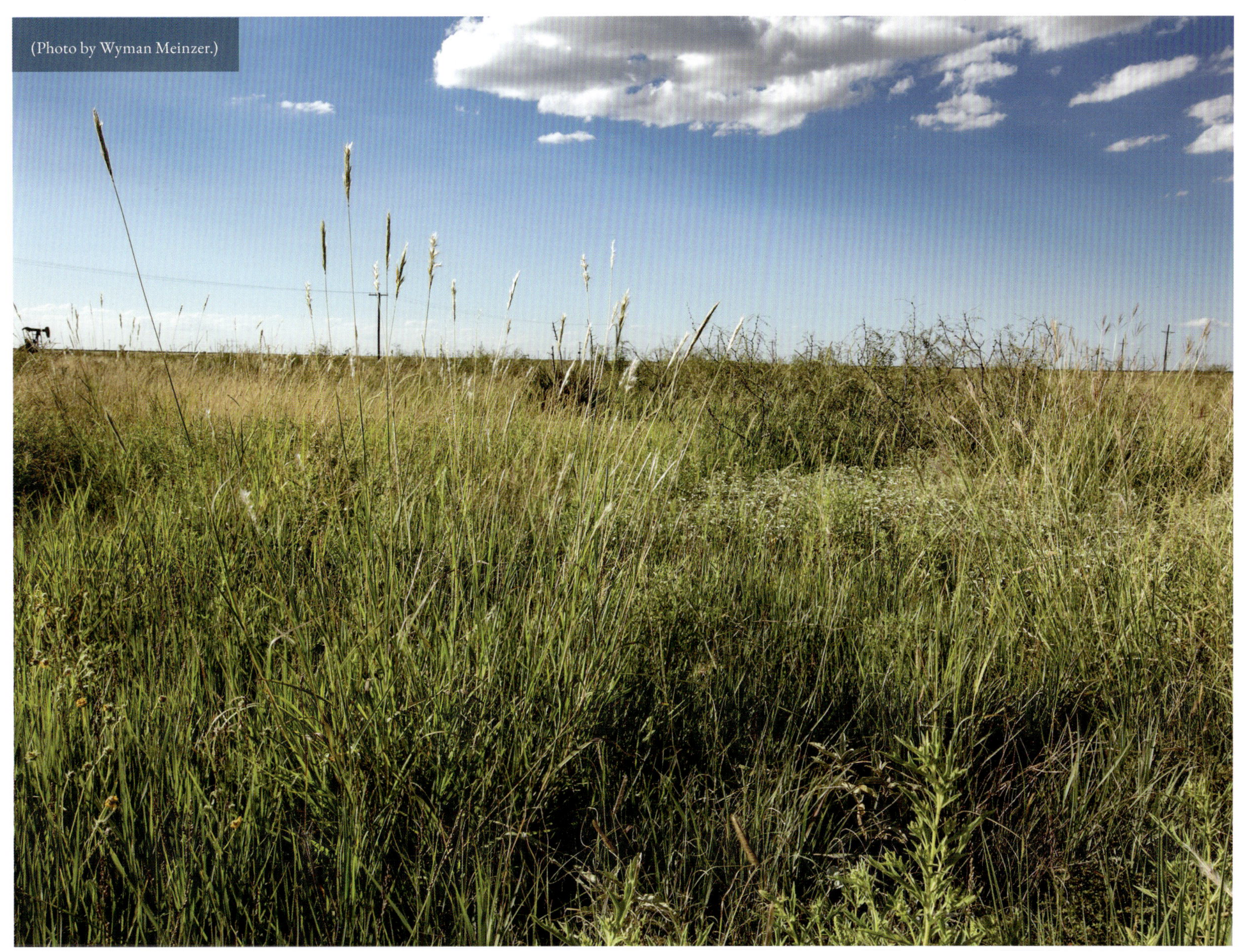
(Photo by Wyman Meinzer.)

Helen DeVitt obviously made every effort to bridge the divide that existed between Florence and David in the DeVitt family. Helen carried on a lively correspondence with her father and had always enjoyed visiting the ranch when she could. She was, however, solicitous of her mother and in many ways closely resembled Florence not only in appearance but also in personality. She shared her mother's pattern of traveling to see various doctors and other health professionals to treat continual bouts with her colon. Spas and health resorts were always open to accepting DeVitt payments to seek a cure.

After her mother and sister left for California, Christine DeVitt lived alone in the family's home in Fort Worth. The eldest of the DeVitt offspring had early in life developed a penchant for independence, stubbornness, and "going on her own." After she graduated from high school in Fort Worth and while the rest of the family lived at the Mallet, Christine went to an all-girls finishing school at Hollins Institute in Roanoke, Virginia. She graduated from the two-year institute in 1905 and then studied music at Forest Park University in St. Louis, which was one of the happiest times in her life. Her mother had instilled in Christine a love for music—specifically the piano—when she was young, and it would be a passion that remained with her the rest of her life. In her later years of philanthropy, she and her foundation contributed millions of dollars to musical education organizations and institutions.

After graduating from Forest Park, Christine came back to Fort Worth and for a while taught private piano lessons until she joined sister Helen and enrolled at Texas Christian where she obtained a teaching certificate. She put that certificate to work teaching music at Fort Worth's Riverside High School for one year and then De Zavala Elementary School the next year. By all indications she enjoyed teaching and likely wished to make it a long career, but after Florence and Helen left for California, Christine must have missed her family. Her father was rarely in Fort Worth by that time, and no records suggest that he and Christine spent any significant time together when he was in Fort Worth. On many of those trips, David DeVitt stayed at a downtown hotel instead of the family home. So, in 1921, Christine decided to visit her mother and sister in California.

Christine probably just intended to have an extended visit when she made plans to go to California. She boarded a train in Fort Worth and first headed north instead of west, traveling through Colorado, Wyoming, Idaho, and Oregon, and then down the northern coastline of California to San Francisco, where Helen and Florence met her at the station in the Embarcadero district of the city. The three enjoyed four days in San Francisco. They then all returned to the rented house that Florence and Helen kept in Berkeley. Christine stayed on in California through the end of 1921 and into 1922, which is when Helen graduated from the University of California. At that point, for reasons unknown, the three then decided to leave the Bay Area and move to Los Angeles. Florence bought a small bungalow in Hollywood. Helen wrote letters to her father that described their life as one of dining at restaurants, enjoying cultural outlets, and a generally luxurious genteel life of three idly wealthy women. David DeVitt continued sending his wife a monthly allowance of $150, although some months—at either Helen's or Florence's request (there are no records of Christine ever asking her father for money)—that figure could climb as high as $300. While Christine had intended only to visit her mother and sister, her "trip" turned into a decade-long stay.

Florence and Christine apparently never traveled back to Texas from California during the time they lived together, but Helen returned to visit in the summer of 1925. It was her first visit to the ranch since 1905. Helen enjoyed spending time with her father and brother—who was, of course, closer to her in age than Christine—but most of all she delighted in meeting new friends and attending the many "socials" in the small towns and at neighboring ranches. She talked her father and brother into holding a party at the Mallet in late June 1925, and at that get-together she met a man named Lee "Bill" Secrest. He lived in Morton and worked as a surveyor for the man who founded the town, Morton J. Smith. Helen began to see Secrest whenever she could the rest of that summer, which did not make her father happy. He believed that Secrest was only interested in his daughter because her father owned the Mallet Ranch. Helen, however, was smitten, and after a very quick romance the two were married in a simple civil ceremony in Tahoka on September 30, 1925. David DeVitt did not attend the wedding, either by his design or by the couple's.

The newly married Secrest couple's marriage was troubled from the outset. Helen relished visiting Texas and the Mallet, but she wanted to live in California near her mother and, now, Christine. Bill Secrest, however, had a good job in Morton and

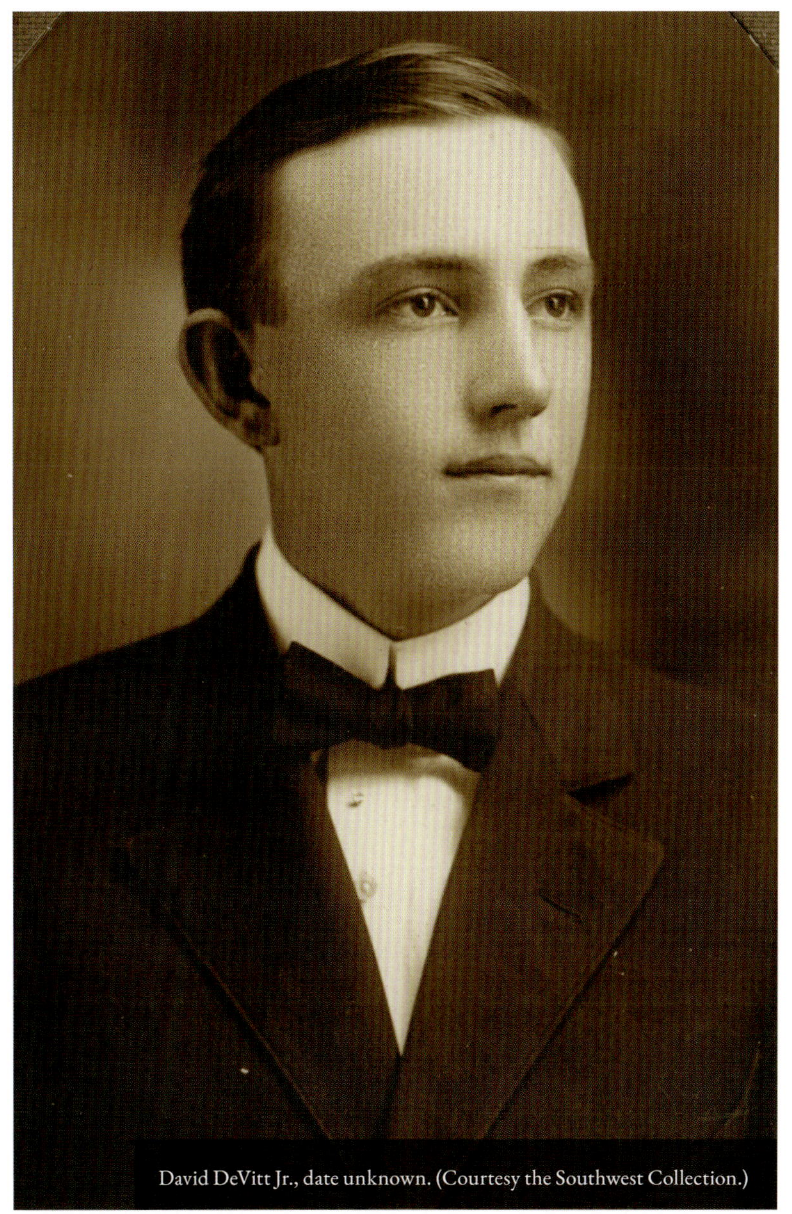

David DeVitt Jr., date unknown. (Courtesy the Southwest Collection.)

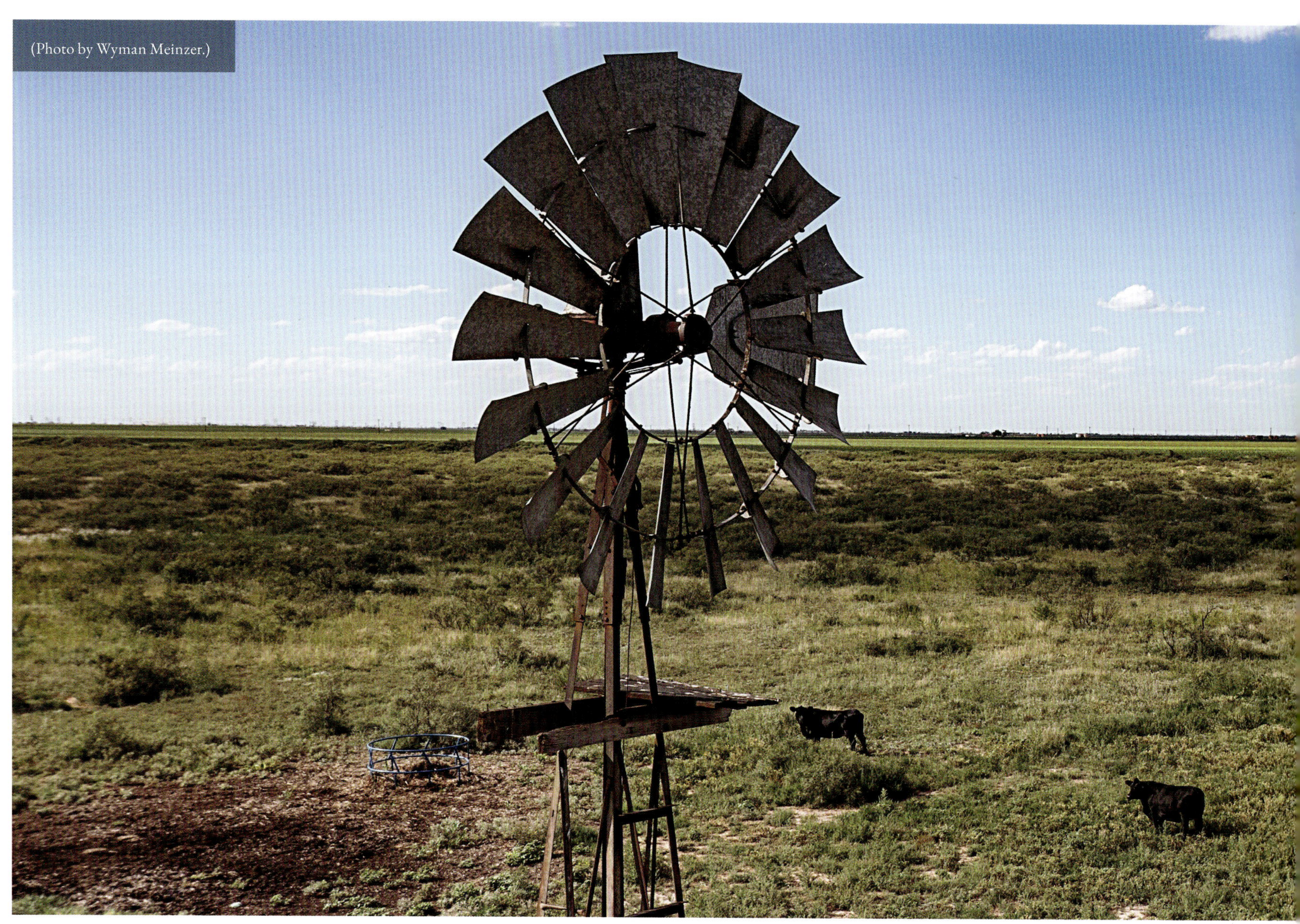
(Photo by Wyman Meinzer.)

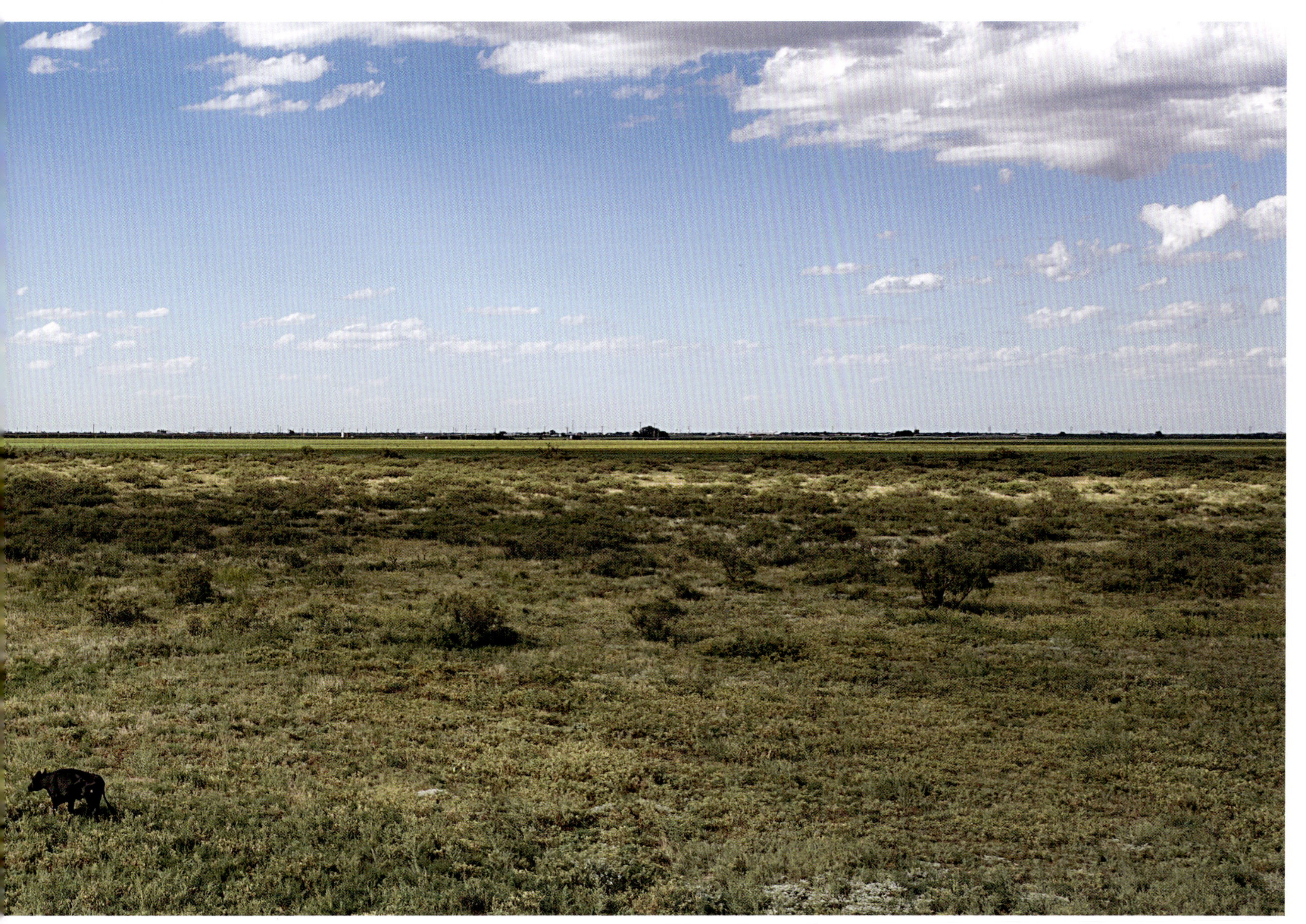

no real desire to uproot and move to California. So, Helen relented and moved to Morton with her husband. It was a much different life than the one she had had in California—slower and not nearly as opulent. Still, she made the best of it until she became pregnant in the spring of 1926. She felt she needed the support of her family, so she returned to Los Angeles to the bungalow in Hollywood to have her child. Bill remained in Morton.

Dorothy Gail Secrest was born on December 23, 1926. After her daughter's birth, Helen wrote to her husband that she wanted to raise her child in California, not Morton, Texas. Bill objected at first, preferring to stay in Texas. He also wanted his family to come back. However, he could not dissuade Helen, so in the interest of marital harmony, Bill agreed to move to California. Bill found a job in San Diego, so after just a few weeks with Florence in Hollywood, the couple moved south. But the arrangement did not stick. Bill Secrest lost his job in July 1930, and he was never happy living in San Diego anyway. The couple and their daughter left California and moved to Lubbock where Bill went to work for the Fort Worth and Denver Railroad. Helen, just as her mother had insisted to her father years earlier, wanted Dorothy to begin school in Fort Worth, not the small city of Lubbock, so she and Dorothy moved back into the DeVitt home in Fort Worth. Separation is never ideal for a marriage, and it can be fatal for one that is already rocky. Helen missed her mother and sister, and she missed California. With Bill in Lubbock, Helen returned to San Diego in 1931. David DeVitt, who had never approved of Helen's marriage to Secrest, agreed to buy Helen and Dorothy a house if they moved to Los Angeles, so they did so in January 1932. Bill and Helen never really reconciled, and letters between the two, while civil, did not contain much of the closeness that husbands and wives should have. Helen filed for divorce from Bill Secrest in 1933 in Reno, Nevada. The court finalized their disunion in December 1933.

It fell to Christine to become Florence's companion after Helen married. The two remained living in the small bungalow in Hollywood. Christine once again took up giving piano lessons to achieve some degree of financial independence, although David DeVitt's remittance still paid the bulk of the household expenses. David DeVitt's visits to California also became more infrequent after Helen moved to San Diego, which further strengthens the evidence of Florence's strained relationship with her husband. He also sent fewer letters to his elder daughter, and Christine mailed even fewer to her father. The connection between mother and daughter was also not always harmonious. Florence, in letters to Helen, complained about Christine's criticism and barbs about her activities, clothes, and—if one reads between the lines—financial frivolity.

The two women likely experienced difficulty in being together so much of the time because they were so different. Florence sometimes lived in a world with some disconnection to reality but also with little regard for how much money she spent. Christine could be just as exasperating to live with. While she could be obstinate and sometimes cutting in her language, she was also a world-class procrastinator, slow to make a decision about almost everything—a characteristic that would continue throughout her life. The two women, although mother and daughter, were almost as close in age as were Christine and Helen. Florence was just eighteen when Christine was born, a woman not that far removed from a hardscrabble existence and married to a man much older than she. As a result, the two women clashed almost like siblings.

While the DeVitt women were in California, the DeVitt men, David and David Jr., continued to concentrate on trying to make the Mallet profitable—a task that had grown increasingly difficult. David Sr. had fought an arduous battle to build the Mallet, dueling with weather, neighbors, the vagaries of a new market, and the challenges of raising cattle in what could be a harsh environment. He had spent most of the first half of the 1920s trying to mitigate personal and ranch profit losses, as well as dealing with an increasingly tenuous family situation. It was trying, but he apparently relished part of it. DeVitt's personality seemed to thrive on conflict, but he was in his seventies as the 1930s approached. Perhaps finished with the battles of trying to make a ranch profitable, he was ready to turn operations over to his son, David Jr.

David DeVitt Jr. had moved into the Mallet headquarters house by 1925 when his father had made him the assistant manager of the Mallet. His title may have been "assistant," but he had assumed most of the day-to-day operations of the ranch by that time. His father had primed David to take over the Mallet from the time he was a schoolboy, and the young man learned the lessons well. By all accounts David Jr. was an impressive figure. He was a hit at dances and other parties, noted for his easy manner and quick banter. He was taller than his father by a bit and much leaner, with dark hair and eyes one admiring lady described as "mesmerizing." He was an effective manager and played a large role in negotiating many of the sales of Mallet land to potential farmers. The only person who did not seem to think highly of David Jr.'s abilities was David DeVitt's new partners in the Mallet, W. D. Johnson and his brother, J. Lee.

When Andrew Drumm had passed away in 1919, his 400 shares of Mallet stock were placed in a trust at the Fidelity Union Bank and Trust in Kansas City—the same place from which DeVitt borrowed money to expand the Mallet herd in 1922. The president of Fidelity was W. D. Johnson, who together with his brother J. Lee also owned the majority stock in the bank. The Johnson brothers were well-known figures in both Texas and Kansas City, men who seemingly had roles in almost every type of business venture between the two places. The Johnsons were born near Brenham, Texas, William Denver in 1860 and Jesse Leon five years later. William left the family home when he was only sixteen and moved to Brown County, where he would eventually work in a general store and the post office and then on to Sweetwater where he worked long enough to save $1,000.

He used his savings to buy a store in Pecos in 1887, a far West Texas train stop town where his older brother F. W. had moved in 1886 to operate a ranch. W. D. entered with his brother into the ranching business, and they were soon joined by their younger brother J. Lee. The ranch was a large operation, stretching over 100 miles on each side of the Pecos River through Loving, Ward, and Winkler Counties. Besides owning a store, the brothers branched out into banking when they established the Pecos Valley State Bank in 1891, an operation that concentrated on loaning money to local ranchers to buy stock. The Johnsons prospered and became some of the wealthiest men in the Trans-Pecos.

W. D. Johnson married Anna Kern, also in 1891, and they had five children in the next ten years while living in Pecos. Much like the DeVitts had decided, W. D. and his wife wanted a better education for their children than the small, isolated town of Pecos could offer, so they sold their interests in the store and bank—but keeping W. D.'s part of the ranch—and moved to Kansas City where he founded the Western Cattle Loan Company. J. Lee Johnson took a similar path. He married a Pecos woman, Dora Allison, the widow of notorious rancher Clay Allison—who gained somewhat of a reputation as a gunfighter—who was killed when a wagon fell on him in 1887. Seven years later, J. Lee and his family moved to Fort Worth where he started a lumber company that within five years became the largest such retailer in Fort Worth and one of the largest west of the Mississippi. He would eventually own more than twenty lumber yards in Texas and Oklahoma.

W. D. Johnson became the president of the Fidelity Union in 1920, and the same year he was either given or purchased one share of Mallet stock, which was more than likely a token gesture that allowed the banker to sit on the Mallet board. He was president of the bank when Marion L. McClure, the

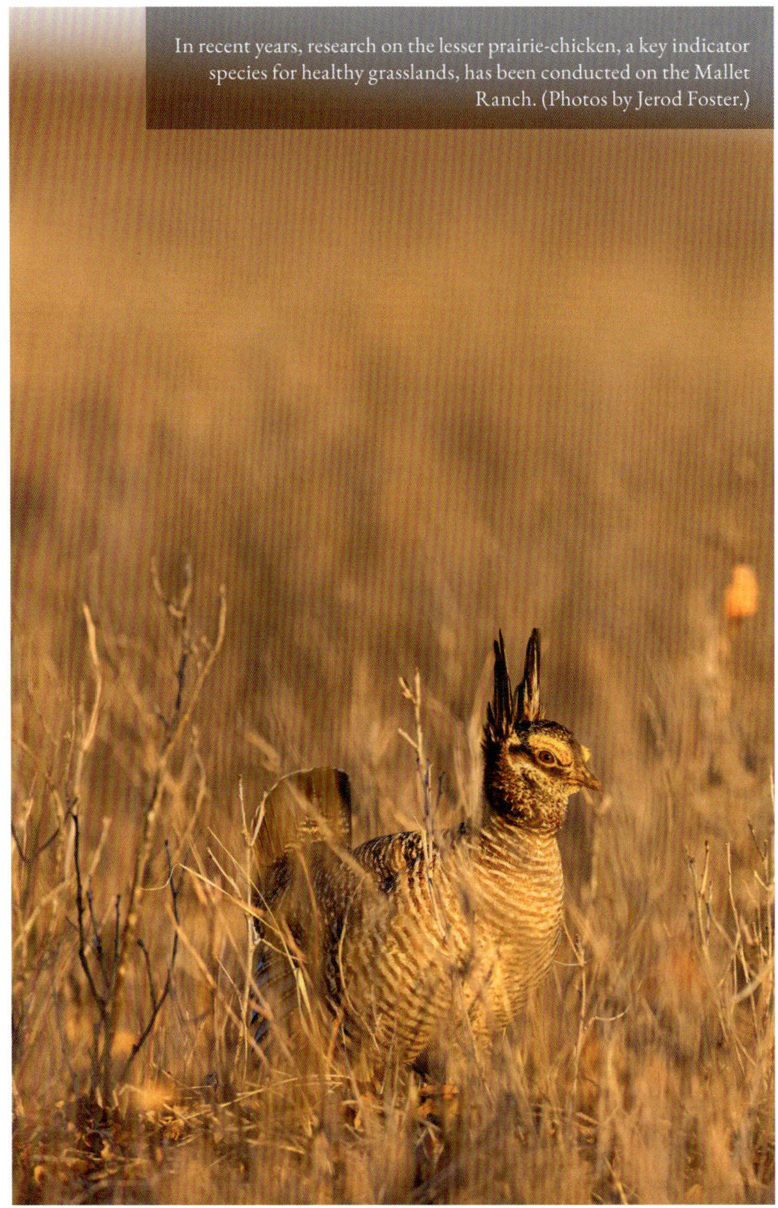

In recent years, research on the lesser prairie-chicken, a key indicator species for healthy grasslands, has been conducted on the Mallet Ranch. (Photos by Jerod Foster.)

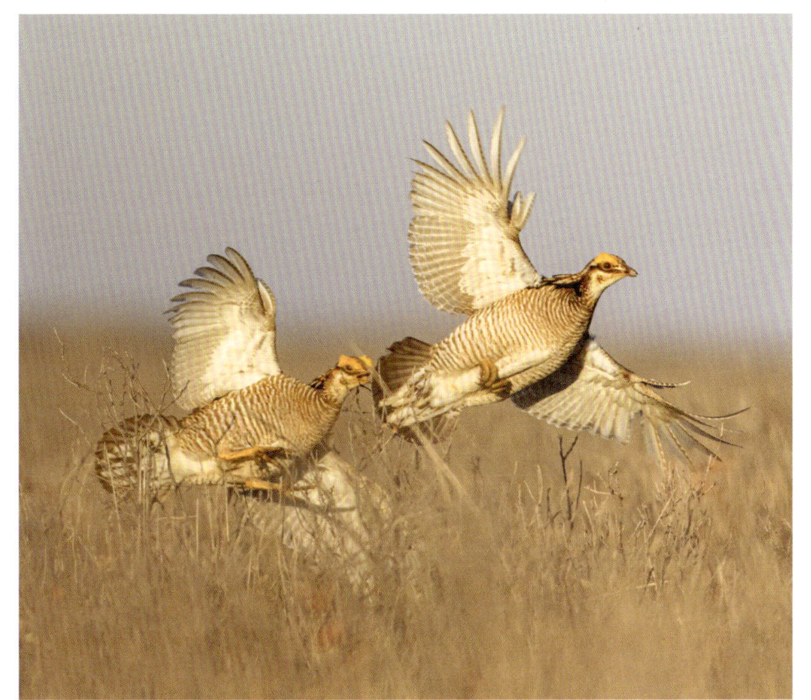

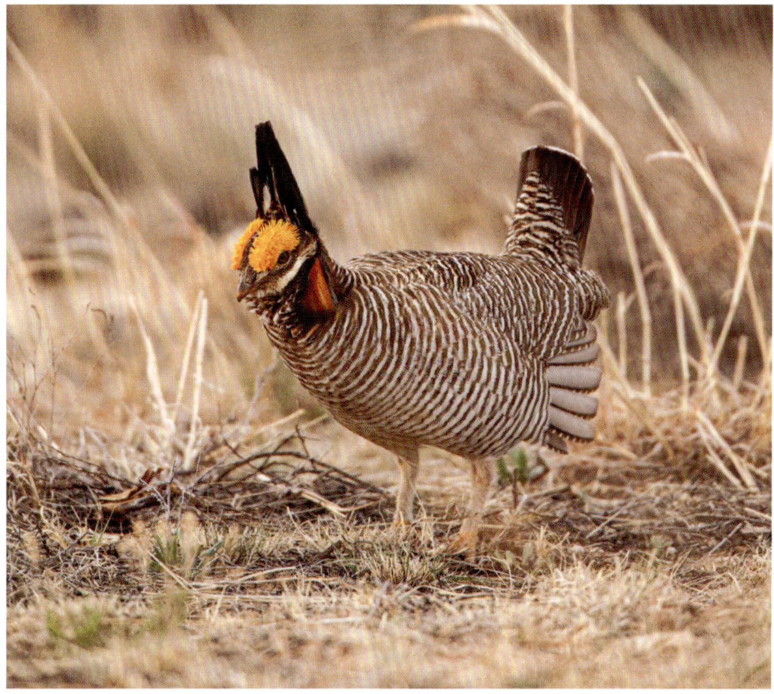

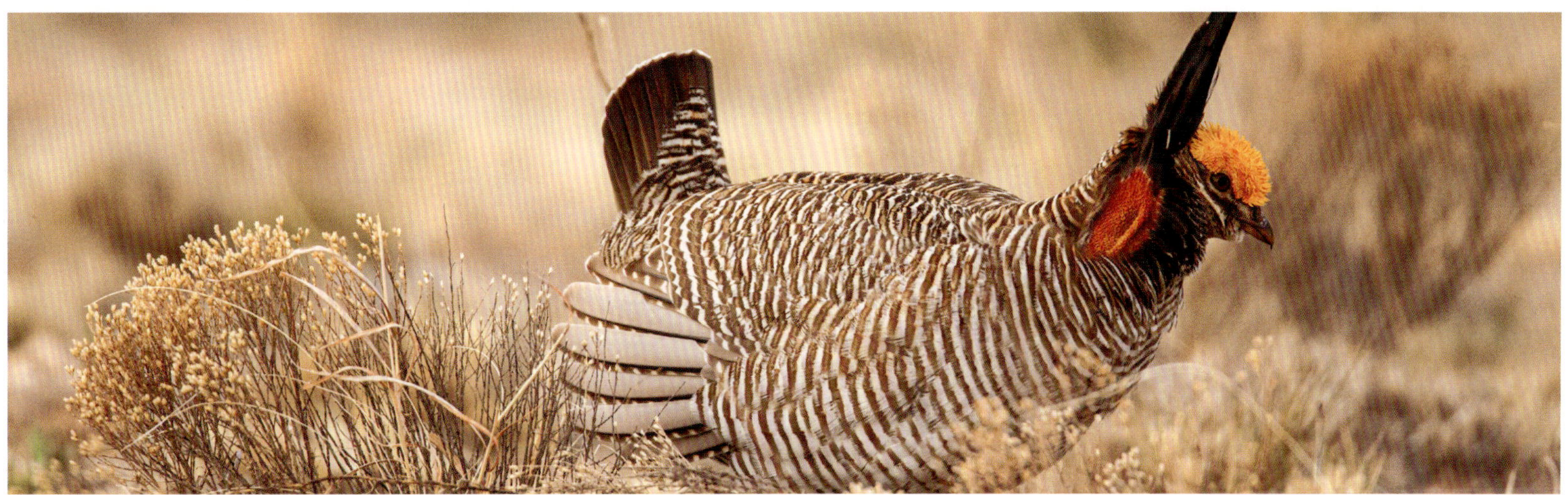

Drumm estate trustee, decided to sell the Drumm shares in the Mallet. The Johnson brothers purchased the shares in 1925—for an unknown amount, as the Drumm Trust records are not publicly available—and thus became David DeVitt's latest partners. Together, the Johnsons owned 40 percent of the Mallet Ranch.

DeVitt, when Flato and Drumm were his partners, essentially had free rein to operate the Mallet as he saw fit, but the Johnsons were not nearly as accommodating. They expected DeVitt to consult them on decisions, and they demanded that they be a part of any financial decisions made concerning the ranch. The Johnson brothers had been the force behind trying to divide and sell the Mallet for farm colonization, and they would also eventually push David DeVitt to make the first leases for oil exploration on Mallet lands.

W. D. Johnson and David DeVitt had a number of clashes, and it seemed that the only times the two men communicated was to object to something the other had done. DeVitt resented the Johnsons' hands-on protection of their minority share, and the Johnsons did not like some of DeVitt's methods of operating the ranch. One of their most fervent disagreements concerned David Jr.'s role and salary as assistant ranch manager. David Jr. had married Louise "Billie" Shelton in June 1929, and Billie came to live at the Mallet headquarters. David, presumably using Mallet funds, had built a needed addition to the very modest house. David was, in almost every way, the operator of the Mallet by that time and deserved a salary commensurate with his duties, but J. Lee Johnson apparently did not concur. He wrote a scathing letter in the summer of 1930 to David DeVitt insisting that he stop paying David Jr. the $250 a month stipend for his duties out of ranch ledgers. "If you want to put your boy on a pension, you will have to pay the pension unaided by your minority stockholders," J. Lee wrote. He also demanded that David Sr. cut his salary—something he had already done five years earlier—and that if DeVitt did not comply, Johnson would "apply for a receiver for the Mallet Company."

Johnson's letters and demands exasperated David DeVitt Sr. and no doubt added to the stress he felt. In a letter to daughter Helen in August 1930, he lamented that his disagreement with J. Lee would keep him from coming to California for a few months, and in a letter to his lawyer at about the same time, he wrote that he was "harassed and overwhelmed with worries . . . with the welfare of the Company, [and] Mr. Johnson's letter simply adds a hundred fold to my cares and worries." What DeVitt did not realize was that his cares and worries were about to grow exponentially.

David Jr. was at the ranch in October 1930 helping with the fall roundup. He and his wife had gone to Levelland on Friday, October 24, and after spending most of the day there began to drive to Lubbock. Reports had David Jr. driving "rapidly," perhaps in an attempt to get back to town before sundown. He never made it. Just east of Levelland he struck a truck. He was badly injured and likely unconscious, while Billie suffered only minor scrapes. He was rushed to Lubbock and a hospital, but it was too late to save his life. He lingered, unconscious, through Friday and Saturday, but then David M. DeVitt Jr. died on the morning of Sunday, October 26. David's mother and sisters came from California and, along with David Sr. and just a few close friends, held services at the home of Mallet bookkeeper L. B. Wright. David Jr.'s death would change the course of the Mallet Ranch, at first toward an uncertain fate, but eventually to a future brighter and more profitable than anyone could imagine.

David Devitt Fighting for His Life Here

Little Hope of Recovery Is Offered for Wealthy Young Ranchman Injured in Auto Accident Friday Night

Critically injured in an automobile accident Friday night, David M. Devitt, Jr., 25, wealthy young cattleman, of Lubbock, had not regained consciousness late Saturday night, attendants at Lubbock sanitarium reported.

Physicians conceded Devitt virtually no chance of recovery. He suffered a severe fracture at the base of the skull, laceration of the brain, a compound fracture immediately below the left elbow and lacerations about the face.

Shortly after sundown Friday, a heavy sedan driven by Devitt struck a truck operated by W. E. McCarter, of Levelland, on the Levelland Lubbock highway, about six miles east of Levelland. Mrs. Devitt, who was riding with her husband, escaped serious injury.

Neither McCarter not Jack Smithee, who also was in the truck was hurt. The automobile hit the truck at an angle, after McCarter had turned his front wheels into a ditch to avoid the collision, the truck driver said. Devitt was believed to have been injured as the top of his car was torn away. He was not thrown from the machine.

Devitt is a son of D. M. Devitt, wealthy ranchman, of Lubbock, and owner of the Mallet ranch in Hockley county.

CHAPTER 4

OIL SAVES THE MALLET

David Mantz DeVitt was seventy-four years old when David Jr. died and no doubt knew he was entering his final years on earth. He had lived a full life, moved from New York to Texas, traveled across that state to establish a ranch that stretched almost to the New Mexico line, and at the same time was able to accumulate some semblance of wealth and live a life of relative luxury. Now, in the evening of his life, it looked like all that accomplishment was withering away. His ranching empire teetered on the verge of shrinking acres, limited profits, and an uncertain future. His business partners questioned his performance as ranch manager, and his family life was tension-filled—at best. It was a burden, for sure, and added to it now was the despondency he felt at the loss of his second son, the one he was training to take over for him and continue the legacy he had so doggedly built.

In many ways, DeVitt never got over the death of his second son. He wrote letters to both of his daughters, and his tone was one of grief and a resignation that all he had fostered was about to crumble. The daughters must have noticed the changes in their father who, for all his faults, had at least always demonstrated confidence and surety in how he tackled life. Now he seemed irresolute and unable to cope with what life had dealt him. It would not be an understatement to assert that David DeVitt had become a broken man.

Defeated or not, DeVitt still had a ranch to run, but it was one that was careening toward insolvency. While beef prices as well as other agricultural commodities had been declining since early in

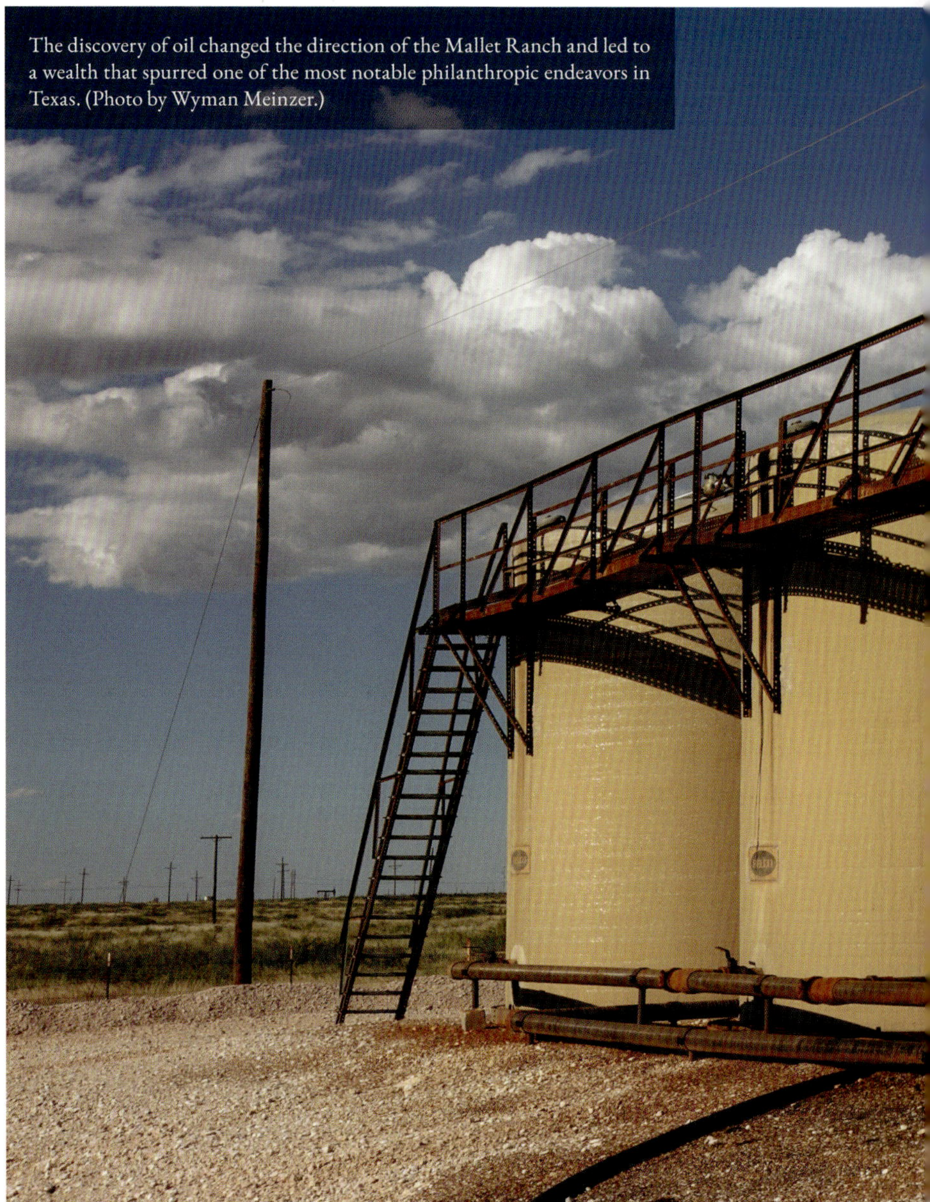

The discovery of oil changed the direction of the Mallet Ranch and led to a wealth that spurred one of the most notable philanthropic endeavors in Texas. (Photo by Wyman Meinzer.)

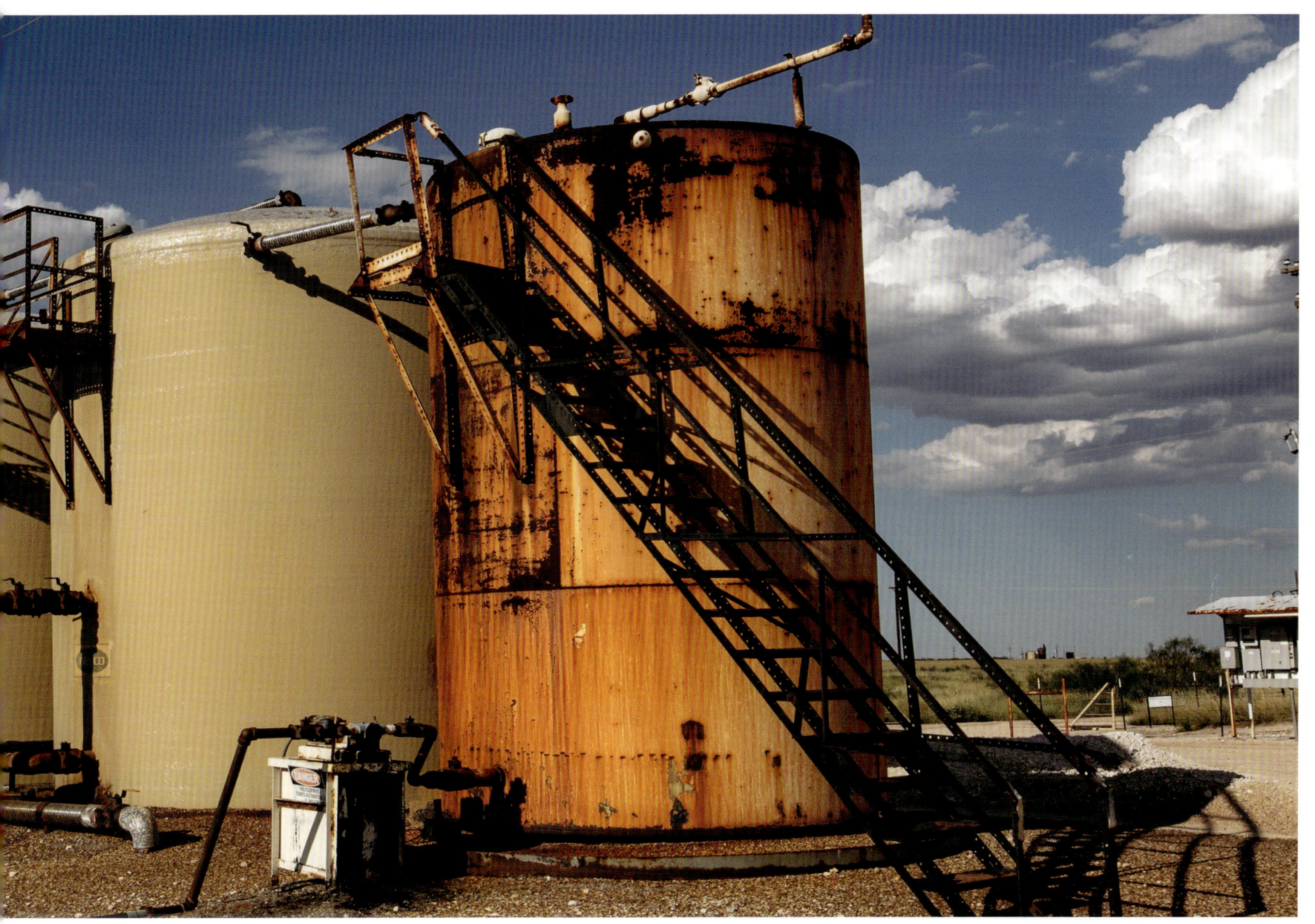
DANGER

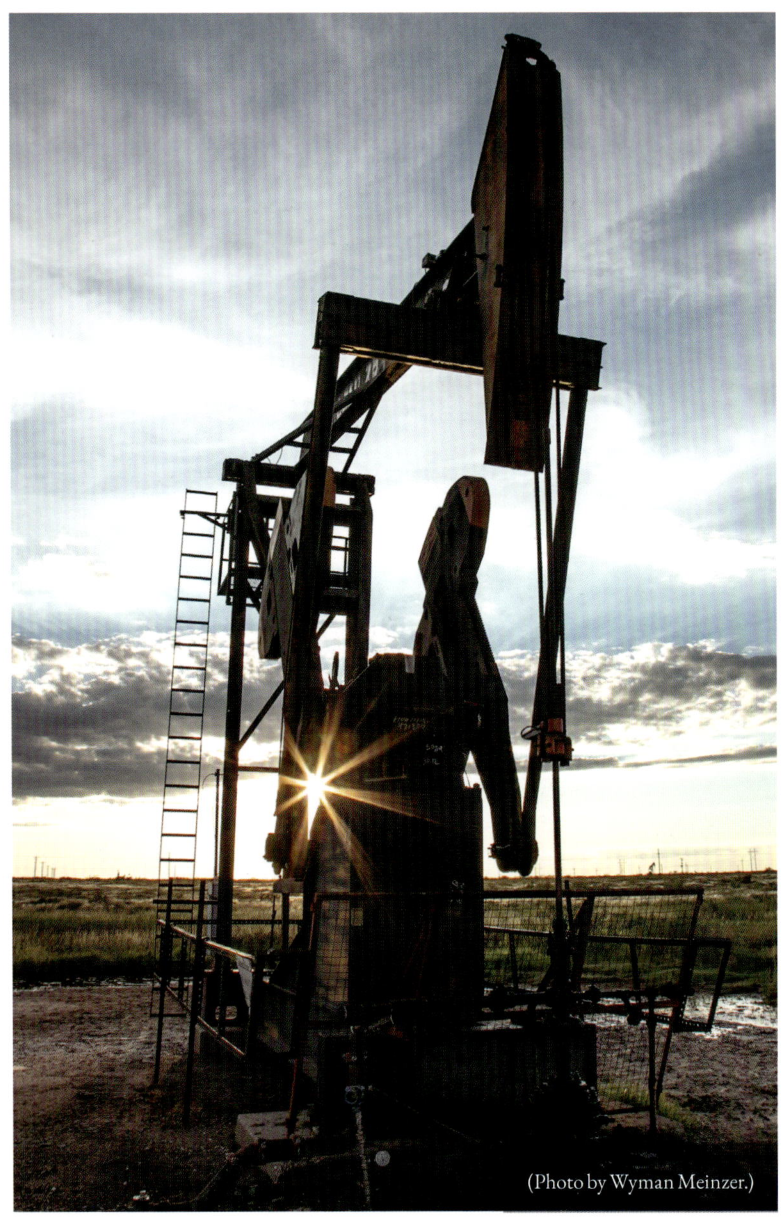
(Photo by Wyman Meinzer.)

the 1920s, the full onset of the economic downturn that would eventually come to be known as the Great Depression came in 1930–1931. The Mallet lost almost $70,000 in 1930 and nearly $80,000 ($77,456 when all accounting was finished) in 1931. Nineteen hundred thirty-two was even worse, as the Mallet losses neared $100,000; adding insult to injury, because Texas uses property taxes as the primary revenue for county and state government, those taxes for a spread as large as the Mallet actually rose. The Mallet Land and Cattle Company Board members met once a year, usually in January, and when they gathered in 1933 they demanded that DeVitt provide them with some plan that would rescue the Mallet Ranch. Particularly sharp in their wording to the ranch manager were the Johnson brothers. W. D. inquired as to why the company was not receiving payments on the notes they had provided to the farmers to whom they had sold land during the colonization efforts. David DeVitt Jr. had been the one originally responsible for collecting past due rent and payments from farmers, but after his death that duty fell to his father. The senior DeVitt had little stomach for dunning farmers for past due payments and was even less inclined to evict people who had nowhere else to go. He often allowed past due remittances to go a full year before he would take any action, and when he did it was generally in a half-hearted manner. He eventually hired a man, J. A. Stroud, to take over the duties, paying him a 15 percent commission on whatever he could collect.

During the 1933 stockholders' meeting, DeVitt likely surprised his partners when he told them he had decided in 1932 to sell the Mallet and had engaged Lubbock real estate agent

Tom Jones to act in that capacity. DeVitt and Jones were good friends, and Jones had served as pallbearer at the 1930 funeral of DeVitt's son. The two men were frequent companions in enjoying whatever merriment Lubbock, Fort Worth, or Kansas City had to offer (Jones accompanied DeVitt on trips). DeVitt was ready to leave Texas and take up permanent residence in California, although whether he would live with Florence was up in the air. So, Tom Jones got busy looking for a buyer for the empire David DeVitt had built. Their contract called for Jones to ask at least ten dollars an acre, for which he would receive a 5 percent commission. DeVitt informed the board of the deal and then left Kansas City. He went to California, where he booked a room at the Alexandria Hotel for an indefinite stay.

There remained one last shot for DeVitt to save the Mallet. W. D. Johnson, as early as 1928, had begun to urge David Sr. to be open to leasing Mallet land to petroleum speculators. DeVitt was not sold on petroleum extraction and no doubt saw drilling crews, derricks, and equipment roads as detrimental to using his lands as pasture, so he resisted Johnson's entreaties. However, as the Depression worsened and the Mallet's fortunes began to decline, DeVitt gave in and signed a number of leases. The oil companies, however, moved slowly and did not get around promptly to making explorations on the Mallet acres; after 1930, and the inauguration of the massive East Texas Oil Field with Columbus "Dad" Joiner's discovery at the Daisy Bradford #3 in the Piney Woods not far from Henderson in Rusk County, they were busy exploiting that find and moved resources from West Texas. Petroleum would not help DeVitt out of his predicament in 1933, but it would one day be the savior of the Mallet Ranch.

David DeVitt made it clear to Tom Jones that he wanted the sale of the Mallet to proceed as quickly as possible. He was now seventy-six, his son and successor was dead, and the rest of his family was in California. Now he wanted to join them permanently. Perhaps he was tired of the lifestyle that had led to his estrangement from his oldest daughter and wife, or perhaps he knew this was the last chance he had to live in California, a place to which he had always talked about moving. So, he directed Jones to sell the Mallet and went first to Kansas City to tie up loose ends—where he likely met with his partners, the Johnson brothers, but there is no record of what they discussed—and then he traveled to Los Angeles.

Jones had little success in finding a buyer for the Mallet in the depths of the Depression, and DeVitt had to extend his contract with the real estate man. Finally, in spring 1933, Amarillo businessman J. A. Whittenburg expressed interest in buying the ranch. Whittenburg's life narrative followed the same pattern as so many others who had come to Texas in the late nineteenth century. At just twelve years old, Whittenburg had made a perilous trip from Missouri to Texas to work alongside his brothers at Ben Slaughter's ranch in Parker County. Through thrift after working as a drover on the Great Western Trail, he accumulated a small herd that he ran on leased acres in Young County. Drought and poor timing caused him to go bankrupt after a few years, and he and his wife, Tennie, became traders among the Comanche in the Fort Sill, Oklahoma, region. They accumulated enough savings to claim land in Roberts County in the Panhandle. From that beginning, Whittenburg built a sizable ranch and expanded into banking and other enterprises in Amarillo. In the early 1920s his lands became part of the rich oil and gas discoveries in the Panhandle, making J. A. Whittenburg—like David DeVitt—a very wealthy man in his seventies.

Jones believed he had found the man to buy the Mallet. In letters to DeVitt, he described meeting with the Amarillo rancher at least twice in the spring of 1933. DeVitt also traveled to Amarillo from Kansas City to see Whittenburg and sent a telegram a month later offering to show him the ranch and entertain an offer. Whittenburg did not take DeVitt up on his offer at that time, but in October 1933 DeVitt once again quoted Whittenburg a price of ten dollars an acre cash for all 52,000 acres of the Mallet. Whittenburg declined making a decision at that time but did not entirely dismiss the idea.

While Tom Jones searched for other buyers for the Mallet, David DeVitt enjoyed his time in California. He had spent two months in a hospital in Lubbock for a respiratory ailment and then convalesced at his suite in the Hilton Hotel until June 1933 when he made his trip to Kansas City to oversee the Mallet spring sale of cattle—transactions that did not yield a profit. He then took a train to Los Angeles, but he did not move into the house with Christine and Florence. Instead, he checked into the Alexandria Hotel. He pestered Tom Jones with telegrams and letters inquiring about the progress of the sale. Jones also had taken over collecting rents from the farmers on Mallet land, and DeVitt scolded Jones for not moving more quickly to collect back payments. If he contacted his partners at all about his dealings during this time, no record exists of any such correspondence. He did, however, inform his Kansas City attorney, David A. Murphy, that he was looking after ranch business despite being in California. He knew Murphy would report the same to the Johnson brothers.

DeVitt enjoyed his three-month sojourn to California and wrote numerous letters to Jones and another friend, Sam Arnett, about his many visits to the beach and other Los Angeles sites. He does write of seeing Helen, but he does not mention Christine or Florence. He had a flare-up of the illness that had confined him to a hospital bed in early August. This delayed his return to Texas until September. He had hoped that the September sale of Mallet cattle would help to ease his financial worries, but cattle prices continued to hover at less than five cents a pound, which was not enough for the Mallet to break even. He hinted to Jones that he might have a buyer for the Mallet from "Kansas parties," but if he did have an inquiry, it went nowhere. When David DeVitt returned from the cattle sale and Kansas meeting in October 1933, J. A. Whittenburg ended his interest in buying the Mallet. DeVitt once again boarded a train to California.

The Mallet Ranch, by the fall and winter of 1933, had reached a crossroads. Just as for a number of other large Texas stock operations that had begun in the late nineteenth and early twentieth centuries, the realities of a changing market, an uncertain climate, soft commodity prices, and now a worldwide economic depression had brought the Mallet Ranch to a crisis point. David DeVitt and his partners with the Mallet Land and Cattle Company could very well squeeze small profits out of the spread if conditions were absolutely ideal, but that was an experience that had proven elusive. The Mallet, like some of the other Texas ranches of the period, faced a future of division and then dissolution.

Still, David DeVitt searched for a solution. He sent Jones a telegram telling him that he wanted to sell the ranch only to Whittenburg. At the same time, in November 1933, he left California for Fort Worth with another scheme in mind to save the Mallet. He made the rounds of oil company offices in Fort Worth, trying to interest them to lease a large tract of the Mallet for petroleum exploration. However, most of the drilling companies in Texas at that time were heavily invested in the East Texas field, and the Depression had also sapped some of their resources and capital. Most of the offices DeVitt called on showed no interest at all; one, the Stanolind Oil Company, expressed some curiosity, but they eventually also turned down DeVitt. He left Fort Worth for Kansas City, where he almost immediately once again was hospitalized for a month. The diagnosis this time included "exhaustion," which in that era could imply stress or depression. If so, the travails of the Mallet could certainly be blamed.

In late January 1934, David DeVitt once again made a trip to California for rest and recovery. He was almost seventy-eight. When Helen saw her father's weakened condition, she convinced him to stay with her and Dorothy so that they could nurse him back to health. He planned to return to Lubbock in March, probably after he celebrated his March 2 birthday with Helen and Dorothy. He never got the chance and died of a heart attack on March 6, 1934, in a bedroom in the small house he had bought Helen after her divorce. His family did not return him to Texas or even to his birthplace of New York but buried him in Los Angeles. It was the end of the life of the former New York journalist who took a wild chance to leave that life behind and establish a stock operation in Texas. He had done well, achieving a degree of wealth, but in his final days he agonized over whether the results of his hard work would vanish under a veil of debt and changing times.

His death meant that now his family either had to find a way to make the Mallet work or sell everything and leave Texas behind. The latter seemed to be the easier choice; Florence, Christine, and Helen had already left Texas and appeared to be content living in Los Angeles. After all, they had taken little interest in the Mallet Ranch thus far, so why should they now have to struggle with trying to keep their father's dream alive? Tom Jones certainly thought that would be the decision as he wasted little time after David's death in letting the DeVitt women know that he would continue to pursue the sale of the Mallet Ranch. What no one could foresee was that circumstances—both intentional and through chance—would allow Christine DeVitt, with the acquiescence of her mother and sister, to chart a different course and keep the Mallet Ranch in the DeVitt family. That decision would also create a celebrated fortune, one that would become one of the most notable philanthropic funds in Texas history. That fortune, though, would come not from the stock and the pastures that David

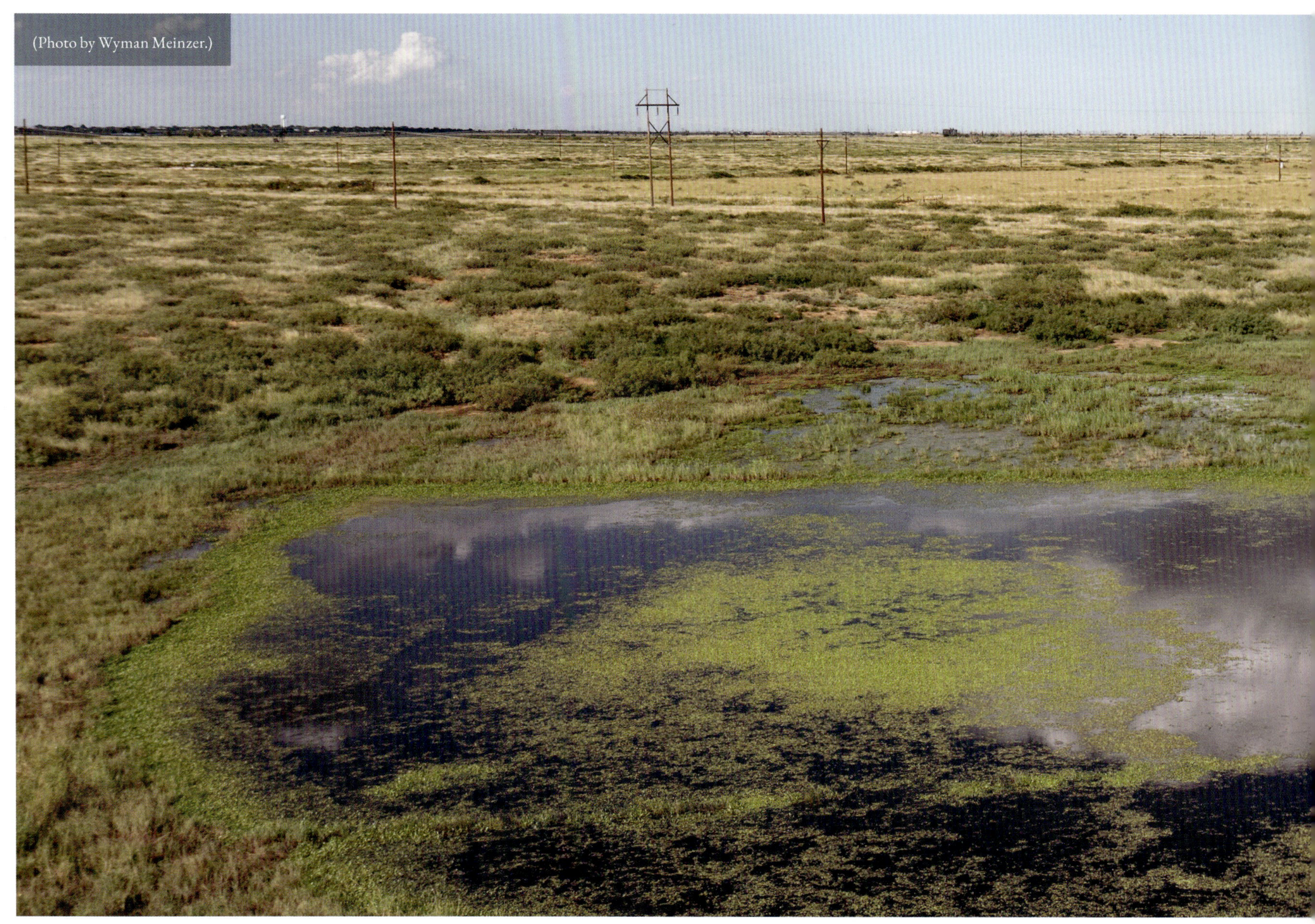

(Photo by Wyman Meinzer.)

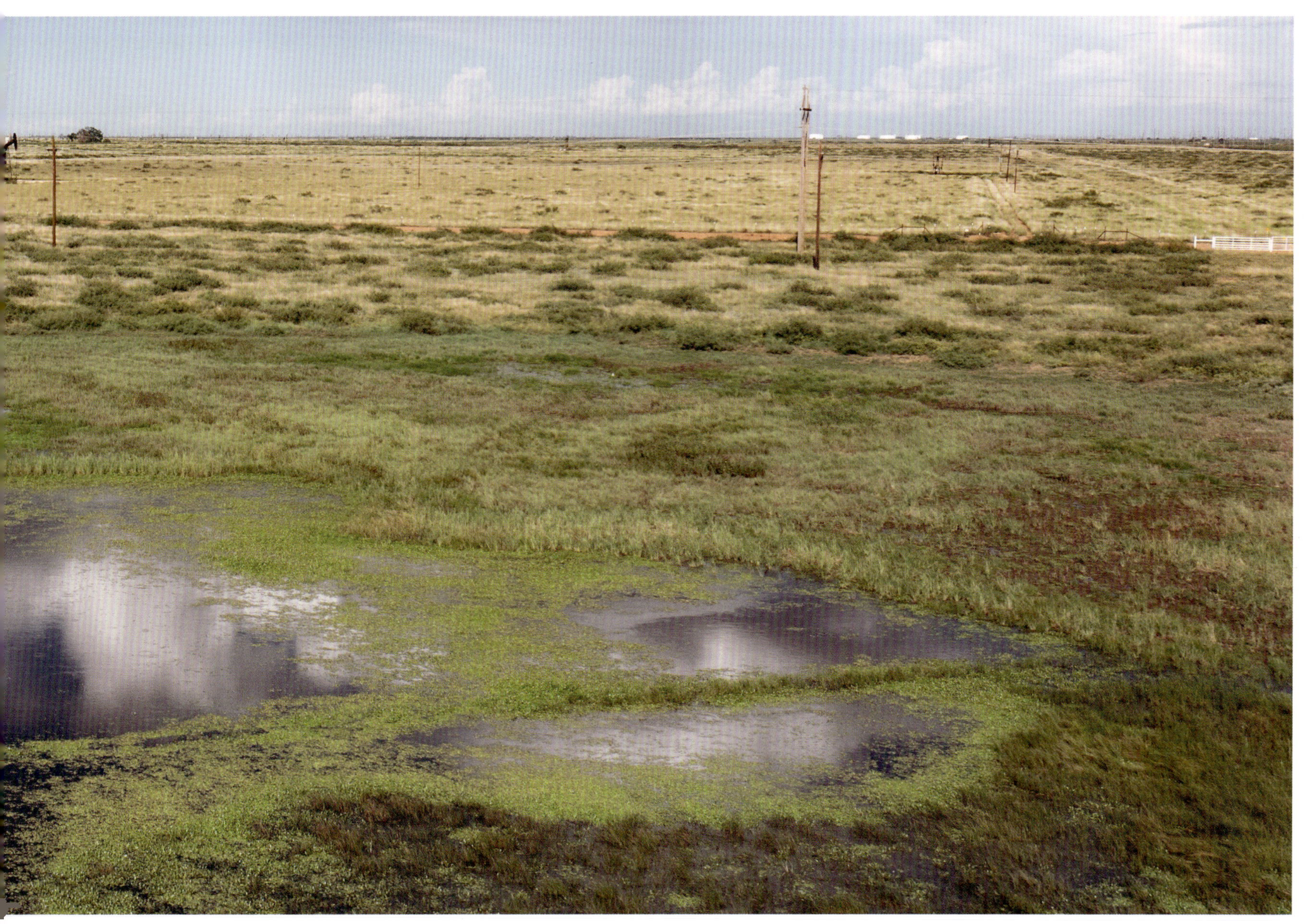

DeVitt built up, but from the minerals that lay underneath those pastures.

Some of the earliest European explorers who ventured into Texas reported a sticky asphaltic substance floating on the waters of the Gulf of Mexico, bubbling up from underground springs and sometimes permeating the surface of the ground. What they saw, of course, was petroleum, or crude oil, and while they occasionally used it to caulk their boats and ships and grease the wheels of carts and mills, mostly they viewed it as a nuisance. Little did anyone know that there would come a time when that gooey, oozing element would revolutionize the world and make Texas a wealthy and important state.

Edwin L. Drake drilled the first commercial oil well in the United States in Titusville, Pennsylvania, in 1859 and the industry progressed slowly from there with most wells drilled in the upper Appalachian region. Texas had its first oil well in 1866 when Lyne Taliaferro Barret completed a well near Oil Springs in Nacogdoches County. However, it was never a large producer, and a decline in prices caused him to abandon production. There were small, sporadic discoveries through most of the remainder of the nineteenth century, but true commercial development of the petroleum industry in Texas did not come until there was a significant discovery near Corsicana in 1894. The Corsicana Field would eventually produce almost a million barrels of oil through 1900 and lead to Texas's first modern refinery, but the most significant discovery in the state's history—and perhaps the most economically significant event ever in Texas—came in 1901.

Exploration in the upper Gulf Coast region began as early as 1892 but with little success. One of the drillers involved in the play near Beaumont was Anthony F. Lucas, who gained a reputation as a man who could "find oil." The Gladys City Oil, Gas, and Manufacturing Company hired Lucas in 1900 to drill in a salt dome they controlled just south of Beaumont. Lucas spudded a well in October 1900 and began to drill. It came in as a "gusher" on January 10, 1901, blowing almost 100,000 barrels a day onto the coastal prairie for five days before they could cap it. Spindletop, as it was called, ushered in a new age in petroleum exploration in Texas. Speculators and wildcat drillers rushed to the region, and the Spindletop oil field was soon producing an amazing 17,500,000 barrels of oil a year in 1902. The beginnings of some of the most notable contemporary oil companies, such as Texaco and Gulf, can trace their origins to this significant discovery.

The industry spread out from the upper Gulf Coast to the central plains with a series of significant discoveries at Sour Lake, Humble (which spawned the Humble Oil Company that later through mergers and acquisition became global giant Exxon), and Goose Creek. Such activity also expanded the industrial capabilities of the region, as refineries and other industrial concerns began to grow in the Houston–Port Arthur–Beaumont region and also made the Houston Ship Channel possible and viable. The industry would begin to spread to the north central region of the state and into the Panhandle and Permian Basin the 1920s, but movement into West Texas would be interrupted when the biggest discovery of them all would come not far from where Lyne T. Barret had drilled that first oil well in 1866. Columbus M. "Dad" Joiner and his partner A. D. "Doc" Lloyd began to drill a well they called the Daisy Bradford #3 in western Rusk County in the summer of 1930. Joiner was convinced there was oil in East Texas but thus far had not been able to make a significant find. However, his luck turned on October 6, 1930, when his well inaugurated what would be the largest single oil field in US history until the vast deposits in Alaska came online in the 1960s. The East Texas Oil Field spread forty-three miles long and almost thirteen miles wide underneath the Piney Woods of East Texas. Oilmen from all the oil regions of Texas almost ceased production everywhere else and rushed into East Texas to take advantage of the new boom area.

There were problems with boosting oil production in West Texas. While finds in the Panhandle and the Permian Basin would eventually produce some major exploration, most oilmen found West Texas—the Panhandle as well as the South Plains and the Permian Basin—not as hospitable to petroleum production as the rest of the state. One of the most persistent barriers was the lack of effective transportation to get oil to a refinery. Most places in West Texas had just one rail line and these were busy transporting stock, which made a switch to hauling oil problematic. That meant they needed to construct pipelines, which greatly cut into profits. Also, much of the petroleum in West Texas contained sulfur, paraffin (which congealed at temperatures below fifty-five degrees and made it difficult to pipe) and other elements that made it more expensive and more challenging to refine. Such conditions meant that larger, well-capitalized firms, such as the Texas Company, Phillips, and Magnolia, would come to dominate the early exploration in West Texas, especially in the Panhandle.

The Permian Basin—the oil-producing area most contingent to the South Plains and the Mallet—carried additional problems besides all those associated with the rest of West Texas. Geologic knowledge of the Permian Basin was scant, which made oil firms reluctant to sink substantial funds into what would surely produce a number of dry holes. Still, in the early 1920s, wildcat drillers found oil at Texon in the eastern part of the Permian Basin in 1923, which ushered in the Permian Basin oil field. The region was the site of a boom period in the late 1920s. The vast Yates Field came online in 1926, and production in and around those two finds continued until the Great Depression and the Daisy Bradford #3 in East Texas caused oil speculation to shift away from West Texas—precisely at the time David DeVitt had begun to seek out potential leases on the Mallet.

Before any attempts to exploit Mallet lands for petroleum could proceed, David DeVitt's family had to first sort out the intricacies of David's will as well as deal with how the ramifications of his death would affect the Mallet Land and Cattle Company. The matter was complicated by DeVitt's estrangement from his family. Florence and David had barely communicated—other than dealing with Florence's request for support—in the last twenty years of his life. It goes without saying that she knew very little about his affairs, financial

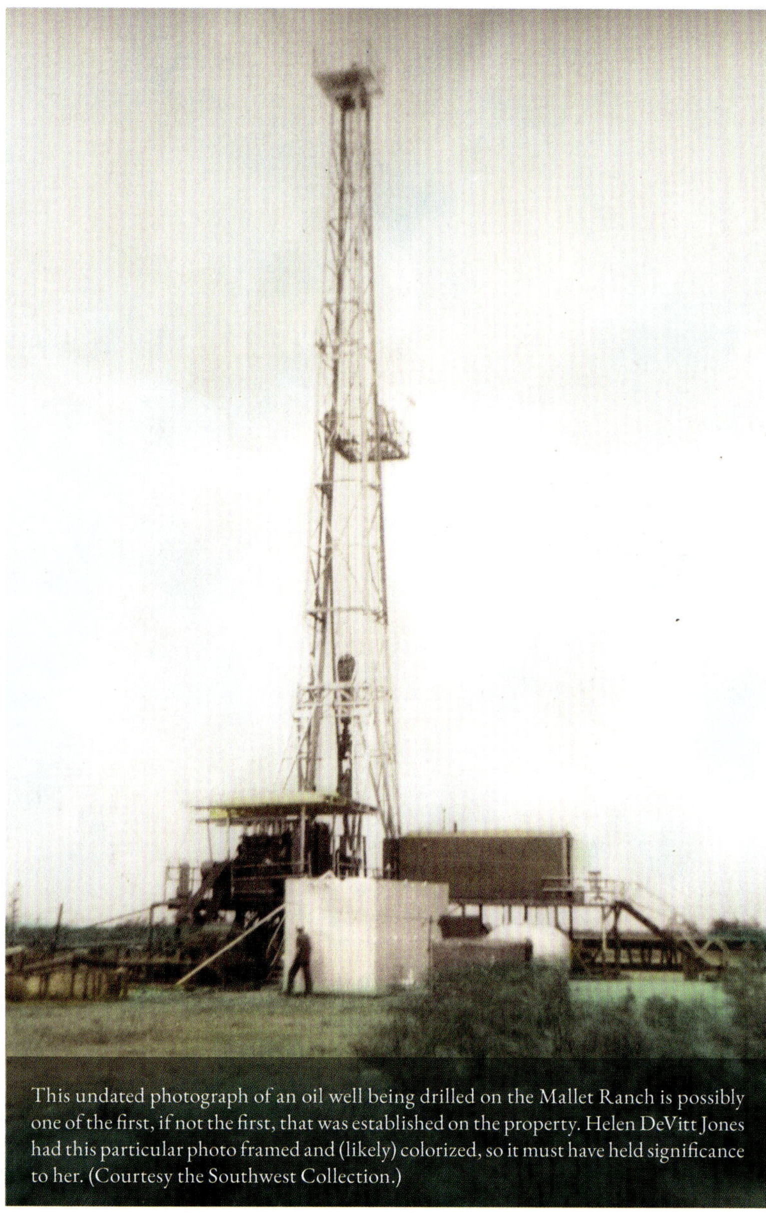
This undated photograph of an oil well being drilled on the Mallet Ranch is possibly one of the first, if not the first, that was established on the property. Helen DeVitt Jones had this particular photo framed and (likely) colorized, so it must have held significance to her. (Courtesy the Southwest Collection.)

or otherwise. Florence, Helen, and Christine had all lived in California since 1921 and had little to do with the actual operation or financial decisions of the Mallet Ranch. However, all three certainly had a vested interest in what would become of David's estate since he had been their only means of support. David DeVitt had left the disposition of his affairs in the hands of co-executors: David Murphy, his Kansas City attorney, and friend and Lubbock banker Sam Arnett.

Christine, particularly, took a keen interest in how her father's estate would be settled. She was forty-nine years of age, had never married, and had given up her career to live with and care for her mother. She realized that she needed to be present when any execution of the will happened, so for perhaps the first time in her life she did not procrastinate and made plans to take a train to Lubbock shortly after her father's services. Florence, nearing seventy and still complaining of multiple maladies, needed some clarification about the estate as she certainly could not support herself. At Christine's urging, she hired an attorney, Ralph G. Lindstrom, to oversee her interests in the estate. Helen, younger and much more passive, seemed content to allow her older sister to take the lead for the family.

David DeVitt's death signaled a change in the direction of the Mallet to W. D. Johnson. As long as David controlled the majority of Mallet shares, Johnson had to defer to the ranch manager on many fronts, but now he began to assume control. He took over as president of the Mallet Land and Cattle Company. Johnson then tapped Sam Arnett to serve as the on-site manager of the ranch and vice president of the company. There is little doubt that Johnson expected the DeVitt heirs—all women, after all—to become silent partners and allow him to make whatever decisions he thought needed to be made. Mr. Johnson would be sorely disappointed.

Christine checked into the Hilton Hotel in Lubbock where her father had often stayed and where she would live for almost fifteen years. Christine met with Sam Arnett shortly after arriving to discuss the will and final dispensation. Christine DeVitt was forty-nine when her father died, and her life was somewhat adrift. She had taught school for a bit after college but had lived in California with her mother since 1921 and not pursued much beyond caring for and being a companion to Florence. While the allowance David DeVitt had provided his family permitted a comfortable living, it was certainly not one that included luxury. Christine was now ready for the "rest of her life" to begin. When she left California for Lubbock, the transformation was underway. The change would result not only in the altered fortunes of the DeVitt heirs but also those of the Mallet Land and Cattle Company investors, Texas Tech University, and countless individuals who would eventually be the beneficiaries of the DeVitt sisters' philanthropy. However, having the mercurial Christine drive the car would make for a bumpy ride.

The will had left DeVitt's share to Florence, and while Florence certainly had her own ideas about the Mallet, she also had no desire to make any decision without her children's consent, especially that of her elder daughter. Thus, Christine took control of deciding for the family how to move forward on her father's assets and, most important, filling his place on the Mallet Land and Cattle Company Board. Such a situation produced a decade-long bout of determination, conflict, and battles between Christine DeVitt and her newly acquired partners, especially the Johnson brothers.

When Christine DeVitt met with Arnett for the first time in his Lubbock office, it became apparent that she would be no passive partner. Arnett was not only the co-executor of David DeVitt's will (along with David Murphy) but also served as the day-to-day operations manager of the Mallet after David's death. He encountered in Christine a woman who was not only prepared to ask questions about dispensation of the estate but also had her own ideas about how the ranch should be run. Christine was not afraid to voice her objections to how Arnett was conducting affairs. Most significantly, Arnett let Christine know that both Johnson brothers, as well as he and David Murphy, thought it was the perfect time to sell the Mallet. Christine wasted no time in letting the Lubbock banker know that the DeVitt women—she, as well as Florence and Helen—would block any such notion of selling what her father had built. Christine DeVitt had taken an adversarial stance with her partners for the first time. It would not be the last.

While Florence DeVitt had given her approval for Christine to travel to Lubbock and speak on her behalf with Mallet Land and Cattle Company partners, she was not willing to acquiesce totally to Christine's whims. She hired California attorney Ralph G. Lindstrom to be her advocate in settling David DeVitt's estate. Lindstrom caught a train and traveled to Lubbock. He also met with Arnett, discussed

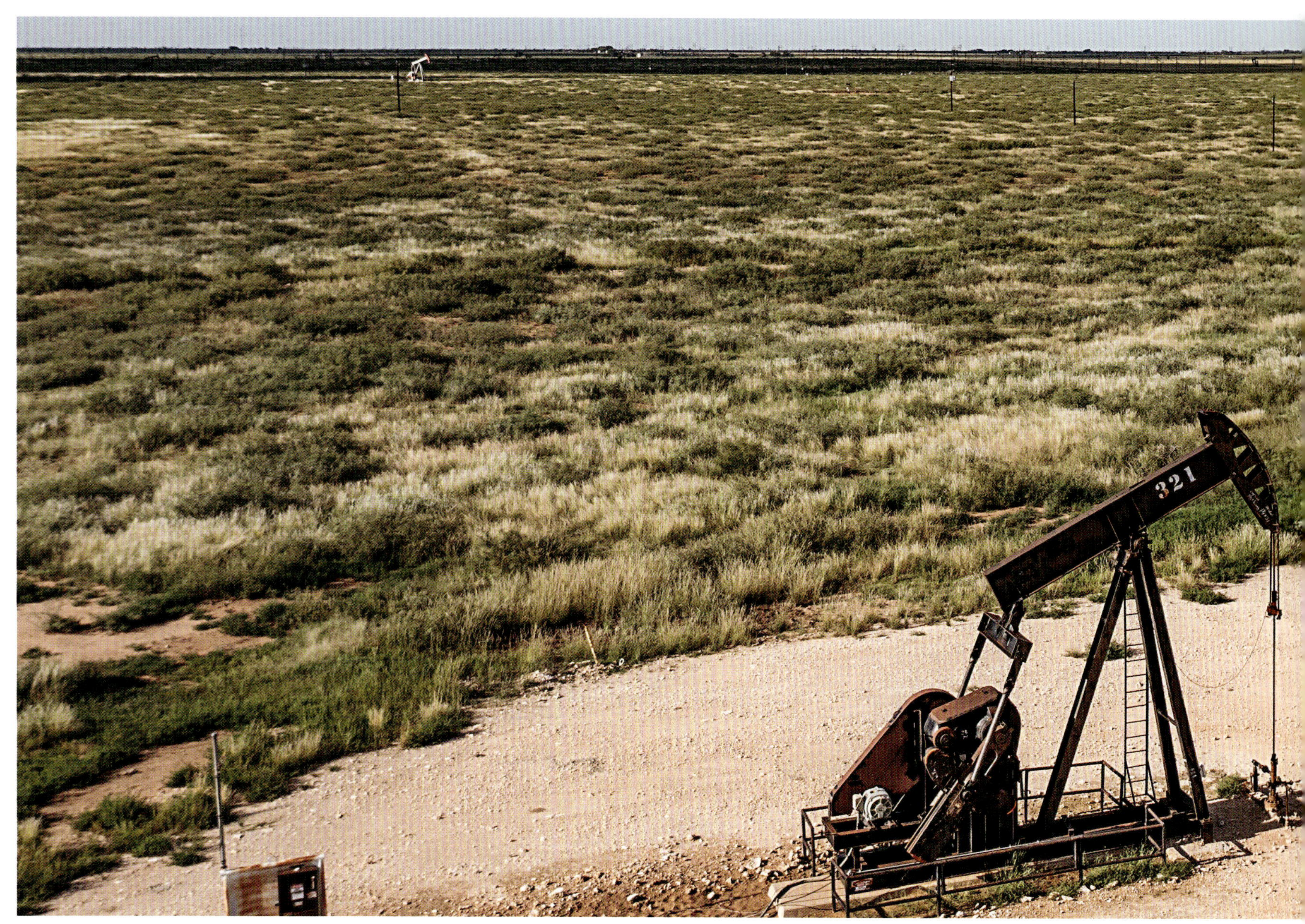
321

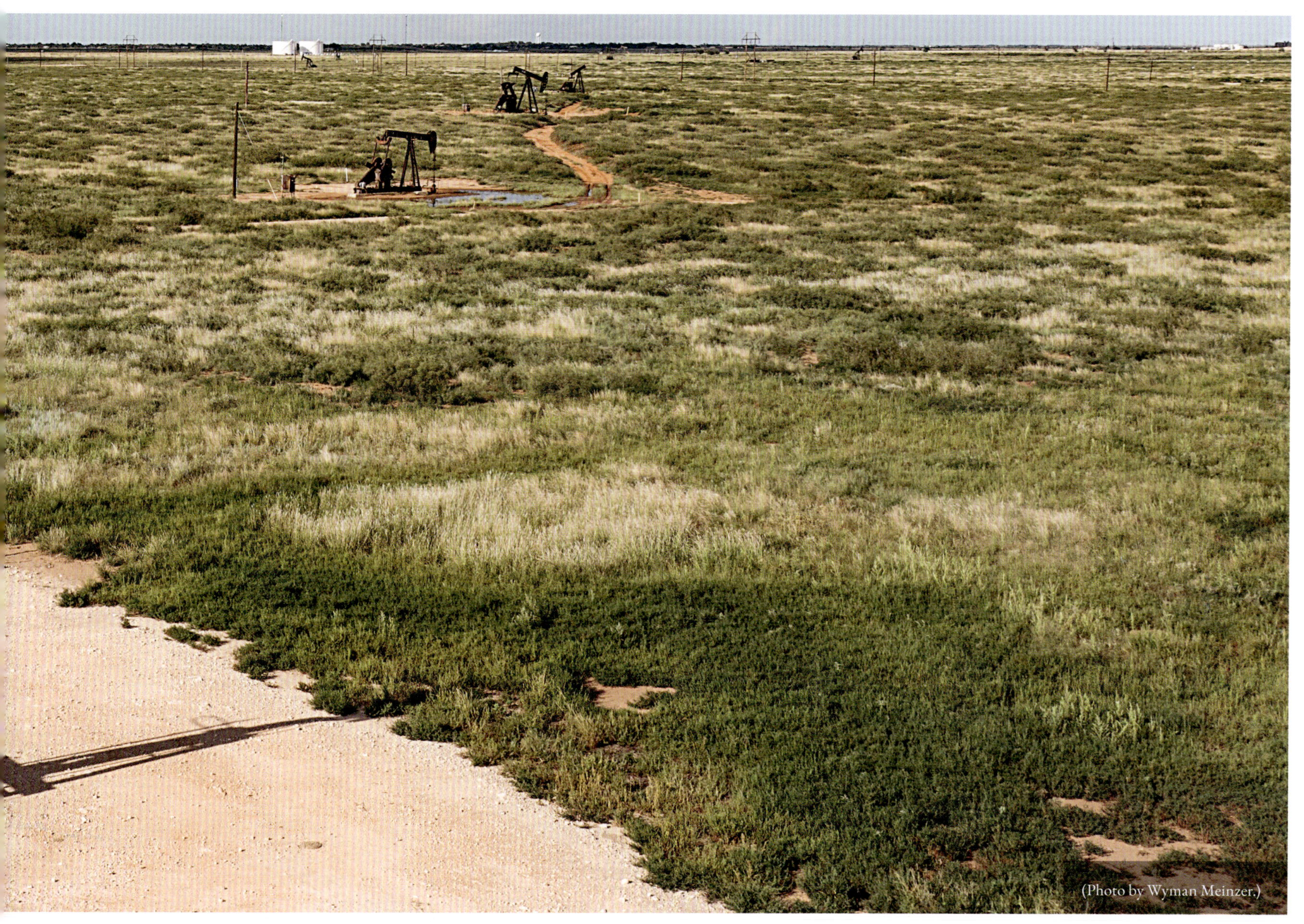

(Photo by Wyman Meinzer.)

the DeVitt estate, and examined the document. He found nothing out of order and reported to Florence that in his opinion "the handling of the will by the executors is satisfactory from what I can see." He also saw nothing amiss in how the Mallet Board had made decisions since her husband's death. He did report that he had encountered one problem in Texas from an unexpected source—or perhaps, in Florence's eyes, one not so astonishing. In both letters and telegrams to Florence, Lindstrom complained about Christine's "constant criticism" of how he was handling her mother's affairs, how he had agreed with the execution of the will, and—most of all—how he had charged Florence a 25 percent fee for his services. Complaining about service fees would become a pattern for Christine.

Christine was not the only concerned party who thought Lindstrom's presence and representation were not needed. David DeVitt's executors also voiced their opposition to Florence regarding the California attorney. Their argument was that Florence's husband had trusted them enough to make them estate executors and, for that reason, they were now advocates for all the DeVitt women. That circumstance also determined why, they wrote to Florence, she needed to persuade Christine to give up her campaign of obstinacy. Florence eventually did drop Lindstrom's services, but she could do little about Christine. She was in favor of selling and let Christine know it. Florence had likely stopped caring at all about the Mallet Ranch the day she moved away from the lonely headquarters house and back to Fort Worth, and she was now a committed resident of California and certainly had no interest in worrying about an isolated ranch on Texas's South Plains. She wanted to sell, and she had convinced her other daughter, Helen, that getting rid of the DeVitt interests in the Mallet Ranch was the right thing to do. Florence could have made the determining decision to sell the Mallet; she was the named heir, and it was her call to make. However, she did not wish to make such a decision unless Christine agreed. Florence DeVitt's elder daughter, as well as Helen and Florence herself, would continue to own a struggling stock operation in the middle of the Great Depression. Christine would continue her opposition to just about everything the executors or the Mallet partners attempted for the next two years. It was almost a virtual war between all parties.

Two of the more interesting insights one could gather from the years immediately after David DeVitt's death were the deteriorating relationship between mother (Florence DeVitt) and daughter (Christine DeVitt) and the loveless aspects of Florence and David DeVitt's marriage. Communication between Florence and her elder daughter contained very little affection after Christine returned to Texas. She castigated her daughter's stubbornness and accused her of hastening her mother's journey to being a "pauper." She also implied that she allowed Christine to take the lead on dealing with the executors and the Mallet Board not because she thought Christine competent but because she did not want to be subject to Christine's criticism and wailings. She once wrote to her daughter, "I'm for selling, but not without your consent for I'm just as well to be a poor dog . . . as to be deviled out of my life by your refusings and abuses as I've suffered thru the past years. I can't stand up under it any longer." Florence and Christine had somehow managed to live together in California for over a decade, but proximity did not seem to foster fondness. Perhaps Florence felt abandoned. After all, Christine had left for Lubbock after her father's death. Except for a few brief trips back, she had no idea of ever returning to California and Florence. Florence DeVitt's husband had essentially abandoned her by the 1890s, and perhaps she felt that her daughter was now repeating the pattern. More likely, she had simply become bitter since during these years she also directed ire toward Helen, supposedly her "favorite" daughter. She once wrote to Christine that Helen was "always on hand to use me for her own convenience and profit." In letters written in 1936 and 1937, Florence went so far as to denigrate the looks and appearance of both daughters. In another letter she acidly wrote that Christine had lived a "wretched life, empty of anything."

Florence DeVitt's unpleasantness toward her daughters was rivaled only by the acrimony she seemed to hold toward men, no doubt a product of her dreadful married life. David DeVitt—especially after 1905—had essentially deserted his wife. He spent more time away than he did at home. Her unhappy marriage had left Florence with an unhealthy distrust of—even hatred for—*all* men, which she often intimated in various letters she wrote in the years after her husband's death and during the ongoing settlement of his estate. She once wrote that she and her daughters would "be skinned by the 'dozens of men'" and that they (the DeVitt women) "will gradually pay out of our own purses." She also wrote about how much she distrusted David Murphy and how he would probably use his "manly charm" to convince Helen to "side with him." In a letter to Christine, Florence admitted she had hated her husband, he had mistreated her, and she was "left with no one to love her."

The almost constant skirmishes between Christine and executors of the will, mother and daughter, and the DeVitt women against the Mallet Board as well as Sam Arnett and David Murphy entered a new phase in 1936. Christine began to insist that she be appointed manager of the ranch. The debate among Christine, the co-executors, and the Mallet Board over that question delayed the settlement of the estate until May 1936 when Arnett and Murphy presented to a Lubbock court the final settlement. Christine lost her bid to become the ranch manager as Arnett continued in that role. Florence DeVitt received the majority shares in the Mallet Land and Cattle Company—the shares her husband had held—but neither she nor Christine were placed on the Mallet Board. Mother and daughter then turned their attention to suing Arnett and Murphy for mismanaging their role as executors and charging a $100,000 fee as executors. The two women hired a Lubbock attorney to handle their case and filed in Lubbock County district court, but a judge ultimately dismissed the case. Christine continued to hound the Mallet Land and Cattle Company Board about their management of the ranch, directing most of her vitriol toward David Murphy, whom she and her mother had decided was the villain in the settlement of David DeVitt's estate. Murphy grew so tired of the hounding that he gave up his seat on the board in favor of Christine at the June 1937 board meeting.

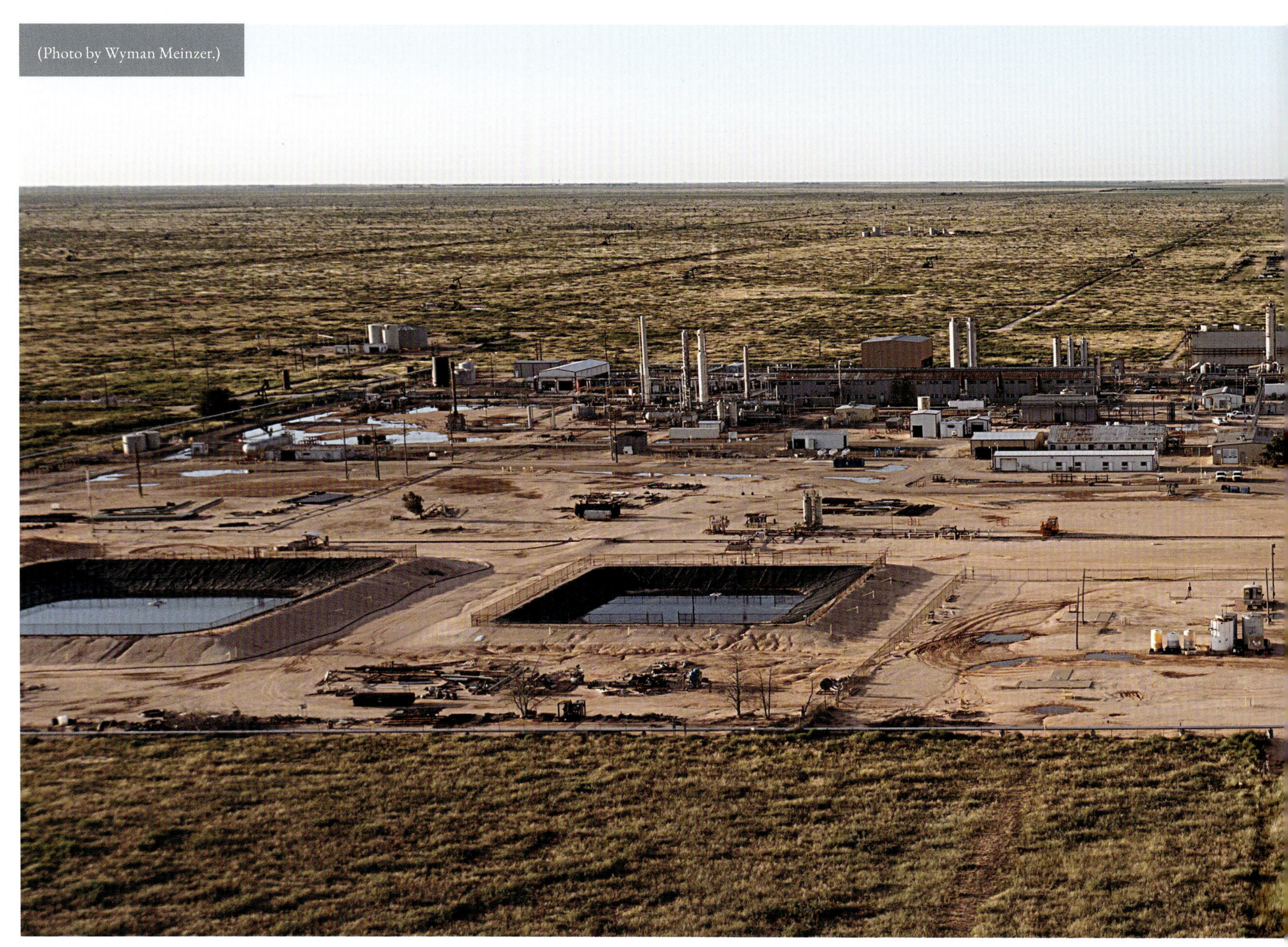

(Photo by Wyman Meinzer.)

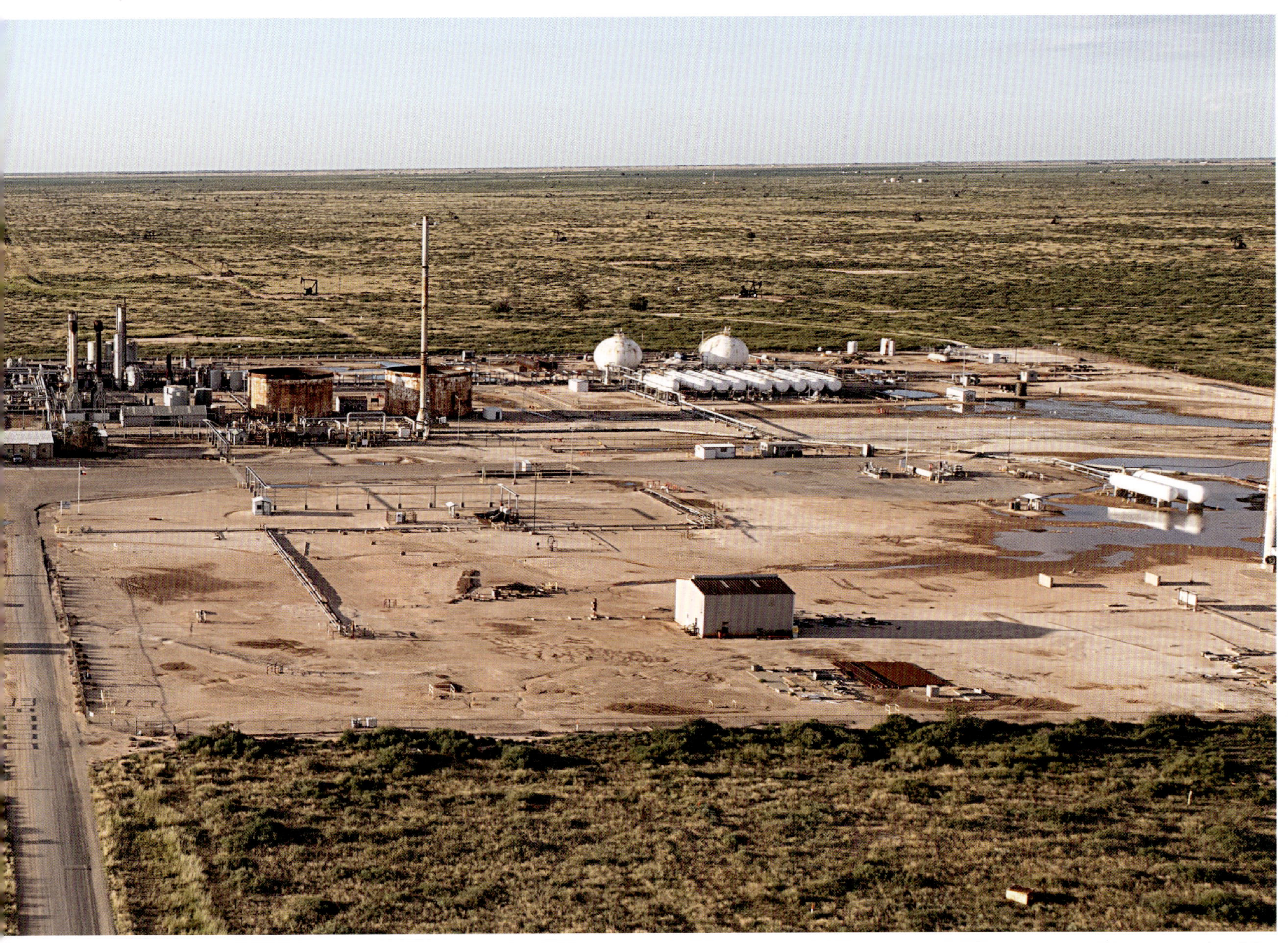

David DeVitt's daughter now sat on the Board of Directors of the Mallet Land and Cattle Company. If her partners thought Christine would cause less consternation inside the tent than on the outside, they would once again be mistaken.

David DeVitt had tried to take advantage of the potential for oil deposits under Mallet land in the early 1930s when he was searching for a way to make the ranch profitable. He had solicited leases, mostly from Fort Worth firms that he was familiar with, but oilmen during that period were first more interested in pouring investment into the vast East Texas Oil Field and, as the 1930s wore on, in protecting assets from the worsening Great Depression. DeVitt died not knowing that he was correct about what would save the Mallet Ranch. It was just that his timing was off. Producers had stayed away from West Texas during the early 1930s because there was no need to even try to compete with the East Texas gushers. Also, West Texas sour crude was much more expensive to refine than the sweet crude coming from the East Texas wells.

But oilmen came back to West Texas in the mid and late 1930s. The major corporations led the way because they could outlay the tremendous costs to drill deeper as well as transport what they found, but by 1936 and 1937, the "majors" began to sell many of their leases to smaller independents, and it would be those oil firms that would lead the new production attempts first in West Texas and then on the South Plains where the Mallet lay. West Texas farmers and ranchers began to welcome these oilmen with open arms. The long drought of the 1920s, the falling commodity prices, and then the blow of the Great Depression had devastated the region. It would be the search for petroleum that would bring the region back from the brink of economic ruin.

The initial discoveries of petroleum near the Mallet came on land formerly owned by DeVitt's old rival, C. C. Slaughter. Oil speculators first became interested in what would become known as the Slaughter Field in the late 1920s when a California company—Honolulu Oil—drilled test wells in 1927. They only found small deposits before conditions forced them to end speculation in 1930. Two different operators returned to the region in 1936, one exploring in Hockley County and the other in Cochran. Cascade Petroleum enlisted Honolulu and Devonian Petroleum as partners to defray costs, leased thousands of acres of land in Cochran County, and began to drill in February 1936 while the Texas Company began to drill in April of that year in Hockley County. The Cascade play, known as the Duggan No. 1-A, brought oil at just over 5,000 feet in October 1936. It would produce almost 400 barrels of oil per day for more than a decade. The find began a mini-boom as drillers leased and explored southeast into Terry County, and subsequent wells could produce nearly 40,000 barrels of oil a day by the end of 1937.

Efforts of the Texas Company in Hockley County south of Cascade's well in Cochran County produced a significant find on former C. C. Slaughter land with the Bob Slaughter No. 1 well. It also hit oil at just over 5,000 feet and produced 512 barrels of oil a day. The Texas Company began to move into other areas and acquire leases, including one on the Mallet, and then to drill numerous wells in what became known as the

Slaughter Field in 1938. Eventually—after the Texas Company discovered oil on Mallet lands—it became apparent that the Duggan and Slaughter fields were not separate pools but two parts of one pool, and the entire producing area became known as the Slaughter Field, one of the most valuable oil-producing discoveries in Texas history, a field that still produces oil today.

W. D. Johnson, who had tried to convince DeVitt to be more aggressive in pursuing petroleum opportunities, became more successful in such entreaties after Sam Arnett took over management of the Mallet after DeVitt's death and with Texas oilmen once again considering West Texas oil plays as a possibility. Arnett, with David Murphy acting as legal adviser, negotiated a lease with the Texas Company. The company began to drill the first oil well on Mallet land that David DeVitt had secured in 1899, Scurry County school land west of the Hockley County line. The Texas Company's 1-A Mallet Land and Cattle Company struck oil in May 1938, a well that would produce more than 700 barrels a day. It also was their discovery that led the Texas Railroad Commission to link the Duggan and Slaughter Fields into one pool. Companies would continue to explore on Mallet lands. Thirty-four producing oil wells were on the Mallet by 1940, generating 175,000 barrels of oil between 1938 and 1940. The oil discovery would change the direction of the Mallet and lead to an accumulation of wealth that not only sustained the DeVitt sisters for the duration of their lives but also spurred one of the most significant philanthropic endeavors in Texas history. Eventually getting to that point, however, would be anything but easy and would begin a war between the partners of the Mallet Land and Cattle Company that would cause a complete reorganization of the corporation.

When Christine DeVitt assumed David Murphy's position on the company's board, she immediately began to question Arnett's and Johnson's direction, decision-making, and conducting of Mallet business. Among the primary focuses of her ire were the leases that Arnett and Murphy had negotiated. Christine, as well as her mother, obviously resented the influence and control that Johnson and Arnett wielded on the ranch their father and husband had founded. Christine in particular thought that W. D. Johnson had taken advantage of her father late in his life and intended to do the same to her mother. Both women believed that the men eventually wanted to move them out of any ownership or control over the Mallet and secure it wholly for themselves. Florence expressed as much in a number of letters to Christine—temporarily transferring her ire from her elder daughter to the two officers of the Mallet Land and Cattle Company.

Christine, both before and after she came on the Mallet board, had made it a habit to oppose and criticize almost every oil lease that Arnett negotiated and Johnson signed. In fact, Johnson would complain in a letter that "Christine opposes everything we do," and for the next three years the Mallet Land and Cattle Company partners found little agreement on anything to do with the Mallet Ranch. Every dispute also had the same model: Christine (and Florence) on one side and the other partners on the other. The text of letters between Florence and Christine as well as correspondence between Christine and

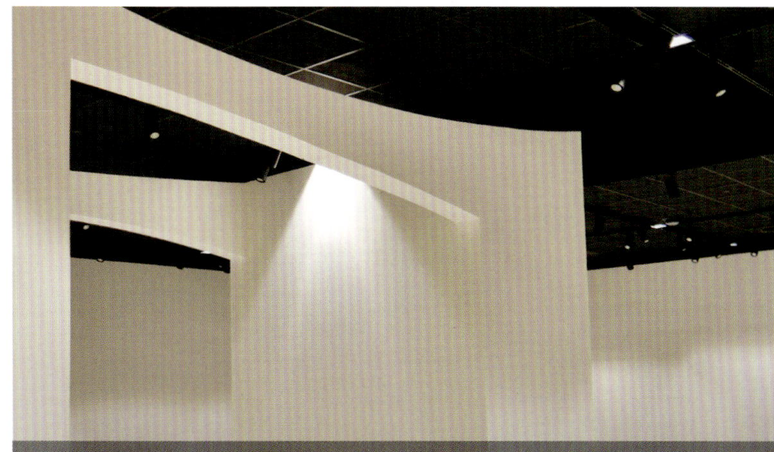

The Helen Jones Foundation, Inc. has supported a new wing to house the collections of Dr. Robert Neff and Louise Willson Arnold. The Arnold Wing displays the couple's extensive art collection, while also expanding collection storage and office space for the Museum of Texas Tech University, which provided these images.

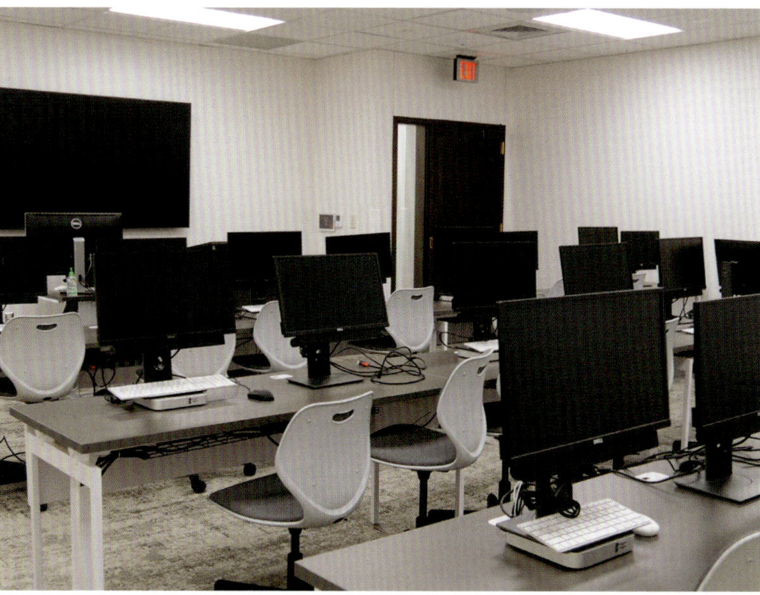

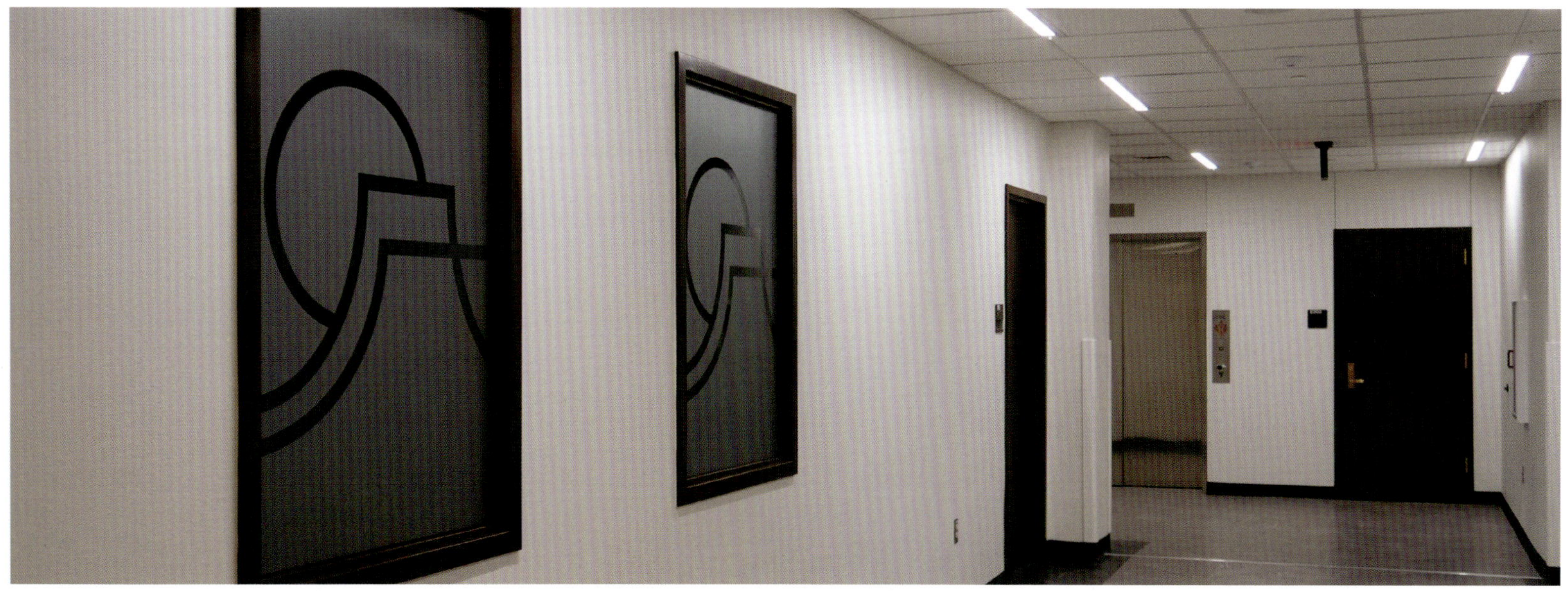

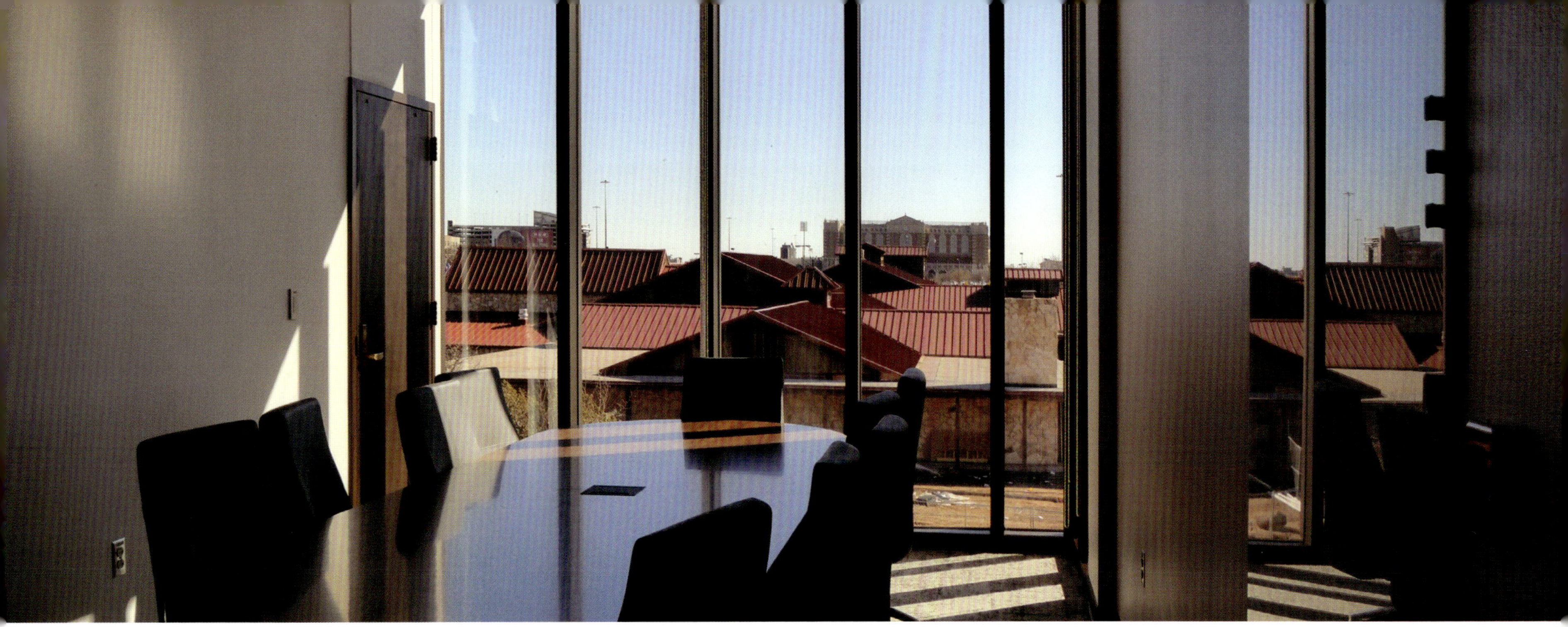

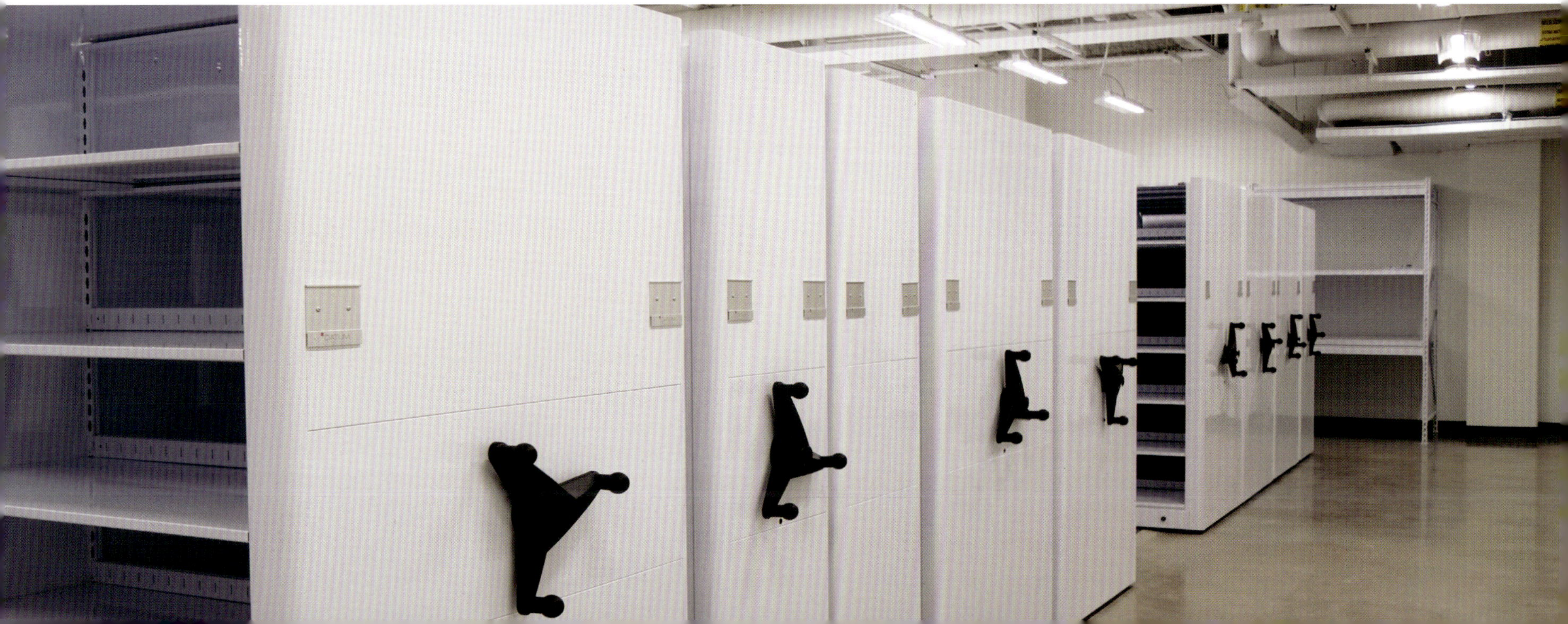

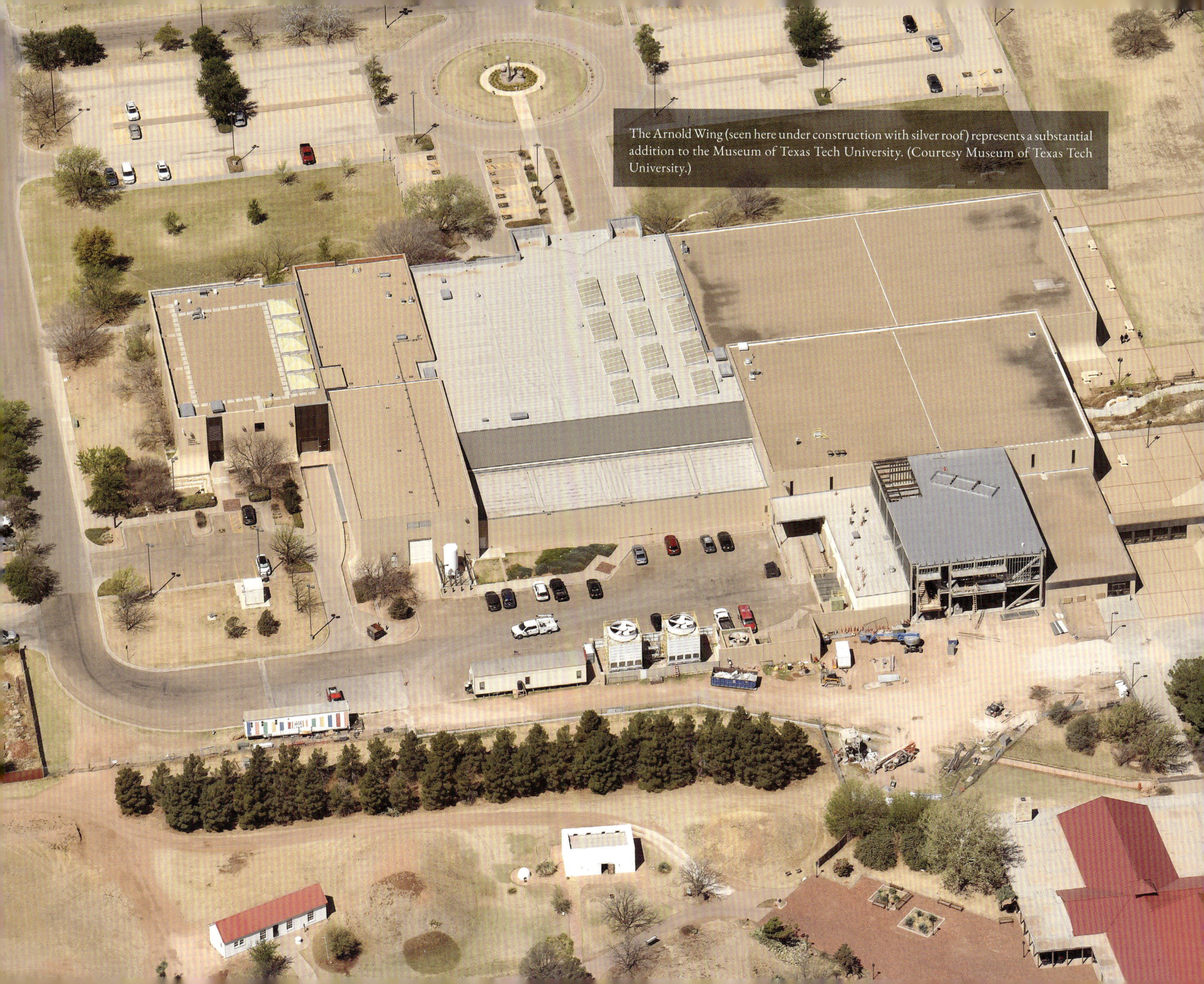

The Arnold Wing (seen here under construction with silver roof) represents a substantial addition to the Museum of Texas Tech University. (Courtesy Museum of Texas Tech University.)

board members carries some of the same tone of both women not trusting men—any men—they encountered in their lives. When Florence DeVitt received a letter from David Murphy that gushed about the news of the oil strikes, she wrote to Christine that while she welcomed the news, she thought that Murphy "has good, even better reason to be pleased than we have," suggesting—again—her suspicion that the men were either hiding something from Christine and Florence or working nefariously to make sure it benefitted them more than the DeVitt heirs.

While Florence and Christine DeVitt wrangled over the estate, oil leases, and other Mallet Land and Cattle Company business, Helen DeVitt Secrest, after her divorce, seemed content to live out her life in Los Angeles with her daughter Dorothy. Helen and Christine had a relationship that vacillated between distant and close, but because of their age difference the bond between the two women was more like that of mother and daughter than two sisters. Helen, like her mother, allowed Christine to hold her proxy in any votes within the Mallet Land and Cattle Company Board—proxies that gave Christine her power and forced Johnson and the board to quite often give in to her wishes. Helen took very little interest in Mallet business other than to make sure that she received her share of any profits the company produced. Helen and Dorothy did not live extravagantly. Their house in Los Angeles was certainly not grand, but neither did they subsist as paupers. Just as she did when her father was alive, Helen occasionally asked her mother and/or sister for additional funds beyond what her shares of the Mallet produced. Christine usually took the opportunity to lecture her about living frugally, but she presumably complied with Helen's request.

Florence DeVitt obviously favored Helen, who visited her often in her small bungalow in Los Angeles. Both women shared an affinity for visiting various sanitariums, health resorts, and doctors for personal wellness. Mother and daughter had lunch together often and their conversation, if it resembled many of their letters, likely centered on complaining or wondering about Christine, how she was living in Lubbock, and the tension with the Mallet board. Still, Helen preferred to remain in the background, although that would change as she would be thrust, along with her mother and sister, into another fight for the control and direction of the Mallet Ranch. Once again, there would be disputes between partners, sides to take, and a battle over who would control the ranch and the business. The fight in the future would once again transform the direction of the Mallet Ranch, the DeVitt family, and decades of philanthropy on the South Plains of Texas.

CHAPTER 5

CHRISTINE IN CONTROL

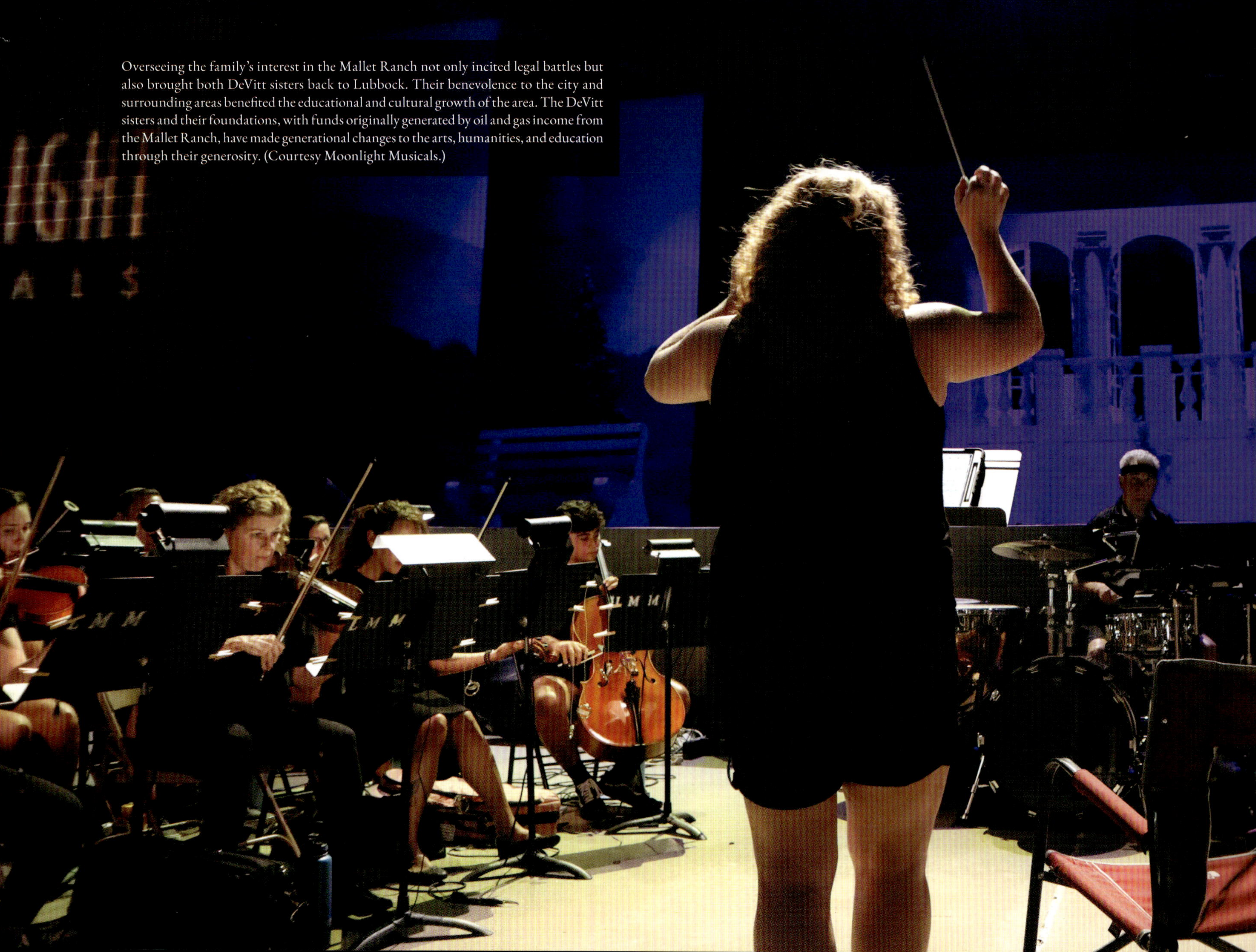

Overseeing the family's interest in the Mallet Ranch not only incited legal battles but also brought both DeVitt sisters back to Lubbock. Their benevolence to the city and surrounding areas benefited the educational and cultural growth of the area. The DeVitt sisters and their foundations, with funds originally generated by oil and gas income from the Mallet Ranch, have made generational changes to the arts, humanities, and education through their generosity. (Courtesy Moonlight Musicals.)

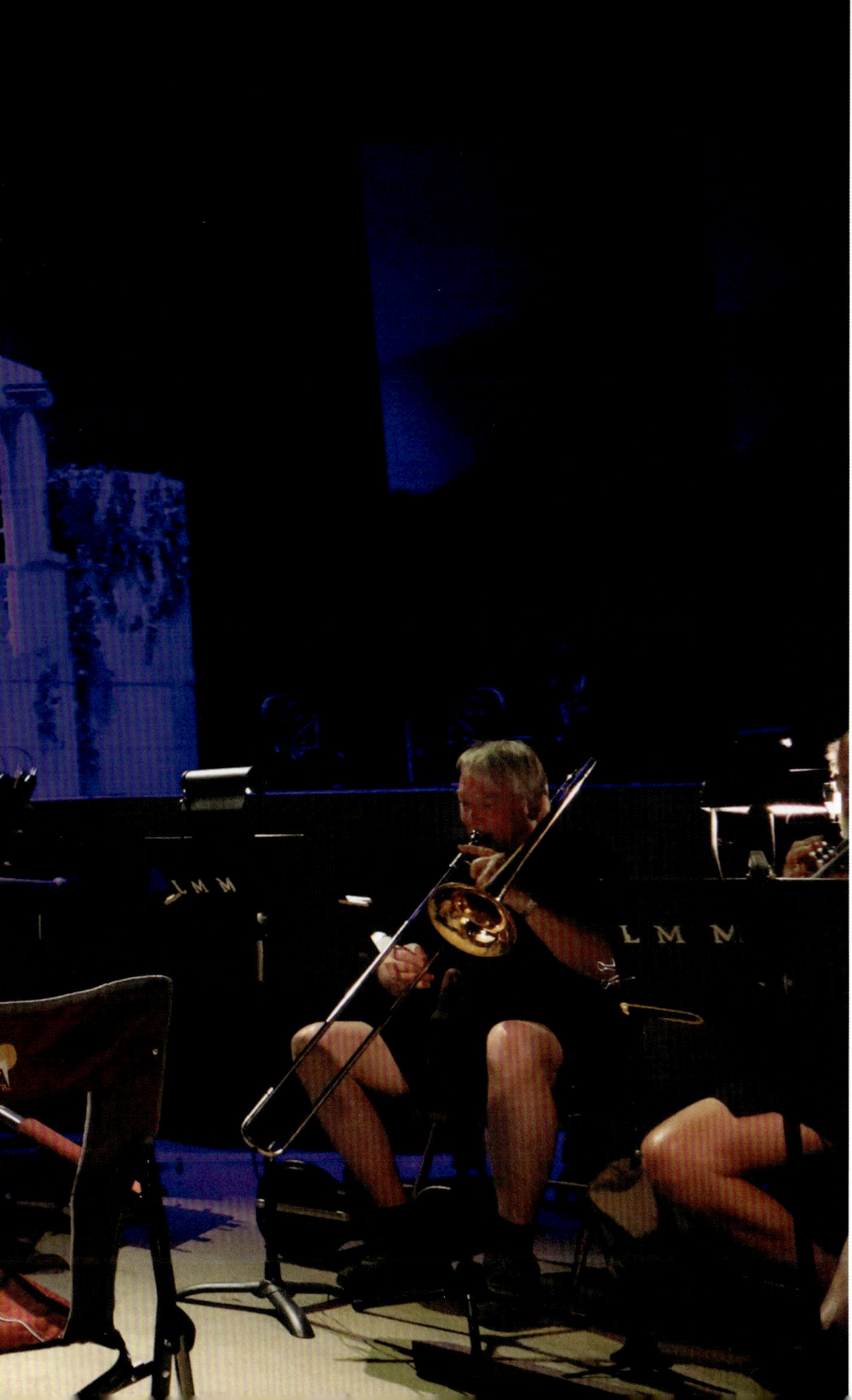

When Christine DeVitt left California and traveled to Lubbock after her father passed away in 1934, she made no sign that she would be once again taking up residence in Texas, especially not in Lubbock. She may have visited a time or two before—although that is not exactly clear from the records—but Lubbock was not a place where she had ever indicated any desire to reside. She had seemingly left Texas behind and all that it contained when she departed in 1921 to join her mother and sister in the Golden State. David DeVitt, whose primary Texas residence was the Hilton Hotel in Lubbock, also had begun preparations in the last days of his life to leave Texas for California as soon as he could sell the Mallet Ranch.

Christine DeVitt was forty-nine when her father passed away. She was unmarried in a time when women of such an age who remained single were subject to whispers and innuendo, and often referred to by the derisive term of "old maid." Most of all, Christine had spent her childhood years living in a home in which her mother's and father's relationship was distant, at best, and likely contentious most of the time. She had briefly escaped such a life when she left home for school and subsequently taught for a brief period in Fort Worth, but she was drawn back into having to be a companion and care for her mother once again when she was in her mid-thirties. Such a reality meant that Christine's ambitions and plans for life once again took a backseat to familial obligations. Christine no doubt loved her father and mother as only a child can love their parents, but she also resented the turns her life had taken and seemed to blame both her parents for the outcome. Her father often left his family alone to pursue his economic ideas, and when he did take time away from running the Mallet he spent most of it in the company of his male friends as well as younger females whose ages meant they were anything but peers. Her mother—a woman whose fate to live within a lonely marriage had made her an angry, unhappy companion—often took her bitterness out on her elder daughter, and Christine learned to give back as good as she got.

Christine most likely had every intention of overseeing the family's interest in her father's estate and then returning to California—or, perhaps, securing her inheritance and returning to reside in Fort Worth once again. However, once in Lubbock she found some contentment, a place in which she could be independent, control her fate, and enjoy life as a woman of means, and doing so in Lubbock would be much easier than in Los Angeles. Thus, Christine found a home, a place where she would live for the remaining fifty years of her life. She would become the wealthiest person in the city, and her adopted hometown would become the most significant beneficiary of her philanthropy in her later years.

Lubbock, Texas, was younger than Christine herself. As early as 1884 a post office denoting "Lubbock" existed at Singer's Store in Yellowhouse Canyon. The city of Lubbock came into existence through the "merger" in 1890 of two earlier settlements: "old" Lubbock and Monterey. The new unincorporated town took the name of the county, which was organized in 1876 and named for Thomas S. Lubbock, a Confederate colonel who died of typhoid fever in Kentucky during the Civil War. He was the brother of Texas governor Francis R. Lubbock. The town grew slowly but steadily after its founding, primarily due to its location in the center of the South Plains, thus its moniker of the "Hub City." The influx of stock operations and farmers in all directions of the city made Lubbock a marketing center. The key change for the settlement came in 1909 when first the city incorporated in March of that year, and then in October when the Santa Fe Railroad came through. Lubbock now grew more rapidly, and by 1920 its population had almost tripled in twenty years to 4,051. The town gained a regional hospital (what would become Methodist Hospital, now Covenant Medical Center) in 1917, and in the same year opened a state-of-the-art electrical plant. The crowning jewel in Lubbock's ascension from rural frontier town to a burgeoning city of regional importance came in 1923 when the Texas legislature authorized the building of Texas Technological College (now Texas Tech University) in the city. From that point on the city's growth began to skyrocket, and by the time Christine DeVitt came to Lubbock its population had risen to almost 50,000.

When she came to Lubbock, Christine moved into the downtown Hilton Hotel, where she would live until she was famously evicted in 1948 for paying her rent late on numerous occasions and leaving trash and other detritus in her room. Her presence in Lubbock meant that she was ready to apply her authority not only to the settling of her father's estate but also to

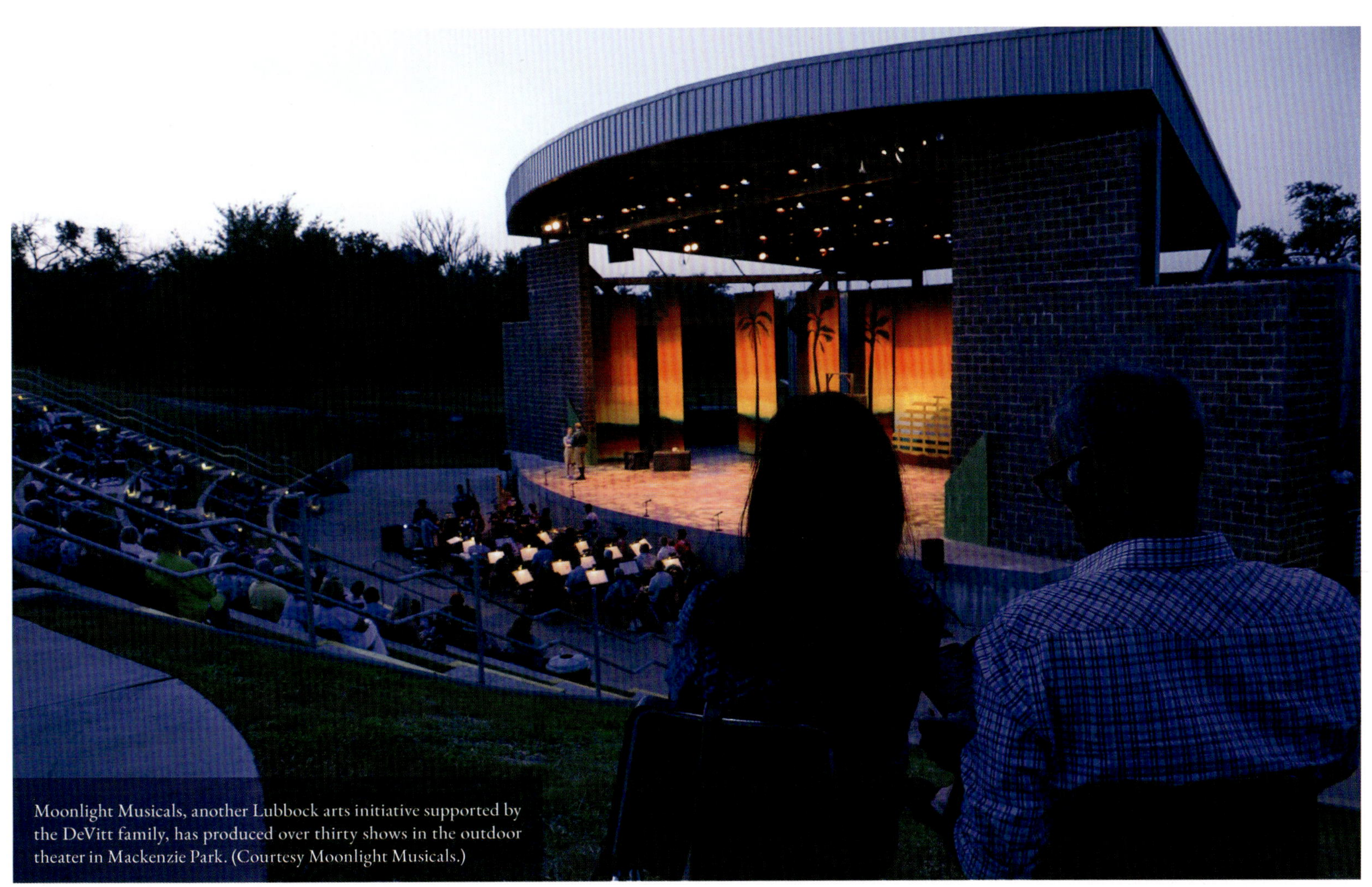

Moonlight Musicals, another Lubbock arts initiative supported by the DeVitt family, has produced over thirty shows in the outdoor theater in Mackenzie Park. (Courtesy Moonlight Musicals.)

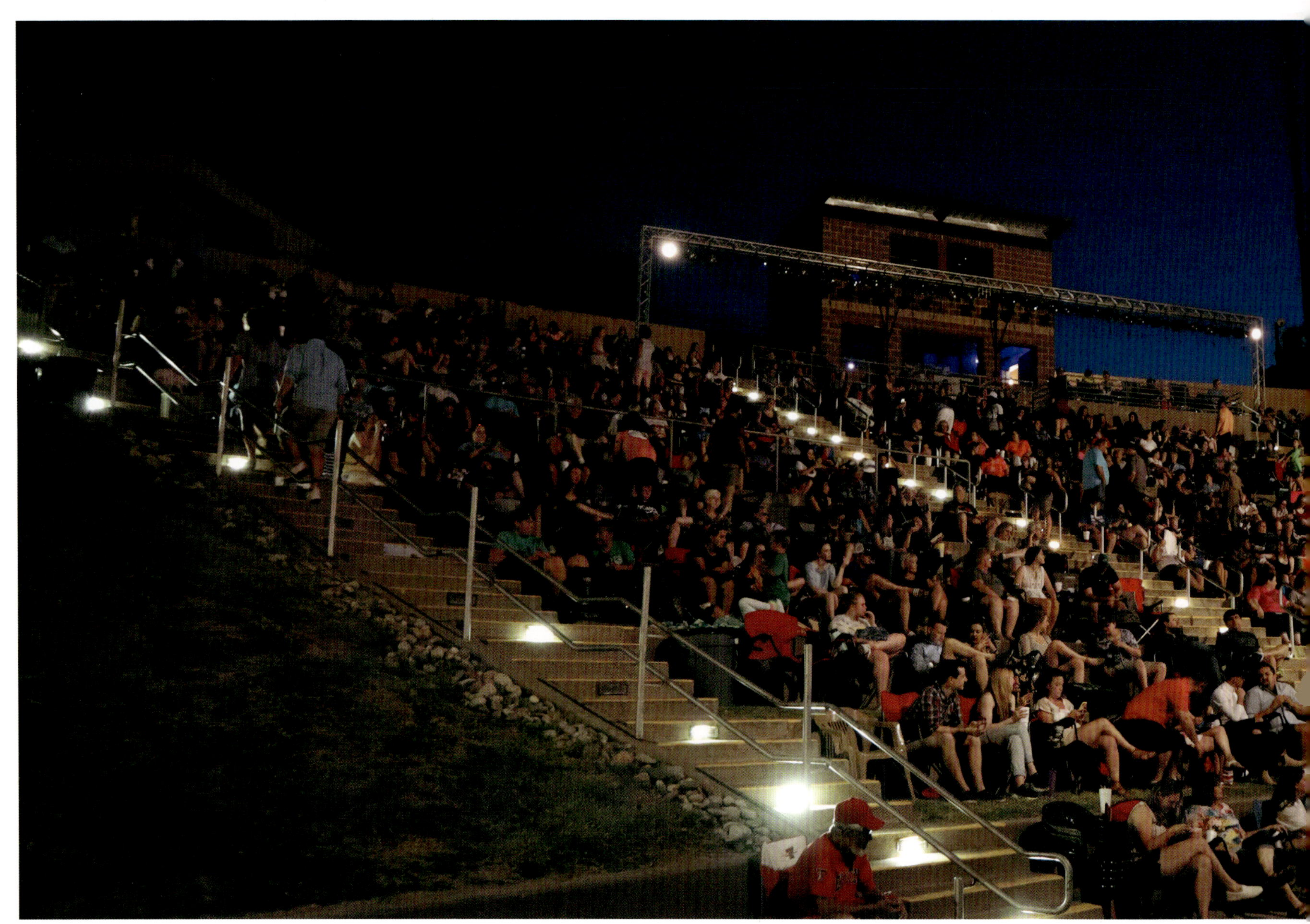

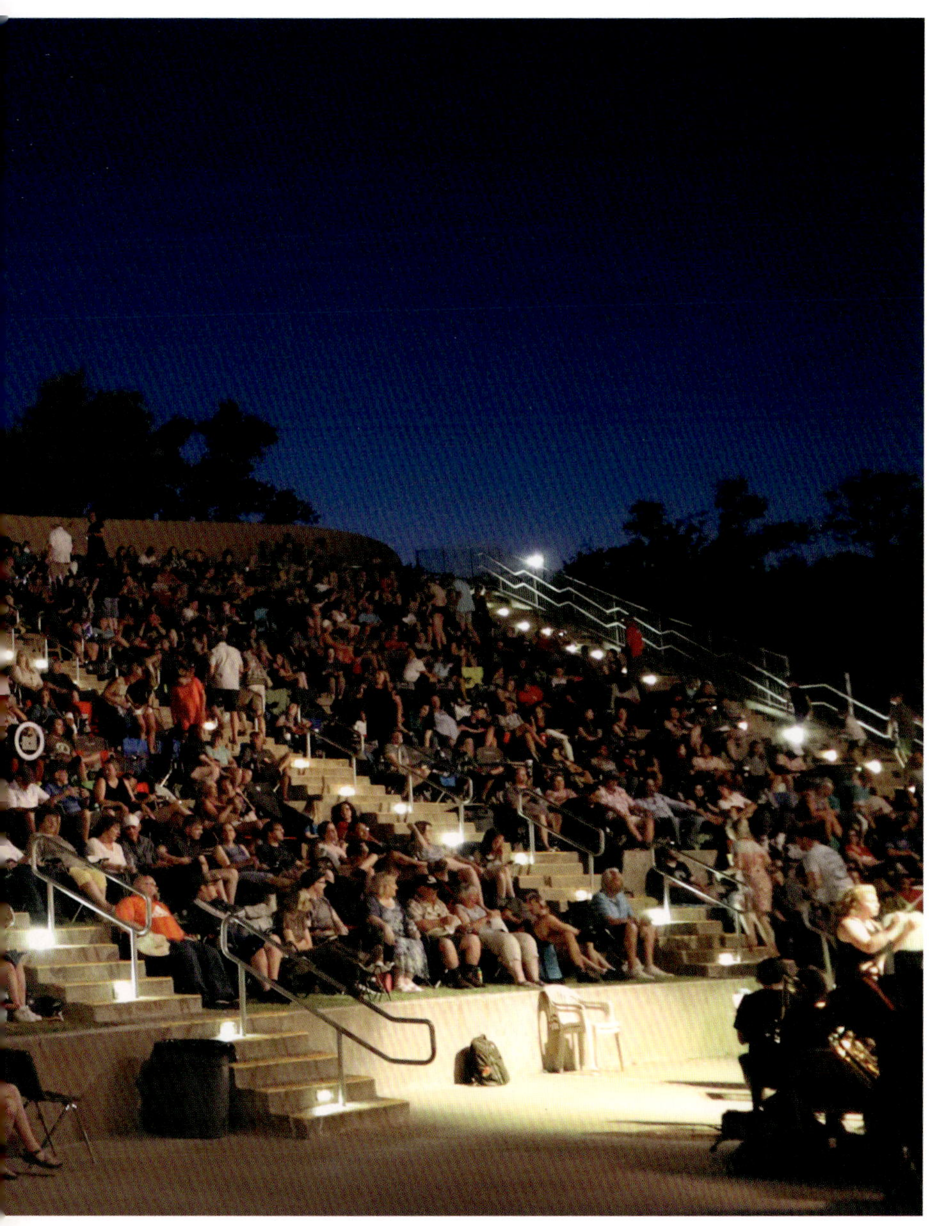

the business of the Mallet Land and Cattle Company; she made it no secret that what she wanted was not just influence but control. Her ascent onto the Mallet board only increased such a desire. In many ways Christine's approach to her spot on the Mallet board was a metaphor for the new direction of her life: she was going to exert command over her economic life just as she had begun to exert more supervision over her personal life.

Christine's insistence on influence and to be taken seriously on the Mallet board had its greatest effect on the relationship with oil companies now that the Mallet was in the middle of large-scale petroleum exploration. Oil deposits had saved the Mallet. The total net income for the Mallet Ranch in 1935 was only $19,035, but by 1939 that net income had boomed to over $150,000, almost entirely due to the wells that the Texas Company had begun to produce in 1938. After the proof of oil on the Mallet, oil companies were now clamoring to obtain leases to explore for petroleum underneath Mallet lands.

The steps required before any oil well is drilled take time, but generally drilling companies—if they are convinced oil is present—want to move as quickly as possible. What has to happen early in the process is the negotiation of a lease with landowners to get permission to conduct geological tests, drill test wells, prepare a drilling site, then—finally—begin to drill a well. Paramount to beginning the process is to agree on a lease for a certain price per acre (often called "bonus money"), which involves a contract and signatures by all interested parties. Sam Arnett, with assistance from W. D. Johnson and David Murphy, had handled the bulk of negotiations for the Mallet since the first well on the ranch, and Johnson, as president, had signed the leases. When Christine DeVitt took her place on the board in 1937—replacing David Murphy—that process began to slow, primarily because Christine insisted on checking every paragraph, sentence, word, even punctuation mark in each lease. Reviewing the language in any transactional contract is good business sense, but Christine took this examination to another level.

Christine DeVitt, much like her mother, did not trust men. Lawyers met with some of her most intense disdain. She also, especially, did not trust oilmen, and she had particular distrust for her business partners with an intense wariness of W. D. Johnson, whom she regarded as wholly self-centered and engrossed only in removing the DeVitts from any interest in the Mallet. Johnson, for his part, could be overbearing and used to getting his way, but his leadership of the Mallet as well as the myriad other businesses in which he had interest consistently produced profits. It would be natural that he and Christine would clash. Christine had another proclivity that would not only drive her partners crazy but also become a part of any business she conducted the rest of her life: she was a world-class procrastinator. She operated on her own time, and nothing could make her move any faster.

Christine's suspicious nature, combined with her proclivity to meticulously—and slowly—analyze any and all business documents, caused Mallet decisions on oil, or any other matter before it, to grind to a virtual halt. She stalled every oil lease that came before the board and even hindered the little stock and farm business that remained on the ranch. W. D. Johnson, who as president perhaps could have pushed Christine more firmly to give her approval, began to avoid direct confrontation with his partner. He often fumed about Christine's reluctance in private correspondence to Arnett and Murphy, who still served as the Mallet Land and Cattle Company's attorney, but publicly he treated Christine with kid gloves, which was easier since Christine was on the board but not an officer. Johnson still held a lot of power.

The business of leases on Mallet land slowed due to Christine's fastidious nature, but events and conditions in the nation and the world meant that the search for oil would rapidly expand. Japan had begun to move to take and control the rich oil fields of South Asia as early as 1938, and by the time Germany invaded Poland in 1939 the world was on the way to being plunged into World War II. A full-scale war of the size that now raged across Europe greatly increased the demand for petroleum, and huge reserves of that commodity waited for recovery beneath hundreds of thousands of acres in Texas, including huge swaths of the Mallet Ranch. The Texas Railroad Commission (TRC) realized the potential for the extraction of Texas oil and how the skyrocketing demand had caused an equal rise in the price of oil, outlays that could begin to refill the state's treasury that had been so depleted by the Great Depression. So, the TRC responded in what seemed to be a curious fashion, but one that made sense on some levels. The TRC's primary method of regulating oil and gas was to practice "prorationing," or restricting, how much petroleum a single well could produce. They restricted the number of days a well could pump on the theory that they could then control production of Texas oil—the richest oil fields in the world—and thus control

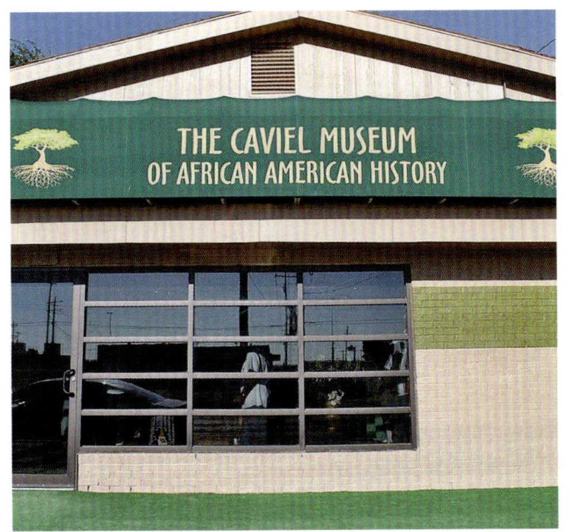

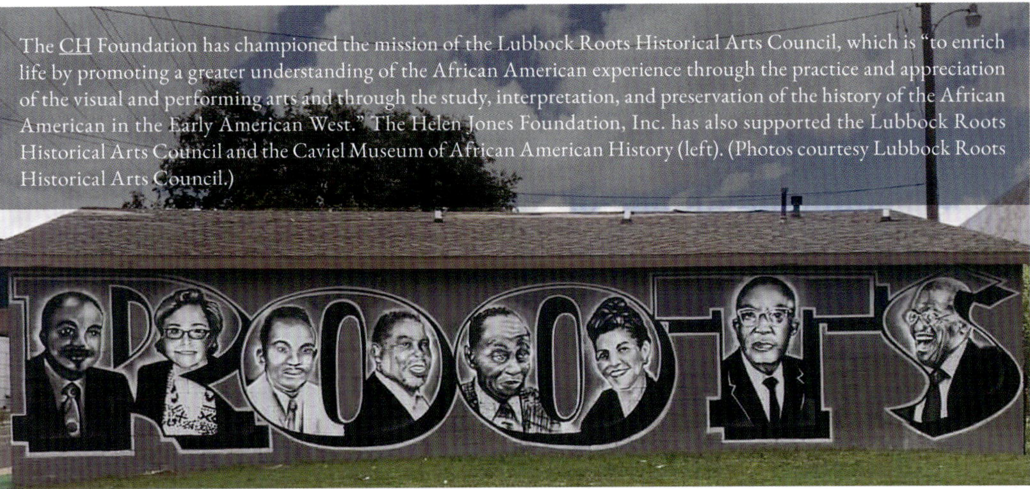

The CH Foundation has championed the mission of the Lubbock Roots Historical Arts Council, which is "to enrich life by promoting a greater understanding of the African American experience through the practice and appreciation of the visual and performing arts and through the study, interpretation, and preservation of the history of the African American in the Early American West." The Helen Jones Foundation, Inc. has also supported the Lubbock Roots Historical Arts Council and the Caviel Museum of African American History (left). (Photos courtesy Lubbock Roots Historical Arts Council.)

the price of oil. This is akin to what the OPEC+ nations do in the current market.

Prorationing meant that oil drilling companies wanted to secure and drill as many wells as it possibly could; more wells meant—even with the restrictions of prorationing—more production. Thus in 1940 and 1941 the Mallet Land and Cattle Company was inundated with requests to lease and drill oil wells, and by the end of 1940 the Mallet Ranch was dotted with more than a hundred wells and was seemingly fully on its way to tripling, even quadrupling, that number. The Mallet Land and Cattle Company office in Kansas City was inundated with requests for leases, but Christine DeVitt now stood as an obstacle to swift transactions. She had replaced Sam Arnett as vice president of the board in 1940, and as an officer she now moved to exert as much control as she possibly could over Mallet business.

True to her nature, she questioned and stalled every lease that came before the board. With Arnett no longer an officer of the company, W. D. Johnson took on the task of negotiating leases, and he began to work on a substantial one with the Canadian Texas Oil Company. Johnson was a wealthy man whose yearly income exceeded the DeVitt family's total by several times, which caused him to have very different personal concerns over the language in the contracts. The United States government, in 1940, placed a hefty tax on income such as oil lease "bonus money," and depending on the transaction, that tax could be as high as 75 percent. Johnson wanted to avoid that tax as much as possible, so he negotiated language that waived bonus money for a higher royalty from the oil company. The oil companies were happy with such language as it saved them a cash outlay before any production of oil; bonus money came upfront and was thus paid whether the company drilled a dry hole or not. Johnson was happy to avoid income tax. Christine DeVitt, on behalf of her mother and sister, was not happy with such an arrangement. Their income depended solely on revenue from the Mallet, and the bonus money—even with the high tax applied—represented a large part of their yearly income. Johnson, backed into a corner by Christine's persistence, agreed and let Christine take over negotiations with Canadian Texas. His decision would soon have repercussions and send the Mallet Land and Cattle Company into a serious legal tussle.

As wells from previous leases began production on the Mallet, many of which Christine contested but eventually signed off on, negotiations with Canadian Texas stalled. It was Christine who was primarily at fault. Her procrastination was in full bloom, and she would go months without answering the oil company about certain clauses and insertions in the potential contracts. W. D. Johnson noted in letters to his other partners that Christine's delay was potentially costing the Mallet significantly. Drilling had escalated along with the war in Europe throughout 1940, but the lease with Canadian Texas on untapped land on the periphery of the Mallet went unsettled.

Johnson grew tired of waiting on Christine to take action, so he called an unscheduled meeting of the Mallet Land and Cattle Company Board of Directors to convene in Kansas City in January 1941, but Christine, backed by her mother and sister, refused to attend. With no quorum, Johnson had to reschedule more than ten times, and it was not until July 31 that the stockholders gathered. The agenda was a single item: a reformulation of the oil policy of the Mallet Land and Cattle Company.

While Christine dickered with W. D. Johnson over holding the board meeting, a crack began to open in the façade of solidarity within the DeVitt family. The relationship between Christine and her sister Helen had long been erratic. The age difference made it difficult for each to relate to the other, and Christine's habit of criticizing Helen's choice of almost anything—something she shared with her mother—often strained their bond. In many ways Helen adored her sister, which made submission to her natural. Helen's nonconfrontational character also tended to make her more tolerant of Christine's demands, but Christine's personality often subsumed Helen's quieter nature. Christine resented the more affectionate relationship that existed between Helen and Florence and took that resentment out mostly on Florence, but it sometimes leaked onto Helen. Still, when it came to most family decisions, Helen continued to accede to Christine's wishes until it came to the Canadian Texas oil lease. Then she did not.

David Murphy, the former board member and attorney for the Mallet Land and Cattle Company, began corresponding with the younger DeVitt daughter and, while not overtly critical, began to lobby Helen to reconsider giving Christine her share proxy so that company business could move more swiftly. Those proxies were important. With the combined proxies of all three DeVitt women, Christine could cast a majority vote on any Mallet business and had done so numerous times. Murphy's entreaties worked, though, and Helen startled her sister by attending the July 31 meeting. If Christine was surprised to see her sister in Kansas City, she was likely flabbergasted when it came time to vote. Helen voted with Johnson and against Christine. She was rewarded for her loyalty to the board president by then becoming a member of the Mallet Land and Cattle Company Board of Directors along with two other new members. One was Helen's ex-husband Bill Secrest, who because of his engineering experience was pushed for inclusion by W. D. Johnson. The other was J. Lee Johnson Jr., nephew of W. D. and son of former partner J. Lee, Johnson, who had died in 1937.

Christine vehemently protested the actions, but this time she did not have the votes. She continued to call for another vote, this time for all the directors to be voted on individually instead of collectively. Then she claimed that J. Lee Johnson Jr. "threw her across the room," although no one present corroborated her account. Christine next moved to remove W. D. Johnson as president and replace him with Bill Secrest as co-president and manager of the Mallet operations. She lost that one as well. Helen then moved that J. Lee Johnson Jr. become board vice president, replacing her sister. The board complied, and they then removed Christine from the Oil Lease Committee and restored to W. D. Johnson the power to negotiate leases. The Mallet Land and Cattle Company board members believed they had removed Christine DeVitt as a power on any decision-making concerning the Mallet. It also seemed as if the Johnson family—this time uncle and nephew—had returned as the nexus of power within the Mallet and perhaps harmony would reign. Again, as had happened so many times, such a thought was sorely incorrect. In fact, instead of harmony the Mallet was about to be thrown into a decade of turmoil, legal wrangling, and infighting that would once again threaten to destroy the ranch and its business.

W. D. Johnson and the other Mallet Land and Cattle Company Board members had staked out their position: they were making sure they controlled the business of the Mallet, and they wanted the DeVitt heirs to be nothing but silent partners. W. D. and J. Lee Johnson Sr. had accepted David DeVitt as their partner rather out of necessity than preference, and they were not reluctant to voice their opposition to many of his decisions as the operating partner. However, since David DeVitt had controlled the majority of shares, short of a legal challenge they could not remove him or go against his wishes. W. D. felt acutely that David's conservative management—particularly his lack of aggressive movement toward pursuing oil interests in the later years of his life—and continuance of "traditional" methods of running a stock operation had cost the brothers significant profits. DeVitt could have made more astute moves in the late 1920s and the early 1930s when the Mallet's fortunes began to sag. He was distracted by his desire to move from West Texas, but he likely also was drained from years of working to build the operation, struggling against the elements, and fighting legal battles with C. C. Slaughter and the Lazy S. In the last years of his life and faced with the Great Depression and other uncertainty, DeVitt may not have been up for another long battle. What he had wanted to do was sell the Mallet, leave Texas, and live the rest of his life in whatever luxury he could afford.

The DeVitt heirs faced fewer options and had begun to look at the Mallet differently. As long as the income from the operation sustained their lifestyle while David DeVitt was alive, the DeVitt women were content to sidestep the strain of dealing with ranch business. After his death, Florence's first instinct—and in many ways that of Christine and Helen—was to sell the ranch and continue to live in California. Florence had indeed urged Christine to agree to sell, and the latter initially seemed amenable to the idea, but that notion changed when she arrived in Lubbock. Perhaps the opportunity she had to survey the actual financial position of the Mallet modified her judgment. The reality was that the price they could have received from the Mallet may have been able to support Florence comfortably for the remainder of her life, but the futures of Christine and Helen would have been much less secure. Christine was nearing sixty by 1942 and not at an age to revive a teaching career, which was the only other occupation she had ever pursued. Or perhaps her change in attitude occurred when she saw for the first time in her life the opportunity to seize control and be an active actor in her life. Whatever caused her to look at the Mallet differently, Christine DeVitt was now committed not only to retaining her position on the board of the Mallet Land and Cattle Company but also to controlling the business and decisions.

After the July 31 meeting, Christine wasted little time in resorting to legal maneuvers. She hired a Kansas City firm to seek a restraining order with the argument that the Mallet officers had held an illegal election that should be voided. Furthermore, the petition stated, J. Lee Johnson Jr. had *physically* prevented her from entering the boardroom and thus "abrogated her rights." The District Court judge agreed with Christine's argument and granted a temporary restraining order that would prevent the Mallet Land and Cattle Company Board of Directors from "taking any action of any kind" until the court could hear from both sides and rule on the merits of the case.

W. D. Johnson, in his position of president, had scheduled a board meeting on August 25. The agenda was to discuss and tentatively approve the oil leases that Johnson had begun to negotiate with Canadian Texas, Honolulu Oil, and the Texas Company. When the members arrived at Mallet offices, they were met by a Jackson County, Missouri, deputy sheriff with the District Court's restraining order in his hand. He presented the order to W. D. Johnson, who told the assembled members that he had no choice but to adjourn the meeting. J. Lee Johnson Jr. was incensed and briefly confronted his uncle, urging him to ignore the order and continue, but the order was clear—it forbade the board from taking any action. Christine had won the first round, but the fight between Mallet Ranch partners was just beginning.

J. Lee Johnson Jr. decided he was going to take the fight directly to Christine DeVitt. Apparently against his uncle's wishes, J. Lee sent his lawyers to the 72nd District Court in Lubbock to file a shocking and potentially explosive petition. Johnson's attorney, J. Lee Klett, presented a brief to the district judge that asked him to take the bold action of putting the Mallet Land and Cattle Company into receivership. He requested that because the board was "hopelessly at an impasse due to Mrs. [*sic*] DeVitt's actions" that the judge appoint a receiver for the company so that the business could continue and the company would "incur no continued revenue loss." Klett, on behalf of J. Lee Johnson, had argued that Christine was "threatening to sue" any company that did business with the Mallet, and that inaction on oil leases could mean that all the oil under the Mallet could be drained by drilling outside the borders of the ranch. Judge Daniel Blair agreed with Klett's argument and appointed—perhaps not to J. Lee Johnson's surprise—Sam Arnett to be the Mallet Land and Cattle Company's receiver. The judge specifically noted in his order that Sam Arnett was to "proceed forthrightly" in negotiating leases with companies wishing to drill on the Mallet. Arnett went so far as to place advertisements in the *Lubbock Avalanche-Journal* inviting companies to submit leases as well as qualifications for potential approval. Arnett would negotiate the leases, but because the corporation was in receivership, Judge Blair would have to give final approval.

Although W. D. Johnson was named as a defendant in the suit, he was obviously aware of his nephew's strategy or at least had accepted it because he and J. Lee hosted Florence and Helen in a September 4 meeting in which they sought each woman's approval of the receivership and the judge's actions. They pointedly did not invite Christine, although Helen had informed her sister of what was to take place. Christine asked her sister in a telegram to "take clear and full notes of everything said." W. D. Johnson opened the meeting by detailing how Christine's delays, procrastination, and outright refusals had cost the company thousands of dollars in lost time and potentially lost oil leases. He claimed that at least "twenty wells" could already have been started if Christine had simply signed off on leases brought to the board. The DeVitts mostly kept silent at the meeting, although Florence did, at one point, state that "Christine was entitled to her turn at having the management." That led W. D. Johnson to explain, "Mrs. DeVitt, she has had control of the board all along," which was accurate since she controlled her shares and the proxies of Florence and Helen.

The Johnsons' exhortations had their effect, as Florence and Helen decided to accept the receivership and cast their lots with W. D. and J. Lee. Helen wrote to Christine that her elder sister had created "disorder" and that Helen and Florence "had no confidence in you whatsoever." At the end of her report to Christine about the meeting, Helen penned, "Don't count on me in your lawsuits." She and Florence signed the document that went to Judge Blair agreeing to the receivership. With all the stockholders in agreement except Christine DeVitt, and after hearing testimony from oilmen recruited by W. D. Johnson and Sam Arnett to state that the Mallet was suffering valuable losses every day that drilling did not commence, Judge Blair made Arnett the permanent receiver for the Mallet Land and Cattle Company, but he ordered Arnett to present each lease he negotiated to him for ultimate approval. Sam Arnett began to negotiate a number of new leases for the Mallet and, once again, it seemed as if the business of the Mallet Ranch would begin to move forward. Once again, perception and assumption would be incorrect.

While Arnett went to work on leases (his first attempt was the subject of more legal wrangling but eventually upheld), Helen DeVitt Secrest added to the legal intrigue and unrest

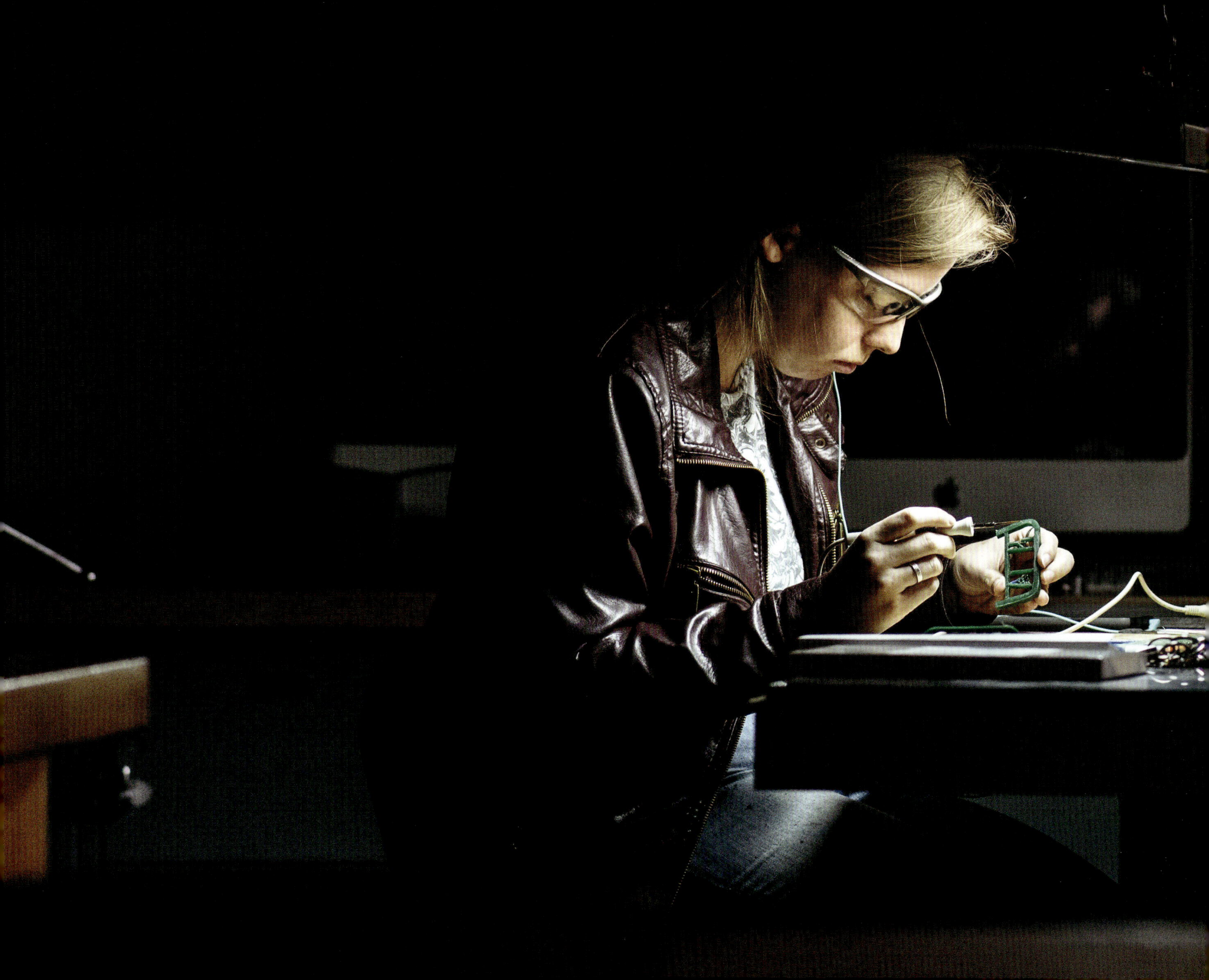

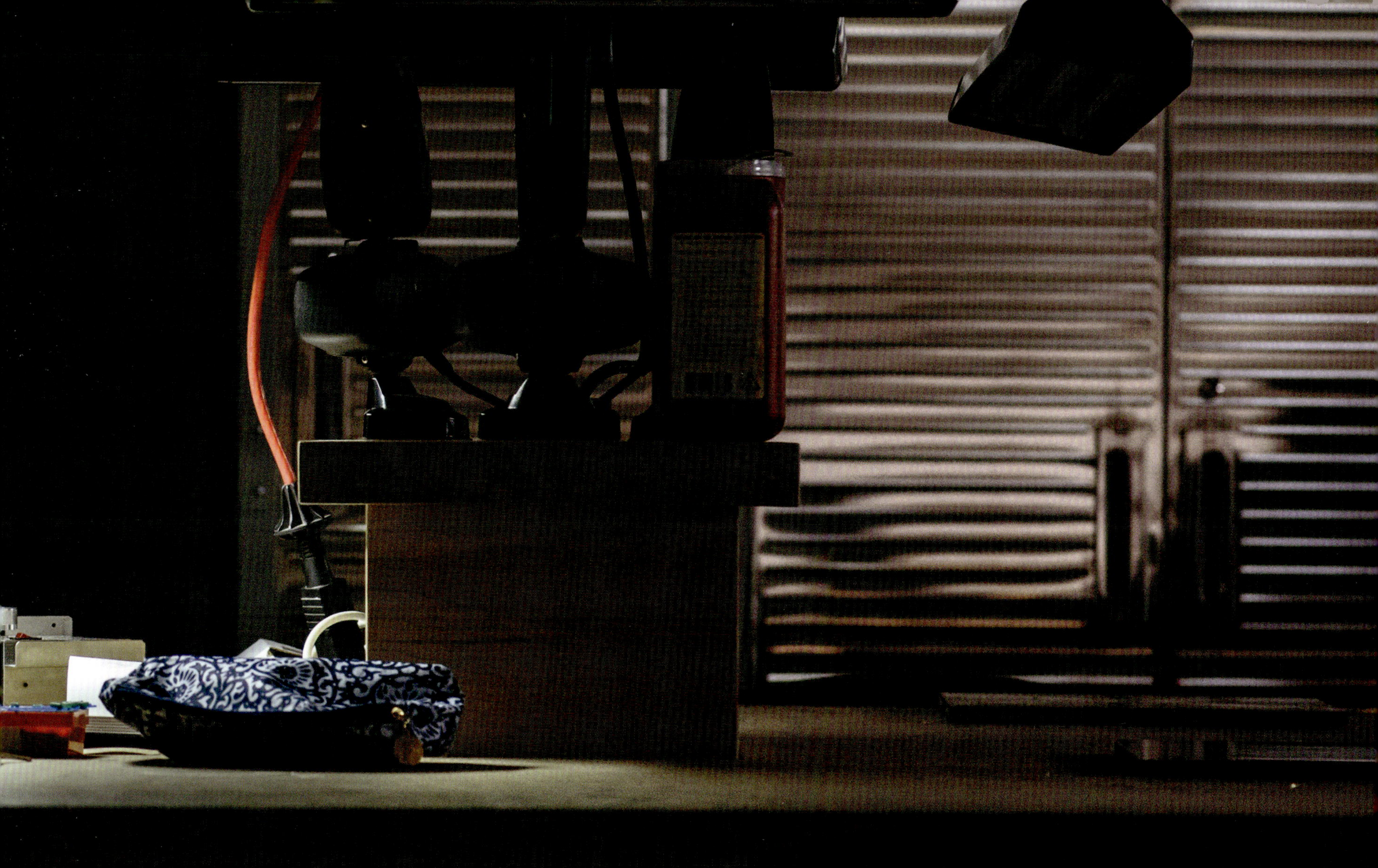

Undergraduate jewelry/metals student working in the 3D Annex Metals Lab within the School of Art, J.T. & Margaret Talkington College of Visual & Performing Arts, Texas Tech University. (Courtesy the J.T. & Margaret Talkington College of Visual & Performing Arts.)

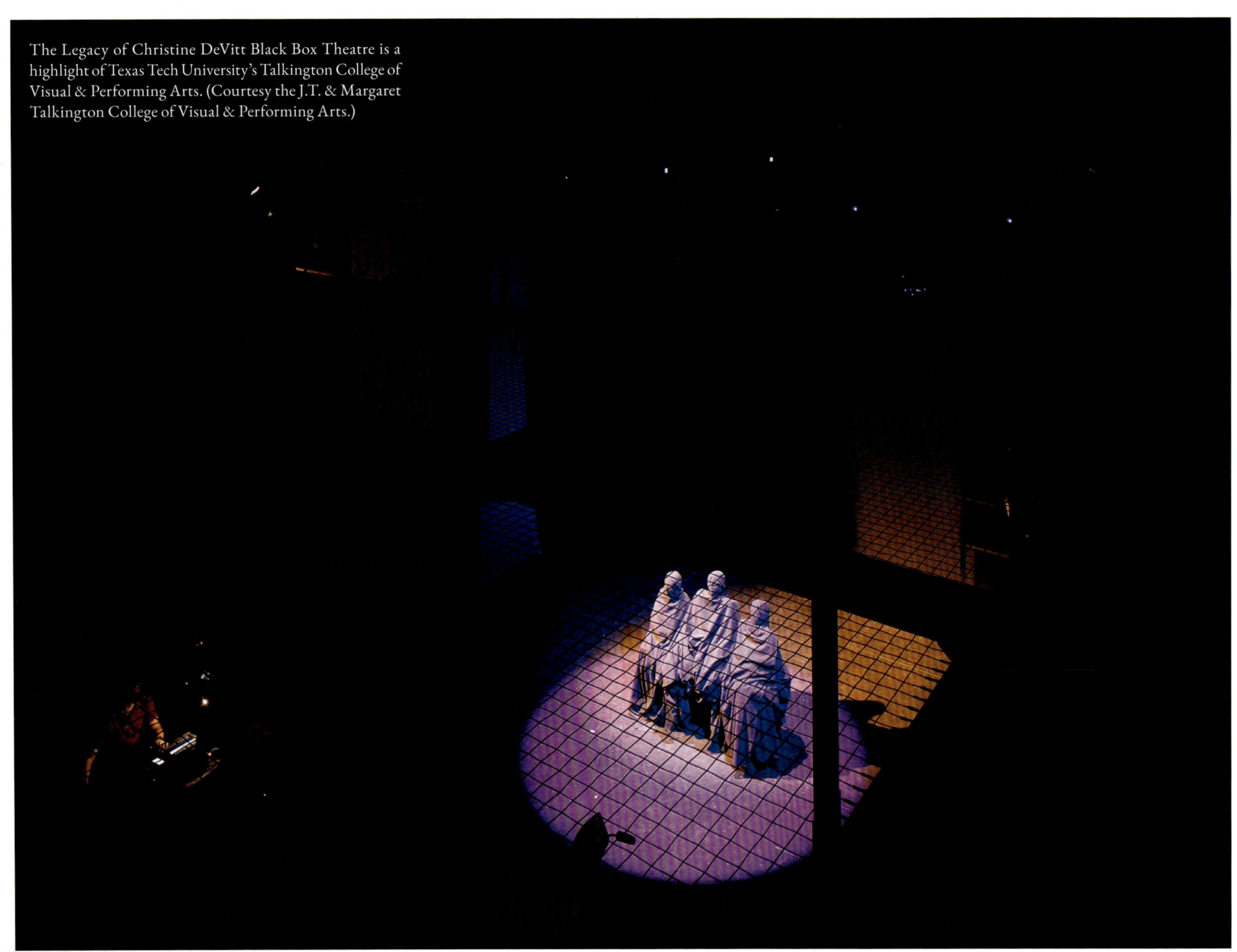

The Legacy of Christine DeVitt Black Box Theatre is a highlight of Texas Tech University's Talkington College of Visual & Performing Arts. (Courtesy the J.T. & Margaret Talkington College of Visual & Performing Arts.)

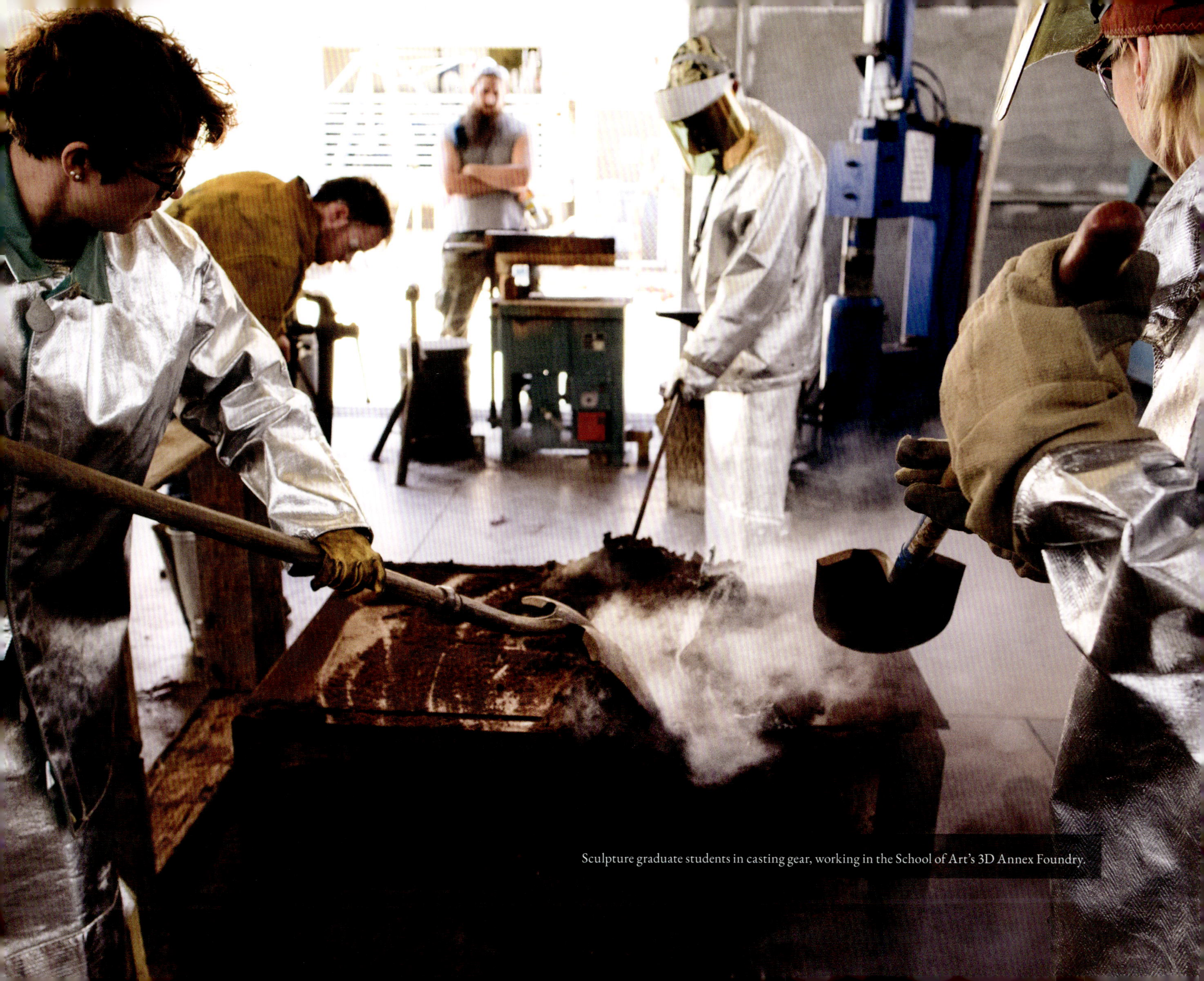

Sculpture graduate students in casting gear, working in the School of Art's 3D Annex Foundry.

surrounding the Mallet board in 1942. Helen had challenged Christine for the first time when she agreed to the receivership, and she now prepared to take an action that would further separate her from her sister. She would also ask for advice from family friend Tom Jones, a man who not only would become a large influence on the younger DeVitt daughter but also would eventually marry her.

Tom Jones's connection to the DeVitt family began long before David DeVitt Sr. made Jones the real estate agent for the ranch. Jones had been a pallbearer at the 1930 funeral of Helen's brother, David Jr. After the 1934 death of David Sr., Jones wrote to Christine saying that "in the loss of both David and your Father I have seen two of my best friends pass away." He had grown up in Georgetown, Texas, but was living in Lubbock with his widowed mother by the 1930s. His mother, Ollie Snyder Jones, was the daughter of Dudley H. Snyder, one of the most famous of the late nineteenth century Texas trail drivers. Snyder ranched in the Georgetown area and became one of the founders and benefactors of Southwestern University. Tom attended both Southwestern and Vanderbilt before becoming a Lubbock real estate agent. His father, William Thomas Jones Sr., had been a prominent doctor in Georgetown before his death in 1911 when Tom was 19 years old. Tom eventually moved with his mother to Lubbock and lived within four blocks of his mother's brother, Fred Snyder Sr. Connections to the Snyder family would be a valuable assistance to both Helen and Christine in the years to come.

Helen had a pattern of allowing men to influence her ideas and path of action, and this case was no different. A Los Angeles attorney, Roland W. Schoettler, who may have been recommended to her by her ex-husband Bill Secrest, came to Helen with a scheme that on the surface would once again consolidate the DeVitt shares. In reality, however, the plan was a vehicle that would allow Schoettler to secure a compensated seat on the Mallet board. Schoettler proposed that Florence, Christine, and Helen once again consolidate their voting shares, but this time do so in a legal trust. A trust would make it difficult for either Mallet board members or the DeVitts to break or challenge Schoettler if he served as the trustee and were placed on the Mallet board. He could then use the DeVitts' majority voting bloc to move the corporation to Los Angeles and take over management of the Mallet Land and Cattle Company.

Helen and Christine remained at odds and their relationship strained. Helen was angry at Christine's lack of full communication on Mallet matters, but she was also irritated that her sister had remained in Lubbock and did not move back to California. With Christine in Lubbock, it fell to Helen to become Florence DeVitt's companion. While Florence and her younger daughter got along much better than did Florence and Christine, tensions and confrontations often surfaced between the two, particularly when Florence chose to use her barbed tongue in Helen's direction. So, Helen wrote a letter in 1942 to Tom Jones, with whom she had begun a social correspondence in 1939, and asked for his opinion on the Schoettler proposal. Jones almost immediately booked a trip from his home in Austin to Los Angeles to meet with Schoettler. Jones met with the attorney and then reported favorably on the plan to Florence and Helen. The two then agreed to Schoettler's proposal, but now they had to tell Christine and get her approval as well.

Helen wrote to Christine and, while the tone was an attempt to bridge the animosity between the two sisters, Helen was still direct with her elder sibling. She lamented that they had seen so little of each other in the previous few years, and when they did see each other in Lubbock at the board meeting, they were on opposite sides. She then got to the crux of her letter, telling her sister that "we know that you will be disappointed." Then she presented the plan Schoettler had drafted. Helen told Christine that she and Florence had already signed the agreement, and they wanted her to sign as well. She ended her letter with a plea: "We want you to help us, and we ask you to come out [to California] . . . but you always just tell us not to do anything, and it does not feel good . . . to do nothing."

Christine was infuriated. She blasted Tom Jones for inserting himself into family business and Helen for even hinting at going along with the plan. She refused to sign, saying there was nothing that would make her accept such an agreement, and then scolded Helen for influencing their mother on the matter. Her recriminations must have worked, because both Helen and her mother rescinded their agreement to the proposal. Helen, to a large extent, then removed herself from Mallet business but pointedly did not give her proxy back to her sister. Instead, she gave it to David Murphy. Helen's personal life did change, however, on November 2, 1942, when she married Tom Jones, a man seven years her senior. As per the pattern, Florence DeVitt enthusiastically approved of the marriage, as she was as charmed by Tom Jones as her daughter had been, but Christine did not favor the union and made sure both bride and groom were aware of her position. Christine DeVitt and Tom Jones had obviously fallen out over some matter not long after her father's death, and their relationship for the rest of Jones's life would be prickly.

The antagonism among the Mallet Ranch partners abated, or at least the nexus shifted. W. D. Johnson and Christine DeVitt began to find greater common ground. They both questioned a number of Sam Arnett's lease negotiations and insisted on changes before they went before Judge Blair, and they agreed that Helen DeVitt Jones and her ex-husband Bill Secrest should no longer be on the board. Johnson and Christine combined to vote J. E. Vickers (Christine's Lubbock attorney) and former member David Murphy onto the board to replace Helen and Secrest. Then they got together and made sure that Vickers would be president of the Mallet Land and Cattle Company Board of Directors. The battle among partners also shifted from Christine DeVitt against everyone to another family affair: W. D. Johnson against J. Lee Johnson Jr. Uncle and nephew were on different sides of almost every issue before the board, but the younger Johnson was clearly outvoted. For the next few years, he would increasingly withdraw from opposition and become less of a voice at board meetings. Perhaps the newly found amity affected Judge Blair as well as because he ended the receivership on March 15, 1943, and returned control of the Mallet Land and Cattle Company to its Board of Directors.

Christine DeVitt had won some significant concessions from her business partners, as well as beaten back a mutiny within her family, but there was something else she wanted to accomplish: she wanted to be an active operator of the Mallet company. She was still not an officer, although her attorney was and certainly listened to her counsel. W. D. Johnson complained to his attorney that Christine "wanted to be advised about everything," evidently with the idea that she could veto any operations decisions with which she did not agree. Johnson apparently told her that he could try, but there was no way that he could fully fulfill her request. Johnson also told Vickers that the company would "never make progress" if they "could not act on our own judgement," which was precisely what Christine did not want Vickers and Johnson to do.

Christine's insistence on more control thus clouded the April 1943 board meeting, and the results indicated either that W. D. Johnson had come to agree with her or that her continued appeals had worn the veteran cattleman so far down that he had decided to acquiesce to most of her demands. The board reappointed Vickers as president and W. D. Johnson as vice president, but then took a curious and vague action when they made Christine DeVitt and J. Lee Johnson Jr. sort of at-large officers for which they would perform "such duties as the President may assign to them." More significantly, while Vickers and Johnson kept their annual salaries of $6,000, the board voted to compensate DeVitt and Johnson the sum of $4,000 annually for those unknown duties.

The other significant development at that meeting was a shift in the administrative function of the Mallet Land and Cattle Company. David DeVitt and Andrew Drumm had formally incorporated the Mallet Land and Cattle Company in 1903. While the ranch was located in Texas, for a number of reasons—primarily for legal and tax reasons as well as access to accounting firms and attorneys that were few and far between in West Texas—the corporation was registered under Missouri laws, and the office (which meant the company accounting books) was housed in Kansas City at the Drumm Commission Company. DeVitt had briefly moved the corporate office to Lubbock in the 1920s, but at W. D. Johnson's insistence the office shifted back to Kansas City. When the Mallet went into receivership, and since Sam Arnett was in Lubbock, the offices once again shifted back to Lubbock, with the understanding—at least in W. D. Johnson's eyes—that when the receivership ended the office would once again move back to Kansas City.

When the board of directors' meeting finished with its business of appointing new directors, the agenda called for a discussion of the location of the corporate office and the company's bookkeeping function. Since the receivership had ended, Johnson assumed that the discussion was merely a formality and that the office would once again return to Kansas City. When Vickers called the item into discussion, Christine DeVitt took Johnson by surprise. In fact, one might say she "ambushed" him. She moved that the board make the office in Lubbock permanent. Johnson immediately objected and argued that Kansas City, with its greater infrastructure, was the home of the Mallet

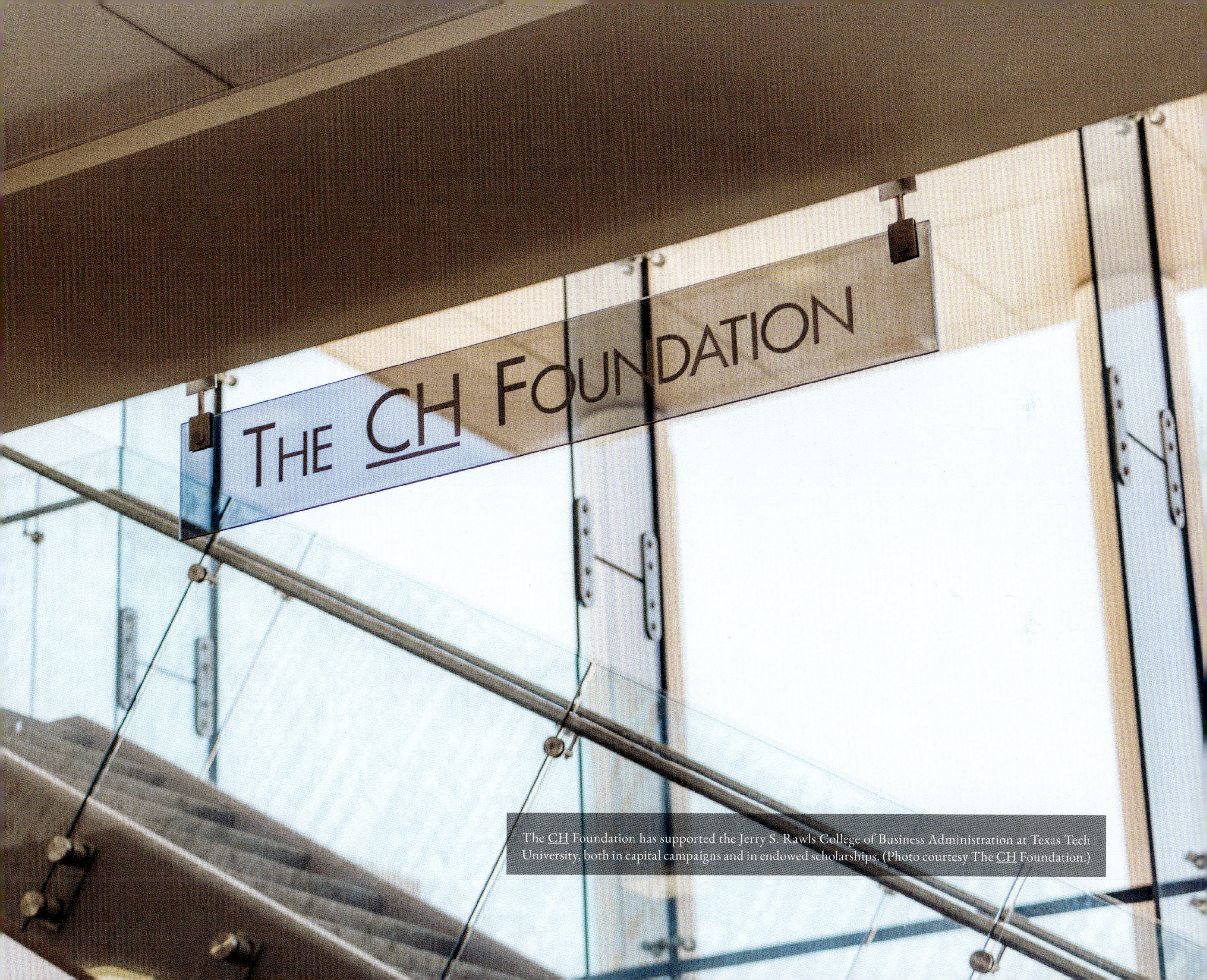

The CH Foundation has supported the Jerry S. Rawls College of Business Administration at Texas Tech University, both in capital campaigns and in endowed scholarships. (Photo courtesy The CH Foundation.)

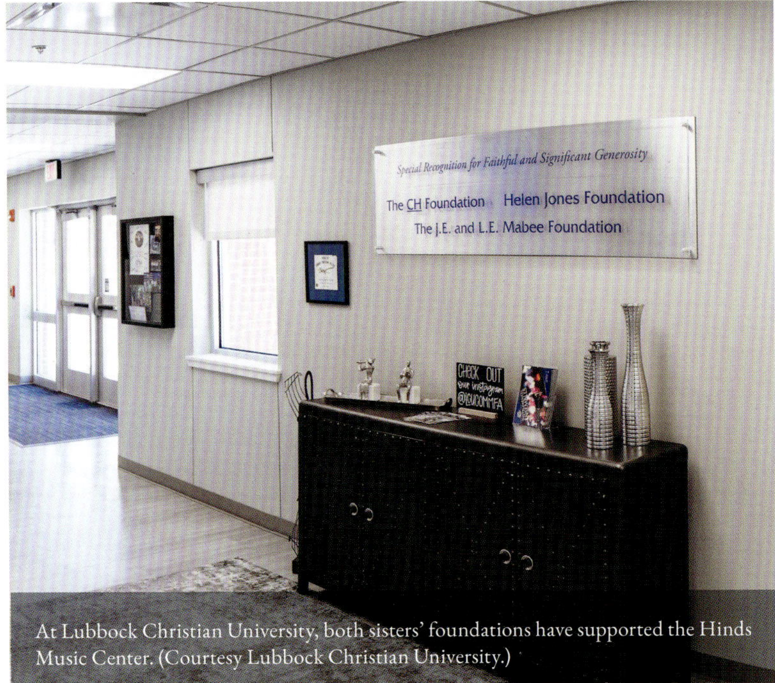

At Lubbock Christian University, both sisters' foundations have supported the Hinds Music Center. (Courtesy Lubbock Christian University.)

incorporation; left unsaid was he could personally oversee the bookkeeping and finances of the corporation. Christine countered with the fact that the records were already in Lubbock and that since the ranch was nearby and the oil companies were also almost all located in Texas that Lubbock was the natural place for the company's headquarters. What *she* left unsaid was that she was also in Lubbock and, like Johnson wanted to do, could oversee the office more closely and have greater influence. Christine had not given up her desire to manage the Mallet, and if the corporation's offices were where she lived that would come more easily. Vickers supported Christine, which meant that Johnson had to relent. Vickers leased new space in the Lubbock National Bank building downtown and the Mallet offices stayed in Lubbock, where they remain today.

While the Mallet Land and Cattle Company board of directors fussed and fought with each other and eventually sent the company into receivership, Sam Arnett did an effective job of managing the ranch, especially when it came to negotiating oil leases. Of course, the Slaughter Field was such a prolific petroleum play that came into production at the exact right time that tremendous profits on Mallet lands were a given. When World War II began, the global demand for oil skyrocketed, and West Texas—as a relatively untapped source for petroleum—suddenly became a focus for oilmen. Oil companies tussled with the Texas Railroad Commission during the first half of 1942 over prorationing and "allowables" on production, but as the war deepened the TRC relaxed some of its restrictions on production, and much of the increases were earmarked for West Texas fields. That was good news for the Mallet Ranch.

Under Arnett, oilmen had negotiated the right to drill more than 90 percent of the ranch's unleased property, which was almost 10,000 acres. These specific contracts were the ones to which Christine had objected so vehemently, but their final approval was critical because they were mostly located in the old Edwards school lands that abutted the former Lazy S lands and were some of the richest petroleum fields in all of the Mallet acres. With the final pieces in place, production soared on the Mallet. The Mallet Ranch had only thirty-two completed wells operating at the end of 1941, but between 1942 and 1943 drillers completed an amazing 466 wells that, according to the final accounting for 1943, pumped 6,364,686 barrels of oil. The Mallet Land and Cattle Company had collected $9,727 in oil royalties in 1940; that amount increased to $578,145 in 1943. Production only continued through the rest of the war years, as by 1945 the Mallet Ranch production totaled over eight million barrels and royalties increased to over one million dollars.

The astonishing rise in the number of wells on the Mallet begs a question: why were so many wells placed over a relatively small expanse? The answer lay in TRC restrictions on how much a well could produce over the course of a month and a year, and where wells could be located. The TRC had established its regulatory rules when oil was discovered in the upper Gulf Coast and in East Texas, which meant that they had done so with quarter sections (160 acres) in mind. Regulations stated that no well could stand within 440 feet of a lease, subdivision, or property line, which made seventeen acres of each labor unusable. Prorationing meant that to raise production the companies had to drill as many wells as they could on the land in which they were allowed. The TRC made a correction in 1946 and began to use Spanish land measurements, which helped some because that meant five wells could be placed on each tract that companies had leased.

The end of World War II did not mean the end or even the lessening of Mallet oil production. The postwar economy continued to grow as Americans frustrated by wartime rationing went on something of a "spending spree" in 1946 and 1947, and one of the items that Americans bought in significant quantities was automobiles. When the auto companies shifted to war production in 1942, they ceased making new cars, but with the end of the war they once again rolled automobiles out of their assembly lines and Americans responded accordingly. More cars meant more gas, which meant greater oil production, and some of that drilling came on the Mallet Ranch. The Mallet Ranch contained just over 6,000 oil wells by 1947. Those wells produced an average of almost 3,000 barrels a day. In addition, the Slaughter Field was deep with oil and geologists predicted that such wells would continue to produce for more than thirty years. When the 1940s ended, Mallet Ranch wells had produced almost fifty *million* barrels of oil since 1938, and the Mallet Land and Cattle Company had deposited almost $12 million in royalties. Mallet directors paid out dividends that came close to 500 percent of the stock's value for each year. The Mallet Ranch—an operation that David DeVitt sometimes struggled to keep afloat—was now awash in cash and profits.

Although the Mallet was making its money primarily from oil, it did not stop being a working stock operation. Just as had happened during World War I, World War II caused a rise in demand for all goods, including food. Also, the US government passed laws and new regulations that called for a large portion of the nation's pork and beef to be set aside for the troops, so while beef was a rationed item at home ranchers sold the majority of their beeves to the federal government. The Mallet Ranch's cattle production, which had reached an all-time low in 1936, rose along with the demand for beef. Yearly cattle income from 1943 to 1946 averaged over $250,000. Farm income from tenants rose right

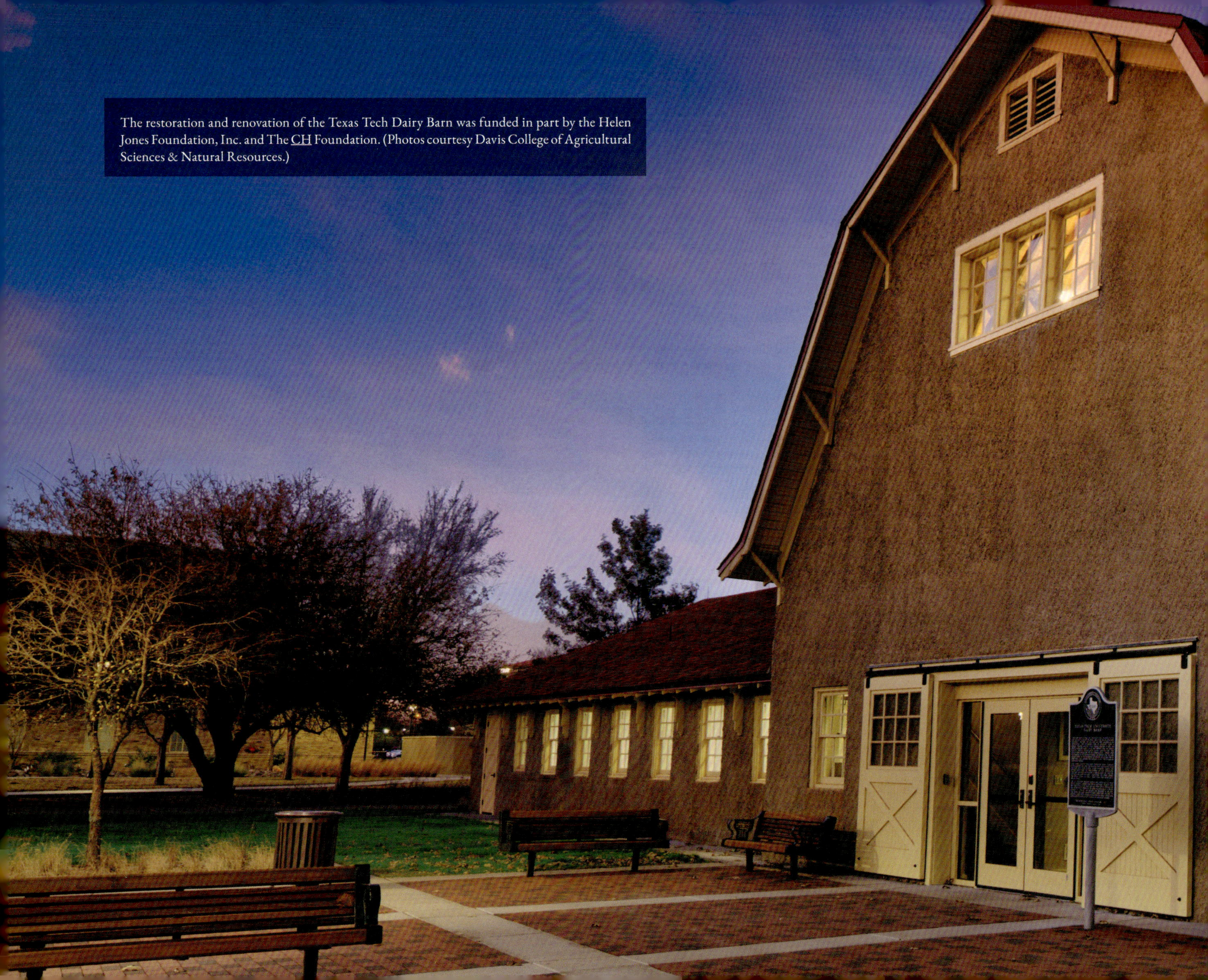

The restoration and renovation of the Texas Tech Dairy Barn was funded in part by the Helen Jones Foundation, Inc. and The CH Foundation. (Photos courtesy Davis College of Agricultural Sciences & Natural Resources.)

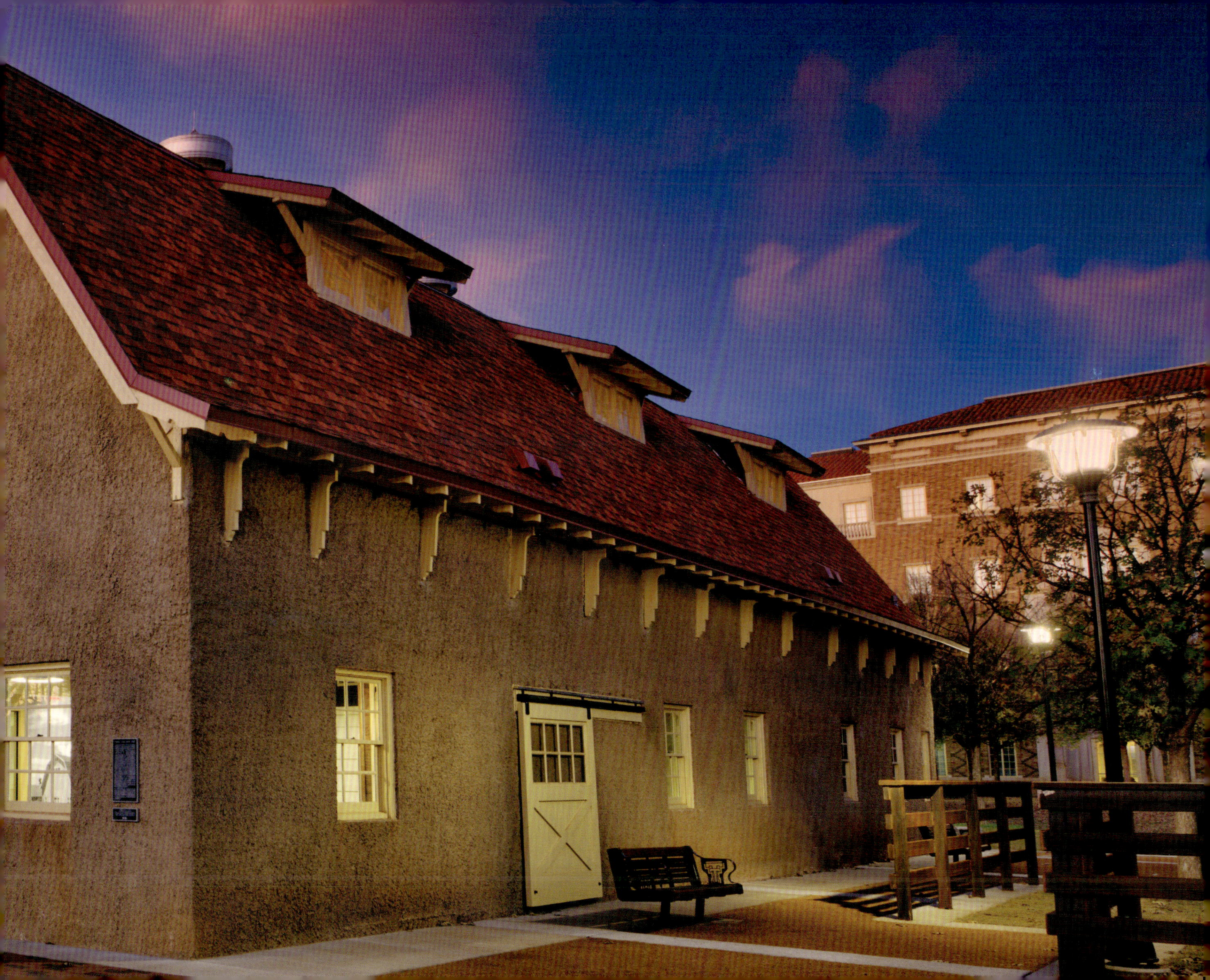

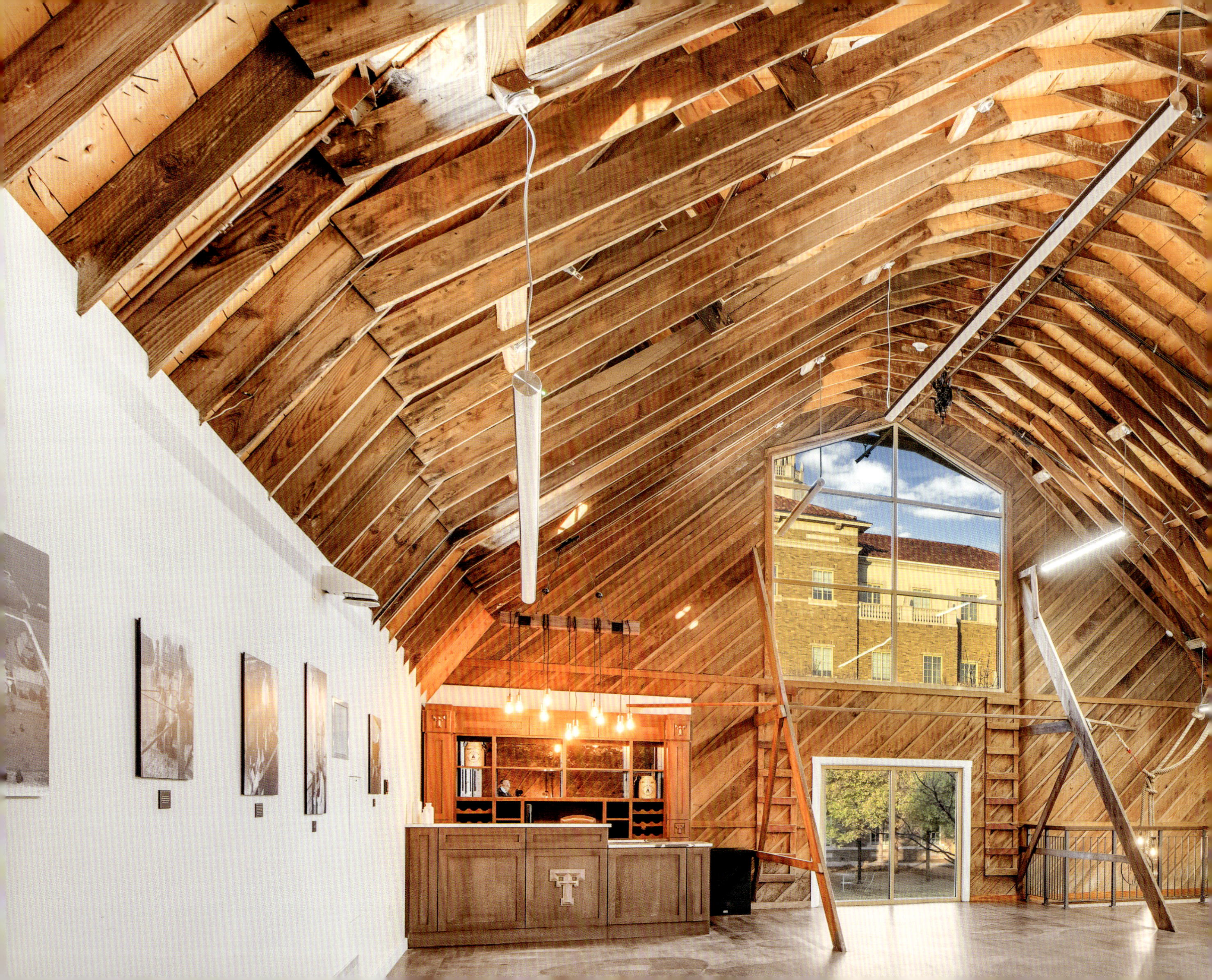

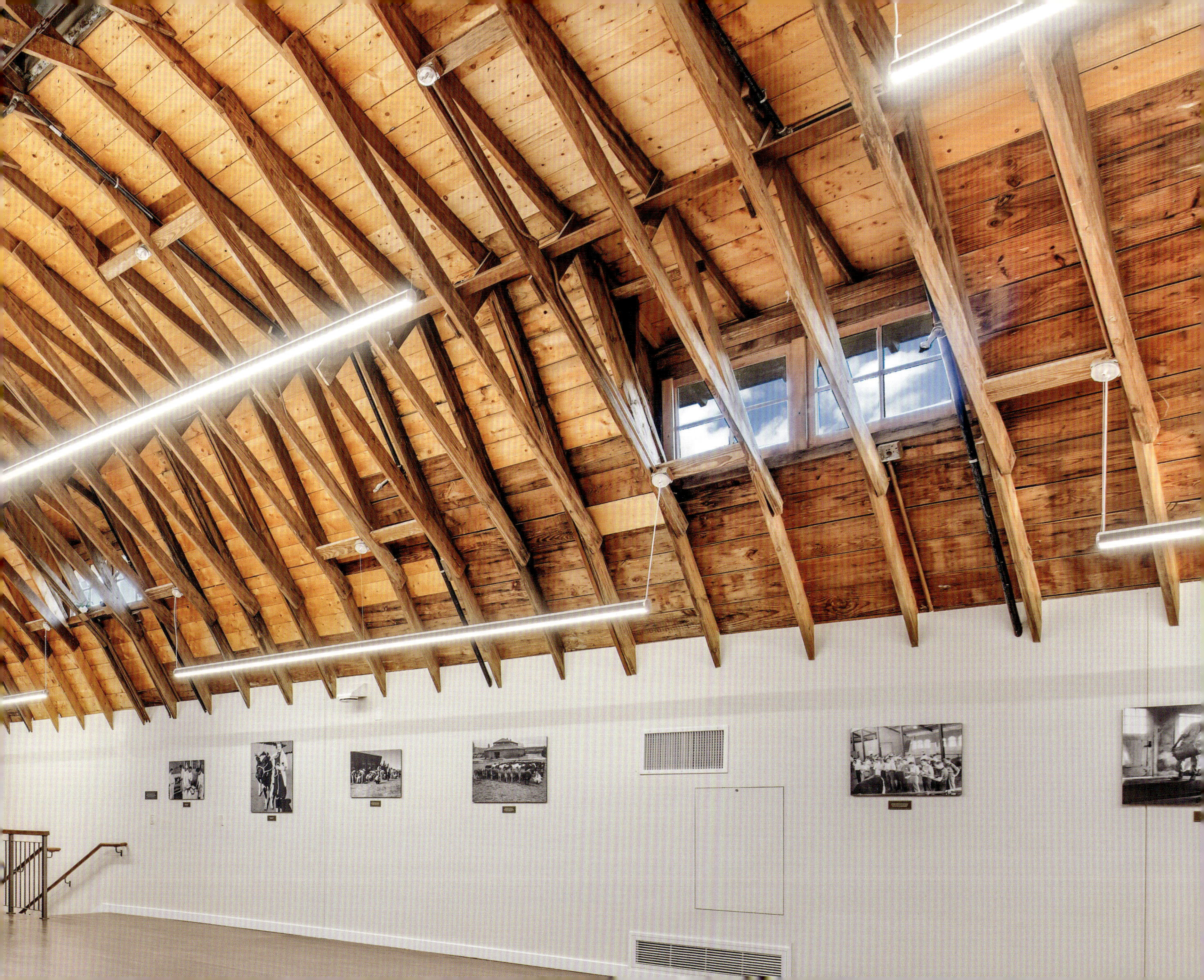

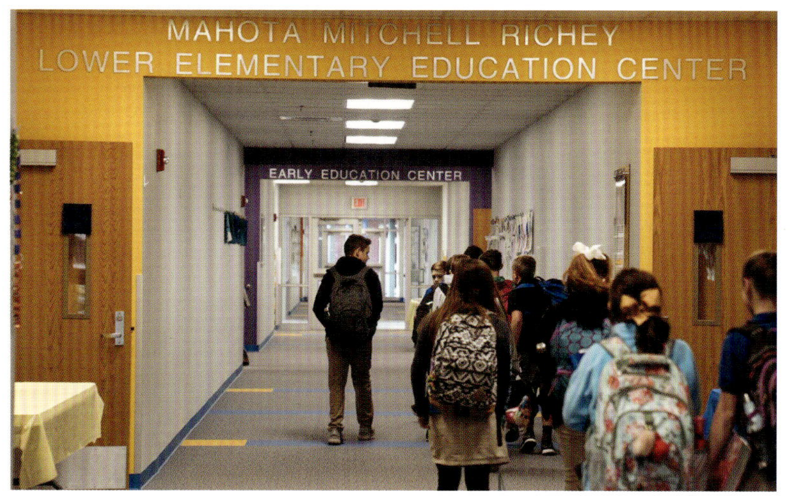

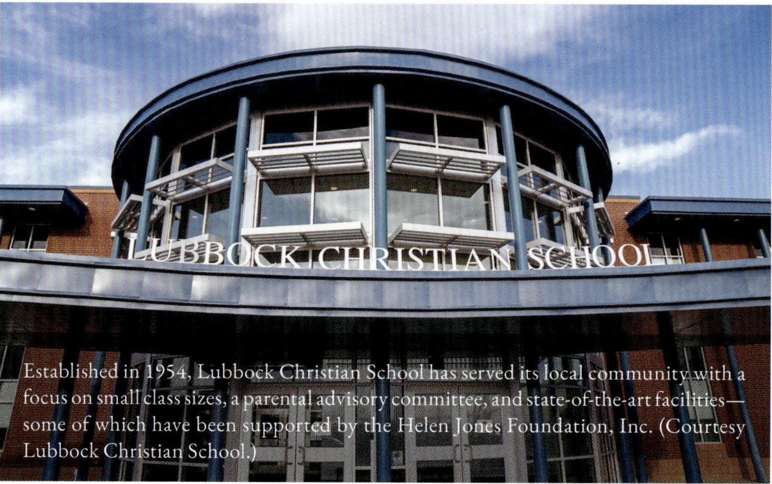

Established in 1954, Lubbock Christian School has served its local community with a focus on small class sizes, a parental advisory committee, and state-of-the-art facilities—some of which have been supported by the Helen Jones Foundation, Inc. (Courtesy Lubbock Christian School.)

along with beef prices, with those producing almost $100,000 annually during the war years. The combination of oil royalties, stock income, and farm rents meant that the Mallet Ranch produced record profits each year of the 1940s and into the 1950s.

The remainder of the 1940s also brought some administrative changes to the Mallet corporation, and the company began to face some serious questions about its structure. One of the "problems" a company faced when producing the profits the Mallet corporation did was taxes. The Mallet, an entity near insolvency in 1935, now had an annual tax bill—property, other state levies, and federal assessments—of over $400,000. That total represented the taxes the corporation paid, but the stockholders—including the DeVitt family—were then subject to federal income tax and, given the high progressive tax rates of the 1940s, that bill was substantial. If that was not enough of a worry, the structure of the Mallet Land and Cattle Company worked against it when it came to United States tax laws. The Mallet, as a corporate structure, was the receiver of the royalties from the oil companies. Corporate income, at least on accounting sheets, can be offset by expenses and other write-offs for tax purposes. However, the Mallet had very few such mechanisms to accomplish that. The corporate expenses were few, just office and administrative overhead and the expenses of operating the ranch, which were never more than $30,000 a year during the 1940s. Thus, the corporation paid an annual average of $165,000 in federal taxes alone during the 1940s—even before the taxman collected his share of dividends from stockholders.

Mallet attorney David Murphy suggested in a letter to President Vickers as early as 1942 that the Mallet could save a significant amount if the directors would agree to dissolve the corporation, then divide the Mallet into shares based on ownership of stock. Such an arrangement would not lessen the

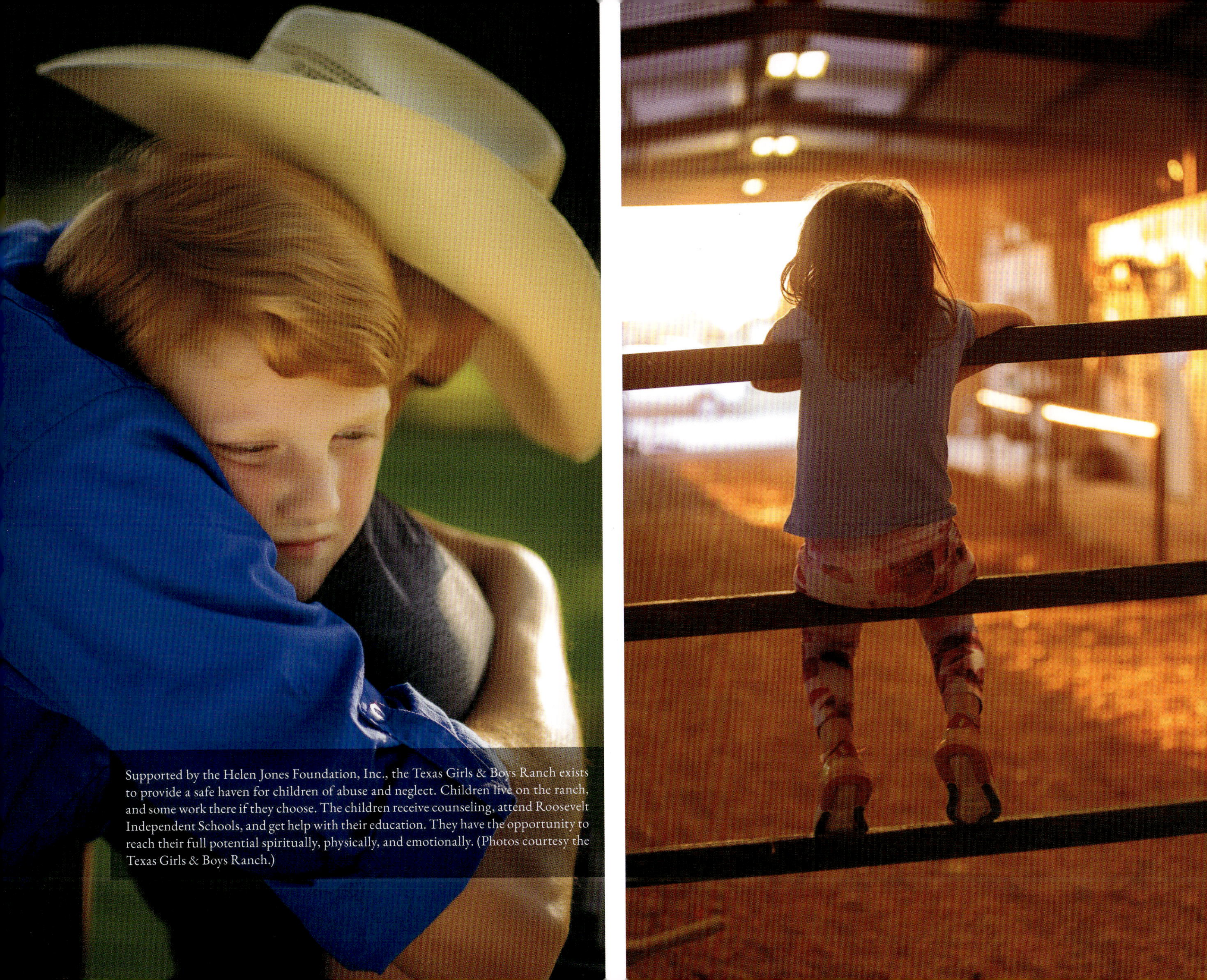

Supported by the Helen Jones Foundation, Inc., the Texas Girls & Boys Ranch exists to provide a safe haven for children of abuse and neglect. Children live on the ranch, and some work there if they choose. The children receive counseling, attend Roosevelt Independent Schools, and get help with their education. They have the opportunity to reach their full potential spiritually, physically, and emotionally. (Photos courtesy the Texas Girls & Boys Ranch.)

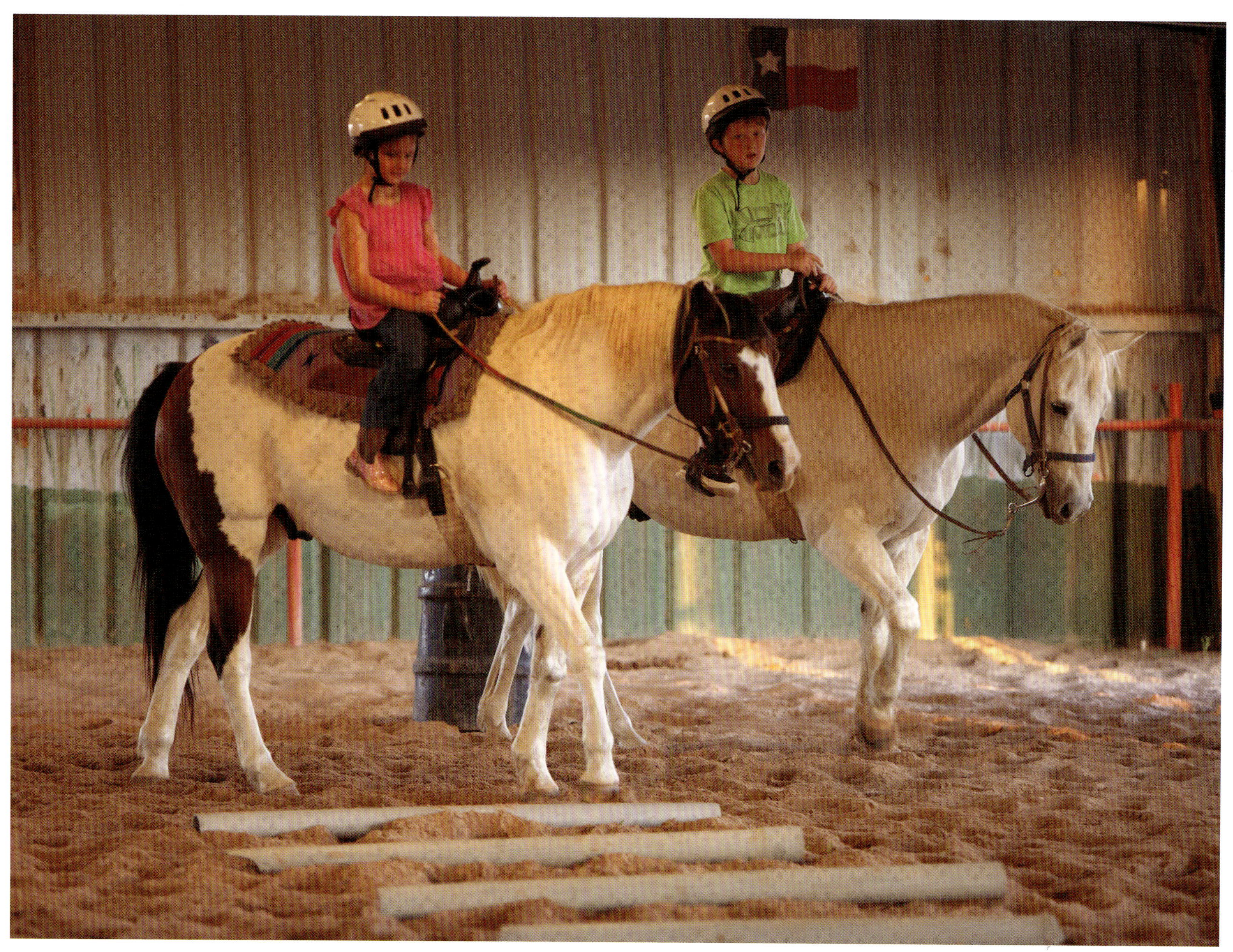

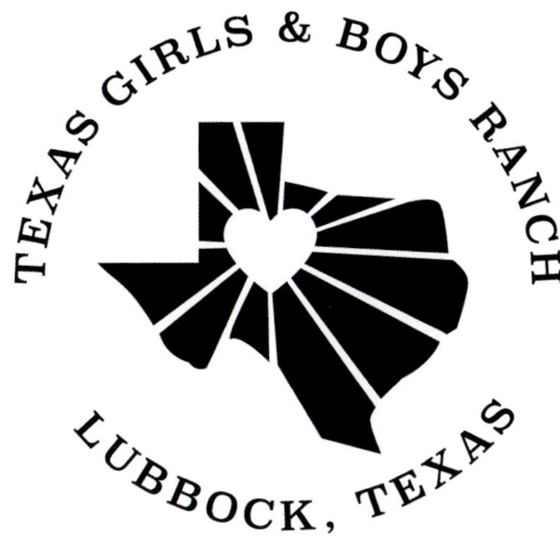

taxation on individuals, but it would stop the "double taxation" problem. Vickers reported Murphy's idea to Christine DeVitt in a September 1942 letter. Vickers would suggest dissolving the corporation again in 1944, this time at a company board meeting. The directors discussed the proposal and also considered simply selling the ranch's royalties for $12 million, but since the operating wells were divided among a number of companies finding a single buyer became untenable, and multiple sales of different parcels would be a jumbled mess. Thus they dropped the proposal for the time being but agreed to revisit the idea when they met in 1945.

Helen DeVitt Secrest's marriage to Lubbock real estate agent Tom Jones in late 1942 produced another change at the Mallet. The newlyweds initially lived in the Hilton Hotel in downtown

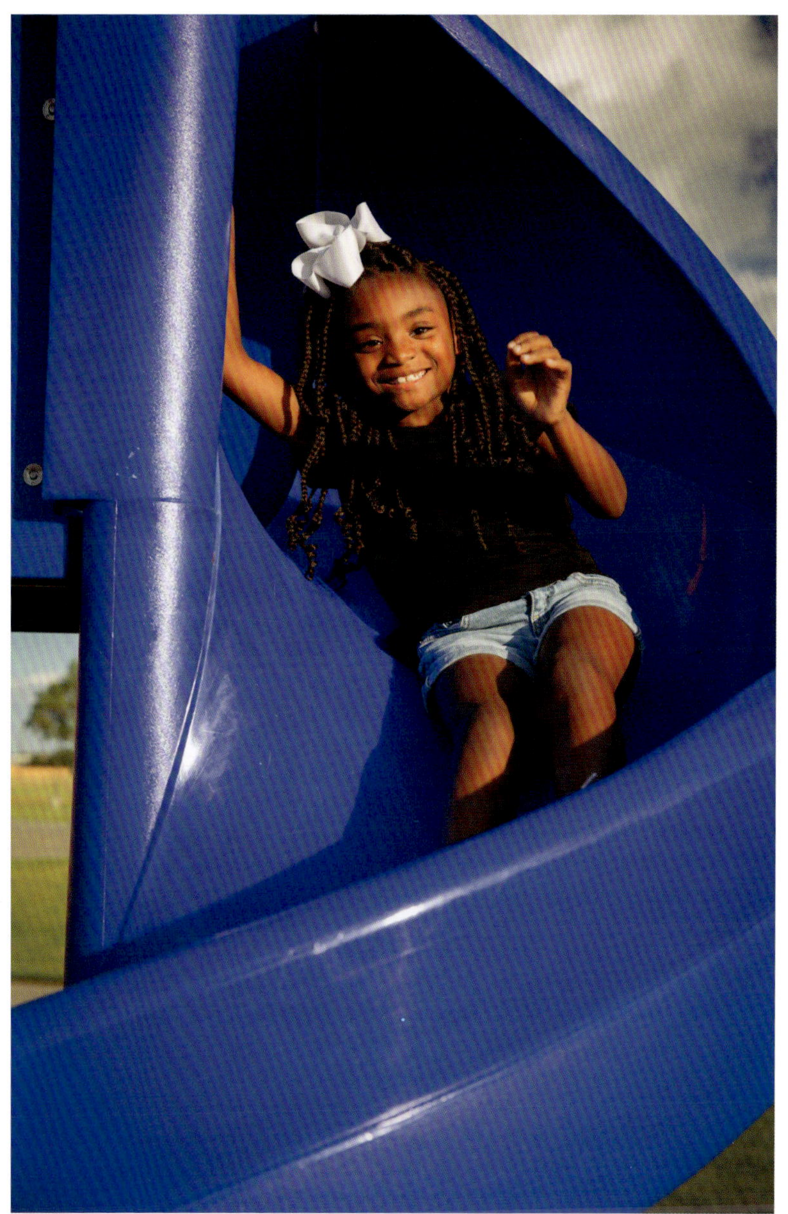

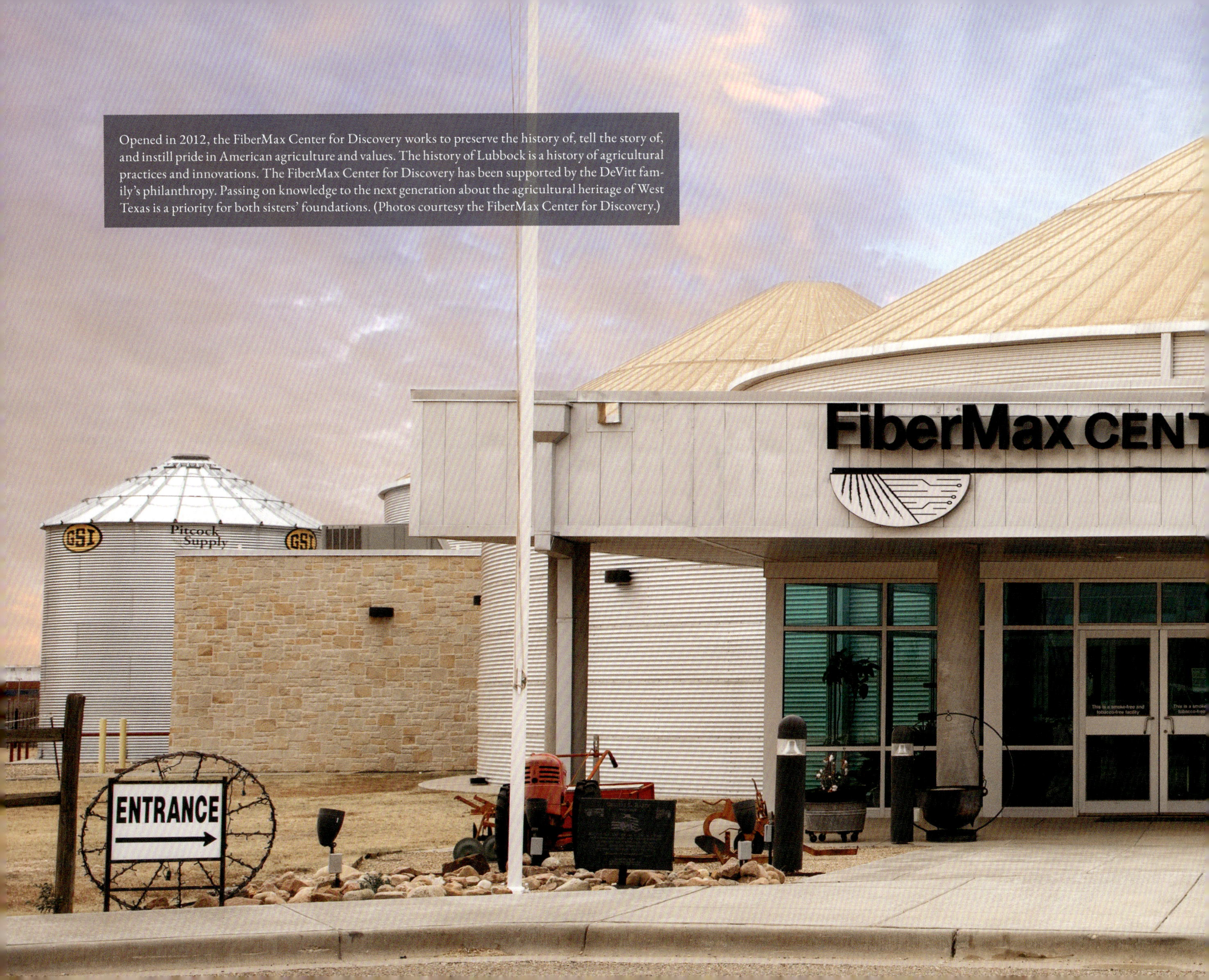

Opened in 2012, the FiberMax Center for Discovery works to preserve the history of, tell the story of, and instill pride in American agriculture and values. The history of Lubbock is a history of agricultural practices and innovations. The FiberMax Center for Discovery has been supported by the DeVitt family's philanthropy. Passing on knowledge to the next generation about the agricultural heritage of West Texas is a priority for both sisters' foundations. (Photos courtesy the FiberMax Center for Discovery.)

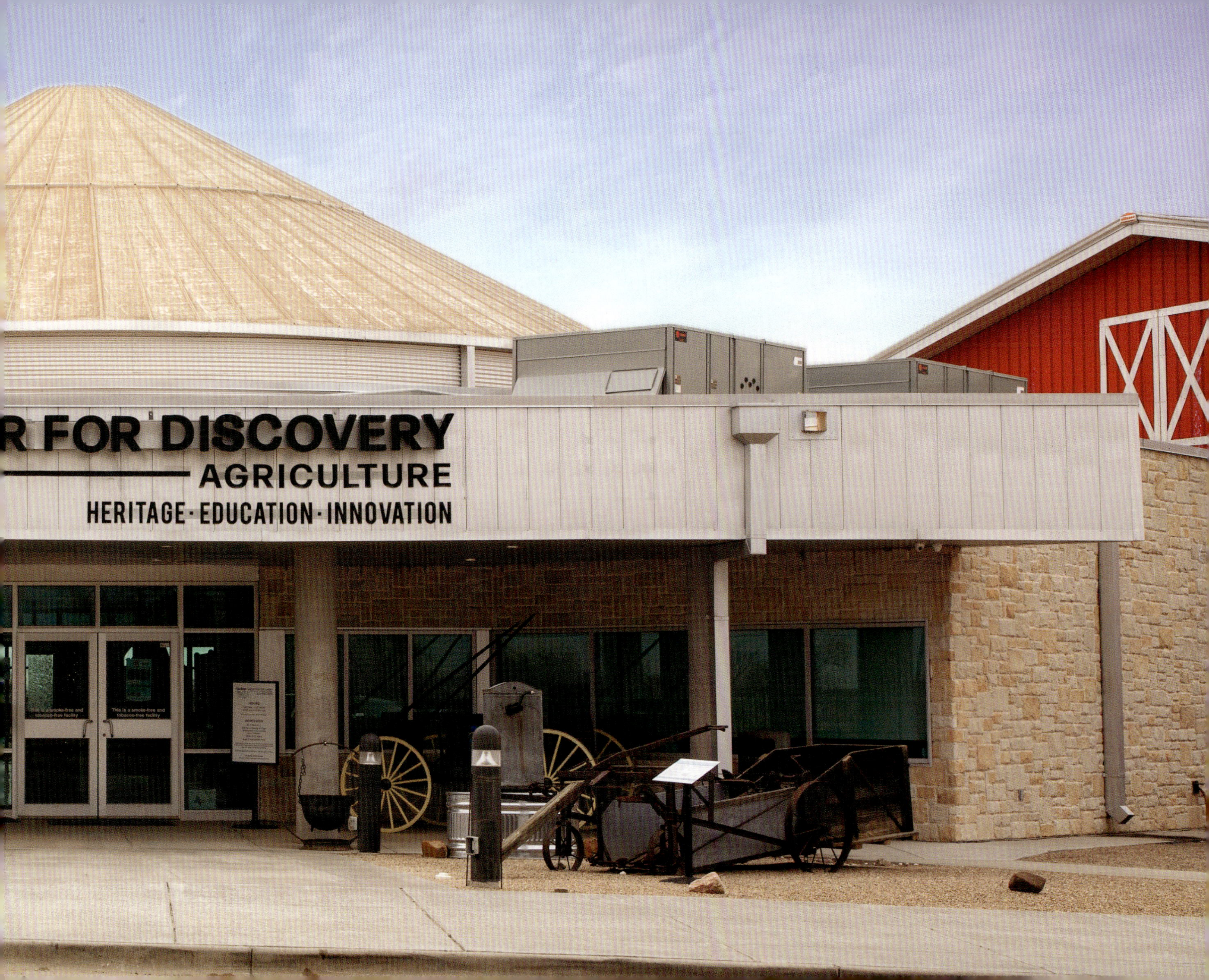
R FOR DISCOVERY
AGRICULTURE
HERITAGE · EDUCATION · INNOVATION

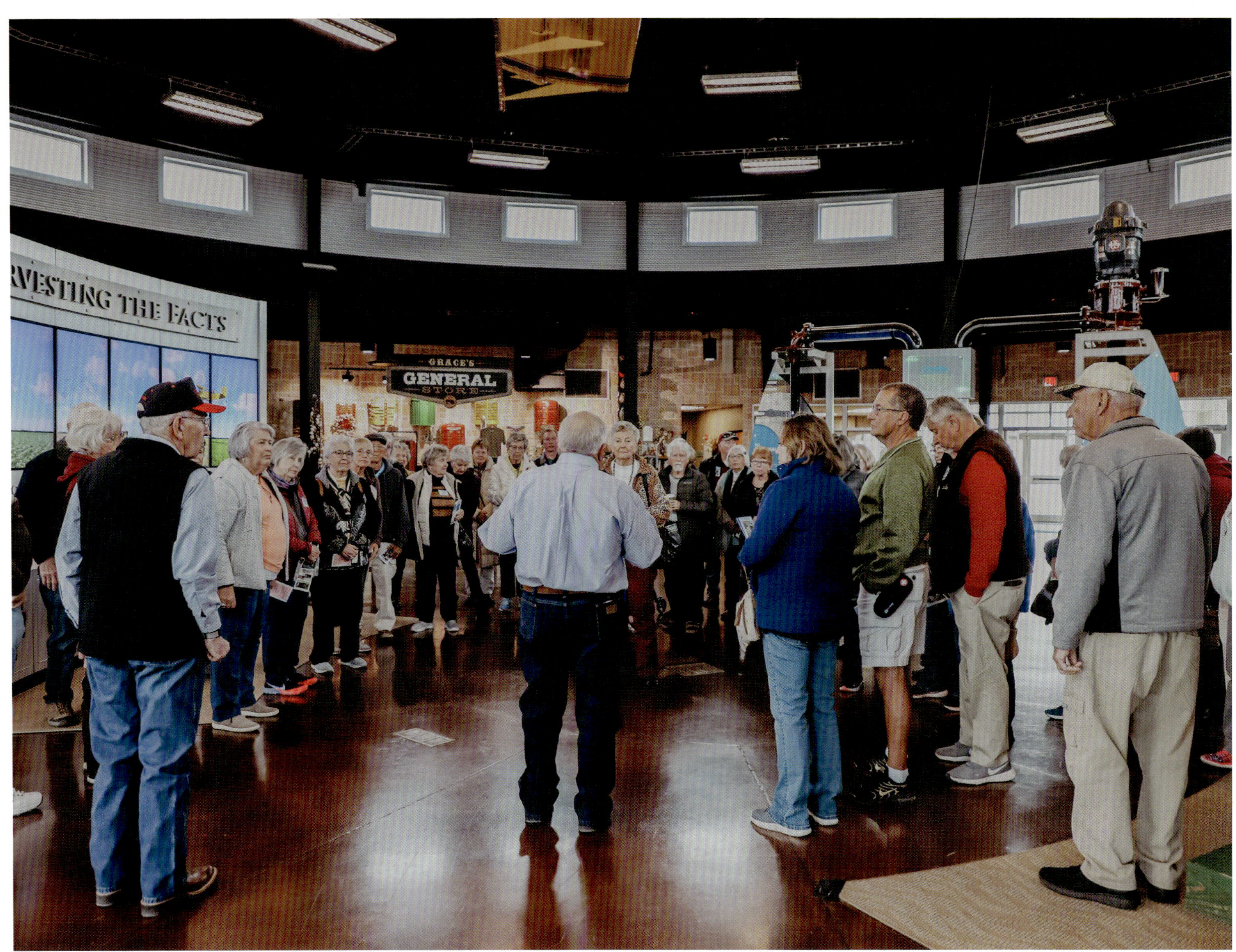
RVESTING THE FACTS
GRACE'S
GENERAL
STORE

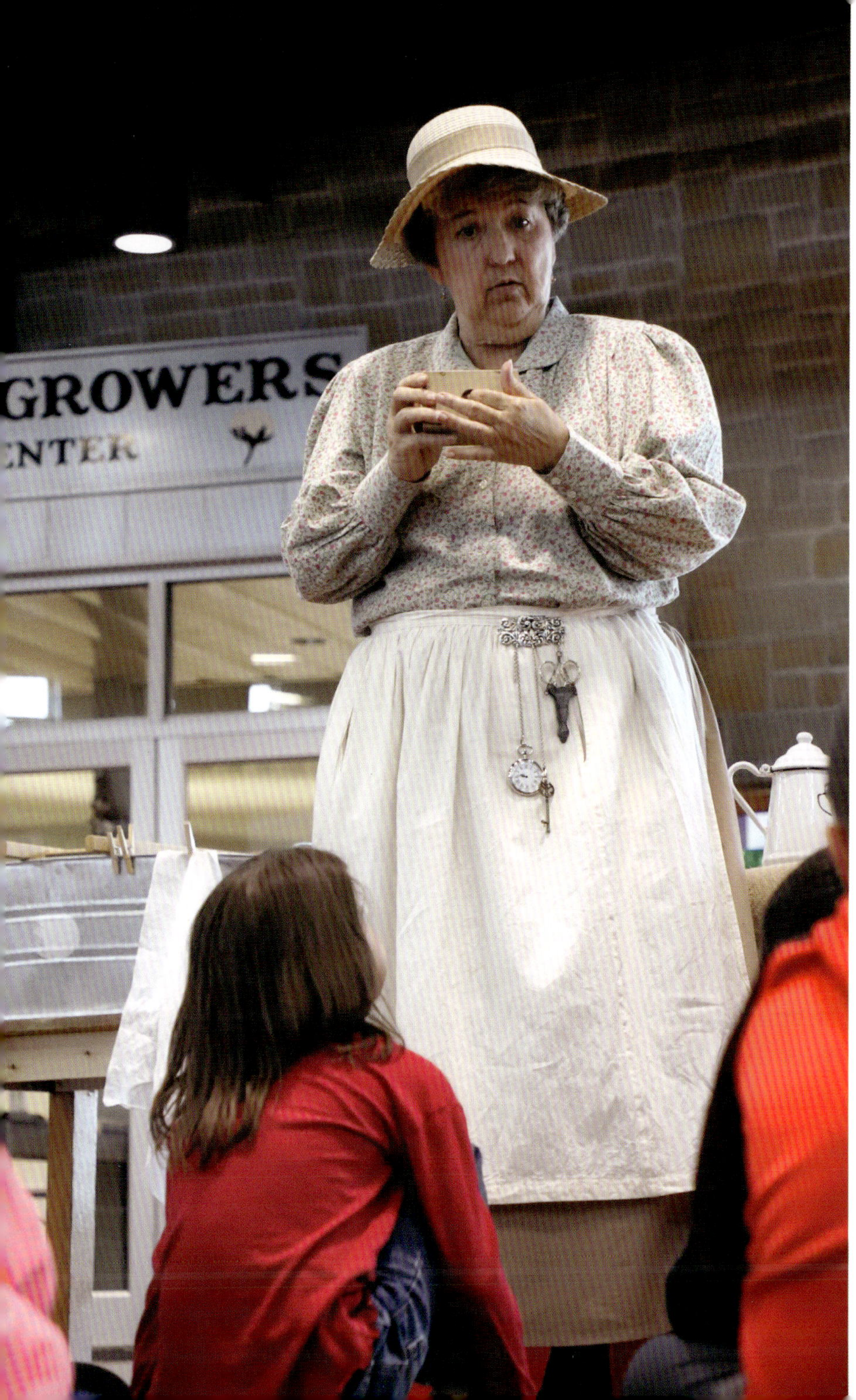

GROWERS

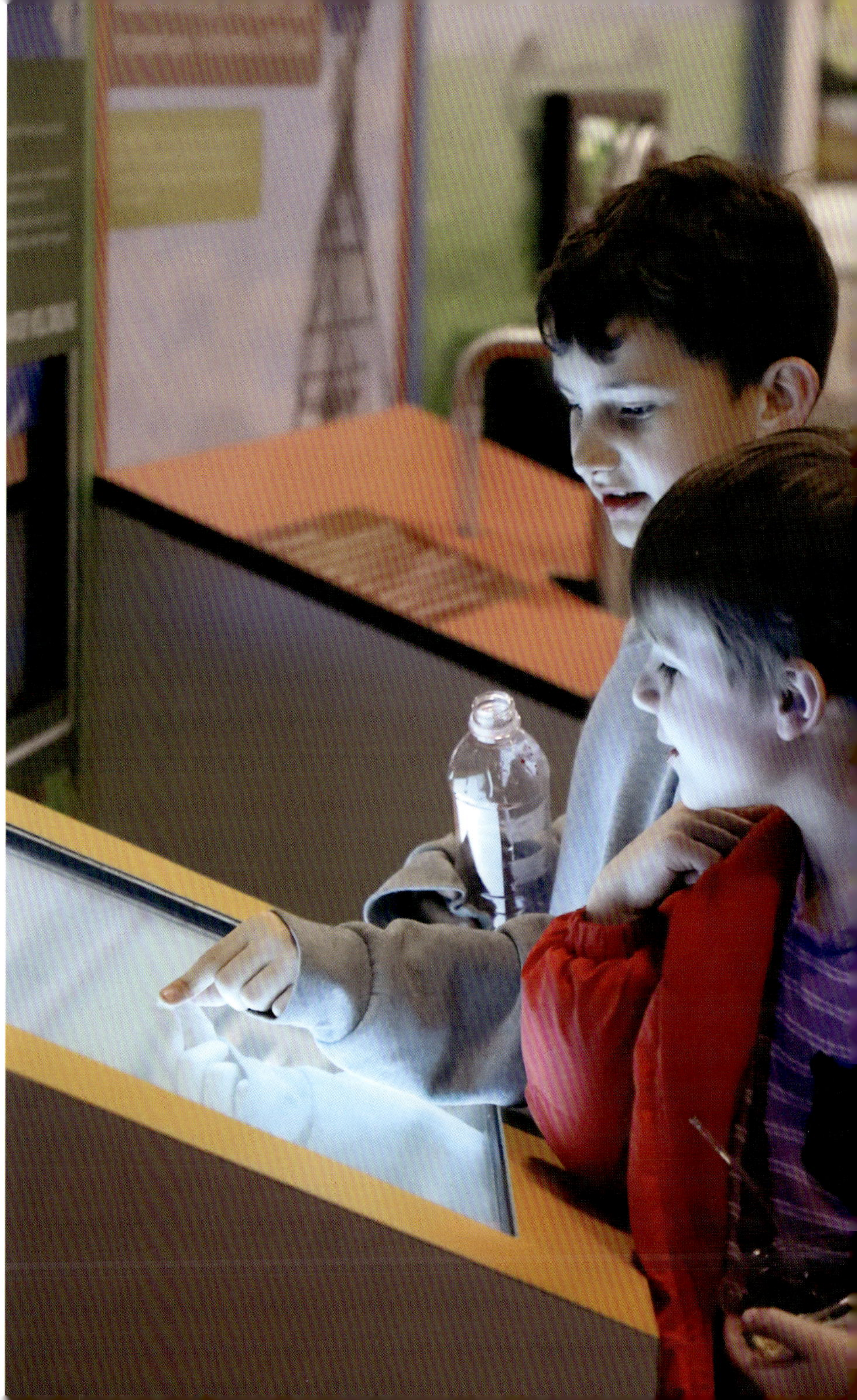

Lubbock, where Christine also lived. Then they purchased a home at 3219 21st street in Lubbock, although Helen retained her California home for visits to her mother and daughter. When her mother would die in 1945, Helen would find herself practically confined to California for the three years it took to settle her mother's estate. This resulted in Helen and Tom Jones almost replicating the long-distance marriage pattern of Helen's parents. In addition to the lengthy closure of her mother's estate, Helen was spending much of her time divided between Los Angeles and Berkeley, where her daughter had enrolled in the University of California and continued to battle with asthma. Tom lived in Lubbock but traveled to California several times for visits. He also made it clear that he wished Helen would leave Los Angeles and come to Texas, but Helen obviously felt that her obligation to her mother precluded such an outcome.

Helen, who had been largely pushed out of any role on the board earlier, wanted her new husband to be given a job with the Mallet. She wrote to Christine numerous times suggesting that she find a place for her husband and pestered company president Vickers with the same question. Christine's primary objection seemed to be that she thought bringing Jones on board as a salaried employee would cause the board to cut her salary. Assured by Vickers that would not happen, Christine relented, but finding Jones a position with the Mallet necessitated some personnel changes. The Mallet board met in May 1944 and fired J. A. Stroud, who had been the farm manager since David DeVitt Jr. had died in 1930. They replaced Stroud with Tom Jones at a salary of $4,000 a year.

The board meeting was another occasion for Christine to voice her insistence that she be made at least a co-manager of the Mallet Land and Cattle Company. Because the board had given her brother-in-law a job, Christine once again, with fervor, asked the board for this appointment. The board relented and named Christine co-manager with Vickers. Her victory, however, was tainted by the board's next action. W. D. Johnson made a motion that severely hamstrung any authority Christine might have exerted over Mallet business. His motion, which the board passed over Christine's objection, stated that "only the President and Vice President shall give orders or directions to employees of the ranch, or carry on any negotiations with any oil lessee." That meant that Christine was a manager in name only and would carry no authority over the day-to-day operation of the Mallet Ranch.

J. E. Vickers tendered his resignation as president of the Mallet Land and Cattle Company Board of Directors in May 1945. His stated reason was that he needed to focus more on his law practice and Mallet business took too much of his time. The real reason was more likely that he—like David Murphy before him—had grown tired of Christine's constant meddling and needling about his decisions. The board, at Tom Jones's suggestion, appointed A. L. Henderson to be president as well as office manager. Henderson was an experienced oil landman, which played a large factor in his receiving the position. Henderson moved to modernize the Mallet's accounting procedures, bringing on a young accountant well versed in the constantly changing US tax laws in the late 1940s. He also effectively managed the Mallet's oil properties.

Florence DeVitt had maintained a constant presence through all the turmoil and infighting that plagued the Mallet in the years after David DeVitt's death. The latter's widow sometimes unleashed her sharp tongue on Christine and questioned her decision-making, but Florence had been a key figure in allowing the family to remain united in pressing decisions about the ranch. Because she was the company's largest stockholder, her percentage made her the most powerful owner in the corporation, a power that Christine—with her proxy—used to her advantage. Despite her insistence for years that she was ill, Florence remained healthy enough to live alone and continue writing letters to both daughters.

Florence's run of relatively good health began to end in late 1943. She entered a hospital near San Diego for surgery for an undisclosed illness. Her recovery was difficult, and both of her daughters took turns comforting her for the better part of two years both in the hospital and when she returned to her home. Helen was, by this time, living in both California and Texas but spent more time in Texas, and she lobbied her mother to leave California and come back to Texas, which she agreed to do in late September 1945. Florence made it clear that she had no desire to live in Lubbock, which only reminded her of those unhappy years on the Mallet. She also would rather not live in Fort Worth, another place that perhaps reminded her too much of her gloomy marriage. So she and Helen made a compromise. Her daughter bought Florence a house in Dallas, but the latter would never make it back to Texas. Florence died on November 30, 1945, at the age of 78.

Mrs. Florence De Vitt Dies In California

Mrs. Florence A. De Vitt, 80, widow of David M. De Vitt, founder of the Mallet Land and Cattle company with ranch holdings southwest of Levelland in Hockley county, died Friday in Los Angeles, Calif.

Mr. De Vitt came to this area in 1880 and began building up the Mallet ranch, one of the earliest ranches in the Panhandle-Plains region, then largely unsettled.

Mrs. De Vitt lived on the ranch and in Fort Worth prior to moving to California.

Survivors include two daughters, Miss Christine De Vitt, Hilton hotel, and Mrs. W. Tom Jones, 3219 Twenty-first; a granddaughter, Miss Dorothy Secrest of California.

Florence DeVitt's death immediately brought about some new and even adverse consequences for her daughters, who became the sole heirs to David DeVitt's stock operation that dated back to 1880 when the New York journalist arrived in Texas. The Mallet Ranch was now a petroleum empire that turned tremendous profits but still faced some obstacles and questions that would fall mostly to Christine but also to Helen as she became more active in Mallet affairs. The bulk of Florence DeVitt's estate comprised her shares in the Mallet Land and Cattle Company. Now, with the stock they inherited from their mother combined with their own, the two sisters cumulatively owned 54 percent of Mallet shares. If they could learn to work together, they could control the board.

The Mallet Land and Cattle Company Board of Directors, reflecting the new reality, elected Helen DeVitt Jones to the board once again in 1948. She replaced attorney David Murphy, who had died earlier that year. Another constant on the Mallet board had effectively lost his voice in Mallet affairs in 1947: W. D. Johnson, probably the most visible and certainly influential member of the Mallet board from the time of David DeVitt's death until the 1940s, suffered a massive and debilitating stroke in July 1947, an illness that left him homebound and virtually unable to manage his personal affairs. The Fidelity Union Bank in Overland Park, Kansas—on whose board of directors Johnson served—managed Johnson's business interests after his assets were placed in a trust at the bank. Fidelity Union would essentially act as not much more than a placeholder for Johnson's interests, and as long as the Mallet showed profits they were content with any decisions the board made. Upon his uncle's illness, J. Lee Johnson Jr. once again became a stronger voice on the board, and he and Christine would often be at odds. Such developments gave the DeVitt sisters virtual monopoly control of the board. W. D. Johnson would eventually die in April 1951 when he was ninety years old.

The possession of controlling shares of the Mallet Land and Cattle Company did not mean that unity and cooperation always existed within the DeVitt family. Helen may have served on the board and held significant voting shares on paper, but as the calendar turned to the 1950s, it would be Tom Jones who began to manage those interests behind the scenes. Jones is a curious and somewhat enigmatic figure within the DeVitt family narrative. He was an old friend of David DeVitt, someone the DeVitt patriarch enjoyed socially. As a real estate agent by trade, Jones seemed to always be on the periphery of Mallet affairs as far back as the 1920s. He became a key adviser to David DeVitt and often helped the latter conduct some of his business. It was Jones who began to negotiate the farm tenant contracts on the Mallet after the death of David DeVitt Jr. and was the brokering agent in attempts to sell the Mallet in the early 1930s.

When David Sr. died in 1934, Tom Jones immediately offered his services to the DeVitt family. He traveled to California to console DeVitt's widow and daughters, offered to advise them as they worked through the DeVitt estate, and began corresponding with Helen and Florence in California. He saw Christine frequently after she moved to Lubbock, and the two may have had a few social engagements that resulted in speculation that they were a "couple," but the reality was that both brought out the worst in each other. Regardless, they did remain somewhat friends. It was often only Jones who could get Christine to move on a decision. Tom Jones continued his correspondence with Helen and began traveling to see her in California after she asked for his advice about how to vote her Mallet stock. Their friendship eventually turned into a courtship, and they married. One must read between the lines of their correspondence to begin to discern some of the foundation of the Jones marriage. Tom Jones was a heavy drinker and Helen DeVitt Jones, like her mother, dealt with a variety of health issues. The couple's frequent separation was likely the best way for the two to deal with the tensions and vagaries of their marriage. Jones's motivations in his relationship with the DeVitts may have been wholly honorable, but it did appear that after he met David DeVitt Sr., Jones seemed to be trailing on the coattails of Mallet assets. Until his death in 1955, Tom Jones would be the actor behind the scenes of many Mallet decisions.

The most complicated facet of Florence DeVitt's death with which the DeVitt sisters had to deal was the complicated California inheritance tax structure. While Christine's and Helen's attorneys argued that Florence was a legal resident of Texas, she had lived in California for more than twenty years and thus the state considered her a resident and subject to that state's much higher and more complicated inheritance tax. California claimed that the estate owed more than $2 million in taxes (at the same time, Christine and Helen owed a combined federal income tax of almost that much), cash on hand that the DeVitts did not possess. Their attorneys began to negotiate a settlement of some kind, but Christine and Helen had no choice but to sell some assets in order to pay the levy. Tom Jones took the lead in raising the money, and he first advised that the only real solution was for the sisters to sell their interests in the Mallet—on which he, presumably, would make a healthy commission. While he entertained some offers, nothing tangible materialized. He then turned to selling some tracts of land in neighboring counties and towns to the Mallet that David DeVitt had personally owned and the sisters had inherited. He was able to sell part of those and raised somewhere near $450,000 for Christine and Helen. Finally, after more than three years of lawyers and legal negotiations, the DeVitt sisters settled with the state of California for just under a million dollars.

While Christine, Helen, and their attorneys dealt with the settlement of Florence's estate, the Mallet continued to produce fantastic oil and gas profits. At the 1946 board of directors meeting, President A. L. Henderson reported that the company had a gross income of over $1.5 million, with a potential dividend to disperse among the shareholders of about $1.4 million. Oil royalties made up more than 95 percent of the company's profits and they continued to rise through the rest of the 1940s, with the company reporting almost $5 million in royalties in 1949.

The Mallet may have experienced enormous profits, but that did not mean the board of directors got along any better. In fact, the removal of W. D. Johnson from active participation on the board may have made relations worse. W. D. and Christine quarreled regularly, and while an outsider might think the two intensely disliked each other, the reality was that there was at least some grudging respect between the two. W. D. Johnson to some degree admired Christine DeVitt's "spunk." Even though she could be somewhat eccentric, Christine was passionate about protecting her family's interests, a trait Johnson shared. Christine, for her part, respected Johnson's vast experience and expertise. They argued and were quite often on opposite sides of issues, but they also compromised for the good of the company more than many people have realized. The relationship between Christine and J. Lee Johnson Jr. was different, however. Christine and J. Lee, with W. D. Johnson sidelined, became the co-signers of all Mallet checks, which set up a number of direct clashes. Christine intensely disliked W. D.'s nephew, and the feeling on the other side was mutual. J. Lee could be an open and vocal misogynist, which did not sit well with Christine's blunt and confrontational demeanor. Her procrastination and reluctance to make a decision without much deliberation also annoyed him greatly and tested his patience.

The adversaries' most divisive and intense disagreement concerned payment of a stock dividend in 1947. The Mallet had experienced a significant profit in 1946 and J. Lee proposed the payment of a fifteen hundred dollar per share dividend to the shareholders. Christine at first, true to her nature, dallied making a decision and answering Johnson's proposal. J. Lee strongly urged her to approve the dividend. Christine responded that she could make no decision concerning such a large disbursement until she could resolve her mother's estate and reach a settlement on the California taxes. Johnson then wrote to other members of the board, including Helen, that he demanded Christine approve the dividend; if she did not, he would execute legal action. Faced with the potential of another legal fight with J. Lee Johnson, Christine relented and signed off on the dividend payment.

The fight over the dividend turned the 1947 Mallet board meeting into another intense affair. Christine and J. Lee got into a yelling match over Christine's suggestion that W. D. Johnson had kept inaccurate books during his tenure as president, causing J. Lee to threaten to destroy the records rather than allow any sort of audit. Christine relented. The meeting agenda also included discussion, once again, of a proposal to dissolve the Mallet Land and Cattle Company as a means to avoid high corporate taxation. Christine had not supported such an action when it was discussed earlier, but even she began to change her mind when a member (likely J. Lee Johnson) pointed out that with the company dissolved she would have sole control over signing any leases that concerned her family's portion of the holdings. On the other hand, if the corporation were to continue, she could possibly be overruled and forced to sign documents with which she did not agree.

Dissolution seemed probable, but objection to such a move came from R. B. Hewitt, the trustee who represented W. D. Johnson's interests. He argued that a corporation was the "best vehicle to use by a group of interests in operating a business." He further contended that oil companies would be reluctant to deal with individual landowners and disagreement would lead to the loss of some leases. The board considered Hewett's ideas, and on the second day of the meeting determined to dissolve the Mallet Land and Cattle Company effective December 28, 1948. They agreed on a liquidation plan that would distribute the corporation's assets to the stockholders. They then voted to redeem the Mallet's United States savings bonds in cash to make distribution easier and assigned J. Lee Johnson, Christine DeVitt, and President A. L. Henderson the obligation to pay the corporation's final taxes and liabilities. Finally, the owners would stop operating the ranch and lease out the pastures to other cattlemen, although they did agree to continue paying a farm manager—in this case Tom Jones—to oversee the Mallet farms.

The Mallet Land and Cattle Company Board of Directors gathered in December 1948 for the last time as a corporate entity to hear a dissolution proposal from Dallas attorney Wright Matthews, who had successfully negotiated the DeVitts' tax settlement with California. There were eighteen stockholders in the Mallet: Christine and Helen DeVitt, who each held 26.6125 percent in shares; W. D. Johnson; the W. D. Johnson Trust; William Jewell College (to whom W. D. Johnson had given 3.2 percent of his shares in the 1930s); and thirteen descendants of J. Lee Johnson Sr., represented by J. Lee Johnson Jr. The stockholders would divide the remaining shares, which came to 2.9234 percent for each stockholder. Of course, the division of more than 700 oil wells, outstanding leases, and about three million dollars in cash was the primary crux of the proposal. The final document divided everything—surface land,

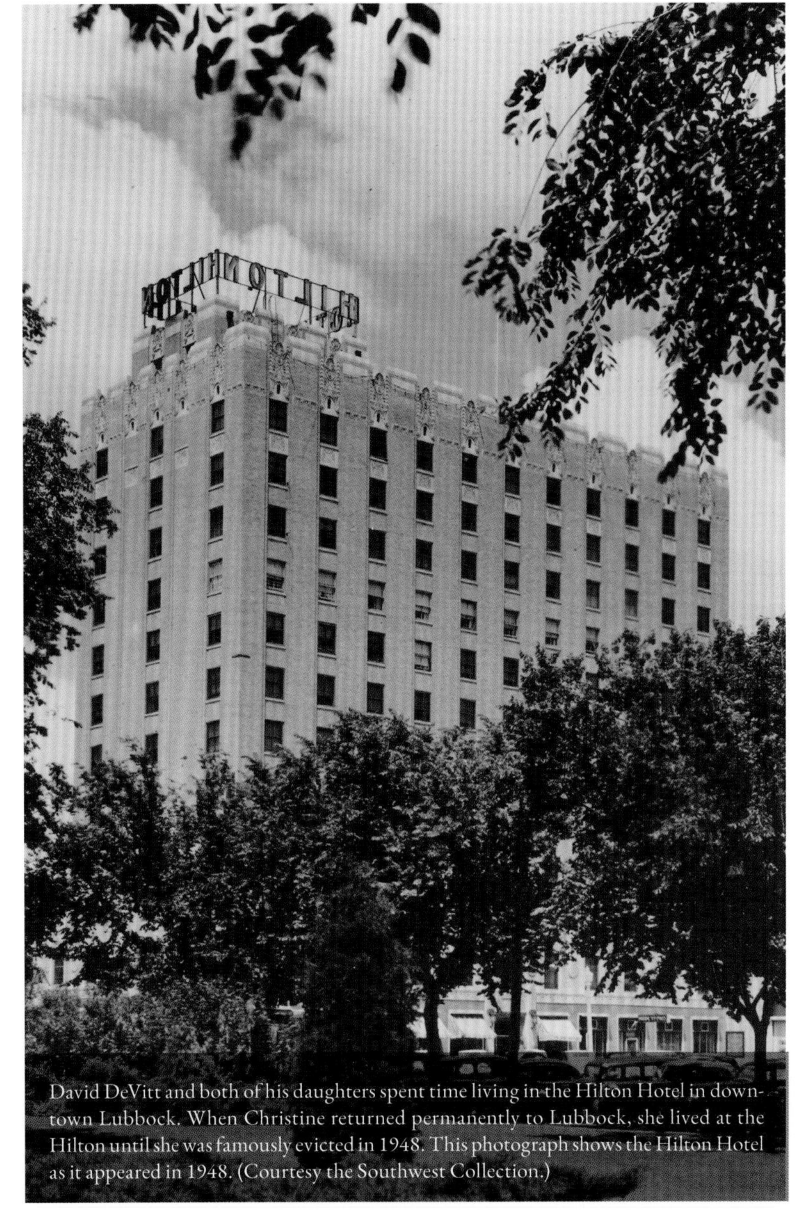

David DeVitt and both of his daughters spent time living in the Hilton Hotel in downtown Lubbock. When Christine returned permanently to Lubbock, she lived at the Hilton until she was famously evicted in 1948. This photograph shows the Hilton Hotel as it appeared in 1948. (Courtesy the Southwest Collection.)

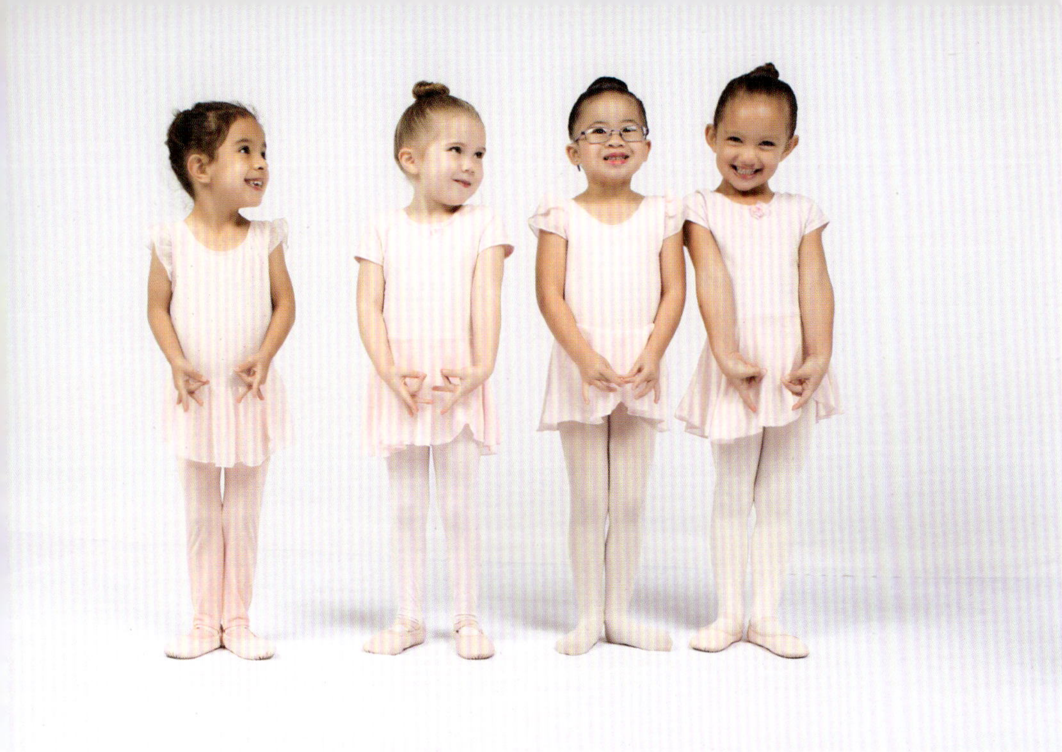

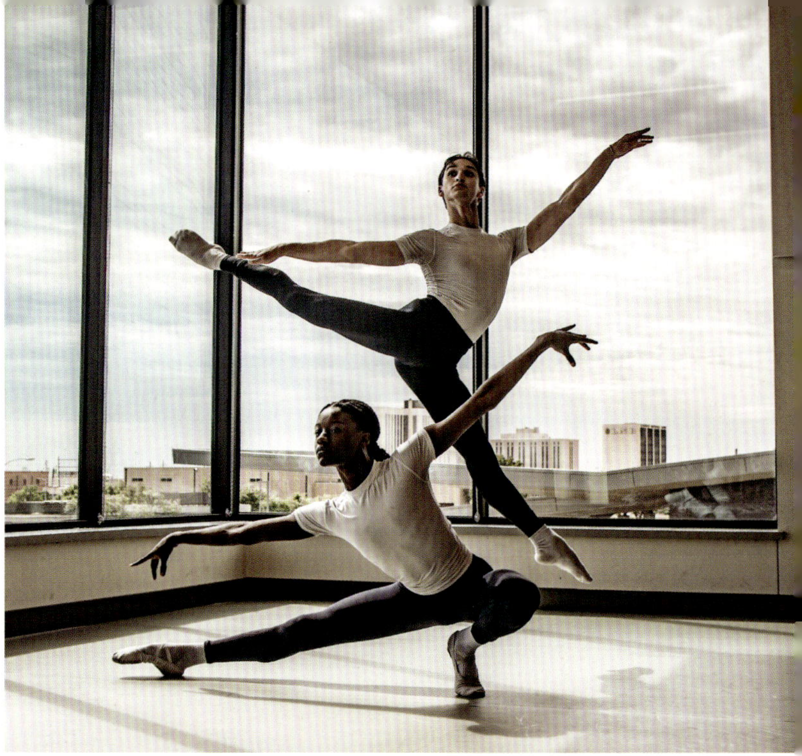

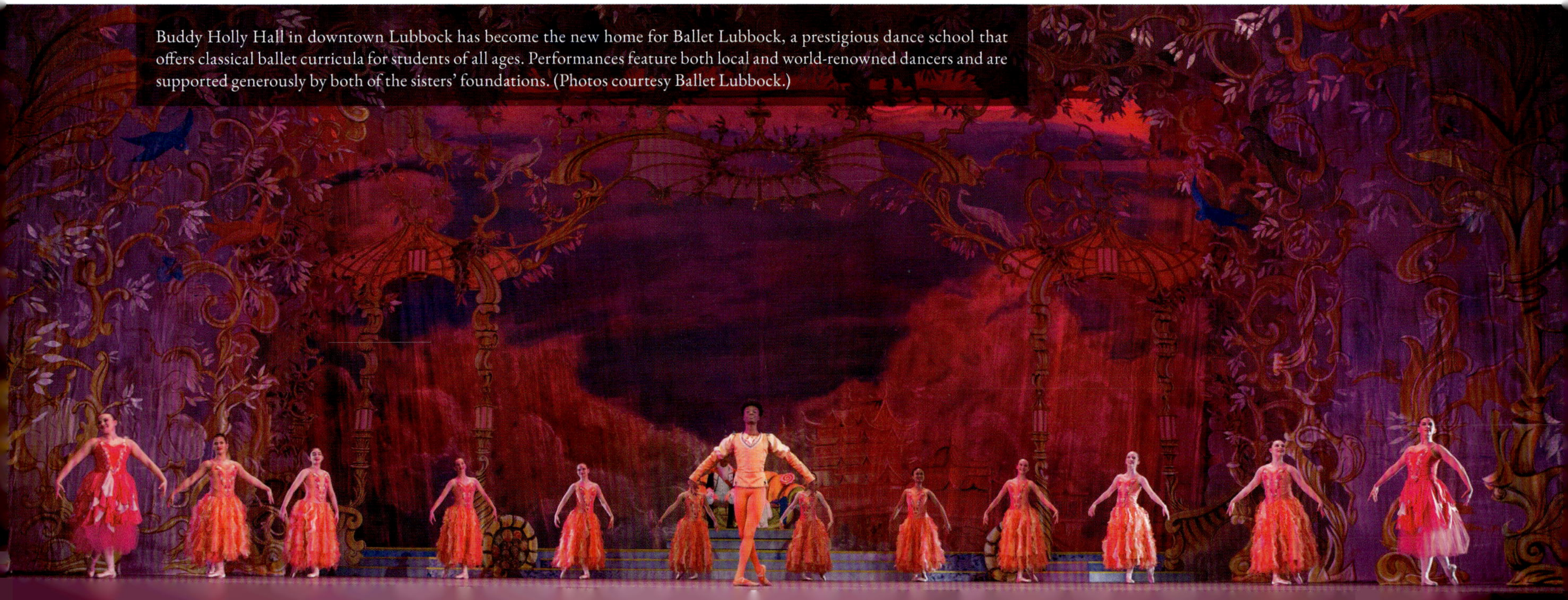

Buddy Holly Hall in downtown Lubbock has become the new home for Ballet Lubbock, a prestigious dance school that offers classical ballet curricula for students of all ages. Performances feature both local and world-renowned dancers and are supported generously by both of the sisters' foundations. (Photos courtesy Ballet Lubbock.)

mineral royalties, outbuildings, and cash into the equal shares indicated previously. Matthews also pointed out how the dissolution would benefit shareholders primarily by lowering each person's federal tax bill.

The final consideration was to resolve how to continue to operate the Mallet Ranch and future oil leases and properties. Since dividing up such operations into shares was impractical and would only serve to carve up into pieces what worked better as a whole entity, the directors agreed they would form an "informal partnership" to operate the ranch and farm operations and to negotiate future oil leases. They named their new partnership simply the Mallet Ranch. A. L Henderson, who had been the Mallet president, was removed largely at the insistence of Tom Jones, and to manage the office they hired Anne Snyder to keep the Mallet Ranch's books and maintain the office. Snyder was Tom Jones's first cousin and a descendant of the pioneer Snyder ranching family. For the next thirty-four years, Anne Snyder would serve as personal secretary for both Christine and Helen and subsequently assume much of the responsibility for the day-to-day operation of the Mallet Ranch.

Tom Jones had his own ideas about what to do with the ranch after dissolution of the Mallet Land and Cattle Company. He wanted to find one individual to lease the entire surface on a lease of at least ten years. The partners, thus, would not have to worry about operating a ranch and all the toils and vagaries that came with it. All they would have to do was collect lease payment for the surface and royalty payments from the oil companies. He even discussed his idea as a *fait accompli* with Wright Matthews and found an interested party in partners Tom Coble and J. A. Whittenburg Jr. of Amarillo. They were receptive to Jones's pitch and began preliminary negotiations to find an agreement, but the men had overlooked one problem that would disrupt their plan: Christine DeVitt had no desire to see the stock operation her father had founded go to someone else to operate. At the age of sixty-four, Christine DeVitt was on the verge of becoming a rancher.

CHAPTER 6

MORE OIL BRINGS MORE WEALTH

When David DeVitt established the Mallet Ranch in 1895, the industry was on the cusp of moving from a frontier operation to a modern model. DeVitt, in many ways, represented the coming of modern operations as he practiced conservation management of his range with a careful eye to the quality of his herd and the most efficient methods of balancing cattle feeding in preparation for marketing. The cattle industry in Texas matured through the 1930s and by the 1950s had begun to employ a number of new techniques that allowed Texas cattlemen to become the most efficient producers of beef in the world. The Texas cattle industry modernized so well that in 1973 the state reached a peak of production with more than fifteen million head of cattle. Texas cattle raising was truly "big business."

Most cattlemen would have been amused if you had told them that a 64-year-old woman with little experience raising cattle and certainly none in operating a range of around 50,000 acres had decided she could become a successful rancher. Christine DeVitt moved to Lubbock after her father's death and began to make frequent trips to the ranch, meeting most of the hands who worked the cattle as well as visiting with their families. Sometimes she even stayed overnight in the headquarters house. In her younger days she and her brother had spent summers at the ranch before her education sent her to other states and then teaching jobs in Fort Worth. In 1921 Christine had ended her brief teaching career and left the family's Fort Worth home to join her mother and sister in California. She was never indifferent to the ranch operations but appeared to

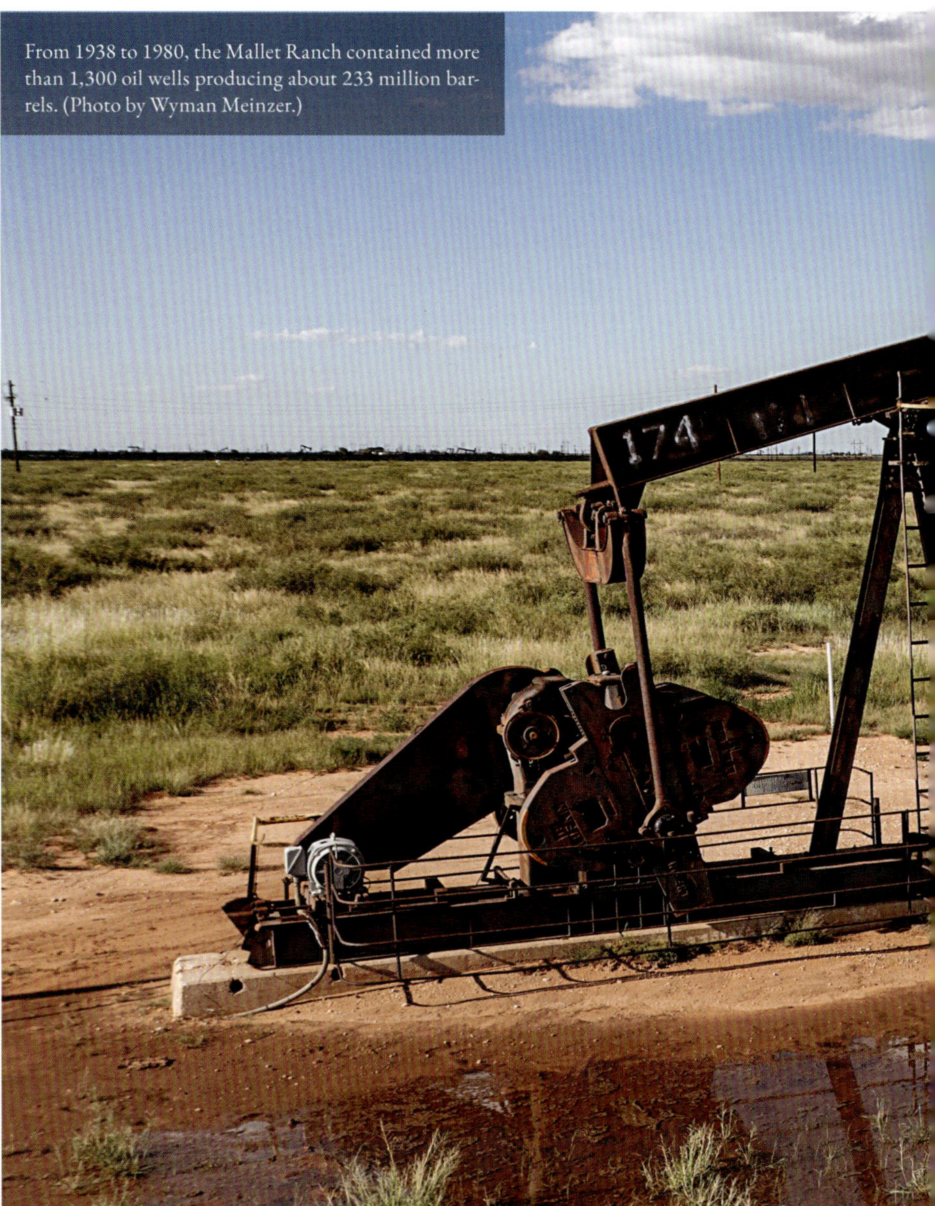

From 1938 to 1980, the Mallet Ranch contained more than 1,300 oil wells producing about 233 million barrels. (Photo by Wyman Meinzer.)

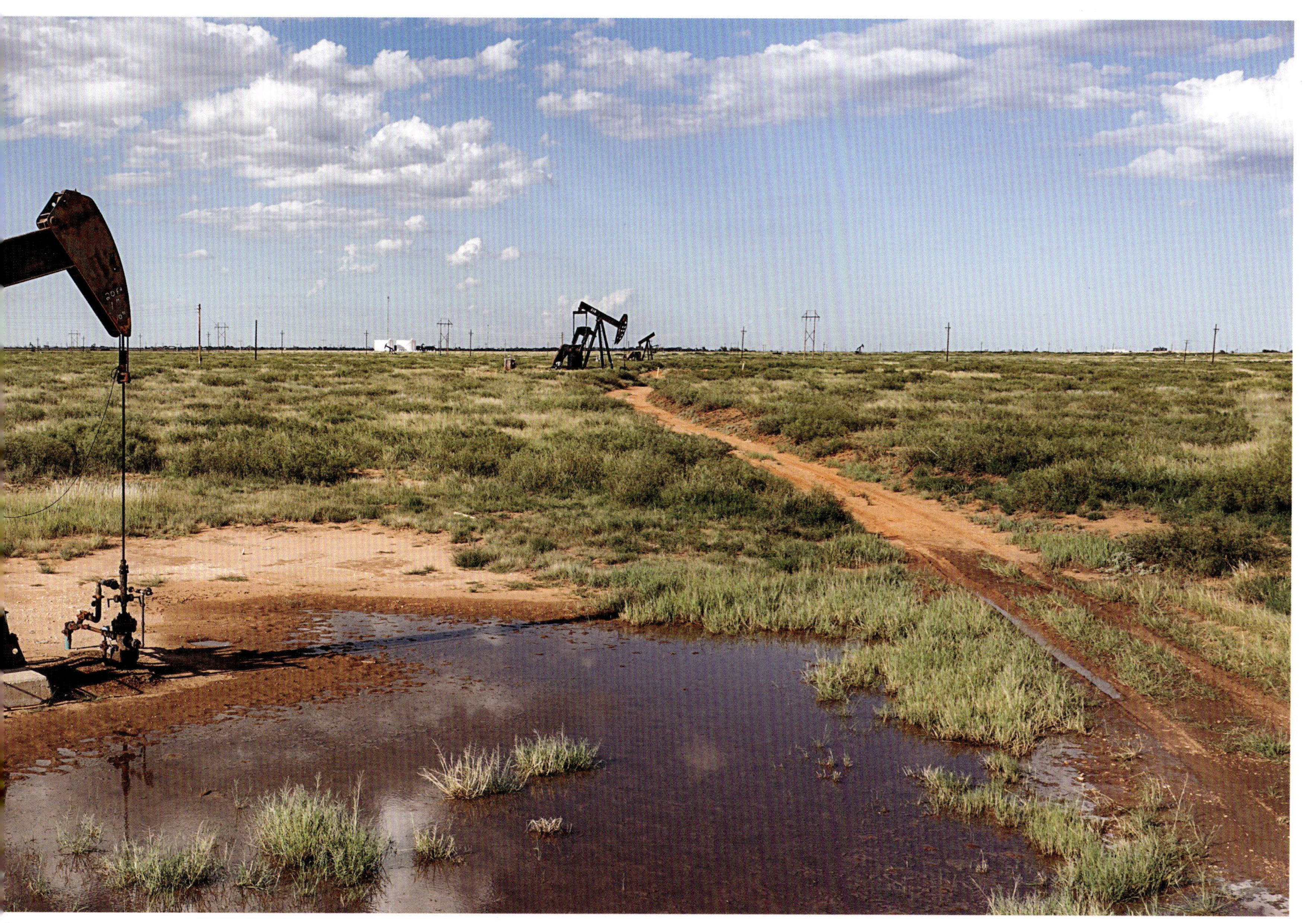

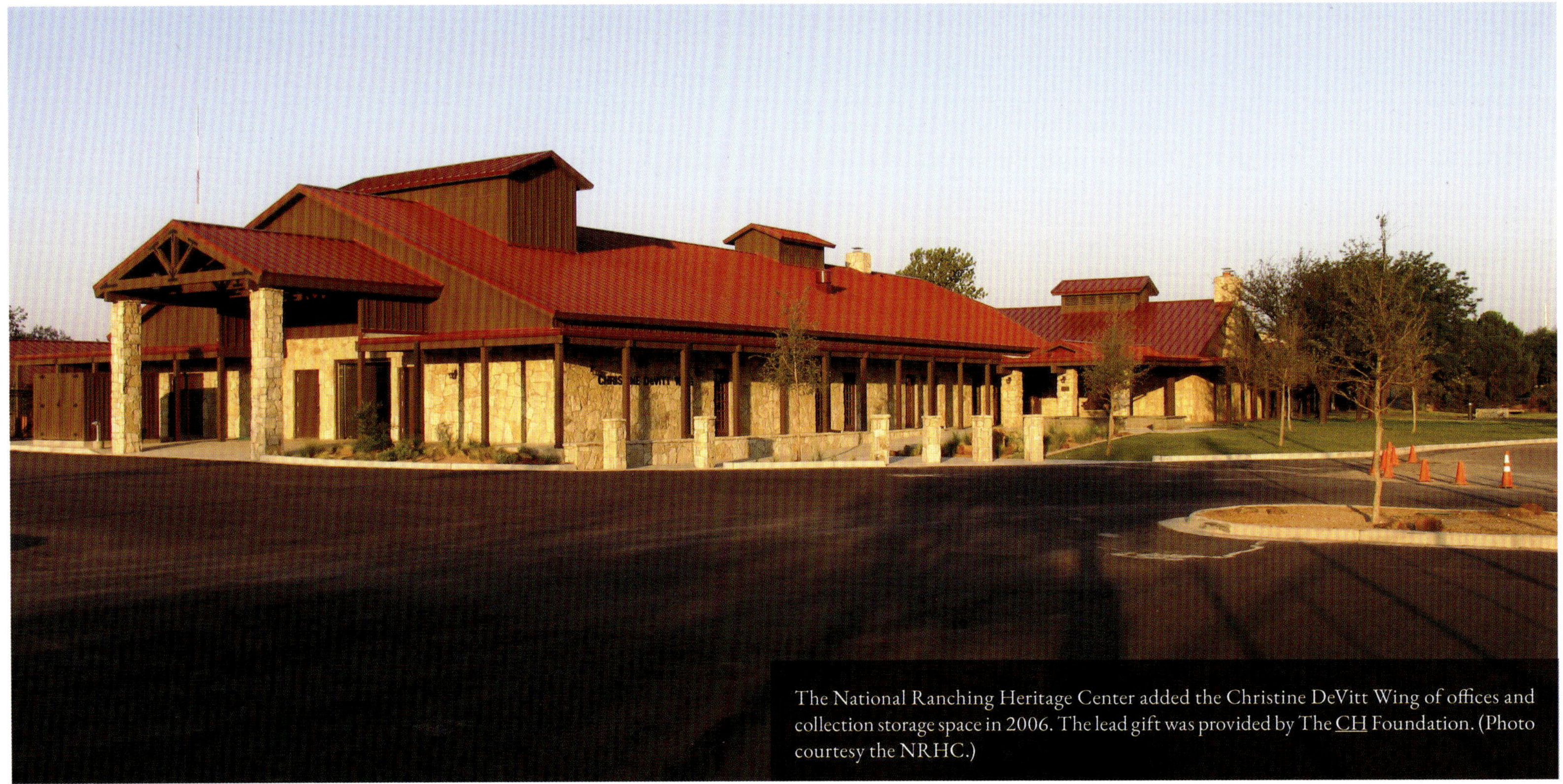

The National Ranching Heritage Center added the Christine DeVitt Wing of offices and collection storage space in 2006. The lead gift was provided by The CH Foundation. (Photo courtesy the NRHC.)

be as much estranged from her father as was her mother. But through the years she had bought and began to keep twenty-five to thirty head of cattle on three thousand acres she and Helen had inherited from their father. This parcel of land was attached to the south end of the ranch and was not shared with their partners. Christine was not as inexperienced or as indifferent as she might have seemed to her partners.

Tom Jones certainly found the idea of Christine's managing the ranch to be ludicrous and wasted no time letting Miss Devitt know that any notion of her taking over the Mallet operation was pure folly. He initially tried to convince her to allow him to lease the ranch to one individual. When she refused and brought up the idea that perhaps she could operate it, he proposed that she only run cattle on a small part of it, at least until she could learn what she needed to do, and then—perhaps—expand operations. As usual, Christine dithered in making a final decision but kept her options open. In the interim while Christine tried to decide, the other partners sold off the entire stock of the Mallet—over 1,000 head—to a New Mexico rancher in February 1949. For the first time since the early 1890s, no cattle grazed on the approximately 50,000 acres of the Mallet Ranch.

Tom Jones, who through his wife and as Mallet farm manager had come to exert more influence on all the partners, grew exasperated at his sister-in-law's failure to come to a decision—any decision—about what to do with the surface operations of the Mallet. He wrote numerous letters to his wife expressing his sentiments. "I talked with Christine today and she still refuses to consider allowing me to find someone to lease the pastures," he declared in one such letter. "She just tells me that she is thinking." In another letter he explained to his wife that "Christine put me off today when I met with her to discuss the ranch. I'm not sure if she will ever make up her mind." Jones did finally find someone, Kansas cattleman A. E. Smith, who was willing to lease the Mallet's pastures. It was a unique lease, however, with Smith proposing to pay by the head instead of by the acre. He planned to place 1,800 head of cattle on the Mallet for $1.50 a head for only one year, which meant the Mallet would have the problem of what to do with its surface acres again in 1950.

Christine rendered that decision moot in the fall of 1949. She had certainly discussed her plan with Tom Jones before she notified her partners because she asked her sister to join in her intention to become a ranch operator. Helen declined. She was content in her current life, which mostly involved traveling and checking into health resorts in an effort to deal with her colon problems. Christine sent each of her partners a letter in September 1949 in which she proposed that she lease the

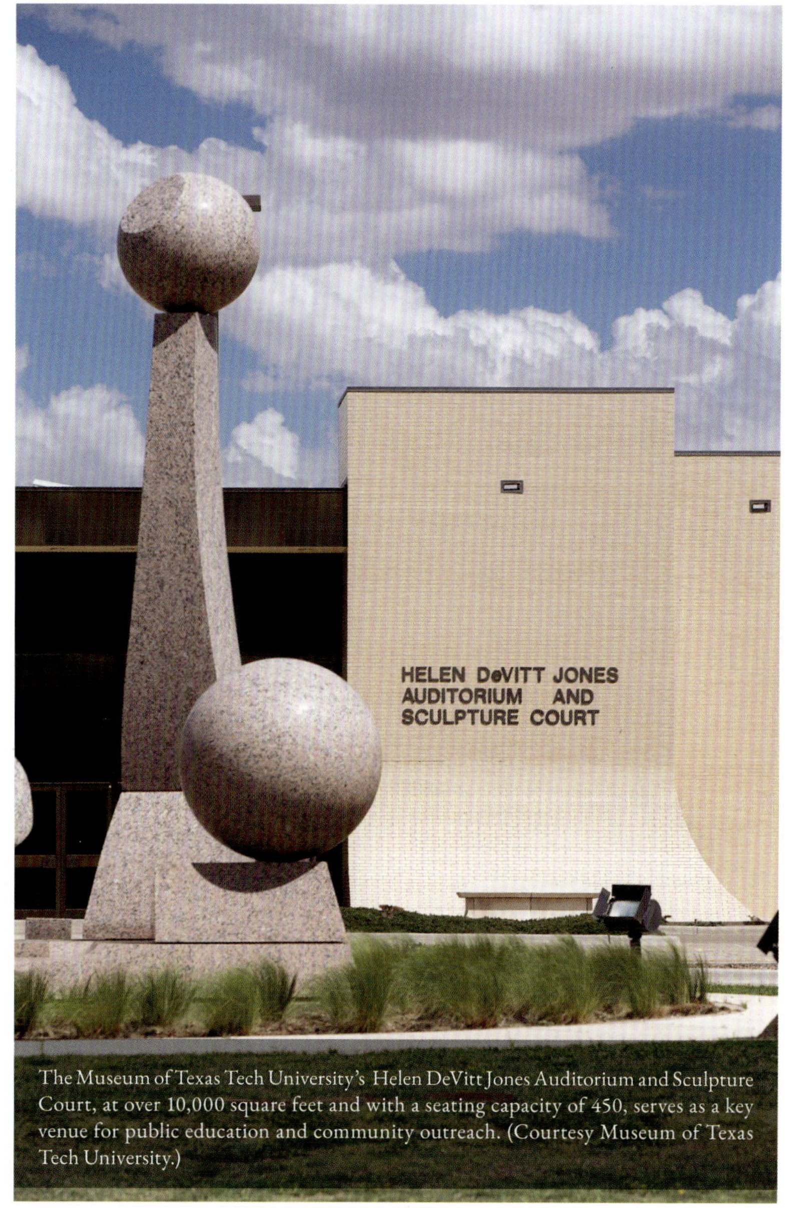

The Museum of Texas Tech University's Helen DeVitt Jones Auditorium and Sculpture Court, at over 10,000 square feet and with a seating capacity of 450, serves as a key venue for public education and community outreach. (Courtesy Museum of Texas Tech University.)

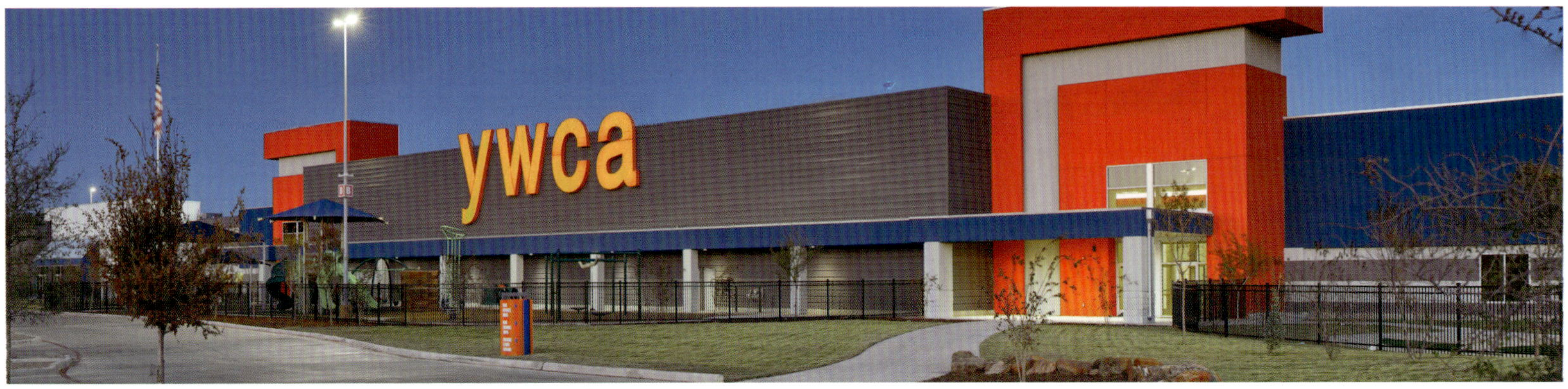

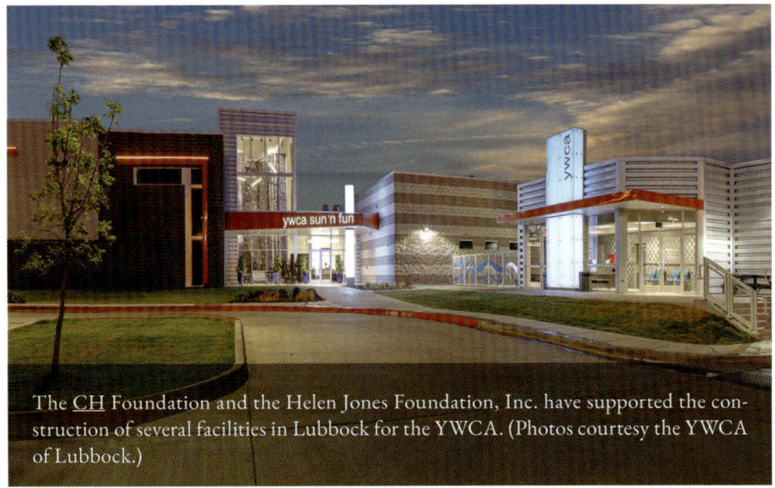

The CH Foundation and the Helen Jones Foundation, Inc. have supported the construction of several facilities in Lubbock for the YWCA. (Photos courtesy the YWCA of Lubbock.)

entire surface of the Mallet Ranch to do with as she saw fit. What that meant to Christine was that she could stock all or part of the Mallet according to her wishes and then sublease the remainder if she so desired. The majority of her partners were amenable, although R. B. Hewitt, the trustee of the W. D. Johnson shares, was reluctant. After some obvious prodding, Hewitt came around and was the one who set the rate of fifty cents an acre per year, a total that was near $25,000. The others agreed and quoted that sum to Christine.

True to her nature, Christine refused to pay that amount because she claimed the many oil wells on the property and the accompanying crew roads and other structures related to oil production rendered much of the Mallet unsuitable to graze cattle. She countered with thirty-five cents an acre. R. B. Hewitt and J. Lee Johnson objected to the figure and wanted to hold firm at fifty cents. Tom Jones by this time realized that not only was the market to lease the Mallet slim but that Christine DeVitt's obstinacy would never approve any other lease brought to the partners after she unhurriedly made up her mind. He wrote to J. Lee Johnson and Hewitt to lobby them to accept Christine's offer and expressed his opinion that Christine would be a good steward for the acres. The partners acquiesced and with Christine signed a three-year lease that gave her complete control over the entire 46,000 surface acres of the Mallet Ranch. Christine paid the $16,000 per year rate—$48,000—up front (a rare agreement for her), but it was renewable for twenty years at Christine's option.

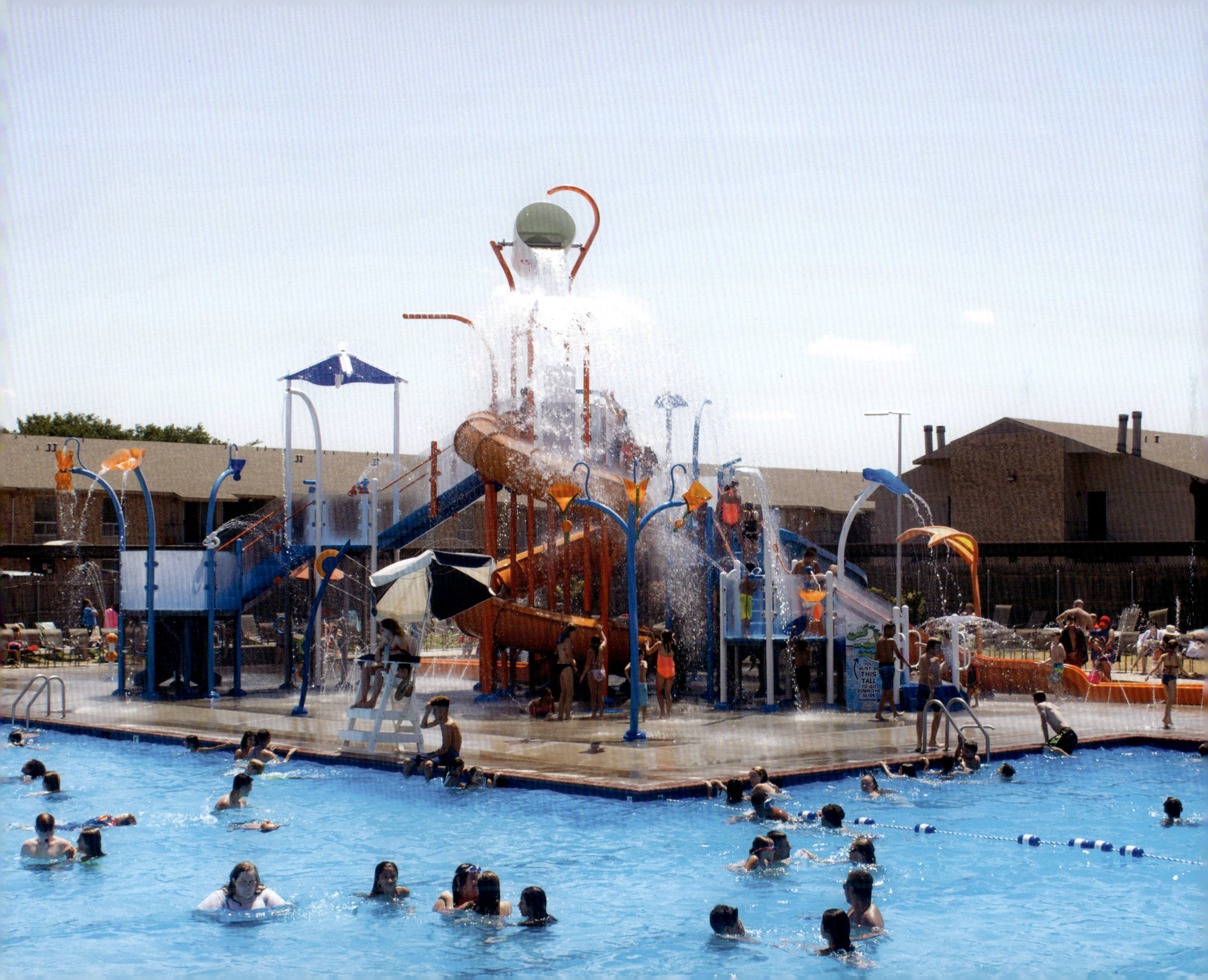
YOU
THIS
TALL
TO GO

In the early years of her control, Christine indeed proved to be a good steward of the Mallet Ranch. She continued to practice her father's conservation ideas. When the drought of the 1950s began to take its toll, she even ceased all leases and allowed the pastures to lie fallow for a year. Then she carefully leased lesser portions to conserve grassland for the next five years. In many ways her operation of the ranch was rather in sentiment for a family business than anything else, but she also had no desire to lose money. She subleased the majority of the pastures, usually at fifty cents an acre for larger tracts of pasture (the rate she had turned down from her partners) and sixty to seventy cents an acre for smaller leases. Such transactions allowed her to collect a personal income from the Mallet with an average profit during the 1950s of just under $3,000, a figure that included losses due to drought of more than $16,000 in 1953–1954.

Christine was a frugal—in some ways miserly—boss. She fired a number of foremen because she felt that they did not keep a close eye on ranch expenses. For years, despite pleas from her many foremen, she refused to install a telephone at the ranch. She finally relented in the 1960s but subtracted the charges for each hand's use of the phone from their wages. Assorted reasons likely explained Christine's conservative fiscal nature. Like for all agricultural economics, stock operations are subject to many factors far outside their operators' control (e.g., weather, the market, the uncertainty of trying to raise living beings for profit). A look at Christine's expenses through the 1950s and 1960s shows how varied they could be. Some years the costs to operate the Mallet were as high as $40,000 while in other years Christine could keep such outlays under $20,000. Christine's ego and stubbornness also might have played a role. Her partners were somewhat condescending when they agreed to allow her to lease the pastures, and as a woman in an occupation that was almost exclusively male, Christine was determined to become successful if for no other reason than to "show the boys" she could do it.

The expense that most infuriated Christine was taxes—of any kind. Just the mention of federal income taxes could make her explode. She put off as long as possible preparing or even signing her tax returns, partly from procrastination and partly due to her ire about having to pay. In fact, Christine often waited until December 31 every year to pay a number of bills and taxes as a quirky form of protest that would continue for the rest of her life. Property taxes also could fill her with indignation. The Mallet was one of the most valuable sources of income for Hockley and Cochran Counties and thus subject to a healthy property tax. When it came to paying those taxes, Christine DeVitt protested more than she did not. On one Cochran County levy for 1972, Christine wrote in the margin "too high, will not pay" and mailed it back to the county. After an exchange of letters, the county agreed to reduce the tax by approximately a third, and she paid it. As she did with her federal income taxes, Christine waited until the last possible date to submit her property taxes. While procrastination was very likely a factor, paying at the last possible moment was no doubt her personal protest at having to pay taxes at all.

Christine spent as much time as possible at the ranch, but she continued to live in Lubbock. She had never driven much and was a notoriously poor driver (as many friends and acquaintances have recounted), but she needed to purchase a car to make the trip from Lubbock to the ranch. After much haggling and the typical quirky Christine demands, such as insisting that the car be shipped to Lubbock by rail, she made her purchase. It was a gleaming 1950 Buick Coupe, one of the few of that model sold in Lubbock that year. Tom Jones reported to his wife that Christine was proud of her purchase, but she did not drive the car very often and one day, not long after she bought the vehicle, she parked it in the garage at the Mallet headquarters/homestead house and never moved it again. The car remains there today— weathered, beaten, and covered in bird droppings.

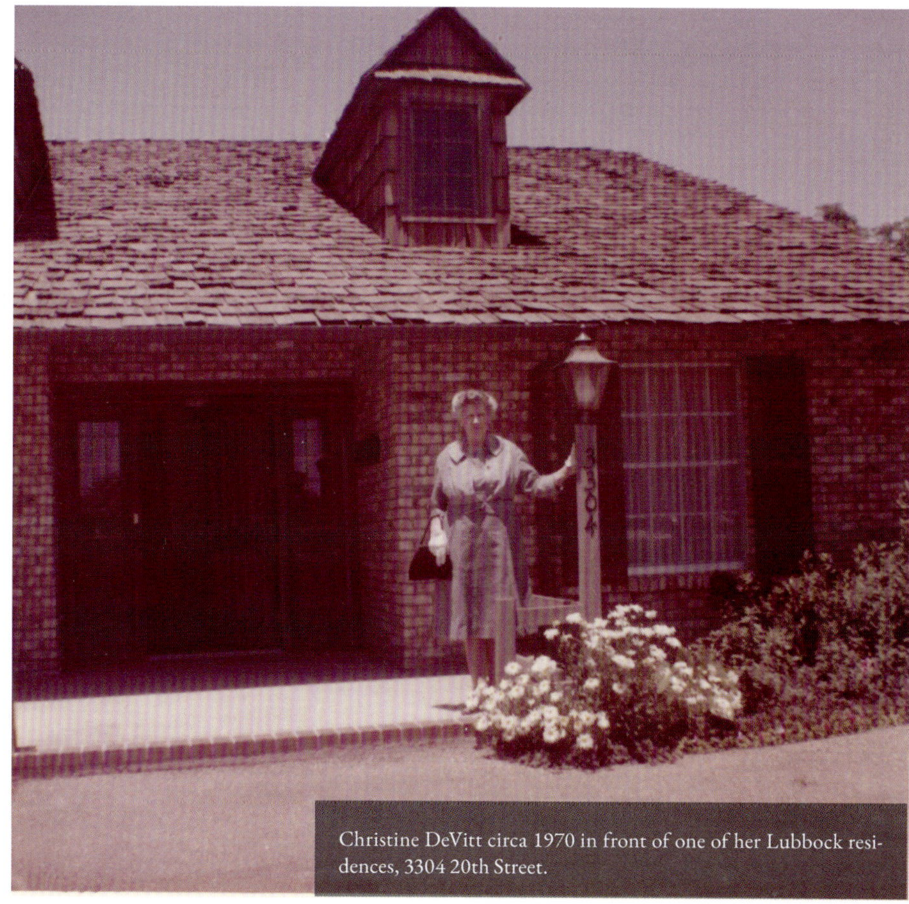

Christine DeVitt circa 1970 in front of one of her Lubbock residences, 3304 20th Street.

No recounting of the life of Christine DeVitt would be complete without mentioning her affection for cats, a fondness that most would call obsessive and some may even label unnatural. While she maintained her residence at the Hilton, she bought a house on 21st Street in Lubbock near the Texas Tech campus in 1944, but she never moved into it. In a legal wrangle that became quite a spectacle among Lubbock citizens, the Hilton management filed suit and evicted Christine in 1948. Christine was frequently late with her rent and cleaning her suite was a chore for the housekeeping staff as she left empty Coke bottles and other detritus all over her room. The Hilton eviction stood, and Christine had to move into her home on 21st Street. Tom and Helen, who had left their residence at the Hilton in 1943 (they voluntarily moved and were not evicted) lived in the house next door. When Christine moved into the home, she began to accumulate cats. She took in any stray that wandered anywhere near her house or any feline anyone would offer her. Cats, like any animal left in a natural state, will produce progeny, and it did not take long for the cats under Christine's roof to number in the hundreds. The presence of so many cats led her to purchase the house next door, which became a home solely for cats. In fact, both houses became so filled with cats that she eventually had to move.

Christine once told her ranch foreman John Sones that her love for cats stemmed from a terrible accident when she left home for a lengthy period and mistakenly locked a mother cat and kittens in the garage. When she discovered they had starved to death, she vowed she would rectify the mistake by caring for any cats that came her way.

Historian David Murrah, who began his research for his book *Oil, Taxes, and Cats* while Helen was still alive, interviewed Helen's daughter Dorothy Secrest on a number of occasions and wrote that Christine and Helen were not close. The fact that their age difference of fourteen years made them closer to being mother and daughter played a role, but Murrah reported that it was more than that. His reasoning considers several other factors. Helen was treated as the "baby" of the family, especially after the death of David Jr., and she was born after David and Florence had lost their elder son, Harold. Florence quite obviously doted on Helen, a fact that she let Christine realize not only in words but also in actions. Helen was also more attractive, something that Christine may have felt created a gulf between them. Tom Jones could also have been a factor. If he and Christine had actually had a romantic interest in each other after Christine's return to Lubbock, the fact that he eventually married Christine's younger, prettier sister might have caused tension between the two DeVitt women.

Helen DeVitt Secrest Jones certainly had charted a much different course than had Christine. Helen did not take a strong interest in the Mallet business, so one cannot investigate her life through a close perusal of the Mallet records or documents surrounding the corporation's dealings as one can with David and even Christine. Helen did leave a significant correspondence record, and David Murrah's interviews and writing are also valuable, and the primary tool, in piecing together Helen's life story. Helen spent a large portion of her early adult years in California shuttling between Los Angeles, San Diego, and Altadena, a small city in Los Angeles County north of Pasadena in the Verdugo Mountains. She moved to Altadena in the hope that of lessening the effects of her daughter Dorothy's asthma, but the need to once again care for her mother brought her back to Los Angeles in 1942.

Helen's concern for her colon problems led her to spend a lot of time and money searching for a cure at doctors' offices, sanitariums, and health resorts. At various times Helen checked herself into sanitariums for undisclosed illnesses in Michigan and Florida. She also virtually moved back to California when Dorothy entered the University of California, Berkeley, repeating a pattern her mother had made with her.

One factor in her constant moving and traveling could have been her reluctance to live with her husband, Tom. Some of the letters are loving and share an obvious affection, while others are terse and almost businesslike in tone. Jones was a heavy drinker,

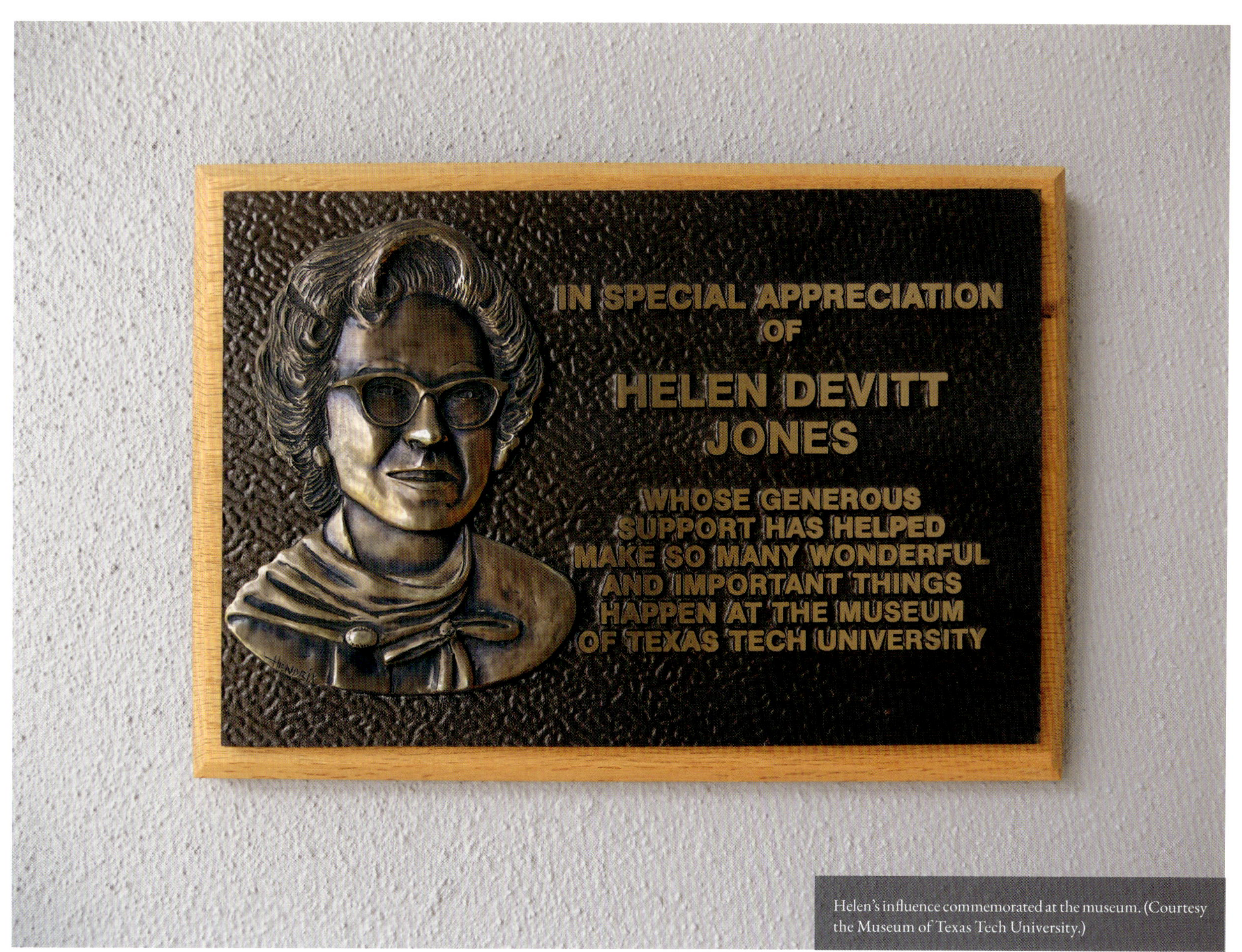

Helen's influence commemorated at the museum. (Courtesy the Museum of Texas Tech University.)

perhaps even characterized as an alcoholic, and a heavy smoker at an average of four cigarettes an hour. He also drank a lot of coffee, adding at least eight to ten teaspoons of sugar a day with his coffee. Furthermore, there are indications that he possessed a healthy temper. Even when Helen returned to Texas in 1950, she did not come back to Lubbock but instead bought a house in Dallas. When her husband had surgery and had to remain homebound for two months in late 1950, Helen did not come back to Lubbock but remained in Dallas with more frequent trips to California. For whatever reason, much of the marriage between Helen and Tom Jones was a long-distance relationship.

Through the early part of the 1950s, Helen rotated between California and Colorado (where she became enchanted with Colorado Springs), and made short stays in Lubbock and Phoenix before buying a house and moving to San Antonio in 1953. One place where she did not spend much time prior to 1965 was Lubbock. Murrah suggests that she avoided Lubbock for a number of reasons, such as the fact that the dry climate and dust exacerbated her health problems, living apart from her sister made life less contentious and confrontational, and her husband's drinking and behavior made her uncomfortable.

Besides contending with her health issues, Helen DeVitt Jones also had to cope with quirky tax laws, particularly California laws. Helen's travels had taken her to California frequently and for extended periods of time, so that state was keen to claim her as a resident; California could impose a significant state tax on Helen's royalty-heavy oil income. The desire to avoid such a tax was the primary reason Helen kept Lubbock as her "official" residence and bought the house in Dallas. At Tom's urging, Helen sought help from Wright Matthews, the attorney who had settled her mother's estate tax difficulties with California. Matthews initially counseled Helen to accept a settlement that would require her to pay a portion of the tax, but Tom Jones would not hear of such an idea. In his mind Helen was a legal resident of Texas and the state of California was trying to take advantage of her. He essentially fired Matthews in early 1953.

California grew tired of trying to collect state taxes from Helen, so in 1957 the Golden State tried to force the Honolulu Oil Company to "collect" their tax for them. Honolulu was a California corporation that held more than a dozen leases on almost 5,000 acres of Mallet land that included almost 200 oil wells, which meant that Helen received significant royalties from the company. California sent a court order to Honolulu that mandated that they garnish Helen's royalties until she paid her debt. Honolulu wrote Helen informing her of the action and dictating their potential legal liabilities. They were particularly worried that Helen would sue Honolulu and that legal action could damage their relationship with the Mallet partners. Helen, through Tom's advice, assured the officials at Honolulu that she would not hold them accountable. With such a pledge, Honolulu rejected California's request and their lawyers eventually received an injunction that quashed the earlier judgment. Honolulu continued to pay Helen's royalties.

The state of California played its last trump card in the case when it sued Helen in 1959 for payment of over $300,000 in

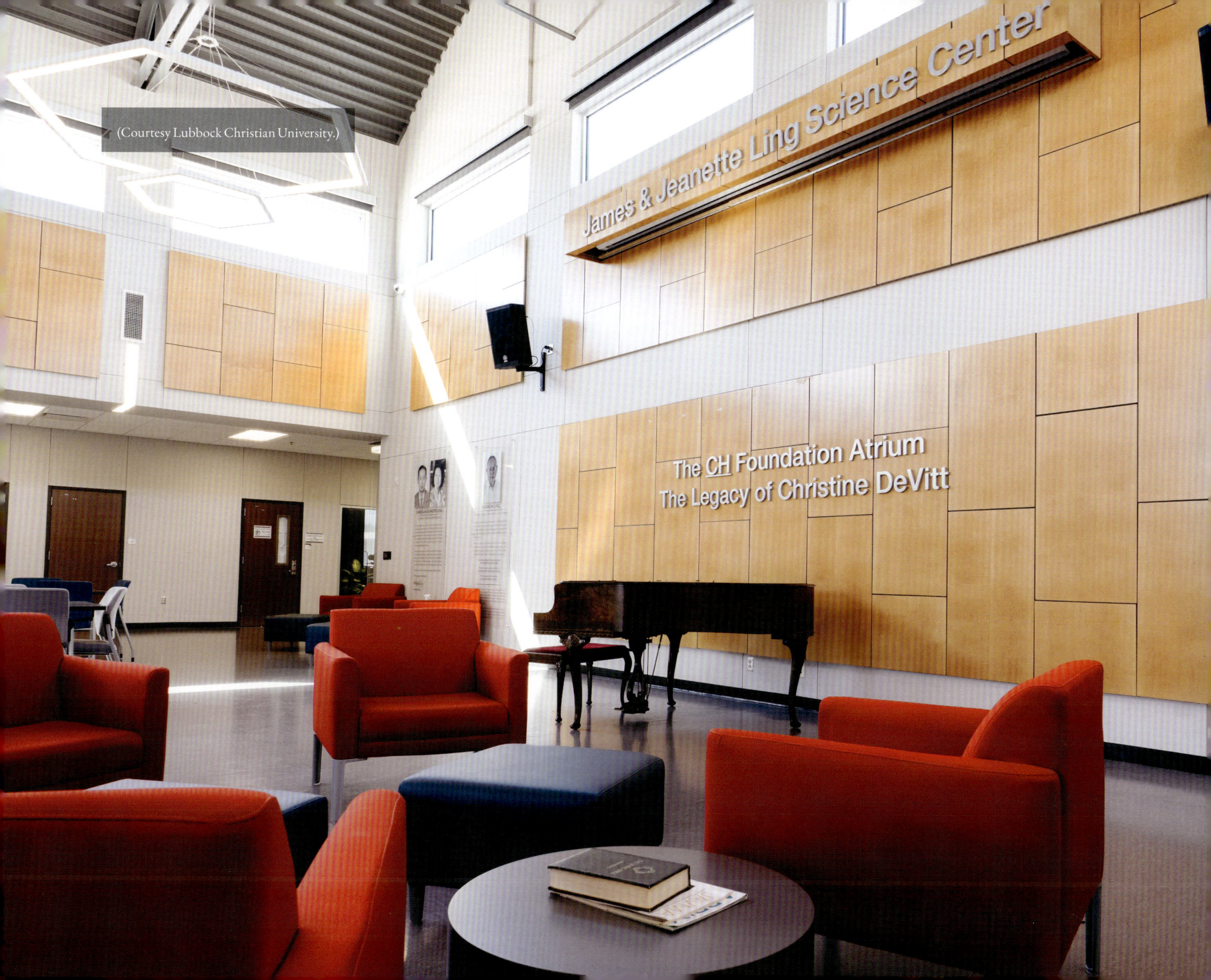

(Courtesy Lubbock Christian University.)

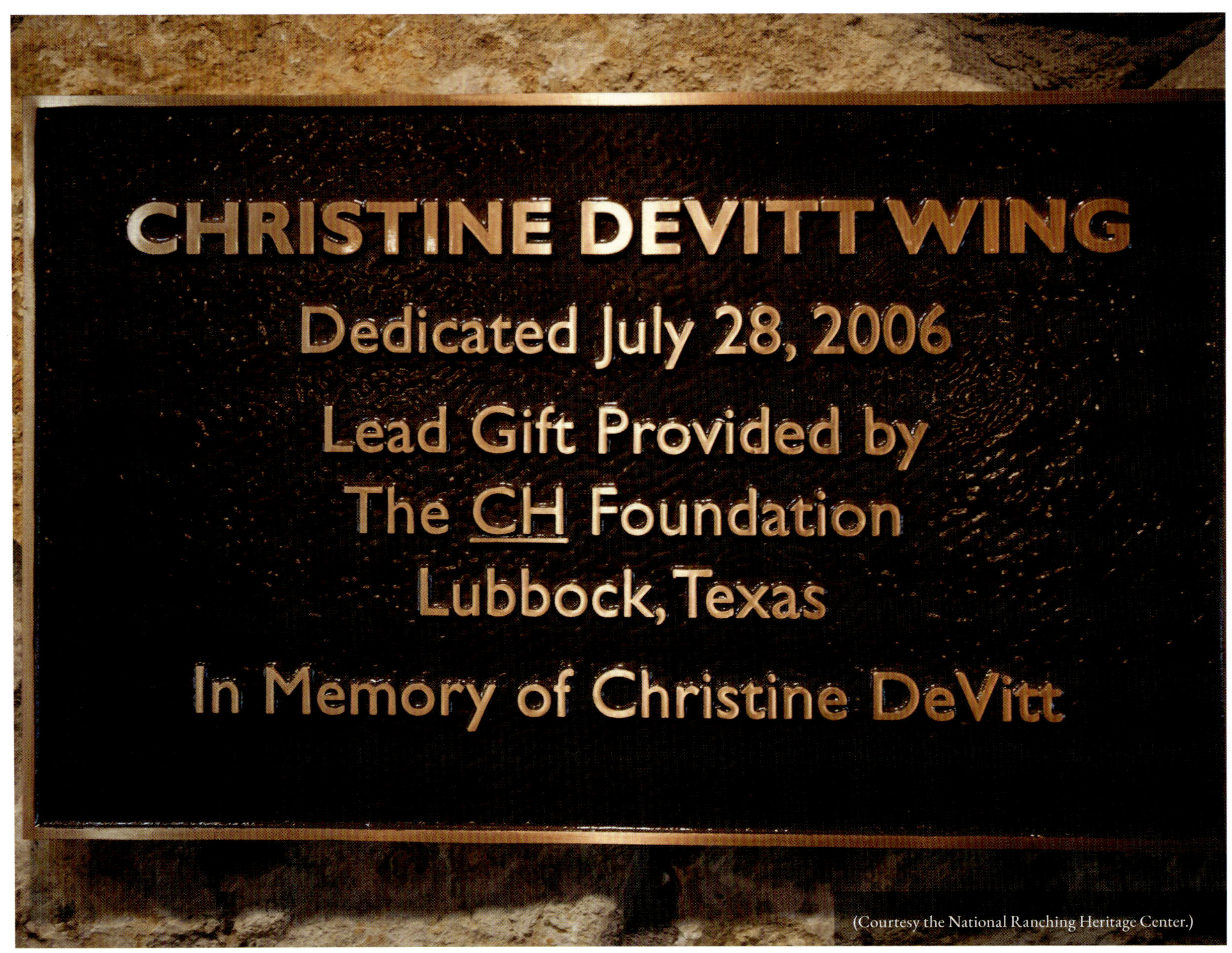

(Courtesy the National Ranching Heritage Center.)

back taxes for the period 1941 through 1960. Instead of turning to Wright Matthews, Helen hired another of Tom's friends, Jim Milam of Lubbock, to handle the suit. Milam negotiated with California authorities for the rest of 1959 and into 1960 before reaching a settlement that required Helen to pay $73,000, which was approximately $20,000 more than she would have paid in 1953 if she had accepted the resolution Wright Matthews had negotiated.

As Murrah details in his work, the episode with California spurred Tom Jones to begin pursuing a deal to sell most—or even all—of Helen's Mallet oil royalties. His intention was two-fold: (1) avoid any such tax situation again—particularly the chaotic and stressful inheritance tax if either Christine or Helen died prematurely—and (2) accumulate cash that presumably he and Helen could live on the rest of their lives. Wright Matthews advised Tom that he should sell Helen's shares and place the proceeds in tax-free bonds that would give the couple a substantial income free from taxes but also keep the principal intact. This strategy also would ensure that Dorothy was taken care of after her mother was gone. In the end, likely because the oil royalties were substantial and had the potential of rising, he recommended she sell only half her royalties. Helen agreed to the plan, and Tom gave Wright Matthews permission to seek a buyer.

Matthews found a buyer in an unlikely place, not an individual but an institution: Southern Methodist University (SMU) in Dallas. Matthews brought an offer of $500 an acre (or $2,500,000) for half of Helen's Mallet royalties. SMU countered with an offer of $350 an acre ($1,750,000). Matthews thought the proposal fair, but Tom initially considered it too low, primarily because he thought oil prices and demand would rise in the future. In the end the couple accepted the offer. Tom's acquiescence may have been due to his being caught up in the paranoid "Red Scare" rhetoric of the period. He told Helen that one reason to take the offer was because "the only bulwark and the only defense we have against Communism is Christian education." Matthews also approached Christine about selling half of her shares. She may have considered the offer but—not surprisingly—never made a decision. The non-decision proved to be a good choice since the recovery of Mallet oil reserves increased by a significant amount in the remainder of the 1950s into the 1960s, and oil prices also increased significantly.

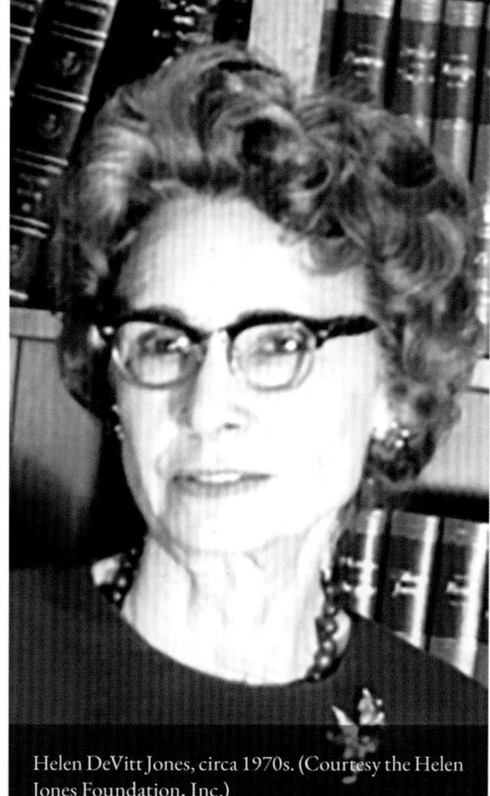
Helen DeVitt Jones, circa 1970s. (Courtesy the Helen Jones Foundation, Inc.)

Tom Jones's lifestyle finally caught up with him when he suffered a sudden fatal heart attack on January 12, 1955, at the age of sixty-three. Tom's death not only removed him from Helen's life—and despite their differences they did seem to have a loving relationship—but it also subtracted someone who had been a huge influence on the business affairs of the Mallet Ranch. Many may question Tom's motives, but while not all the advice he gave Christine and Helen was selfless, his presence did have a positive effect on the business decisions of the DeVitt family and the Mallet. Quite often he was the moderate voice when Christine waged her battles with everyone else on the Mallet board, and he took measures to make sure his wife would be safe as she aged; he was likely aware that he would precede her in death.

Tom's death caused Helen DeVitt Jones to spend some years somewhat adrift. She continued her travels to various locales she had come to enjoy, especially Colorado Springs, and took time to frequently visit Dorothy, who by this time was living in San Francisco. If Christine DeVitt's primary character trait was procrastination, Helen's was avoidance, which was a result of her gentle, nonconfrontational nature. She had never taken much interest in the Mallet or any other personal business and had left most decisions pertaining to them first to her father, then to Christine, and then Tom (who often consulted with Christine). Her method of avoiding not only the reality of her husband's death but also what she should do about her now growing personal wealth was to travel and continue her habit of visiting health spas and sanitariums. She scheduled a visit to the Mayo Clinic in the summer of 1957 determined to finally discover why her health was so poor. She spent six months living

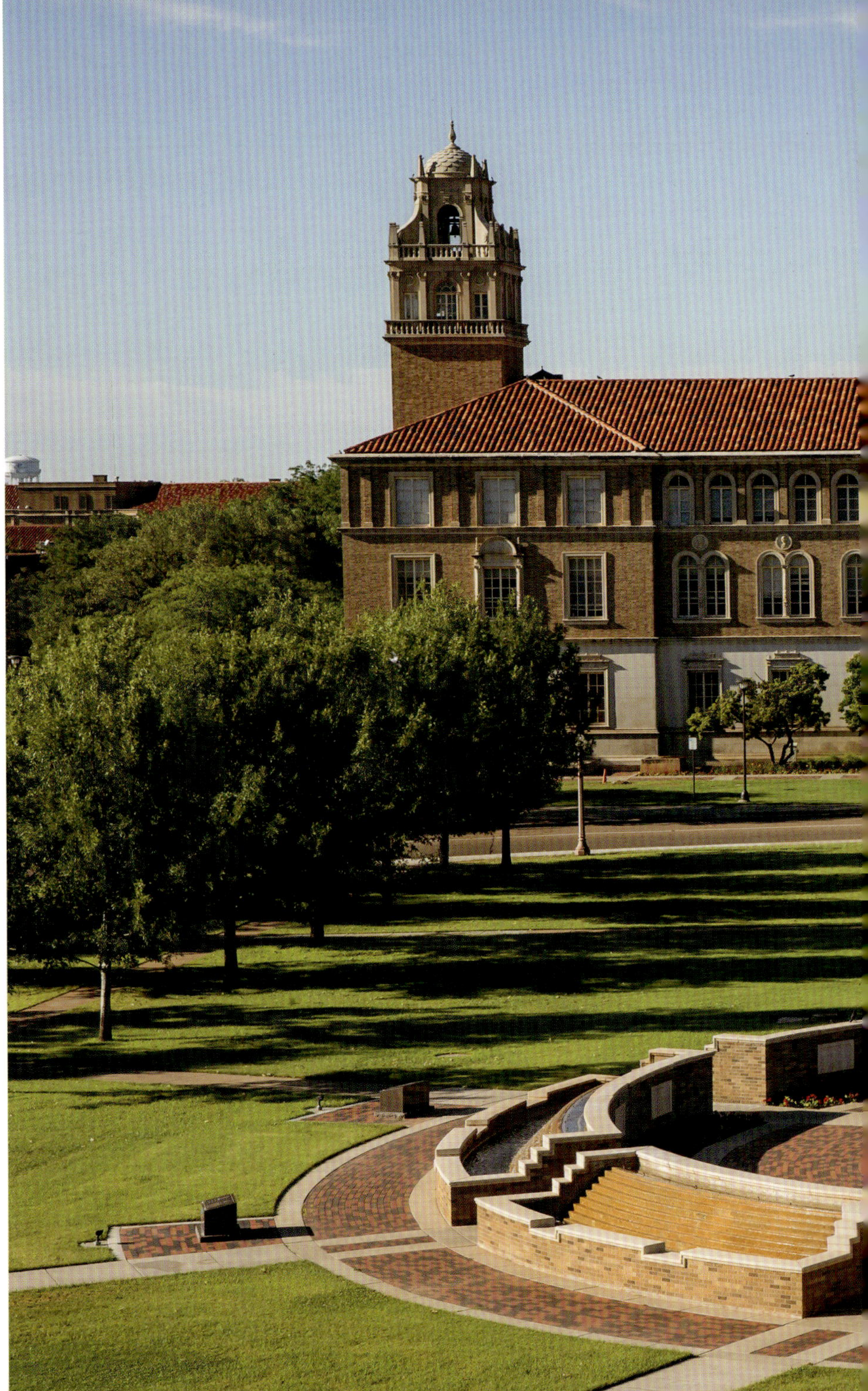

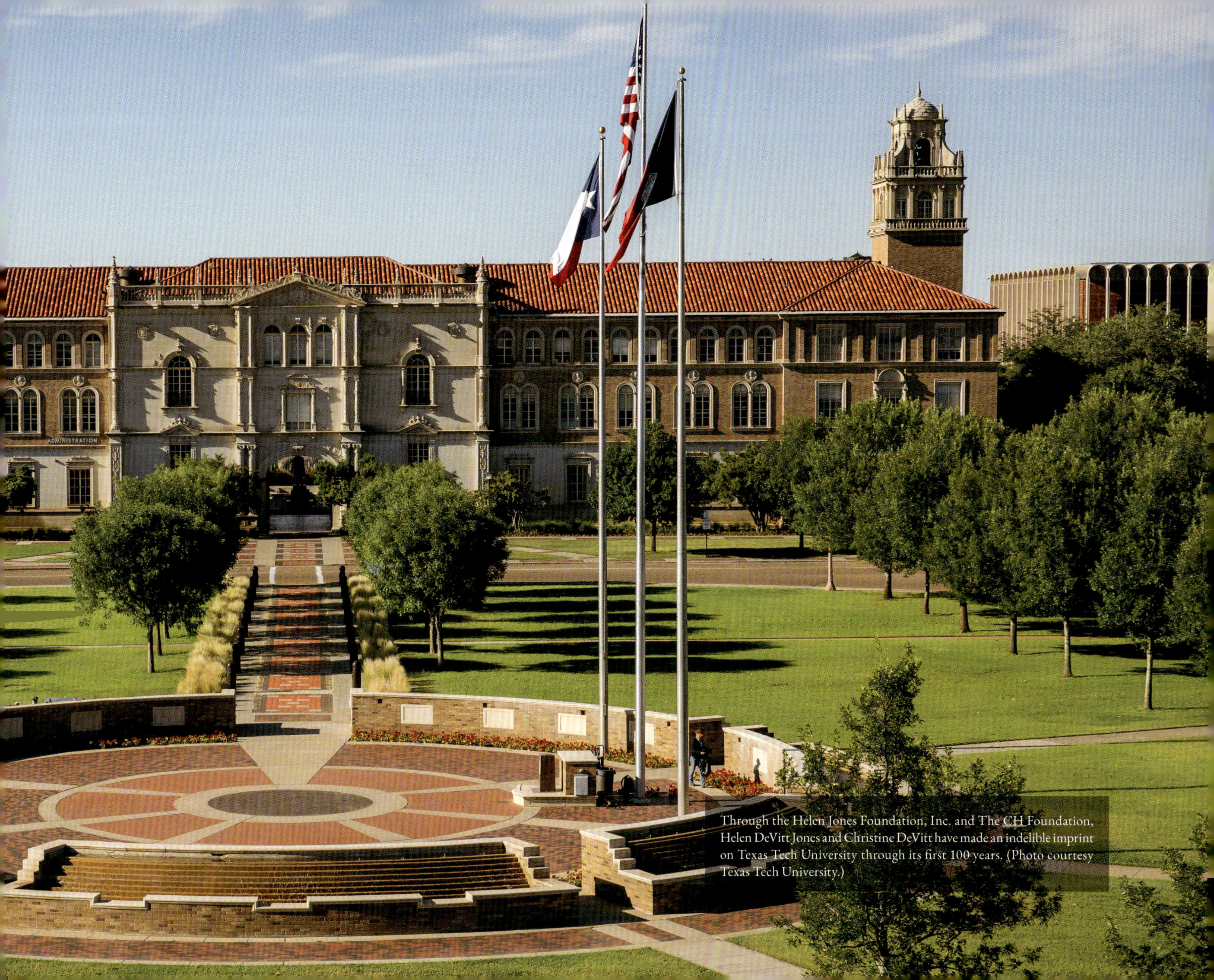

Through the Helen Jones Foundation, Inc. and The CH Foundation, Helen DeVitt Jones and Christine DeVitt have made an indelible imprint on Texas Tech University through its first 100 years. (Photo courtesy Texas Tech University.)

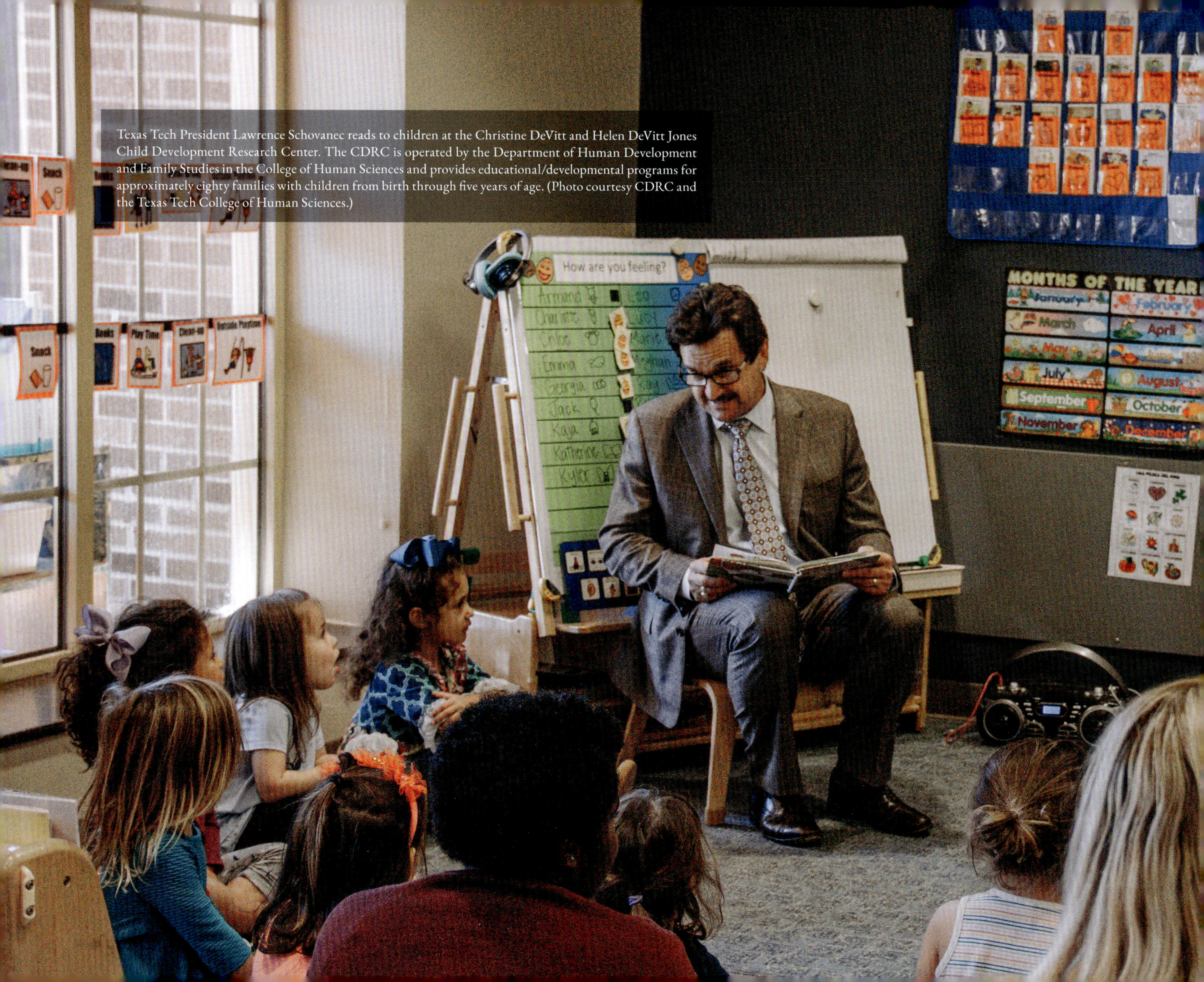

Texas Tech President Lawrence Schovanec reads to children at the Christine DeVitt and Helen DeVitt Jones Child Development Research Center. The CDRC is operated by the Department of Human Development and Family Studies in the College of Human Sciences and provides educational/developmental programs for approximately eighty families with children from birth through five years of age. (Photo courtesy CDRC and the Texas Tech College of Human Sciences.)

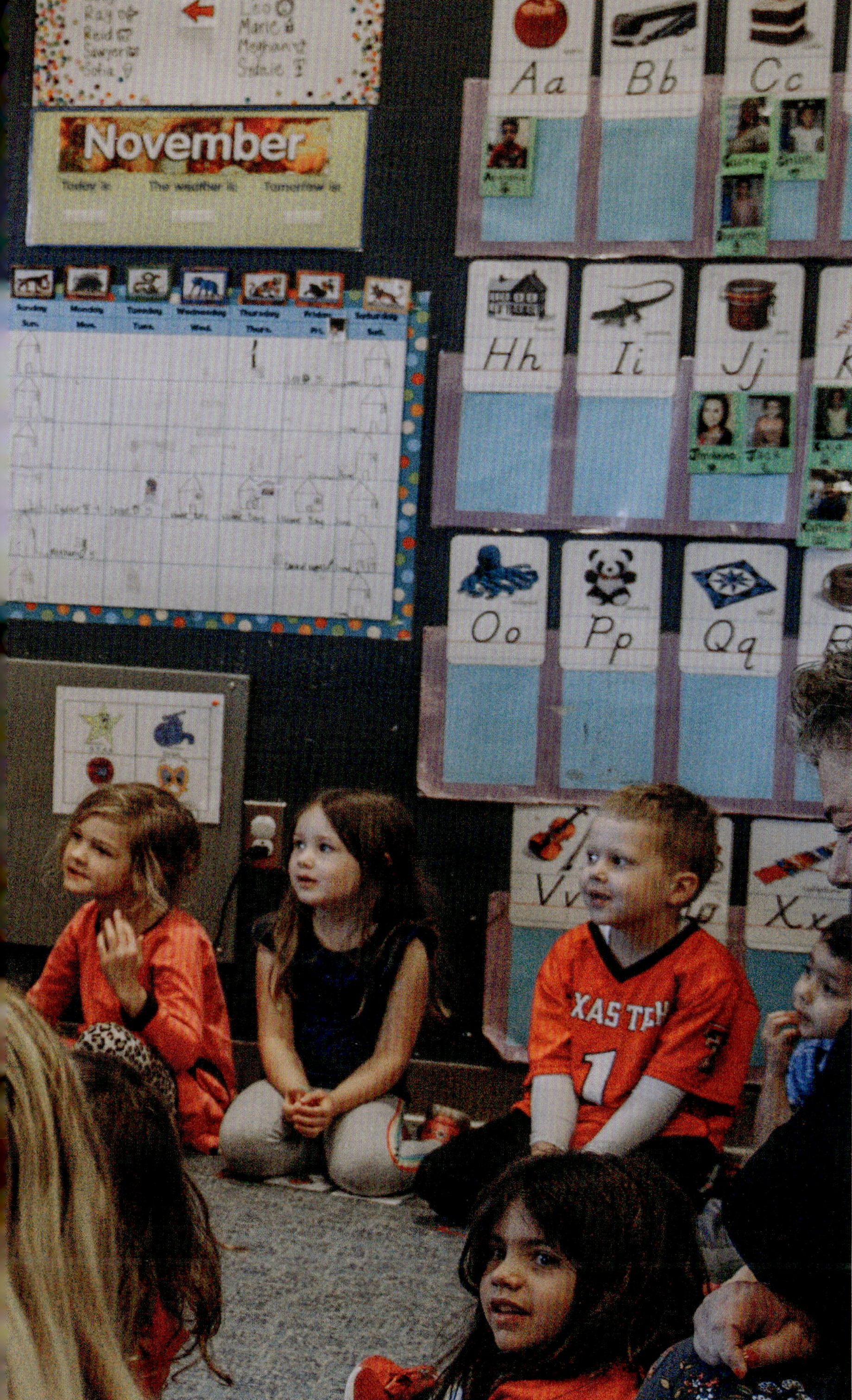

in Rochester, Minnesota, and visited numerous doctors. One of her visits was with a psychiatrist who told Helen, probably for the first time in her life, that many of her health problems were mental, not physical. She was sick and tired of being sick and tired.

Helen continued to travel in the first few years of the 1960s. Between her frequent stays in Colorado Springs, Phoenix, and Santa Barbara hotels and spas, she visited Dorothy in San Francisco. She also supported Dorothy's lifestyle, as her daughter was rootless and perhaps pursuing some of the same answers that her mother had never found. Just as Helen often did when she was young and asking her father for extra funds to help her live in California, Dorothy solicited additions to the generous allowance her mother provided. Perhaps surprisingly, Christine was a doting aunt and sent money to her niece quite often. Dorothy also experienced health issues: she suffered from extreme asthma, which often caused her to have numerous respiratory problems, some of them requiring hospitalization for weeks at a time. Helen, who was a very devoted mother, stayed at her side during those times and served as her primary caregiver as she convalesced.

Dorothy, whose career was as an artist, moved to an artist's colony in New York State in 1959. She would live in New York for the next fifteen years of her life. Helen followed her daughter to the East Coast. Throughout 1960, Helen shuttled between New York City, Boston, Washington, DC, and then back to New York. She bought a house in Woodstock, New York, where Dorothy had settled. Dorothy married in 1961, which relieved Helen of some of her "duties" of caring for her daughter. Helen began to spend more time in Lubbock after that, which meant more time with Christine, who turned seventy-five in 1960. The two DeVitt sisters, beginning in the early 1960s, spent more time around each other than they had since Helen was a very young girl. Helen probably began to feel a greater obligation to care for her sister as she aged. Serving as a caregiver suited Helen's personality. In 1965 at the age of sixty-six, Helen cut back on her travels and generally spent her time in Lubbock living close to her sister.

Christine DeVitt had made moves in 1960 to increase her personal herd on the Mallet and actively involved herself with almost every decision on the ranch despite her advanced years. She continued her pattern of cycling through foremen to run the day-to-day operations at the Mallet, but in 1964 she turned to John Sones to serve in this capacity. Almost as irascible as Christine and a man who shared some of the same philosophies, Sones would be the last foreman of the Mallet, serving for more than twenty years. Perhaps Christine had found her match, but it could be that at almost eighty years old Christine DeVitt had begun to "mellow."

Sones did a fine job in managing the Mallet. Christine allowed him to have greater freedom in running the ranch, and she loosened the purse strings a bit—perhaps due to the fact that the Mallet oil wells were producing more revenue than anyone had ever thought possible. Sones, through the remainder of the 1960s, increased the profits of the Mallet Ranch operations each year, with a high of $26,000 in 1968. In many ways that was not just the pinnacle of beef cattle operations at the Mallet but the pinnacle in Texas and the nation. The economic woes that hit the country in the 1970s may have been even worse for agricultural sectors and some of the worst in history for beef cattle. A combination of nationwide recession, inflation (producing a new economic outcome, "stagflation"), and changes in the tastes and demands of the public led to a serious depression in beef prices. The Mallet saw its net income drop by $10,000 in 1969 to just a bit over break-even in 1970 and losses of more than $10,000 each year through 1975.

While the proceeds of the stock operation ranged from modest to nonexistent, the farm operations of the Mallet were a different story. The latter, which had begun in the 1920s, were not part of the ranch that Christine DeVitt controlled and operated. This was a separate division and had been overseen by Tom Jones before and then after the Mallet Land and Cattle Company dissolved in 1948. The Mallet lands were tenant farms. The standard contract that Tom Jones had farmers sign called for the operators of the farmland to return one-fourth of any cotton crop and one-third of any grains harvested to the Mallet as rent.

Like agricultural crop enterprises anywhere, Mallet farm revenue ebbed and flowed with the caprices of weather, market, and soil conditions. The World War II years were uneven as they coincided with irregular rainfall and an uncertain market. The end of the war brought better conditions; bountiful rains fell from 1946 to 1949, and the conversion of most farms to mechanical implement use brought greater harvests. At that same time, high demand for agricultural products—especially cotton—after the war increased commodity prices. Farm rents for the Mallet in those years averaged near $50,000, culminating in a high of $56,000 in 1949.

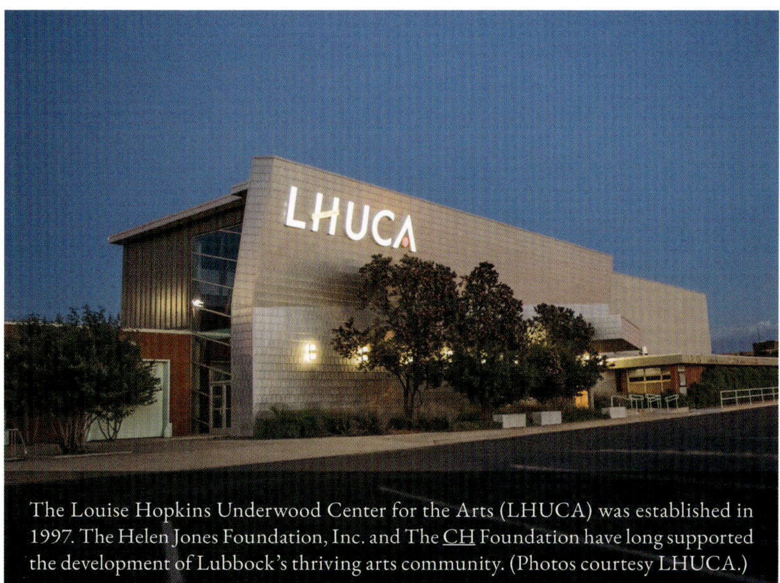

The Louise Hopkins Underwood Center for the Arts (LHUCA) was established in 1997. The Helen Jones Foundation, Inc. and The CH Foundation have long supported the development of Lubbock's thriving arts community. (Photos courtesy LHUCA.)

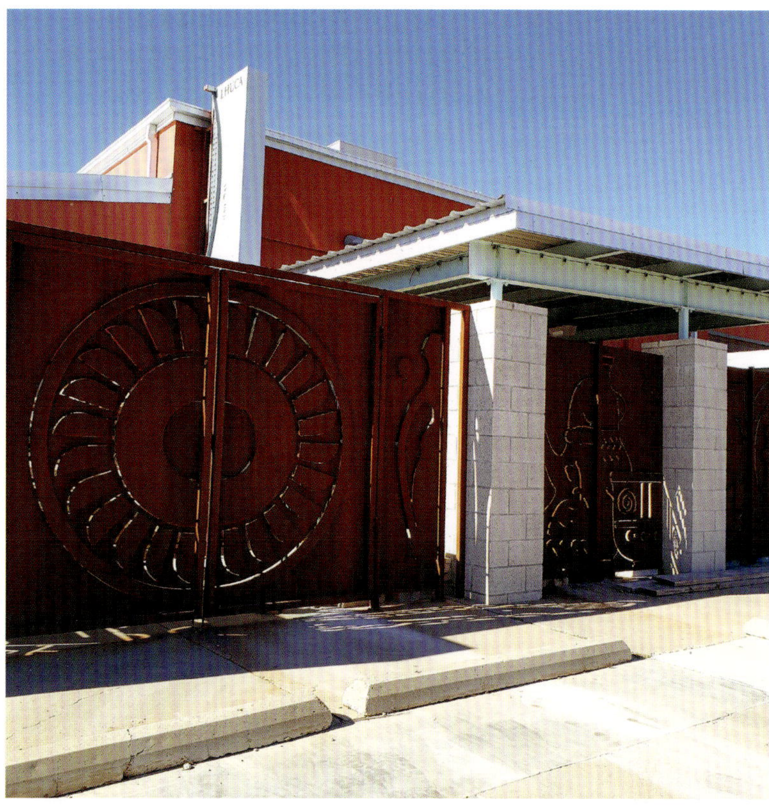

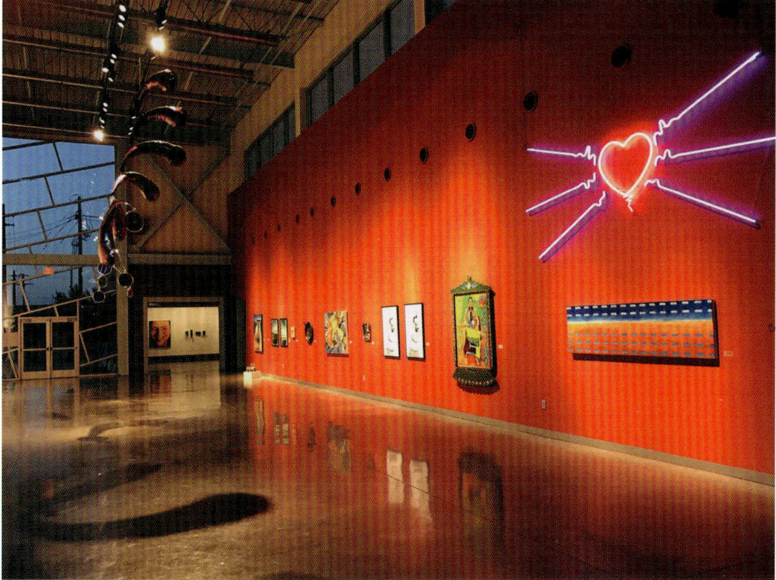

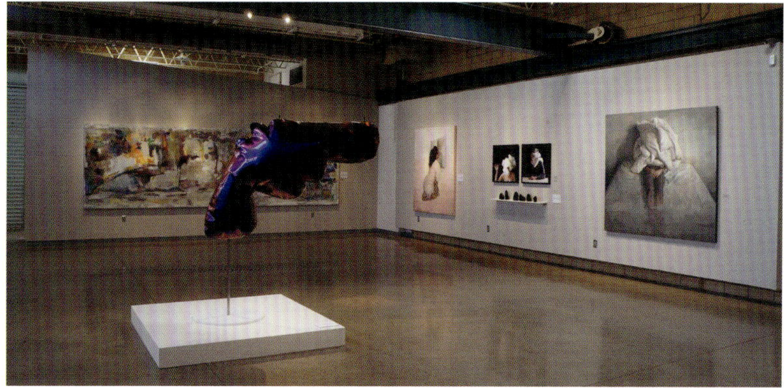

The promise of continued good farm conditions would crash in the 1950s. The increase in demand for agricultural commodities began to cool in the first few years of the 1950s, which depressed prices, but the most devastating blow to farm income in the 1950s would be climatological. Beginning in 1950, and lasting through most of the decade, Texas and all the Southwest was hit with one of the worst droughts on record. Some farmers watched crops wither in the fields, and others just gave up and saw no reason to plant what could not receive ample water. Returns for the Mallet shrunk each year through 1952, with a slight rebound in 1953 and 1954, but nowhere near pre-1950 levels. Whereas the Mallet had collected $56,000 in crop rents in 1949, by 1952 that figure had shriveled to less than $6,000.

When Tom Jones died in 1955, it fell to Christine to find a new farm manager for the Mallet partners. She hired Lee F. York to take Jones's position. York was the former farm loan manager for the First National Bank in Lubbock. He had graduated from Texas Technological College in 1945 and had been at the bank since 1952. His Mallet position, which consisted primarily of negotiating tenant contracts and collecting commissions on the negotiated leases at harvest, did not require him to devote full-time attention to the tasks, so he continued his job at First National. As per usual, Christine's penny-pinching came out in her negotiations with York. Jones's commission in the position had been ten percent of the rents, and York asked for the same. Christine countered with five percent, and they settled on seven percent.

During York's tenure the Mallet should have begun to take the needed step of drilling more water wells so that farmers could irrigate their increasingly parched crops. York approached Christine about doing so, but she was reluctant to spend the money. Long-time tenant Tom Price unilaterally took the initiative and drilled a well in 1955 that caused his crop to increase exponentially. Price's irrigation efforts led two other tenants to begin to irrigate, and that step produced in 1961 a record profit for the Mallet farms of $106,000. After more than a year of Price's asking and then almost bringing legal action, Christine agreed to pay part of Price's costs of drilling. Unfortunately, Christine refused to make any more outlays to drill water wells, which blunted conversion to more irrigation. The three earlier farmers became the only farmers on Mallet land to practice irrigation. The remainder dry-farmed, a difficult proposition at best on the increasingly dry South Plains. It seemed as if that would not be a factor with the end of the drought in the late 1950s, and combined with good rains in the early 1960s, the Mallet farm operations returned to profitability. York urged Christine to use some of the capital to drill more wells, but she did not see the need.

Her reluctance to spend on additional wells cost the farm operations. As it so often does, drought returned to the South Plains in the mid-1960s and with it cut Mallet farm income in half, averaging just less than $30,000 annually for the remainder of the 1960s. The lack of water for irrigation hurt the Mallet farmers trying to practice dryland farming throughout the decade. Three of the Mallets farmers who had rented land since the 1930s let their contracts lapse by the end of the 1960s and two more decided it was time to retire, which meant there were only ten farmers leasing almost 6,000 acres, with one of them—Tom Price—cultivating almost one-third the total. Despite the reduction of returns, Christine still refused to pay to drill more wells.

Christine's management of the Mallet, in addition to her domination of her partners as the voice for her own and her sister's shares, caused her partners to decide to let her be on decisions concerning both the Mallet Ranch and the oil properties. The Mallet produced an abundant amount of oil and all the partners collected handsome dividends, thus there was no immediate need to engage in any confrontations with Christine. For her part, Christine had returned to her earlier practice of either refusing to sign almost all leases the oil companies placed before her or just never answering queries. J. Lee Johnson Jr., who represented his father's heirs' interests, was aging and had likely tired of fighting with Christine during the receivership and dissolution days, and since the Johnson family had a number of other interests that required his attention, he receded from actively trying to take a role in Mallet affairs. Besides, as he said to John Archer in 1973, "[I]f any oil company wanted to do anything on the Mallet Ranch, we [meaning Miss DeVitt] were opposed." It was not just requests for new oil exploration that Christine ignored and delayed; besides insufficient irrigation groundwork for the farms, the Mallet Ranch's infrastructure—corrals, pens, windmills, and more—was aging and deteriorating from neglect and a lack of upgrades. Christine had allowed her conservation ideas and techniques to slip by the 1960s, and many of the Mallet's pastures were becoming overgrazed. Others were even losing grass altogether.

How much of the condition of the Mallet's surface and lack of movement on new oil exploration was due to Christine's refusal to sign agreements or her habit of procrastination is open to debate, but the situation would have no doubt continued and severely hurt the ranch and the partners' assets if a new voice that represented the Johnson heirs had not—perhaps unwittingly—decided to be the latest man to challenge Christine DeVitt.

W. D. Johnson's Mallet shares had been placed in a trust with all his other assets when he died in 1951. Johnson's son, W. D. Jr., had taken little to no interest in the Mallet portion of his father's estate as he busied himself overseeing the many other parts of the vast financial empire his father had accumulated in his long life. As far as the younger Johnson was concerned, the trust was managing the Mallet shares well enough. As long as those oil royalty checks arrived every quarter, he and his family were content. Their lack of attention had given Christine virtually free rein over all Mallet business decisions.

That began to change in the 1970s. The trust document governing Johnson's Mallet shares expired in 1971. His heirs, at the direction of W. D. Jr., all established new trusts for their Mallet shares at Columbia Union National Bank in Kansas City. The trust eventually came under the management of John Archer, who decided that he needed to travel to Texas, meet with Christine, see the Mallet properties, and get an idea of what he was managing. He met with Christine in October 1971, and the cantankerous octogenarian greeted him as she usually greeted those men she thought questioned her judgment—with contempt. Convinced that he would get nowhere with her, Archer went back to Kansas City and allowed Christine to continue to manage the Mallet unopposed by any of the partners.

Archer decided to make another attempt at discussing Mallet affairs with Christine in 1973. He would also at this time come armed with a bit more firepower as William Jewell College, to which Johnson had given Mallet stock in the 1930s, agreed to allow Archer to speak for their interests as well. He first made an inspection tour of the Mallet and what he saw concerned, even angered, him. As he reported to J. Lee Johnson later, the ranch's infrastructure was woefully inadequate, the pastures in poor condition, and most of the farms barely able to be cultivated. Christine dismissed his concerns and derogatorily referred to his age when she spoke of him (Archer was in his early thirties). Archer needed to make some kind of stand that would make Christine realize that he was serious about wanting her to improve the Mallet's surface. He did so when, on behalf of Christine's Johnson partners and William Jewell College, he refused to approve Christine's new grass lease. In his mind, Christine had been taking advantage of her partners by paying only thirty-five cents an acre for her lease for over twenty years. At the same time, she had failed to improve the ranch, which had reduced its value. She had also allowed the oil companies to use Mallet ground water without any fees (assessment of those fees was standard in almost all land contracts), and finally she had failed to provide the means for the Mallet farms to practice full irrigation. In short, he charged that she was a poor steward of the ranch.

He wrote Christine a letter in February 1974 that stated his worries, which included all the above concerns and other shortcomings she had when it came to the Mallet. He added that she "[had] not been a fair and open partner." Christine responded as she usually did when she received such communication: she exploded in anger. (Tom Jones once wrote to Helen that Christine just "does not respond well to things written down.") She did agree to meet with Archer and the Johnsons in February 1974 in Lubbock. At the meeting, Archer laid out his critique, which mirrored what he had written earlier. He was prepared to make Christine three offers. The first would allow her to continue to lease the entirety of the Mallet, but at the rate of $1.50 an acre; if she would agree to that, the Johnson family would authorize the Mallet to spend $200,000 on capital improvements to the ranch. Second, Christine could allow the Johnson family to lease and operate the ranch for the same $1.50 an acre and they would undertake the improvements. Or, third, the ranch would be divided among all the partners, who could operate their shares as they desired.

Christine and her attorney, George McCleskey, met with Archer and W. D. Johnson's grandson David Frayman in McCleskey's office. The only record of the meeting comes from Archer as Christine either took no notes or did not preserve what she did. Archer, in his report to the Johnson family, called the results of the meeting "mixed." He said that Christine was "interested" in taking on the required improvements but made no firm commitment. She did agree to review his suggestions and promised to respond by April 10. Surprisingly, given her habit of procrastination and cancelling meetings, she did so. McCleskey indicated to Archer that Christine wanted to continue leasing the Mallet surface and operating the ranch, and he implied that she would agree to at least some of Archer's conditions. He made it clear that he thought that Christine had done all she could in managing that ranch and asked that the young banker refrain from "criticism" as with Christine it would not be "productive."

Christine did begin some improvements, mostly on windmills and fencing; she still was reluctant to drill for water. Archer, with six of the Johnson heirs, journeyed back to Lubbock in October 1974 and met with John Sones and Lee York to get their opinions and ideas about the ranch. But when Archer met with Christine, the barbed and disagreeable side of her personality got the best of her. She belittled Archer, primarily about his age, but in the end the parties came to an arrangement. Christine would agree to the improvements if her partners agreed to a new lease, and she would also pay the new rate of $1.50 an acre. She would allow the Soil Conservation Service and the Texas A&M Agricultural Experiment Station to survey and make recommendations about how to improve and maintain the ranch's pastures. The parties left the meeting thinking they at least had the framework for agreement, and after a few more starts and stops, John Archer agreed to sign a new lease and Christine was once again the operator of the Mallet Ranch. Unfortunately, the partners never settled on how to make improvements on the Mallet farms, and irrigation projects lagged.

The proposed improvements on the Mallet did not begin in earnest until 1976–1977. John Sones convinced Christine to improve and increase her herd in the late 1970s and by the end of that decade almost 700 head of cattle grazed on the Mallet; by 1981 that number had increased to almost a thousand, the most on the ranch since 1949. The ranch had lost money every year since 1973, but in 1982 the Mallet Ranch cattle operation made a profit of almost $150,000.

During the years between 1938 and 1980, the acres within the fences of the Mallet Ranch contained more than 1,300 completed oil wells. Those wells produced in those years an astonishing amount of oil, approximately 233 million barrels. Such a prodigious amount of oil made all the partners of the Mallet Ranch very wealthy individuals, but no one made more money from the Mallet than the DeVitt sisters. Both women became multimillionaires. Being awash in cash is a nice problem to have, and such a development led the DeVitt sisters to become two of the most generous philanthropists in Texas history.

CHAPTER 7

DeVITT SISTERS SPREAD THE WEALTH

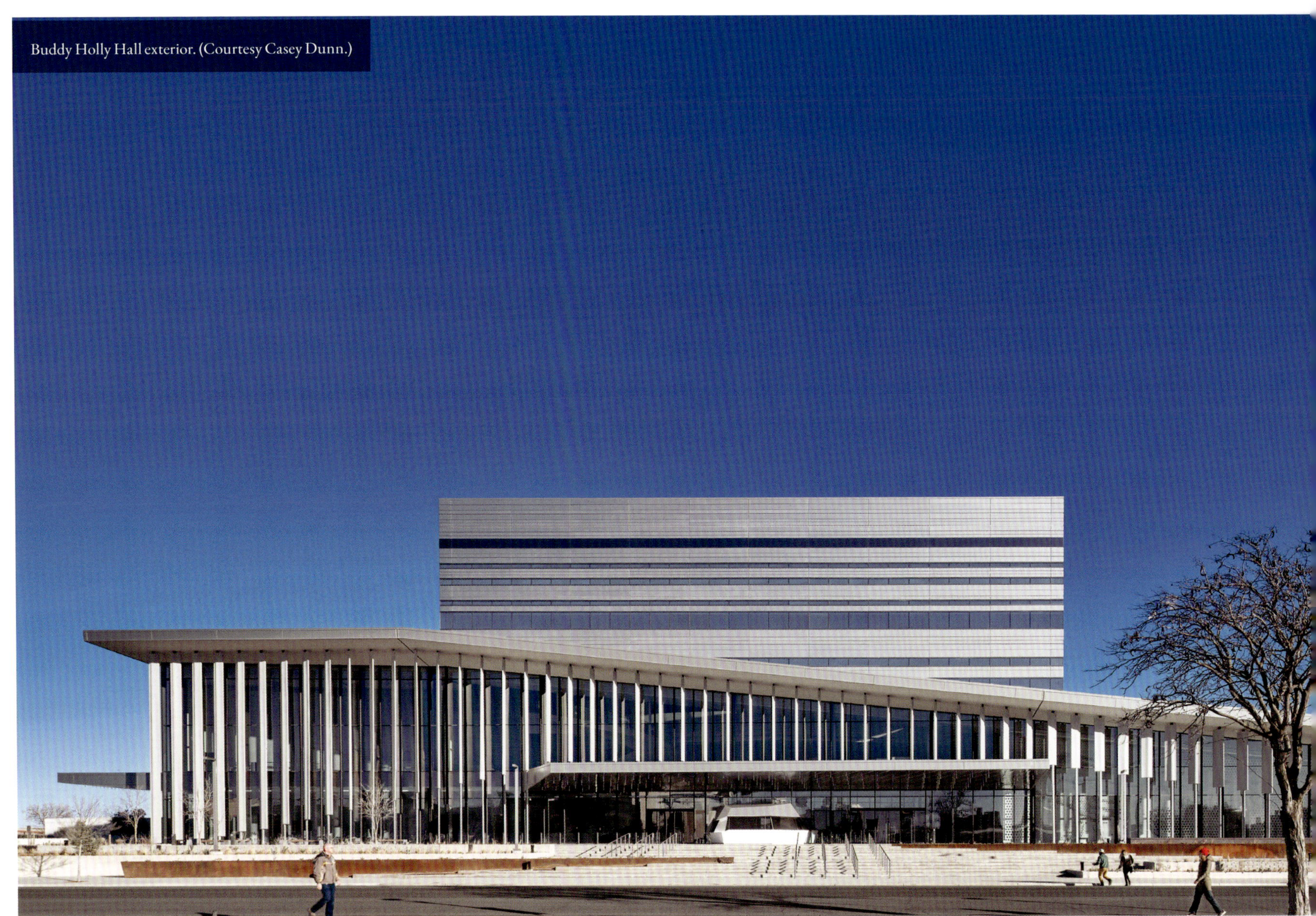

Buddy Holly Hall exterior. (Courtesy Casey Dunn.)

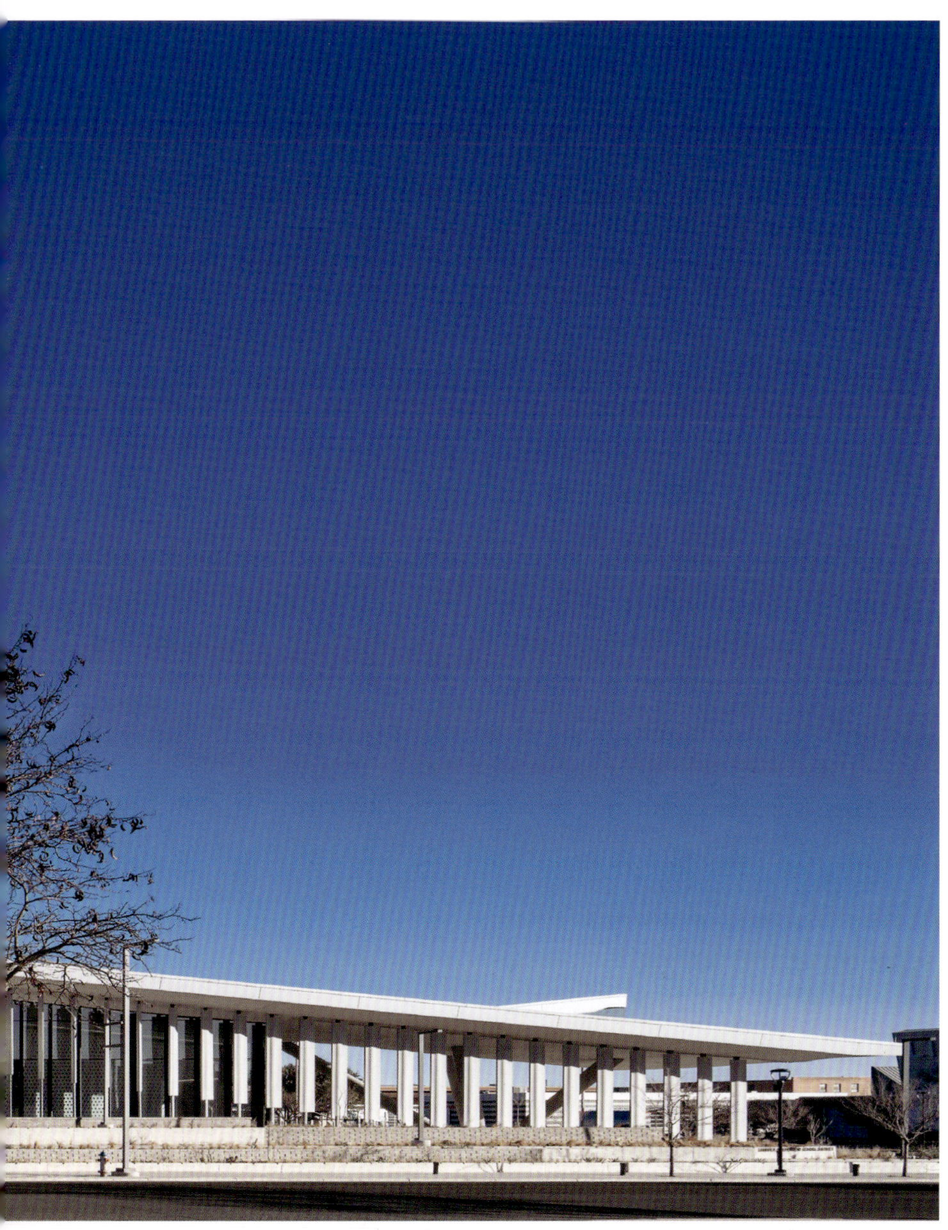

Because of the circumstances of their lives, neither Christine nor Helen had large families to inherit their wealth. As a result, both women donated millions of dollars to a multitude of organizations, institutions, and even individuals during their lifetimes. At the end of their lives, they willed the vast majority of their fortunes to fund two philanthropic entities with an outreach extending primarily throughout the South Plains. Christine DeVitt created The CH Foundation, and her sister Helen established the Helen Jones Foundation, Inc. Dorothy Secrest, Helen's daughter, received a sizable inheritance from her Aunt Christine and created The Plum Foundation, which operates primarily in California and Oregon.

Many people often saw Christine DeVitt as a cantankerous and sometimes miserly businesswoman, but that was not a complete picture of her nature. Christine, for example, had a deep affection for her niece Dorothy Secrest, sending her money even when she did not ask. Christine held a great interest in her employees on the Mallet and took time to get to know them. Despite her outward frugality when it came to ranch expenditures, she at times gave her ranch hands cash, especially at Christmas, to buy presents for their families. Behind the outward granite-like façade of a blunt, hard woman, Christine DeVitt had a soft spot for giving, which in her later life would make her the best-known philanthropist in Lubbock.

Christine was reluctant, at least in the early years of her wealth, to engage in public charity. Part of the reason was no doubt her lack of trust in many organizations, especially those run by men. Another reason was that she was a private person and did not want the "line at the door" that often follows those who are public philanthropic patrons. That began to change in the 1950s, partly because her wealth had grown to considerable heights, but primarily because of the United States tax code. The great wealth that the Mallet produced for Christine DeVitt was accompanied by equally substantial federal income tax bills. Christine abhorred paying taxes of any kind, but she especially loathed federal income taxes. She intentionally waited until the last possible moment to file and pay her federal taxes as a form of protest. So, as a way to offset her tax bill, Christine DeVitt began to take advantage of the charitable write-off that the US Department of the Treasury allowed.

Her initial forays into public giving revealed an indication of which causes she would favor throughout the rest of her life: medical institutions and education. Interestingly, and perhaps reflecting her innately private nature, Christine made her early gifts somewhat anonymously. In 1958 she contributed $10,000 to the School of Nursing at the Methodist Hospital in Lubbock. In fact, that hospital would remain one of Christine's most favored establishments for contributions. Before the formation of The CH Foundation, she directed over a million dollars to the Methodist Hospital, and her foundation would later continue the tradition.

The heftiest amount of Christine DeVitt's generosity went toward educational institutions, particularly Texas Tech University. She made her first donation to Texas Tech in 1959, a gift of $20,000 to the West Texas Museum (now the Museum of Texas Tech University). Christine had formed a close relationship with Texas Tech historian and museum director William Curry Holden. They were neighbors, and Christine frequently had lunch with Holden's wife Fran. After her first gift and through the 1970s she contributed more than a million dollars to the museum, becoming its most munificent patron. Holden once said that the Museum of Texas Tech would not have grown nearly as much as it did without Christine DeVitt. The museum honored the DeVitt benevolence when it constructed a new museum building on Texas Tech property on 4th Street by naming the West Wing after David M. and Florence A. DeVitt.

Christine also made contributions to the Texas Tech Department of Music and the larger College of Arts and Sciences. Her funding eventually created the DeVitt Endowment for the Fine Arts in 1979, a fund that continues to provide scholarships for qualified students to study music and the arts. The Texas Tech Board of Regents approved construction of a much-needed new library in 1963, and Christine DeVitt contributed $30,000 as one of the first major donors to that endeavor. The total of her contributions and those of The CH Foundation to Texas Tech University is staggering. She gave almost $3 million personally to the institution before her death in 1983, and The CH Foundation has subsequently given to date $45 million to the main Texas Tech campus and more than $9 million to the Texas Tech University Health Sciences Center through fiscal year 2022. She also made sizable donations to Lubbock Christian University and South Plains College in Levelland as well as a generous donation to William Jewell College in Missouri to honor her old nemesis and partner W. D. Johnson.

One of the projects most dear to Christine's heart was her support of the Ranching Heritage Center, now known as the National Ranching Heritage Center. The center was largely the brainchild of Texas Tech President Grover Murray and began with Murray's conception of an outdoor historic park that would chronicle and preserve the history of ranching in the Southwest. Murray asked William C. and Frances Holden to become the co-chairs of a committee that would plan and conceive his vision and ultimately raise funds for the museum. The couple agreed to take on the task. Their first action was to form a committee composed of grassroots stock raisers as both consultants and potential fundraisers. In addition to the Holdens, the initial committee included David Kritser of the JY Ranch; Frank Chappell Jr. of the Renderbrook-Spade and Chappell-Spade Ranches; Howard Hampton, the second-generation operator of Hampton Ranch; John Lott with the Slaughter U Lazy S Ranch; Watt Matthews, part of the founding family of the Lambshead holdings; Charles Schreiner III, owner/operator of the famed YO family ranch; and D. Burns of the Pitchfork Ranch. They were all appointed to a committee that would "serve to develop the Western Ranch Complex or Complexes for the ICASALS [International Center for Arid and Semiarid Land Studies] Institute and Museum." Holden and Murray designated the group as the "Ranching Headquarters Planning Committee," and the members met for the first time at the Pioneer Hotel in

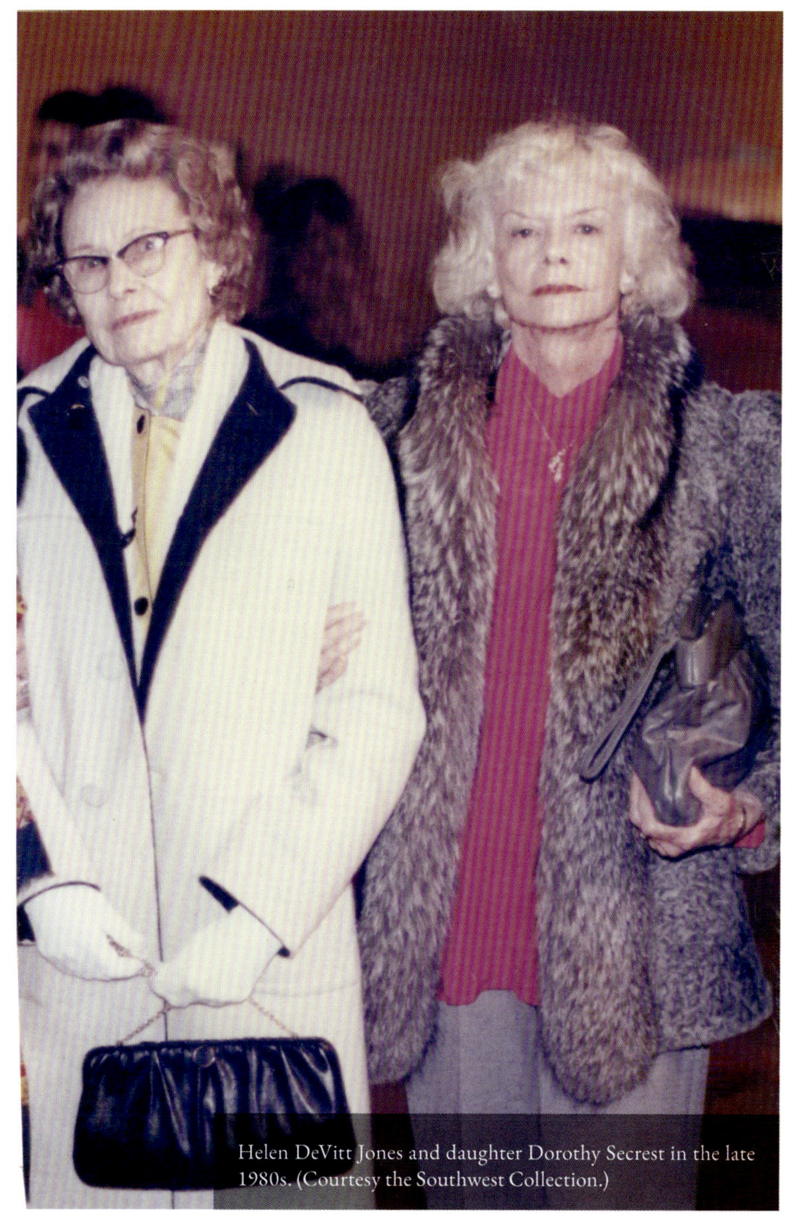

Helen DeVitt Jones and daughter Dorothy Secrest in the late 1980s. (Courtesy the Southwest Collection.)

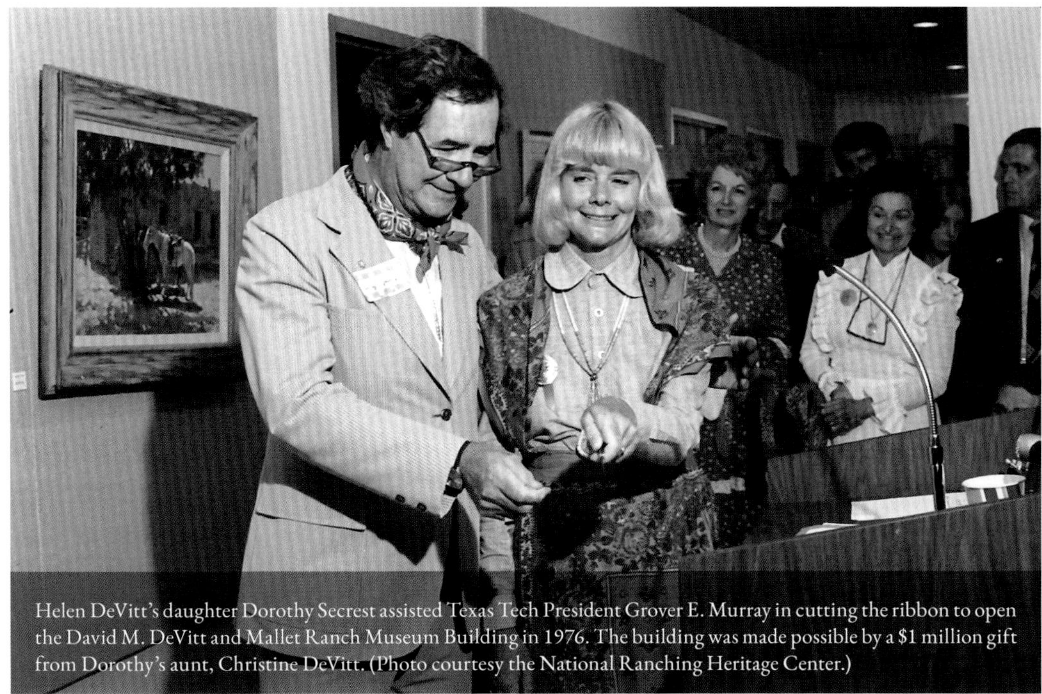
Helen DeVitt's daughter Dorothy Secrest assisted Texas Tech President Grover E. Murray in cutting the ribbon to open the David M. DeVitt and Mallet Ranch Museum Building in 1976. The building was made possible by a $1 million gift from Dorothy's aunt, Christine DeVitt. (Photo courtesy the National Ranching Heritage Center.)

November 1966 in downtown Lubbock to begin conceptually planning the project.

Given her relationship with the Holdens, Christine DeVitt surprisingly was not invited to be a member of the initial committee. The committee members made it clear that they had no intention of being a fundraising outlet and insisted that Texas Tech take the lead in financing the project. Because that was not going to happen, President Murray eventually formed another committee that would become the first members of the Ranching Headquarters Association (RHA), a nonprofit membership organization to support the programs of what would become the Ranching Heritage Center. The committee included most of the original members and was charged with the task of raising money for the Ranching Heritage Center, which was initially called the Ranching Headquarters Center. The members of the committee agreed to contribute to the project, as did a number of local ranch families, including descendants of Burk Burnett at the 6666 Ranch. While many of the "old families" of the region were thrilled with the project and agreed to fund the moving and restoration of the buildings chosen for the site, the committee had failed to attract a major donor through most of 1968—a donor willing to write that "big check" that often serves as the catalyst for such a project. It fell to William Curry Holden to find that first major donor to kick off a round of fundraising that would make the Ranching Heritage Center possible. Holden turned to his friend and neighbor, Christine DeVitt, to become that donor.

Christine consented to become a supporter of the project and in December 1968 agreed to donate more than $200,000, a sum that would eventually grow to almost one million dollars by the time the Ranching Heritage Center opened in 1976. Her contributions largely financed the building of the primary

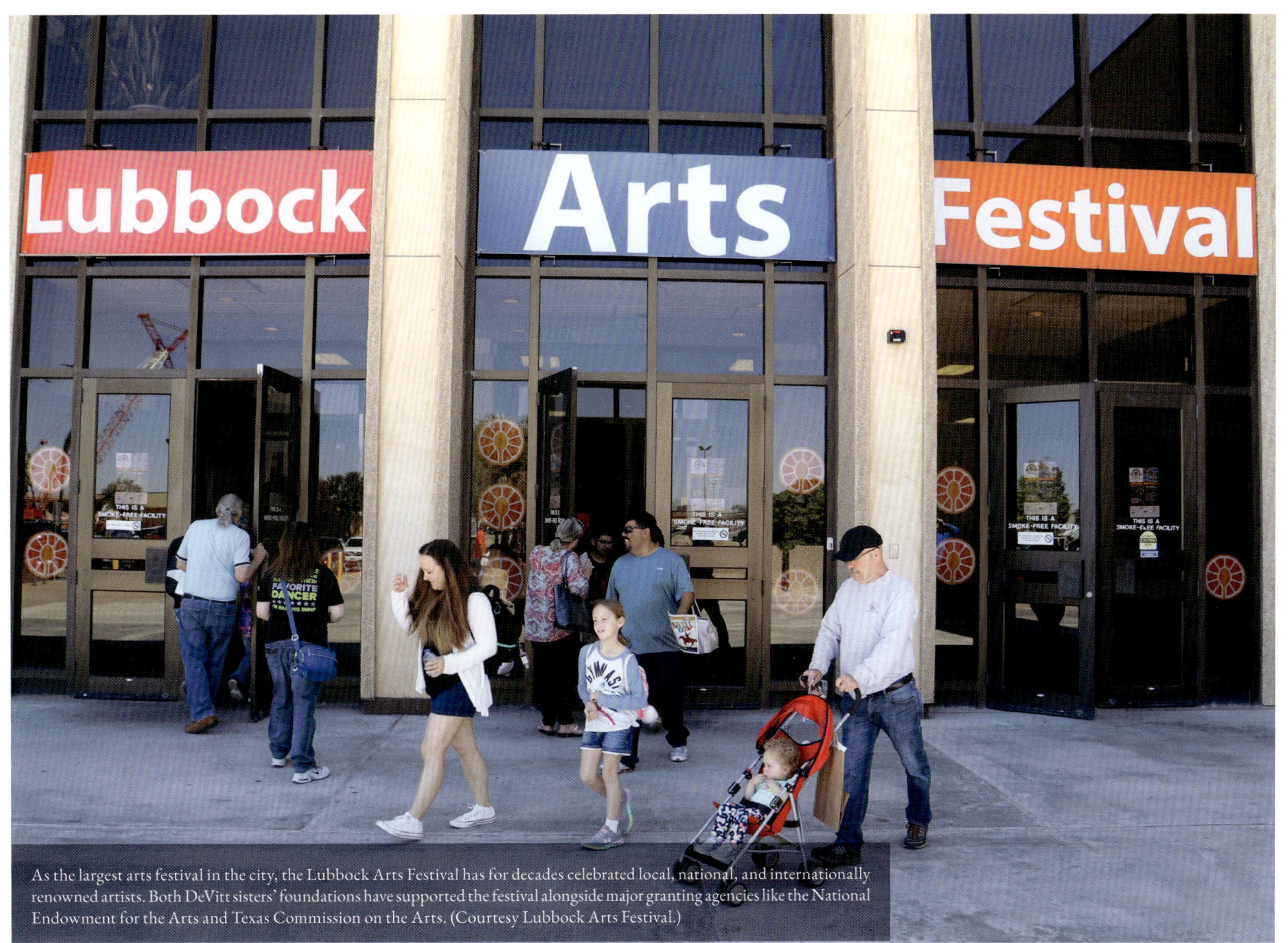

As the largest arts festival in the city, the Lubbock Arts Festival has for decades celebrated local, national, and internationally renowned artists. Both DeVitt sisters' foundations have supported the festival alongside major granting agencies like the National Endowment for the Arts and Texas Commission on the Arts. (Courtesy Lubbock Arts Festival.)

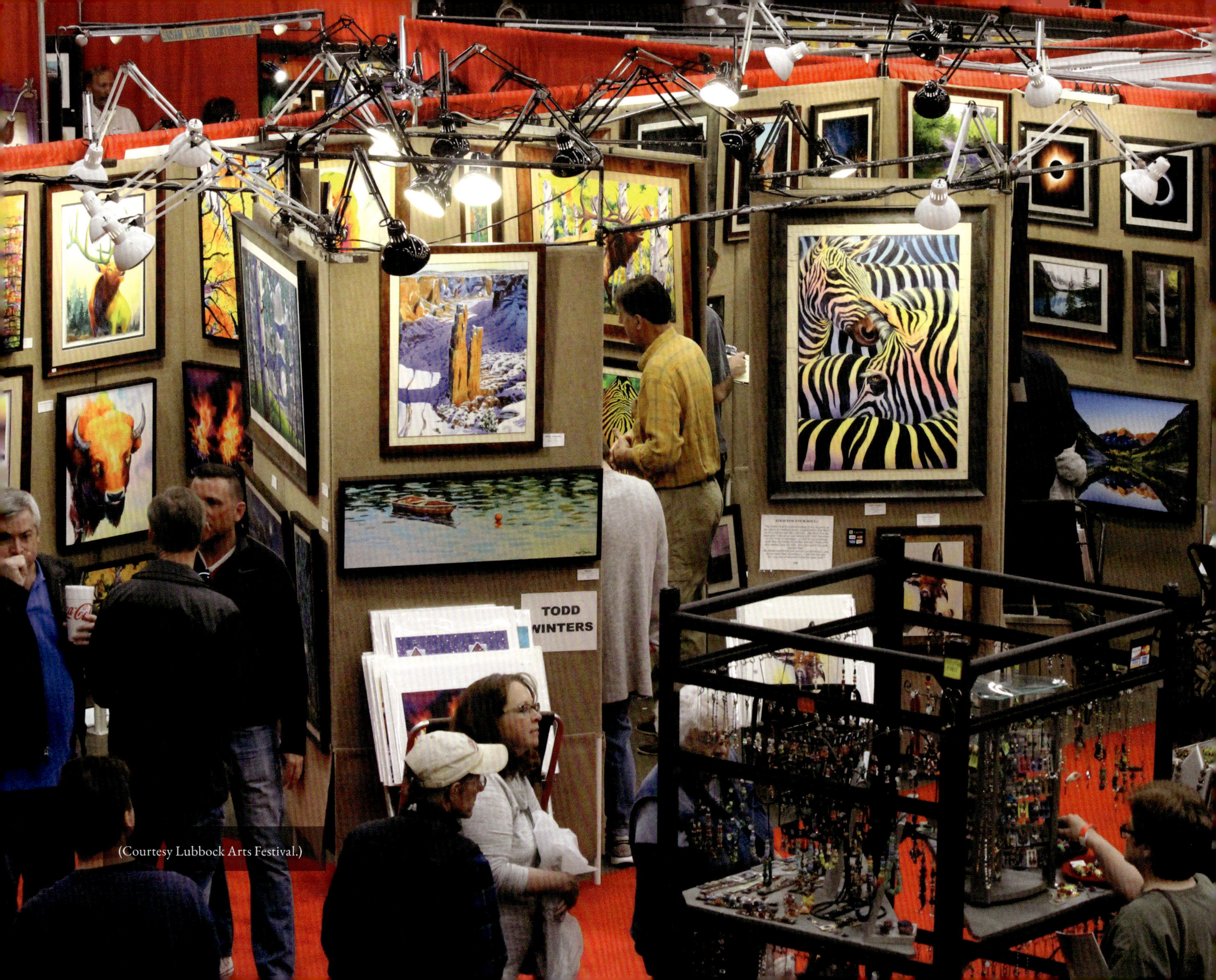

(Courtesy Lubbock Arts Festival.)

museum building. In true Christine fashion, she also insisted that she be immediately added to the RHC Board of Overseers so that, as Holden recounted, "she could keep an eye on how the money was spent." She also stipulated that the administrative and primary building be named after her father and designed to resemble the headquarters structure of the Mallet Ranch. DeVitt's role in establishing the RHC was crucial, which is the reason she was so honored at the opening of the RHC described in the introductory chapter of this book.

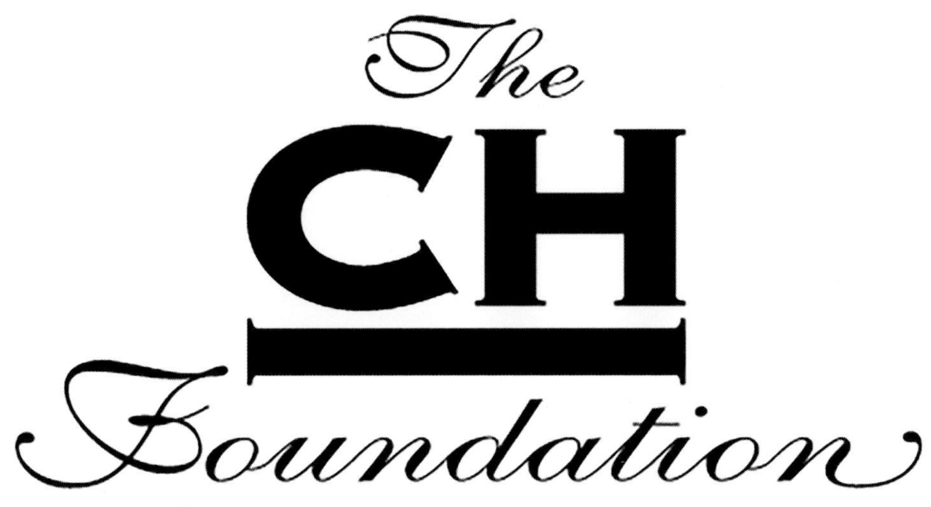

The Legacy of Christine DeVitt

Christine DeVitt turned eighty-four in 1969 and, perhaps for the first time, began to realize that her mortality was close to coming to an end. While she had continued to oversee the Mallet Ranch, she increasingly began to turn the prime decisions over to foreman John Sones after 1964 and devoted more of her time to philanthropy to ensure those enterprises would continue after her death. She also had to be aware of the difficult battles she and Helen had waged with the State of California over inheritance taxes, and while Texas does not have direct state estate taxes, the federal government does, and Christine did not want to see a large portion of her wealth consumed in that manner. To such ends, Christine met with her attorneys to begin plans to form a foundation that would continue her philanthropy. After discussions about funding, tax implications, and the structure of such an establishment, Christine applied for and received a charter that would form The CH Foundation in 1969. When she and her brother Harold were young, her father had purchased and given to his two children a small herd of cattle. He registered their brand as CH using the first letter of each child's name, and that became the name she gave to her foundation. Christine, Helen, and Jack Gray Johnson served as the foundation's trustees. Johnson eventually resigned and Christine replaced him with her niece, Dorothy.

Any Christine DeVitt action would not be customary without delays, and The CH would prove no different. While

Christine had conceived of the idea in late 1969 and expressed her ideas on what The CH would fund in a first draft of her will in 1970, she did not get around to funding and holding the first board meeting of the foundation until 1976. She opened an account in the name of The CH with $10,000. Christine's movements toward actual activity by The CH were further delayed when she had a series of hospitalizations from the summer of 1976 through the early part of 1978. She seemed to make a recovery and returned to her home on 21st Street with her cats, but in February 1979 her health took a dramatic turn for the worse. Her mobility, which had become somewhat restricted after 1974, became almost nonexistent and she was unable to do much more than move from her hospital bed to a desk that Methodist Hospital officials provided in her hospital suite. Christine DeVitt spent the last four years of her life in that suite and during those years gave Methodist Hospital nearly one million dollars.

Christine had filed a will in 1977 that left the bulk of her estate to her sister Helen, but both women's financial fortunes had changed dramatically in the late 1970s and early 1980s. Oil prices had begun to rise significantly with the Arab oil embargo of 1973, and they continued to rise as the world demand for petroleum grew. Christine's oil income alone was almost half a million dollars a month, which meant she was accumulating a sizable fortune. The terms of the 1977 will bequeathed most of her estate to Helen and a smaller portion to Dorothy. Such terms would subject her estate to a tax of over $15 million, a sum that Christine had no desire to see sent to the government. After consulting with attorney George McCleskey, Christine established a trust for both her sister and her niece. At the same time, Christine held the second meeting of The CH Foundation and added George McCleskey to the board.

Christine grew weaker in 1983 as the months passed. By the fall season she could not rise from her bed. Helen visited every day, usually remaining with Christine for hours. Helen and Christine, who had spent most of their lives distant as sisters, grew closer as they aged and perhaps came to understand each other more in those last years of Christine's life. Helen was a prodigious letter writer and left behind substantial correspondence. Christine did not correspond as her sister did, and when she did it was primarily on business affairs. As a result, what we know about the sisters' relationship is slanted toward Helen's view. Helen, it seems, did not understand what "motivated" Christine in life, and the difference in the two women's personalities made it difficult to see how they could be siblings. Christine could be sharp and even aggressive, but Helen was meeker and quieter. Even their mother had once written Helen expressing wonder at "why Christine wasn't cut out something like the rest of us." Despite their divergences, no one who knew them doubted they loved each other. Even when they had found themselves on opposite sides of Mallet business in the 1940s, they continued to speak with each other. Helen once wrote to Tom, when he was urging her to take a position that sided with the Johnsons, that she "did not want to anger Christine." Tom wrote back that Christine was "going to be angry anyway, but she would get over it." Through

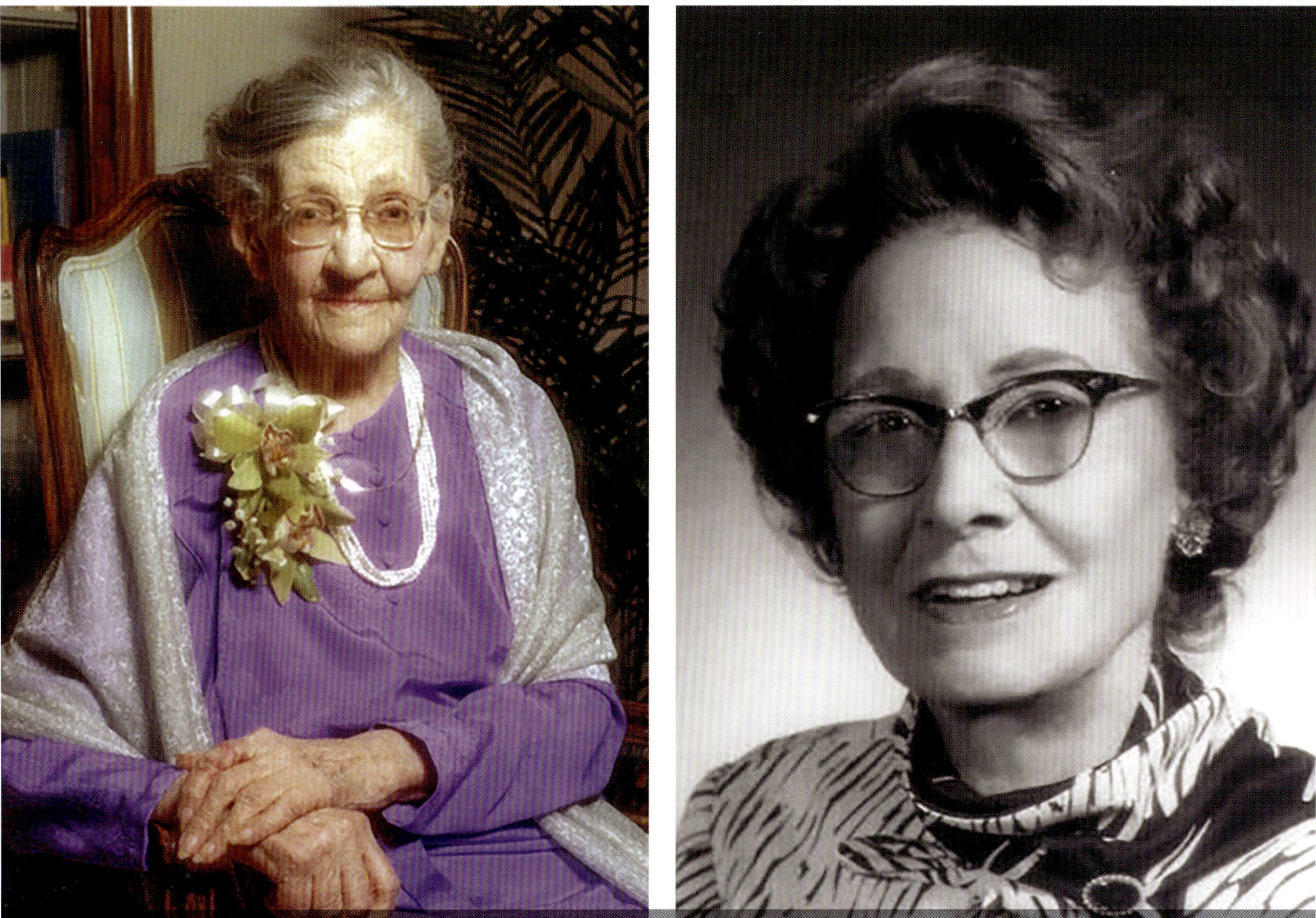

Christine DeVitt (left) and Helen DeVitt Jones (right) were among the last members of a family that founded one of the most historic ranches in West Texas, still in operation today. The discovery of oil on the ranch resulted in both women establishing separate philanthropic foundations that, over the years, have donated millions of dollars to advance education, health, and the cultural arts throughout the South Plains. The region would not be the same without their contributions. (Photos courtesy the National Ranching Heritage Center.)

it all, the DeVitt sisters retained a relationship that neither one ever renounced.

Christine DeVitt died in her sleep on October 12, 1983, at the age of ninety-eight. Her obituary called her a "pioneer area businesswoman," a description that did not even begin to capture her personality or impact. She was eulogized in grand terms but also by those who acknowledged her stubbornness and procrastination. Others praised her private acts of kindness, such as when she quietly helped many of the Mallet hands during difficult times—often after they had ceased their employment. Few people in Lubbock had a larger cross-section of funeral attendees. Some of the most recognizable figures in Lubbock—such as Texas Tech president Lauro Cavazos, Lubbock mayor Alan Henry, and Congressman Kent Hance—attended her services, but some of her cowboys and the nurses who had taken care of her during the last years of her life were also there.

Since becoming involved in the Mallet affairs in 1934, Christine DeVitt had engaged in her share of legal tangles. It was only fitting that her estate and its final allocation would involve a team of lawyers. Helen and George McCleskey were the co-executors of Christine's estate. As they prepared to send the will to probate, they received an unexpected challenge from Helen's daughter, Dorothy, who had married Theo Klein in 1983. According to numerous interviews David Murrah held with Dorothy, Theo insisted that his wife contest the will, which placed her in opposition to her mother and greatly distressed Helen DeVitt Jones. Dorothy resigned from The CH Foundation board, as did her husband, who had been placed on the board shortly after Christine's death. The legal fight lasted six years and involved a fight not only over Christine's will but also over who would eventually look after Helen's affairs.

A Lubbock County court ruled in March 1986 that Dorothy had no standing to challenge Christine's will. Dorothy was represented by one of the most visible attorneys and politicians in Lubbock, John Montford. Montford, a native of Fort Worth, had served the county as district attorney from 1978 to 1982 and then won the Texas Senate District 28 race. He served in that seat until 1996 when he left to become the first chancellor of the Texas Tech University System. George McCleskey and attorneys from his firm—McCleskey, Brazill, and Graf—worked as counsel for the DeVitt estate. Montford appealed the county court ruling to the state court of appeals in Amarillo. The state court reversed the ruling and ordered that Dorothy's challenge proceed. McCleskey then appealed to the Texas Supreme Court, which eventually agreed with the appeals court and ordered a trial to begin.

Before the new trial could take place, lawyers and judges had to settle another legal question. Helen DeVitt Jones was eighty-four when Christine died, and she had leaned on someone for help in conducting her affairs for a good portion of her life. For thirty-four years that person had been Anne Snyder. Christine, at the suggestion of Tom Jones, had hired Anne to run the Mallet office in 1949. As the years went by, Anne essentially became personal secretary for both Christine and, after Tom Jones's death, Helen. Anne took on even more of Christine's affairs after Christine entered the hospital. Perhaps the stress of that responsibility contributed to Anne's having a severe stroke in April 1983. She never recovered and died in 1984.

Without Anne's help with correspondence and personal affairs, Helen relied on a close friendship with Louise Willson Arnold. Their friendship had begun in 1966 when both Helen and Louise were placed on the board of the Texas Tech Foundation. Louise was the wife of Dr. Robert (Bob) N. Arnold, a prominent obstetrician and gynecologist in Lubbock. Although Louise had grown up in Floydada, Texas, and spent two years at Southern Methodist University, she had a degree in home economics from Iowa State University and had invested many hours in fashion and design courses. During the fifteen years that the two women served together on the Texas Tech Foundation board, they discovered they had similar interests in the fine arts and especially enjoyed auditing Texas Tech professor Betsy Sasser's classes on art and architecture history. Sasser was Louise's friend and soon became a friend of Helen DeVitt Jones. Louise was 25 years younger than Helen and although they had a strong bond based on similar interests, their friendship sometimes resembled a mother/daughter relationship. Helen was not very well organized and prone to collecting clutter, with stacks of unanswered mail and unpaid bills. At loose ends without Anne Snyder to help her get organized, Helen asked Louise for assistance as a friend. Instead of going out and paying the bills herself, Louise sat down with Helen and patiently went over each piece of mail and each bill needing payment until the clutter was resolved and the house was back in order. Louise kept Helen organized.

Likely at the suggestion of George McCleskey, who understood that the upcoming legal proceedings with Helen's daughter were going to be lengthy and stressful, Helen filed a Designation of Guardianship of Person and Estate in December 1985 naming Louise Willson Arnold as her guardian if that were to become necessary. Helen also took the step in 1984 of forming and incorporating her own philanthropic organization, the Helen Jones Foundation, Inc., with an initial endowment of \$5 million. For that reason, the full establishment of the Helen Jones Foundation, Inc. came before The CH, which had to wait until Christine's will was fully executed. Helen would eventually endow her namesake foundation with another \$70 million after her death.

One reason Helen moved to name a guardian was that she was in the early stages of dementia and memory loss. In 1989 her condition had advanced so much that in January 1990 a Lubbock county court ordered the conditions of Helen's Designation of Guardianship to take place with Louise Arnold as Helen's legal guardian. Dorothy, however, believed that she should be her mother's guardian and asked the court to name her rather than Louise. Thus, another legal battle began. After one mistrial and another postponement, a jury made Louise Arnold the legal guardian in August 1990 because the jury recognized that Helen was cognizant when she prepared the will.

Of all the lawsuits involving the DeVitts, the guardian lawsuit was the most important to the South Plains because it essentially established the Helen Jones Foundation, Inc., which funds most of its grants in an area from Tulia down to Lamesa over to

Guthrie and west to the New Mexico border. Helen's original $75 million funding has been invested well, and the foundation now has about $240 million in assets and has granted $176,175,032 in total gifts since its inception. Lubbock has received the majority of the grants, including $28 million in capital outlay to the Buddy Holly Hall of Performing Arts and Sciences plus another $5 million in maintenance. South Plains College Vocational Technical Education recently received $4 million. Through 2023, Texas Tech University has received $74,249,975 in total gifts since the foundation was established.

From 1984 until today the Helen Jones Foundation, Inc. has given grants to eleven colleges and universities, nineteen public and private schools, twenty-seven organizations representing the fine arts, fourteen museums, seventeen youth and children's groups, twelve libraries, forty-one human and health service groups, and twenty-eight miscellaneous gifts (e.g., Sherick Memorial Home, Lubbock Heritage Society, Volunteer Center of Lubbock). Although foundation funding is primarily to the South Plains, Helen DeVitt Jones chose to give twelve national gifts before she died (e.g., Southern Poverty Law Center, National Center for Higher Education, The Cousteau Society).

Louise Arnold was the first executive director of the Helen Jones Foundation, Inc. from 1984 to 2005 and charted the direction of the foundation in areas that were important to Helen DeVitt Jones. When James C. Arnold, Louise's son, became executive director in 2005, the foundation was already successfully established. Jim Arnold has guided the investments to an impressive accumulation of assets that will continue to flow out to the South Plains, a region where the wealth was created and where it is now shared.

The final settlement of Christine DeVitt's will was the next courtroom drama involving the DeVitt family, but it did not occur until almost seven years after Helen DeVitt Jones's guardianship was settled. David Murrah wrote that "neither side relished the fight," and Dorothy decided to separate her interests in the matter from her husband's and asked Montford to negotiate a settlement. He sent a twenty-page proposal to The CH Foundation's board and Helen's representatives. Both sides offered minor amendments and changes, but on December 31, 1992—an appropriate date for anything involving the quintessential procrastinator Christine DeVitt—both sides signed an agreement that essentially kept the major provisions of Christine's original will. The battle also may have had another cost as Dorothy Secrest divorced her husband shortly before the document became final.

The CH Foundation was finally able to complete its founding, a process that began in 1977. Helen DeVitt Jones reorganized the first board of directors in 1988 by naming herself president and Louise Arnold, George McCleskey, L. Edwin Smith, and Nelda Thompson as directors. That group finalized the mission of The CH Foundation with a statement that the foundation would be dedicated to "medical, educational, and public charities located in West Texas." Helen continued as the board president until 1990, when she became honorary chairperson. Although the foundation gave its first grant in 1985 for $500 to the Texas Tech PBS television station, no significant

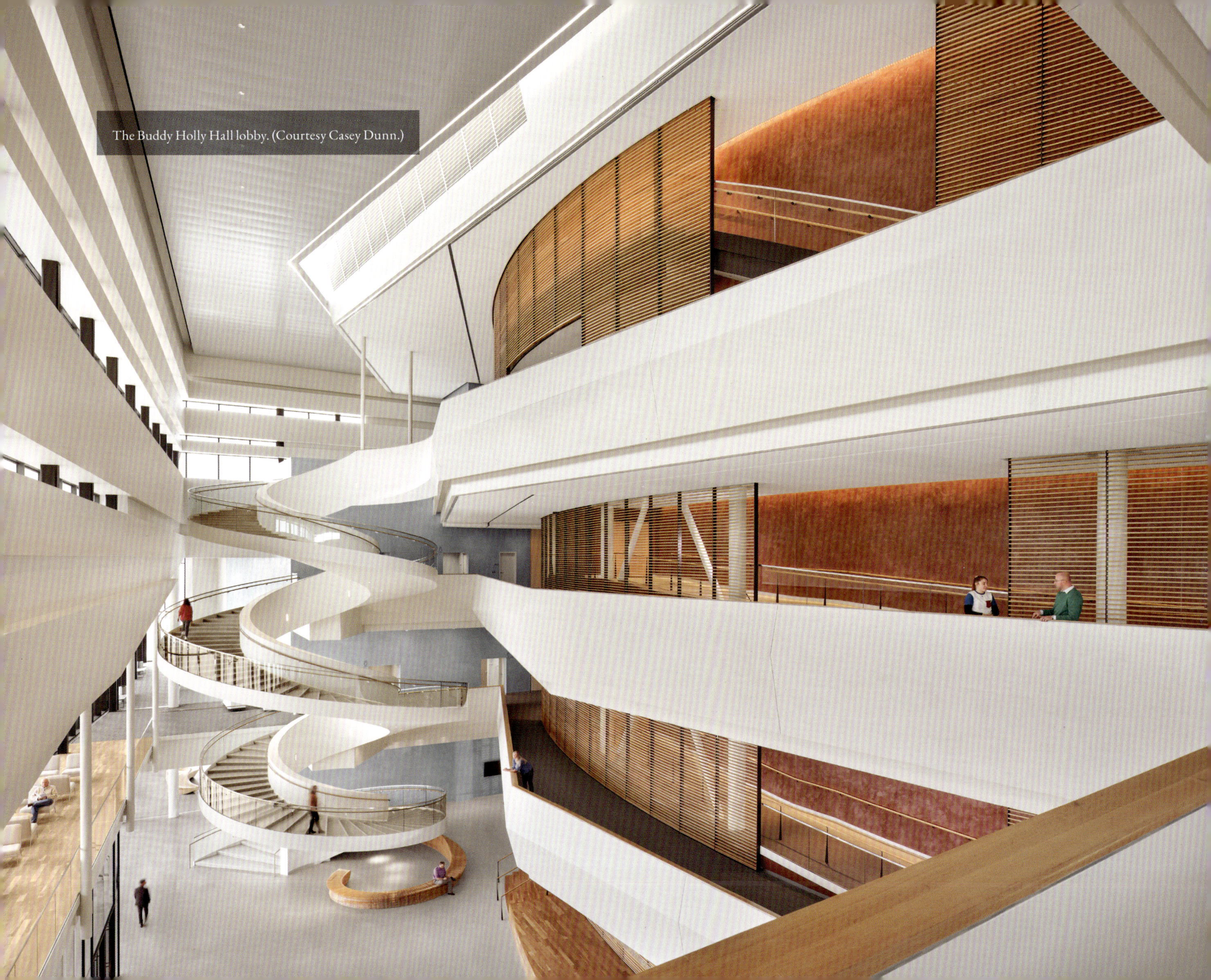

The Buddy Holly Hall lobby. (Courtesy Casey Dunn.)

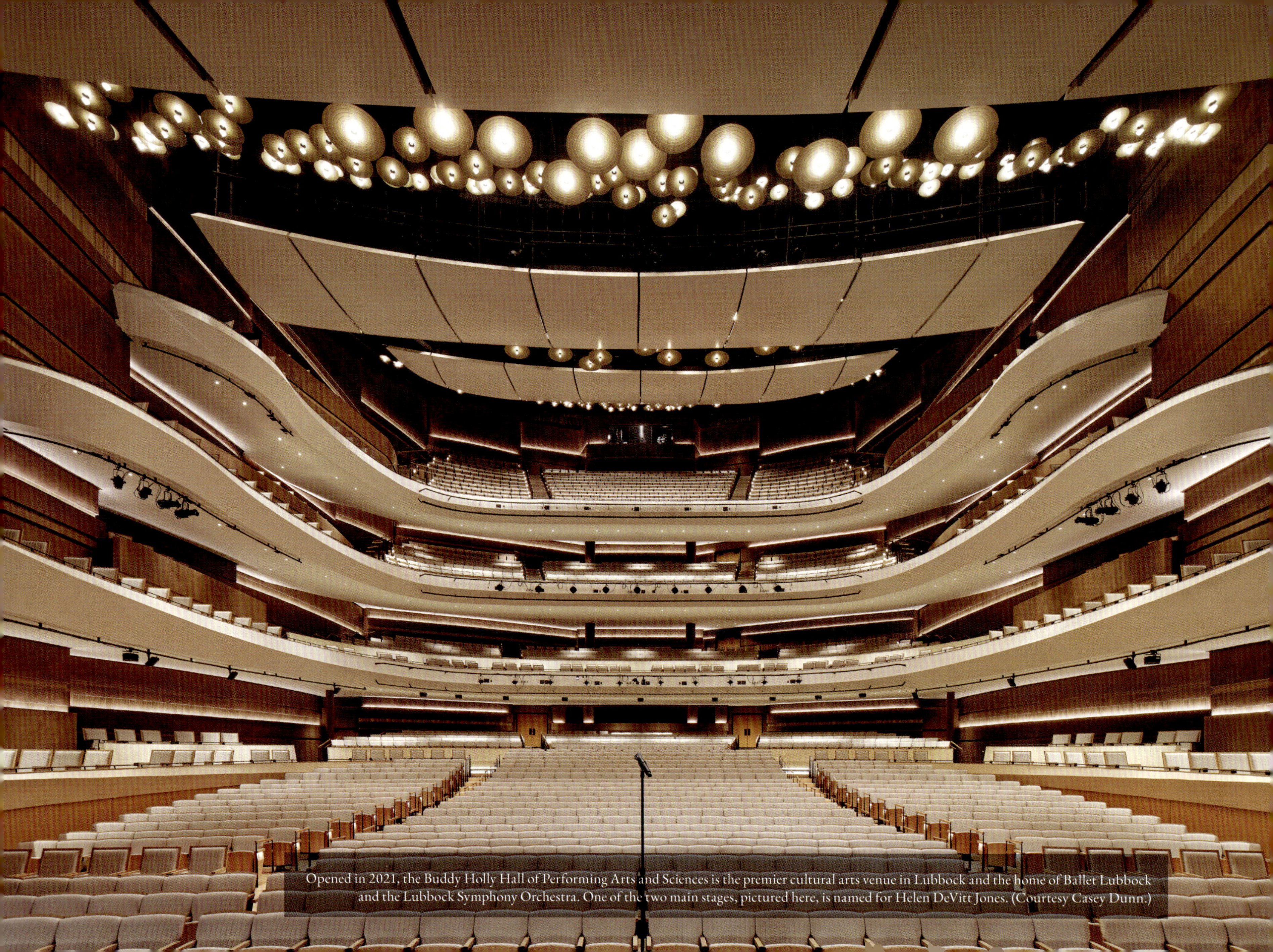

Opened in 2021, the Buddy Holly Hall of Performing Arts and Sciences is the premier cultural arts venue in Lubbock and the home of Ballet Lubbock and the Lubbock Symphony Orchestra. One of the two main stages, pictured here, is named for Helen DeVitt Jones. (Courtesy Casey Dunn.)

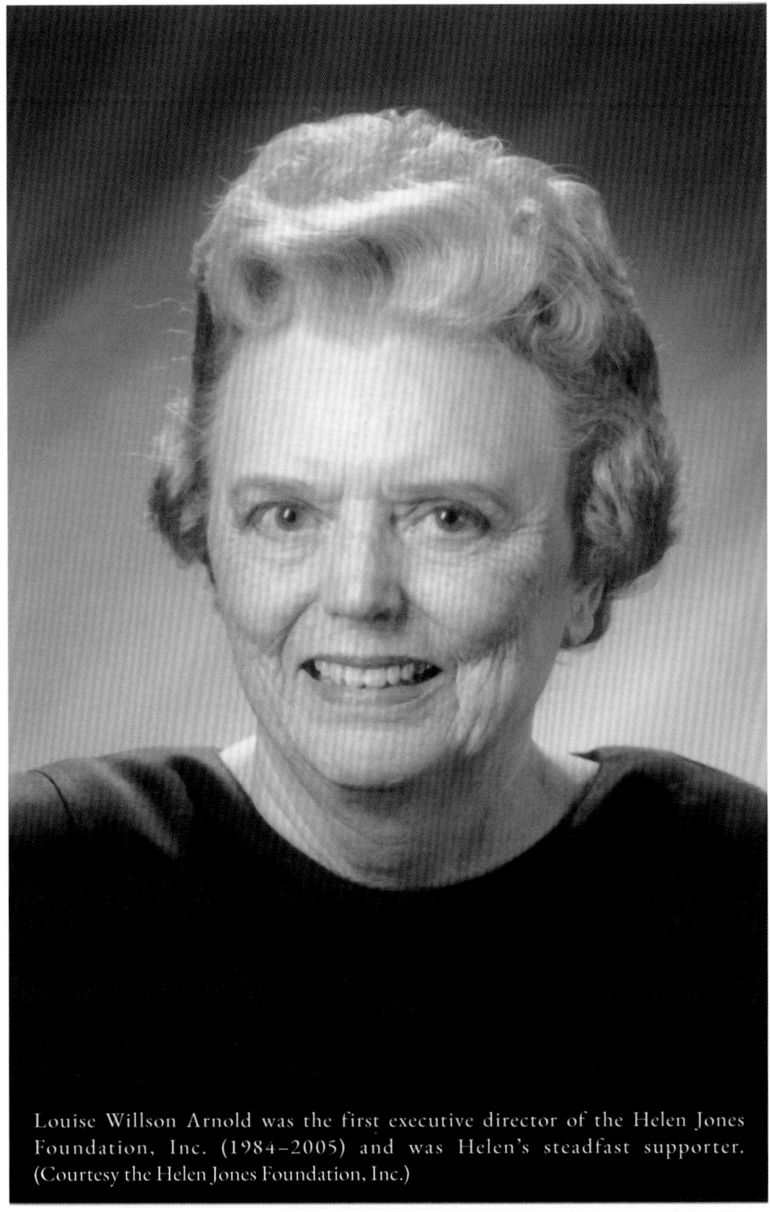
Louise Willson Arnold was the first executive director of the Helen Jones Foundation, Inc. (1984–2005) and was Helen's steadfast supporter. (Courtesy the Helen Jones Foundation, Inc.)

grants were given until 1992 when the foundation was able to grant nearly half a million dollars.

Under the day-to-day direction of Executive Director Sandy Ogletree, Grants Administrator Heather Hocker, and Accountant Cheryl Sanford, The CH Foundation operates in the spirit of Christine DeVitt as a substantial donor to educational and community improvement projects on the South Plains. The total giving since the beginning of the foundation is $191,021,581 with single gifts averaging between $30,000 and $50,000. With total assets of more than $200 million, the foundation has given $37,812,542 to the main Texas Tech campus and $9,059,915 to the Texas Tech Health Sciences Center from its inception through 2022.

Ogletree explained that The CH Foundation considers grants keeping in mind the four R's: the ranch, the range, the royalties, and the rural. Projects that bring a fine arts offering into a rural setting are a double win for The CH. One of the projects funded in 2022 is a new library in the small town of Sundown near the Mallet Ranch. The current library is operating out of a pharmacy but will move to a church building that has been donated for use as a library. "The impact on that little town will be substantial," Ogletree said, "but it's only a $40,000 grant. Sometimes the impact is not equivalent with the dollar value. This foundation definitely has a heart."

The Helen Jones Foundation, Inc. and The CH Foundation each own a portion of the surface area of the Mallet Ranch. The affairs of the ranch are handled by Ben Davidson of McCleskey, Harriger, Brazill & Graf, LLP. The firm executed two new oil

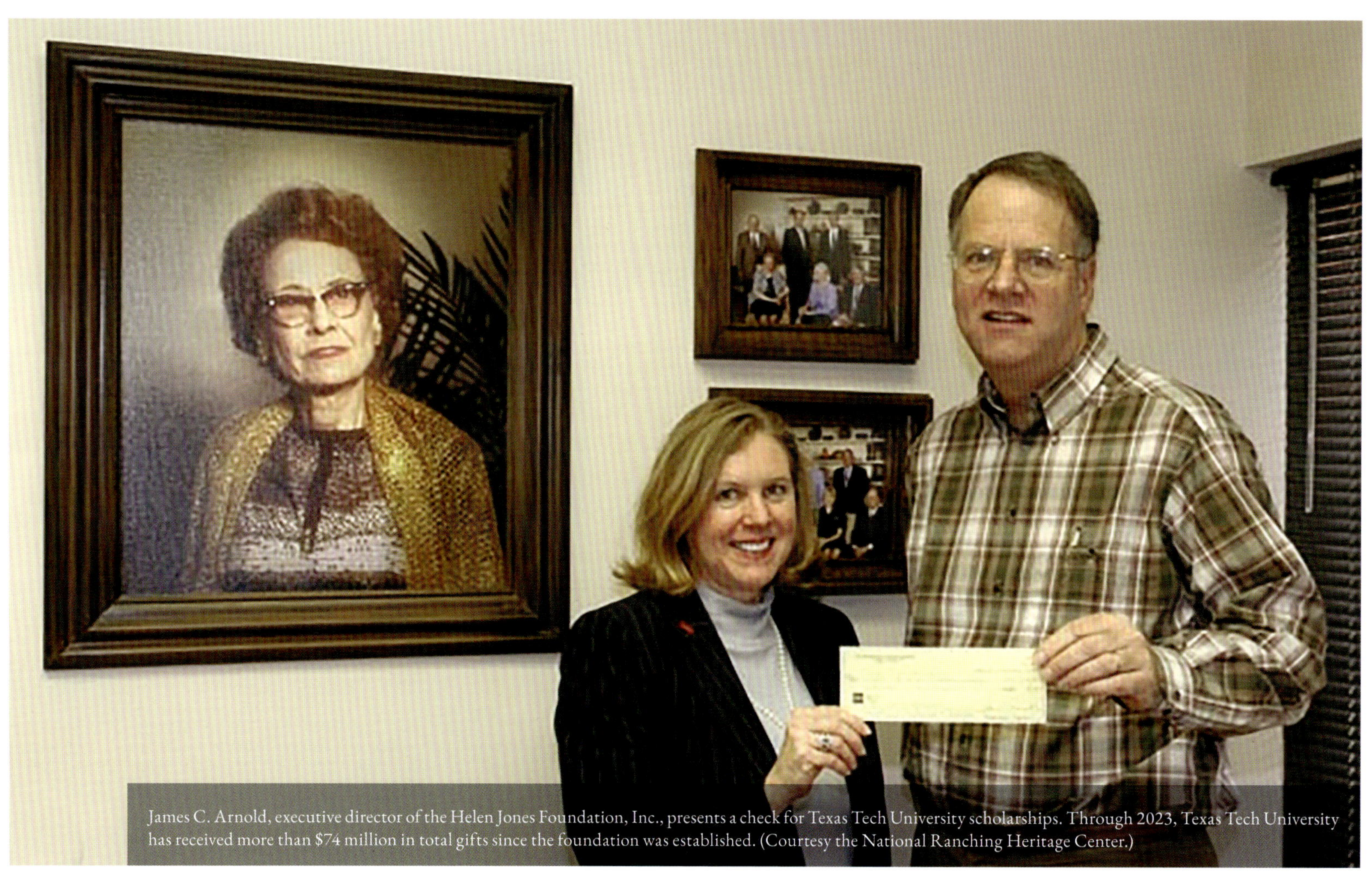

James C. Arnold, executive director of the Helen Jones Foundation, Inc., presents a check for Texas Tech University scholarships. Through 2023, Texas Tech University has received more than $74 million in total gifts since the foundation was established. (Courtesy the National Ranching Heritage Center.)

leases in 2021—the first leases in thirty years. According to Ogletree, the Mallet Ranch is the largest virgin, high plains land still in existence and the largest native grass ranch in the country. "Oil is no longer the primary income source of the foundation, but it was the root of the wealth," Ogletree said. "The cattle started it, then the oil came in and now it's investments. What will come after that? It could be wind. We have an engaged board that's looking forward into what will continue to allow the level of support we have given to the community."

Helen DeVitt Jones, among the last members of the family that founded one of the most valuable and noteworthy ranches in all of Texas, died a few months short of her ninety-eighth birthday on September 28, 1997. Her death came 102 years after her father, David DeVitt, bought his first herd and began a stock operation on land that grew into one of the most prized oil fields in a state full of oil fields. The story of the Mallet Ranch on the South Plains, like so many other Texas ranching stories, is a tale of much more than running cattle.

EPILOGUE

Unlike so many other historic ranches in Texas, the Mallet Ranch remains mostly intact. It has not met the fate of subdivision, bankruptcy, multiple ownership changes, or loss of all vestiges of its former glory as have others like it in Texas. A drive to the Mallet today is almost like a journey back in time. I have made that drive a number of times in the last couple of years. When I left Lubbock, traveled out Highway 62, and turned onto FM 1585, it was almost like I had turned back a page of time. Although climate change, excessive wear, and the pressure of increased use and population has taken its toll, much of the land looks very nearly like it must have looked the first time David DeVitt rode up to survey the potential tracts he would begin to lease and purchase near the turn of the twentieth century.

If you do not feel like you have stepped back in time on the drive to Sundown, you most definitely will when you turn back south onto the packed-dirt ranch road that will take you to the gate that leads to the Mallet headquarters house. While the Mallet still exists as an entity, the headquarters has long been neglected. The house that David DeVitt moved his wife and two young children into in 1905, the one that David Jr. built an addition to for himself and his wife, and the one that formed the center of human existence on the 50,000 acres of the Mallet Ranch, is barely standing. It is listed as one of the most endangered historic structures in all of Texas, but any hope of preservation is likely slim.

I wish David DeVitt had recorded what his thoughts were when he first laid eyes on the land that would become the

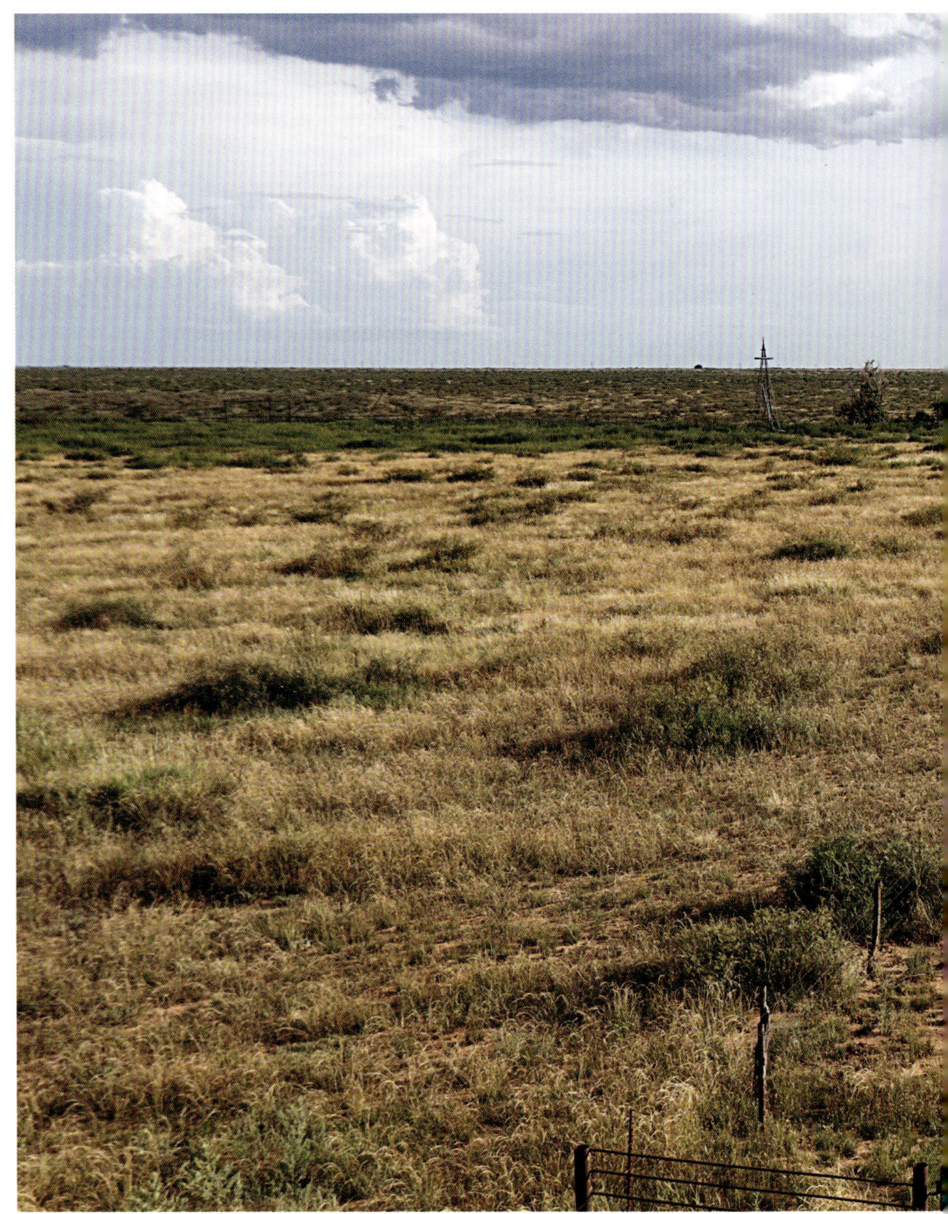

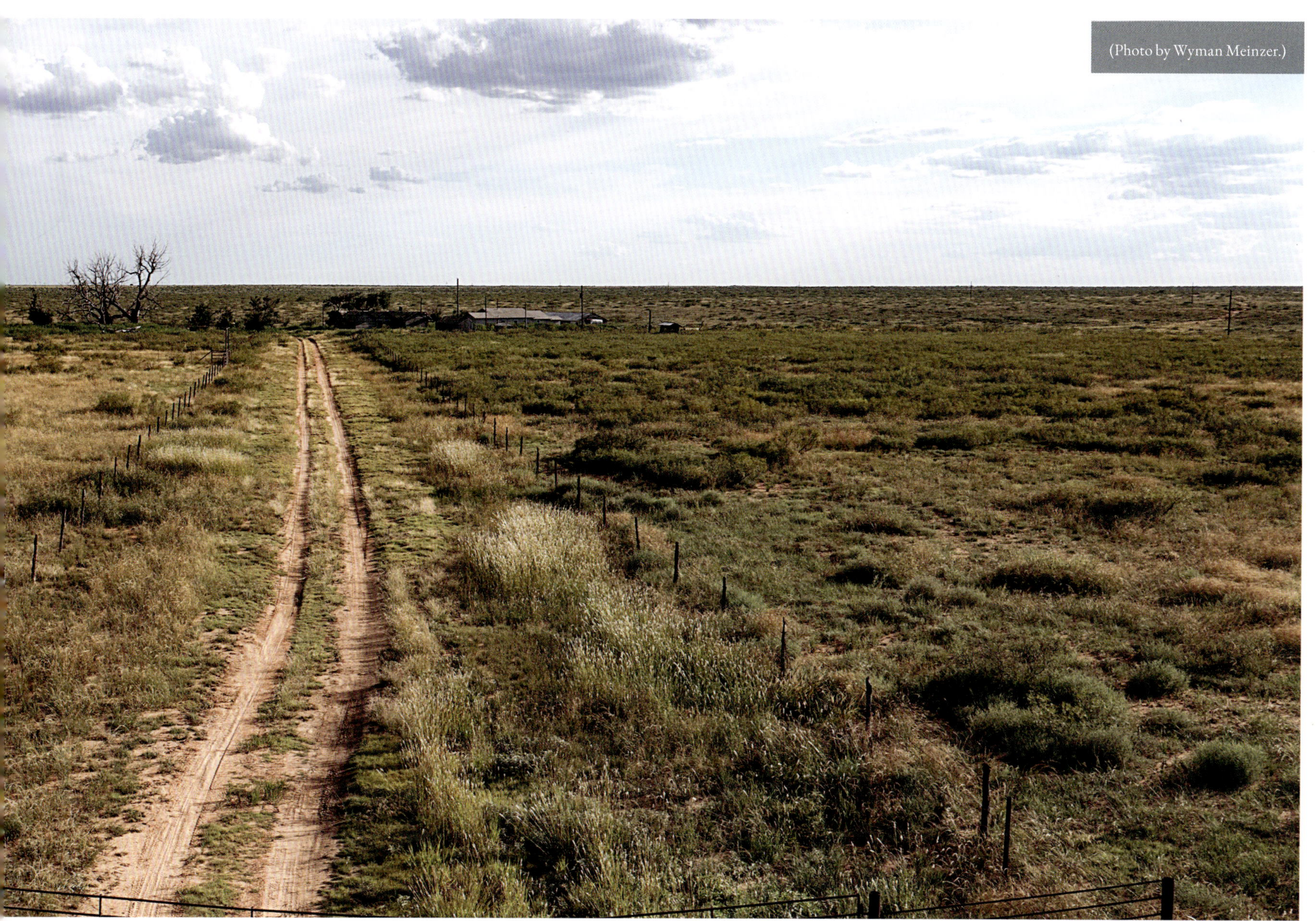
(Photo by Wyman Meinzer.)

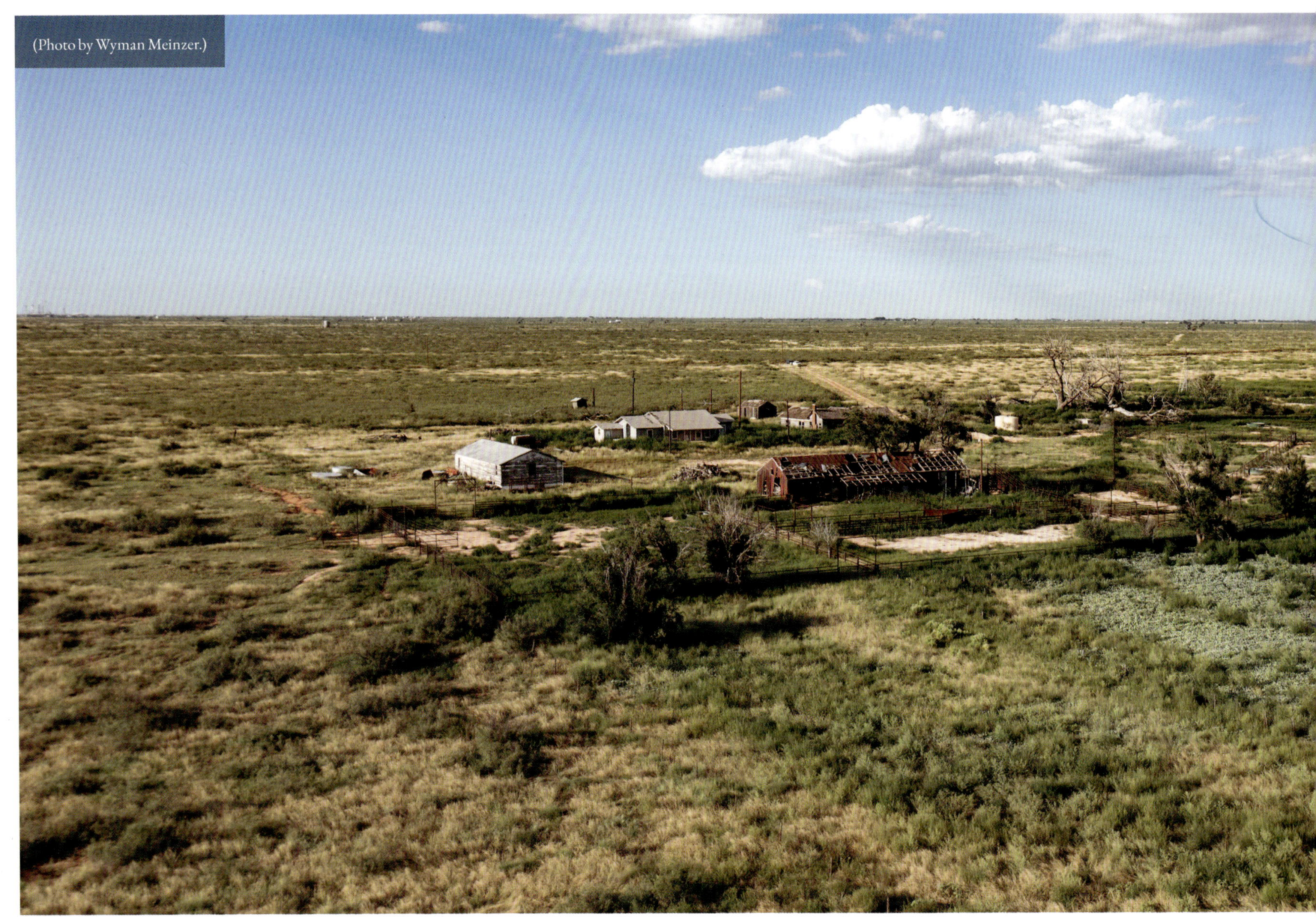
(Photo by Wyman Meinzer.)

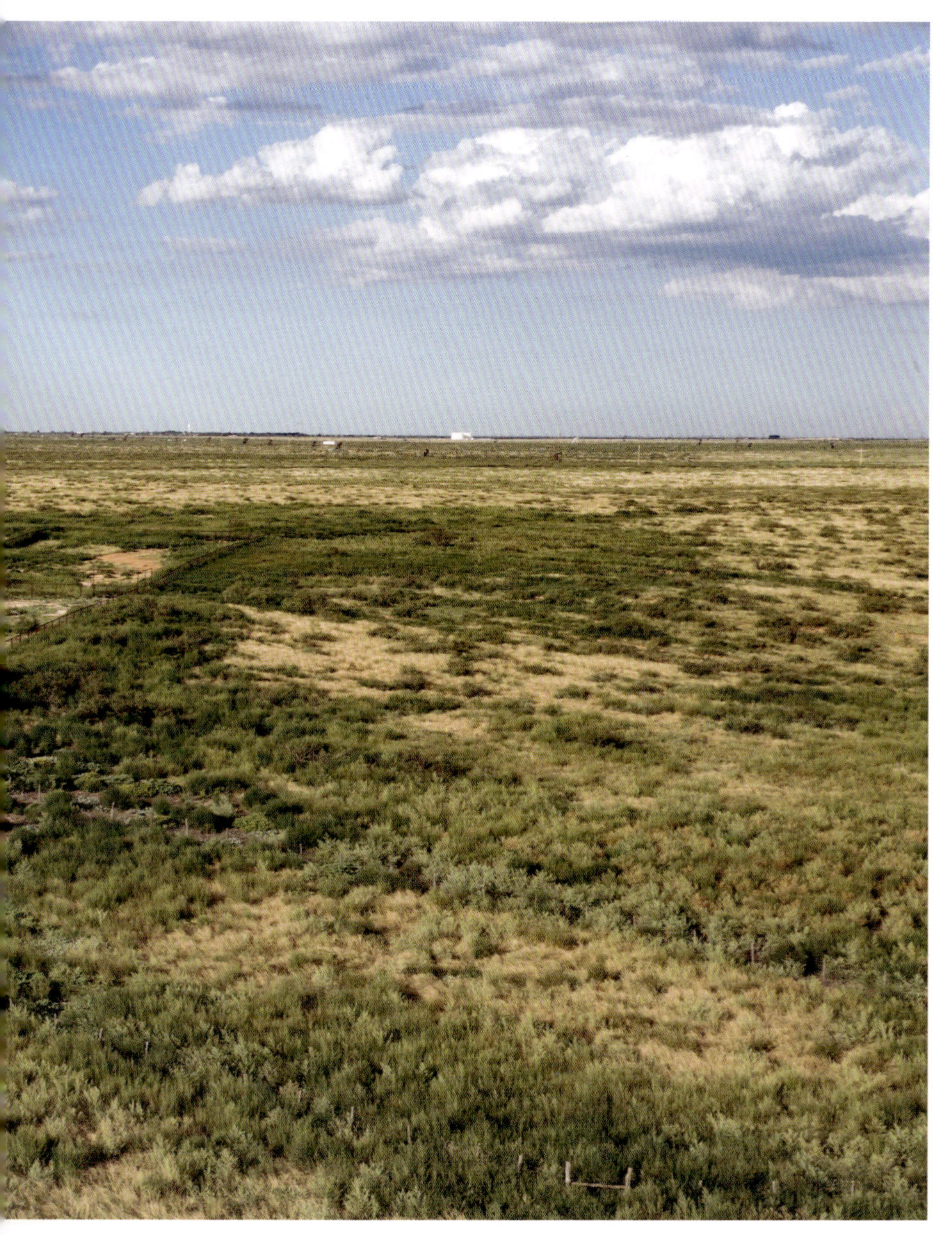

Mallet Ranch. Could he have possibly envisioned what it would become or what future destiny lay in store for his family? There is probably no way he could have, but I wonder if he had any dreams that approached how the narrative unfolded as his life and then that of his daughters progressed. He was entering what was, at the time, truly the last frontier in Texas. The rest of Texas by the 1890s remained mostly sparse, but towns and economic activity had at least penetrated all regions except the South Plains. DeVitt established his ranch in a place that was—to use a word many still use to describe parts of the South Plains—empty. Was it overwhelming for a young man who less than two decades earlier had worked as a journalist in the most populous city in the United States?

As I told David Murrah, a friend and fellow Mallet author, if Hollywood could make a hit like *Yellowstone* out of a fictional ranch story, it should be easy to achieve the same success by telling the Mallet's tale. The story has everything television or movie producers and directors might want: villains, heroes, intrigue, legal fights, violence, money, and romance, all taking place in a land easily associated with the myths and legends of Texas. We could write a screenplay and never have to make up a thing that did not actually happen.

The narrative of the Mallet, and particularly the DeVitt family, is more than a Hollywood fantasy. It depicts a family that, while possessing its share of flaws, overcame them to construct a lasting legacy. The philanthropic contributions of the DeVitt sisters from the riches of the Mallet continue to benefit thousands. If the Mallet is unlike many other historic ranches because it has remained intact, the legacy of the DeVitts is unique because their wealth was not squandered, not lost, and not used for nefarious purposes. Their wealth has been a wellspring of charity and hope for those it has benefitted, a fitting legacy for a man who founded a stock operation that helps many whose aspirations may have been unattainable without them. David DeVitt probably did not have such thoughts as he surveyed those acres in 1895 after making the journey from San Angelo to see for the first time the ranch he had purchased. I would like to think, however, that perhaps a small seed of those thoughts sprouted as he sat on horseback looking at his land. Maybe Hollywood *should* make a movie.

REFERENCES

CHAPTER 1

Primary Source

Mallet Ranch Records, 1865–1992 and undated, Boxes 3 and 6, Southwest Collection/Special Collections, Texas Tech University, Lubbock, Texas.

Newspapers

The San Angelo Standard

Published Material

Austin, Rose. *An Early History of San Angelo*, n.p., n.d.

Campanella, Thomas J. *Brooklyn: The Once and Future City*. Princeton, NJ: Princeton University Press, 2019.

Campbell, Randolph B. *Gone to Texas: A History of the Lone Star State*. New York: Oxford University Press, 2003.

Carlson, Paul H. *Texas Woollyback: The Range Sheep and Goat Industry*. College Station: Texas A&M Press, 2016.

Cornett, James W. *The Chihuahuan Desert*. Albuquerque: University of New Mexico Press, 2013.

Duff, Katherine. *Catclaw Country: An Informal History of Abilene in West Texas*. Austin: Eakin Press, 1980.

Jordan, Terry G. *North American Cattle-Ranching Frontier: Origins, Diffusion, and Differentiation*. Albuquerque: University of New Mexico Press, 1993.

Murrah, David J. *Oil, Taxes, and Cats: A History of the DeVitt Family and the Mallet Ranch*. Lubbock: Texas Tech University Press, 1994.

Patterson, Jimmy. *A History of Character: The Story of Midland, Texas*. Midland: Abell-Hanger Foundation, 2014.

Rich, Harold. *Fort Worth: Outpost, Cowtown, Boomtown*. Norman: University of Oklahoma Press, 2014.

Skaggs, Jimmy M. *Prime Cut: Livestock Raising and Meatpacking in the United States, 1607–1983*. College Station: Texas A&M Press, 1986.

Sosebee, M. Scott. *Henry C. "Hank" Smith and the Cross B Ranch: The First Stock Operation on the South Plains*. College Station: Texas A&M Press, 2021.

Specht, Joshua. *Red Meat Republic: A Hoof-to-Table History of How Beef Changed America*. Princeton, NJ: Princeton University Press, 2019.

CHAPTER 2

Primary Source

Mallet Ranch Records, 1865–1992 and undated, Southwest Collection/Special Collections, Texas Tech University, Lubbock, Texas.

Newspaper

Lubbock Avalanche-Journal

Oral History

Interview with Hiley Boyd Jr. by David Murrah and Lauren Liljistrand, May 22, 1992, Southwest Collection/Special Collection, Texas Tech University, Lubbock, Texas.

Published Material

Campbell, Randolph B. *Gone to Texas: A History of the Lone Star State*. New York: Oxford University Press, 2003.

Carlson, Paul H. *Texas Woollyback: The Range Sheep and Goat Industry*. College Station: Texas A&M Press, 2016.

Jordan, Terry G. *North American Cattle-Ranching Frontier: Origins, Diffusion, and Differentiation*. Albuquerque: University of New Mexico Press, 1993.

Murrah, David J. *Oil, Taxes, and Cats: A History of the DeVitt Family and the Mallet Ranch*. Lubbock: Texas Tech University Press, 1994.

———. *The Rise and Fall of the Lazy S Ranch*. College Station: Texas A&M Press, 2021.

Ogle, Maureen. *In Meat We Trust: An Unexpected History of Carnivore America*. New York: Houghton Mifflin Harcourt, 2013.

Patterson, Jimmy. *A History of Character: The Story of Midland,*

Texas. Midland: Abell-Hanger Foundation, 2014.

Skaggs, Jimmy M. *The Cattle-Trailing Industry*. Norman: University of Oklahoma Press, 1991.

———. *Prime Cut: Livestock Raising and Meatpacking in the United States, 1607–1983*. College Station: Texas A&M Press, 1986.

Specht, Joshua. *Red Meat Republic: A Hoof-to-Table History of How Beef Changed America*. Princeton, NJ: Princeton University Press, 2019.

CHAPTER 3

Primary Source

Mallet Ranch Records, 1865–1992 and undated, Southwest Collection/Special Collections, Texas Tech University, Lubbock, Texas.

Oral History

Interview with Hiley Boyd Jr. by David Murrah and Lauren Liljistrand, May 22, 1992, Southwest Collection/Special Collections, Texas Tech University, Lubbock, Texas.

Published Material

Campbell, Randolph B. *Gone to Texas: A History of the Lone Star State*. New York: Oxford University Press, 2003.

McKay, Seth S. *Texas After Spindletop: The Saga of Texas, 1901–1965*. Austin: Steck-Vaughn, 1965.

Murrah, David J. *Oil, Taxes, and Cats: A History of the DeVitt Family and the Mallet Ranch*. Lubbock: Texas Tech University Press, 1994.

Ogle, Maureen. *In Meat We Trust: An Unexpected History of Carnivore America*. New York: Houghton Mifflin Harcourt, 2013.

Rich, Harold. *Fort Worth: Outpost, Cowtown, Boomtown*. Norman: University of Oklahoma Press, 2014.

CHAPTER 4

Primary Source

Mallet Ranch Records, 1865–1992 and undated, Southwest Collection/Special Collections, Texas Tech University, Lubbock, Texas.

Oral History

Interview with Hiley Boyd Jr. by David Murrah and Lauren Liljistrand, May 22, 1992, Southwest Collection/Special Collections, Texas Tech University, Lubbock, Texas.

Published Material

Hinton, Diana Davids, and Roger M. Olien. *Oil in Texas: The Gusher Age, 1895–1945*. Clifton and Shirley Caldwell Texas Heritage Series. College Station: Texas A&M Press, 2002.

Moore, Richard R. *West Texas After the Discovery of Oil: A Modern Frontier*. Austin: Jenkins Publishing, 1971.

Murrah, David J. *Oil, Taxes, and Cats: A History of the DeVitt Family and the Mallet Ranch*. Lubbock: Texas Tech University Press, 1994.

CHAPTER 5

Primary Source

Mallet Ranch Records, 1865–1992 and undated, Southwest Collection/Special Collections, Texas Tech University, Lubbock, Texas.

Newspaper

Lubbock Avalanche-Journal

Oral Histories

Interview with Howard Fowler by David Murrah, June 18, 1992, Southwest Collection/Special Collections, Texas Tech University, Lubbock, Texas.

Interview with David Frayman by David Murrah, November 12, 1992, Southwest Collection/Special Collections, Texas Tech University, Lubbock, Texas.

Interview with Robert Gaston and Anne Gaston by David Murrah and Lauren Liljistrand, September 15, 1992, Southwest Collection/Special Collections, Texas Tech University, Lubbock, Texas.

Telephone interview with Lynn Snyder Hooker by Sue H. Jones, August 30, 2022, Lubbock, Texas.

Published Material

Day, Matthew. *Fueling Victory at Home: How the Mallet Ranch of Texas and Its Relationship With the Oil Industry Helped Reshape the American Southwest in the 1940s*. Lubbock: self-published, 2019.

Murrah, David J. *Oil, Taxes, and Cats: A History of the DeVitt Family and the Mallet Ranch*. Lubbock: Texas Tech University Press, 1994.

CHAPTER 6

Primary Sources

Mallet Ranch Records, 1865–1992 and undated, Southwest Collection/Special Collections, Texas Tech University,

Lubbock, Texas.
National Ranching Heritage Center Collection, Southwest Collection/Special Collections, Texas Tech University, Lubbock, Texas.

Unpublished Source

Sosebee, M. Scott. "The Founding of the National Ranching Heritage Center," presented at the West Texas Historical Association Annual Meeting, March 2022, Lubbock, Texas.

Oral Histories

Interview with John Archer by David Murrah, July 17, 1992, Southwest Collection/Special Collections, Texas Tech University, Lubbock, Texas.
Interview with David Frayman by David Murrah, November 12, 1992, Southwest Collection/Special Collections, Texas Tech University, Lubbock, Texas.
Interview with Robert Gaston and Anne Gaston by David Murrah and Lauren Liljistrand, September 15, 1992, Southwest Collection/Special Collections, Texas Tech University, Lubbock, Texas.

Published Source

Murrah, David J. *Oil, Taxes, and Cats: A History of the DeVitt Family and the Mallet Ranch*. Lubbock: Texas Tech University Press, 1994.

CHAPTER 7

Newspaper

Lubbock Avalanche-Journal

Primary Sources

Mallet Ranch Records, 1865–1992 and undated, Southwest Collection/Special Collections, Texas Tech University, Lubbock, Texas.
National Ranching Heritage Center Collection, Southwest Collection/Special Collections, Texas Tech University, Lubbock, Texas.

Unpublished Source

Sosebee, M. Scott. "The Founding of the National Ranching Heritage Center," presented at the West Texas Historical Association Annual Meeting, March 2022, Lubbock, Texas.

Oral Histories

Interview with John Archer by David Murrah, July 17, 1992, Southwest Collection/Special Collections, Texas Tech

University, Lubbock, Texas.
Interview with James C. Arnold by Jim Bret Campbell and Sue H. Jones, August 2, 2022, Helen Jones Foundation, Inc. Office, Lubbock, Texas.
Interview with David Frayman by David Murrah, November 12, 1992, Southwest Collection/Special Collections, Texas Tech University, Lubbock, Texas.
Interview with Robert Gaston and Anne Gaston by David Murrah and Lauren Liljistrand, September 15, 1992, Southwest Collection/Special Collections, Texas Tech University, Lubbock, Texas.
Interview with Sandy Ogletree and Heather Hocker by Jim Bret Campbell and Sue H. Jones, August 9, 2022, The CH Foundation Office, Lubbock, Texas.
Telephone interview with Lynn Snyder Hooker by Sue H. Jones, August 30, 2022, Lubbock, Texas.

Published Source

Murrah, David J. *Oil, Taxes, and Cats: A History of the DeVitt Family and the Mallet Ranch*. Lubbock: Texas Tech University Press, 1994.

INDEX

Note: Entries in bold refer to images.

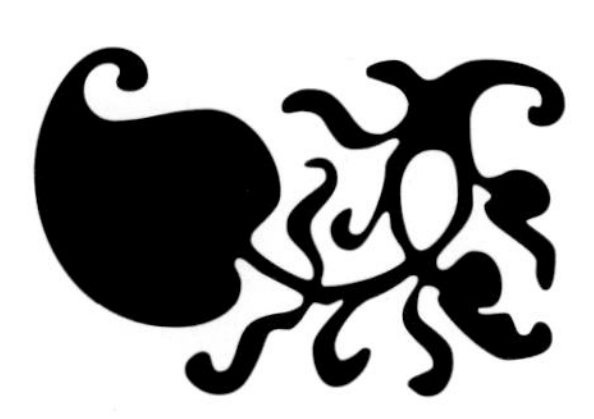

Publication of this book
was made possible by the
generous support of
the Helen Jones Foundation, Inc.

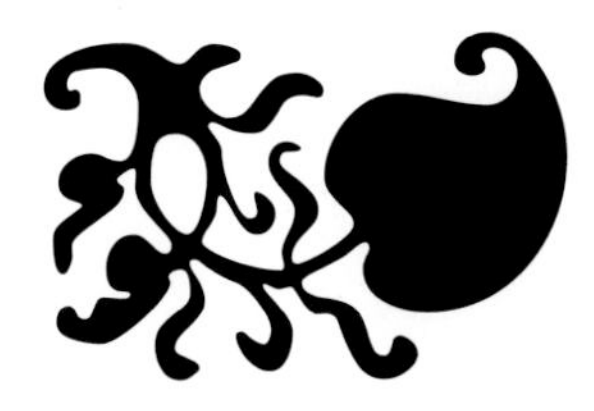

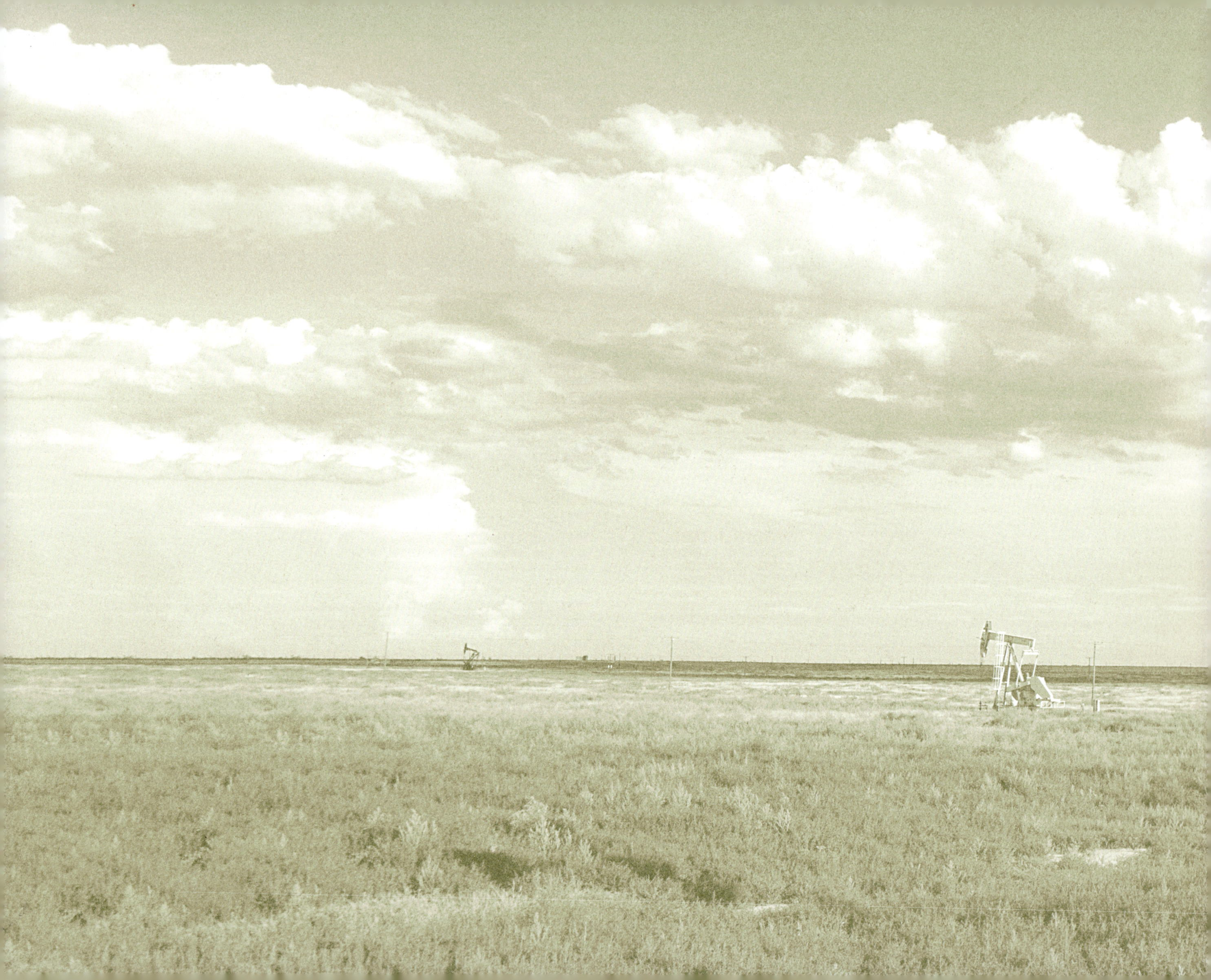